D1482061

The
Unriddling Of
CHRISTIAN
ORIGINS

The Unriddling Of
CHRISTIAN ORIGINS

A Secular Account

JOEL CARMICHAEL

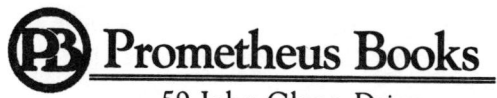 **Prometheus Books**

59 John Glenn Drive
Amherst, New York 14228-2197

Elements of this book appeared in *The Death of Jesus, St Paul's Timetable* (German: *Stehe auf und Rufe Deinen Herrn*), and *The Birth of Christianity: Reality & Myth.*

Published 1995 by Prometheus Books

99 98 97 96 95   5 4 3 2 1

Library of Congress Cataloging-in-Publication Data

Carmichael, Joel.
    The unriddling of Christian origins : a secular account / Joel Carmichael.
      p.   cm.
    Includes bibliographical references.
    ISBN 0-87975-952-6 (alk. paper)
    1. Christianity—Origin. 2. Church history—Primitive and early church, ca. 30–600. 3. Christianity—Controversial literature. I. Title.
BR129.C293   1995
270.1—dc20   95-16635
                                                    CIP

Printed in the United States of America on acid-free paper

Contents

Preface

A Revision of Perspective

The establishment of a religion is also a secular event. In the case of Christianity this obvious statement is complicated by a unique fact—the core of the religion is fused with real-life events, or at least with events whose validity as history is considered a fundamental element of the religion.

This has proved to be most complicated. In fact, the vast literature on Christian origins has produced no realistic account of their secular background.

The complexity and obscurity of Christian origins, attested to by more than half a million books, have become a cliché.

Since the few incontestable facts are felt to be unsatisfactory, it is taken for granted that it is natural for the gap in our information to have been replaced by theories, surmises, speculations, and endless borrowings from other disciplines. Hundreds of thousands of scholars, semischolars and journalistic popularizers have created such a labyrinth that it has become difficult for scholars themselves to discern the events that brought about the most capacious religion in history.

As we shall see, the main reason for the proliferation of the literature on Christian origins is just this combination of scarce data and willful speculations. The constant production of books is fueled by the widespread reluctance to accept as adequate those data that *are* uncontested. The reluctance surely arises out of the tug of some religious longing, however repressed, and in its simplest form is rooted in the powerful aversion to surrendering faith in Jesus as the originator of the religion and, more generally, in the divinity of Jesus himself.

For if the inquiry into Christian origins were to be conducted on the human plane alone—which is possible, after all, even for believers, who must accept the early claim that Jesus, even if 100 percent divine, was also 100 percent human—why should this dissatisfaction with historical conclusions, confirmed by what is already known and is inherently acceptable, have persisted so tenaciously?

There is in fact nothing mysterious about the origins of Christianity. The broad outlines of Jesus' activity during his lifetime, or rather during that portion of it that has survived in the record, as well as of the gradual, piecemeal, and somewhat irregular development of the faith that led to the establishment of a universal Church, are perfectly clear.

It is true that from the very inception two centuries ago of the Higher Criticism of the Bible, the historical approach has been largely cultivated with admixtures, often overwhelming, of large-scale ideas. Not merely were the few historical data not accepted, or wholly disregarded, but any empirical discussion whatever was subject to ideas of one kind or another—philosophical, in the broadest sense, or extrapolated from philosophy in the form of theology, or uncontrollable excursions into a wide range of seductive but quite irrelevant other studies. Hegelianism, Marxism, abstract sociology, literary criticism, theories of cultural diffusion, have all been named. In the modern period especially, literary criticism and abstract sociology have played a stellar role, producing incredibly intricate works whose link to historical events is entirely whimsical.

The origins of Christianity have actually been far more thoroughly explored than those of either Judaism or Islam. The background is far better understood, with a wealth of detail unthinkable either in Islam or even in Judaism, which was, of course, a fundamental factor in the origin of Christianity.

Albert Schweitzer once referred to the "Higher Criticism" of the Bible as a triumph of German theology, but it is also true that the very nature of the theological interest in Christian origins has ultimately led to a feeling of hopelessness in contemplating the results.

The figure of Jesus remains elusive, no doubt because of the reluctance to abandon its theological explanation. Jesus is the only protagonist of any major religion who is considered divine: This simple fact may explain the inhibition in accepting even modest empirical data.

We shall see that the enigma surrounding the person of Jesus is to be explained by specific, definable, and understandable historical events whose mysteriousness lies not in their nature but in the inevitable limits on our knowledge.

A striking feature, generally unnoticed, of all histories of Christian origins, including would-be secular ones, is that the life of Jesus is tacitly accepted as the beginning of the story of Christianity.

This is certainly natural, sensible, understandable, but it can be a beginning only in the rhetorical sense—the first step in a complex exposition. As we shall see, it is by no means a functional, or causal beginning. The life of Jesus did not, in and of itself, lead to the formation of Christian doctrine. The fact that all elements of Christianity were shaped after Jesus' death is the cardinal factor of any serious account.

The very phrases "early Christianity," the "beginning of Christianity" and so on are profoundly misleading. There was a sharp break between two orders of historical factuality. In fact, the essential problem in the genesis of Christianity must be summed up by a simple question:

How was the Kingdom of God, an ancient idea proclaimed in a new form by Jesus and by Saul of Tarsus (St. Paul), somehow forgotten and transformed into a religion revolving around the deification of Jesus?

This would seem to be a simple transition, yet it is this refocusing of the Kingdom of God onto the figure of Jesus that was to create Christianity.

And it was the endless magnification by Saul of Tarsus of Jesus as Son of God that was the source of Saul's further conviction that the Kingdom of God was imminent and *guaranteed* by the resurrection and glorification of Jesus; above all, that the identification of the believer with the dying and rising Christ, Son of God, was the key to immortality.

This was essentially the structure of a new religion that could legitimately be called Christianity. Saul's Letters, accordingly, already constituted the foundations of a wholly new theology, entirely unknown to Jesus and unsuspected by Saul himself.

Vast though the literature on Christian origins is, it represents an attempt to clarify a small collection of writings—the New Testament: primarily Saul's Letters, then the four Gospels and the Acts of the Apostles. For a comprehension of the historical background the works of Flavius Josephus, a Jewish general who defected to Rome in the Roman-Jewish war of 66–70, will also prove essential.

A sudden flurry of interest in the complexities of the first century was aroused by the discovery of the Dead Sea scrolls in 1947, which unleashed one of the most violent controversies in scholarly history, a controversy that subsided a decade or two later only to flare up again to a lesser extent in the 1980s. In addition to the many scholars who leaped into the fray, the huge lay audience, inflamed by various popularizations that had percolated through the agitated academic community, was fascinated by the prospect of illuminating Jesus' person and background.

Yet the scrolls proved disappointing. It is true that many other scrolls, found since the first handful, have amplified the Jewish background, in particular the messianic Judaism of the two centuries spanning the emergence of Christianity, but they have added nothing to the study of early Christianity itself, except negatively: there are no Jewish elements in the genesis of Christianity other than the fundamental ones already indicated in the Gospels, the Acts of the Apostles and Saul of Tarsus's Letters. They have cast no light on Jesus, nor for that matter have they indicated any specific influences that might have influenced the formation of Christianity. They have not, in fact, added anything to the "nuggets" of information embedded in the earliest Christian texts that I shall be referring to often.

Looking back from our own vantage point at the edifice of scholarly criticism concerned with disentangling the origin of Christianity, the very fact, properly understood, that it revolved around the person of its putative founder, Jesus, should have served as a natural division in the inquiry—between Jesus, the living human being, and Jesus the Son of God. Saul's own formula sums up this division: "Unless Jesus was resurrected, our teaching is in vain."

Saul's flat statement highlights, on the one hand, the core of belief underlying Christianity, and on the other the contrast, in kind, between the life of Jesus the man and the significance of Jesus as exemplar of qualities attributed to him after his death—the Christ, the Son of God, Light of the world, Savior of the Universe, and the head of the universal Church.

This simple idea will justify a clear order of exposition—part 1: Jesus before Christ, and part 2: Christ after Jesus.

Since the Gospels and the Acts of the Apostles, and for that matter Saul's Letters, contain many instances of real-life information, we shall see that the establishment of the historical framework will make it possible to extract valid facts even from the traditional texts, since forgery was quite alien to their writers, editors, and compilers.

Accordingly, this book will attempt to explain the sequence of events in which the original belief of Jesus, John the Baptist, and Saul of Tarsus in the imminent Kingdom of God—a transformation of the real world—was replaced by a belief in the divinity of Christ Jesus, Son of God—the foundation of a universal Church, launched by the destruction of the Jewish temple and state in the Roman-Jewish war of 66–70.

Part One

Jesus Before Christ

Introduction

Both Jesus and Saul of Tarsus (St. Paul*) as well as the germination of Christianity itself, cannot be understood without an awareness of a historical factor that has been misperceived for almost 2,000 years—the movement of agitation for the Kingdom of God that culminated in the massive Jewish insurrection against Rome in 66–70. This agitation arose out of the conviction, held by countless Jews during the first century, that while God himself would install his Kingdom, his decision could be hastened by taking action oneself.

It has been misperceived for the simple reason that after the Jewish debacle in the insurrection against Rome the true nature of the Kingdom of God had to be suppressed by the Jews, because it had brought about a disaster, and by the believers in Jesus who were to give rise to the Christian Church because Jesus, who had preached the Kingdom of God, had to be detached from the activists a generation later who actually did what Jesus had only tried to do.

The result has been that the first century is, at present, a vacuum. Even secular historians take as their starting-point an area defined essentially by Christian theology: despite the Jewish origin of Jesus and his immediate partisans, the mythology of the Church has obliged students of its history, all unconsciously, to scrutinize each cluster of events as though they were

---

*Paulus was Saul's Roman name. He calls himself Paul in his Letters.

independent of each other—Christian origins on one side, the Jewish War against Rome on the other.

A further irony is also no doubt the loss to Jewish historiography of the first century, which saw the transformation of the Jews into a Diaspora people. The traditional explanation of the Jewish debacle in the Roman war as divine punishment for delinquency resulted in the absence of any secular history at all, and hence in the de facto acceptance of the Christian version of events.

Yet the documents conveying the traditional Christian story—the four Gospels and the Acts of the Apostles—are, despite the naturalistic atmosphere of the Gospels and the presence of many nuggets of fact—mythological throughout. The genesis of Christianity cannot, in fact, be understood without its historical background.

Without this real-life setting it is impossible to understand Jesus' activity, the relationship between Saul and Jesus, the role played by Jesus' family and followers in the Temple that was destroyed together with the Jewish state in 70 C.E., and its effect on the spread of the new religion.

The basic source of antihistorical distortion in the Gospels was the radical shift of perspective inherent in the theological interpretation of Jesus' crucifixion, i.e., the very germination of the new faith. The failure of Jesus' secular enterprise and his humiliating death brought about a transformation of outlook: that very death gave rise to the conviction that Jesus was the Incarnation of God, Lord of the Universe, Light of the World, Savior of Mankind. All factual recollections were reorganized accordingly and dovetailed into the framework of an evolving cult. This shift of perspective distorted the Gospels *systematically*: the basic ideas interwoven with Jewish life—Kingdom of God, the Messiah, Son of David, salvation—were wrenched out of their true context, national resistance to the pagan Roman Empire.

The transformation is highlighted by the disregard shown the "Mother Church," made up of the immediate family and followers of Jesus himself. Since this Church was destroyed in the cataclysm that wiped out the Jewish nation, no record of it survives: It fell outside the magnification of Jesus' person that is the substance of Christianity.

Saul, too, believed with fervor in the Kingdom of God; he, too, had a vision, perhaps similar to the vision of Simon the Rock, who saw Jesus not only resurrected but glorified at the right hand of God. (Simon was nicknamed Cephas, in Greek Petros [Peter], which means "the rock.") But

Saul's conclusions were different from those of Simon the Rock and of Jesus' small entourage, who had fled to Galilee after his crucifixion.

For that entourage the resurrection and glorification of Jesus were interpreted within a Jewish setting: the Kingdom of God, which they thought had been heralded by Jesus, was postponed for some inexplicable reason, but only for a short time: Jesus would come again, very soon, and this time the Kingdom would surely appear.

But Saul believed in a somewhat different Kingdom of God—ethereal and universal, detached from the need for a restoration of Jewish sovereignty and indifferent to the religious/national Jewish resistance to Rome. Moreover, he was gripped by the notion that a unique event like the resurrection and glorification of Jesus, the Son of God, inevitably had cosmic significance: it *had* to be the very prelude to the Kingdom of God.

For Saul, the delay constituted a baffling problem:

If the Kingdom of God, a cosmic event brought about by the Creator of the Universe, had been launched by the resurrection and glorification of Jesus, why had it not *already* been consummated? How could it have started at all without being instantaneously realized?

Why did the world still look the same?

For Saul this problem had nothing to do with theology, but with real life. Starting out from a calculation that the Kingdom of God would infallibly be installed no later than 40 years from the resurrection, Saul devised a cluster of ideas to bridge the gap between the resurrection and the installation of the Kingdom. These ideas were to become, long after his death, the substance of a religion he could never have foreseen. His starting point, his puzzlement over the delay, was to become meaningless a generation or two after his death, while the theory he devised to explain it became irrelevantly archaic along with the idea of the Kingdom of God itself, now replaced by a universal Church.

Saul died a few years before he could have seen his reckoning confounded: his Letters were tucked into a different framework, the framework of a universal Church

1

The Agitation for the Kingdom of God

Each of the first three Gospels presents Jesus as proclaiming the Kingdom of God that was "at hand." "The time is fulfilled, the Kingdom of God is at hand, repent" (Mk 1:15). This is what launches the Gospels, the story of Jesus. It is a formula, arresting in its simplicity, that is both ancient and historically, no doubt, authentic, especially since it is utterly at variance, as we shall see, with the intellectual edifice that has been erected over it.

The concept of the Kingdom of God is the key to the agitation that from the first century on churned up Jewry until about 135 C.E., led to the destruction of the Jewish state in the war against Rome of 66–70 C.E., flared up in the abortive Bar Kocha rebellion of 132–35, and launched Christianity.

Today its meaning has been transformed: the evolution of Christianity itself had turned the phrase into either a metaphor for ethical behavior or a recondite aspect of theology. But in the generation spanning Jesus' activities the concept was wholly palpable, factual, and dynamic. It meant the transformation by God of the natural world into one in which God's will would conduct human affairs directly and hence restore the fortunes of the Jews, the chosen people.

The Kingdom of God was rooted deep in the Jewish past. In sharp contrast with the dense intricacies of paganism, in which a wide variety of natural phenomena enjoyed degrees of divinity explained by complex mythologies, the religion of Israel was anchored in the simple idea that the whole of the universe had been brought into existence by the will of a single Being, himself subject to nothing whatever—neither other beings, nor a preexistent order, nor fate, nor hazard.

This supreme Being—Yahweh or Jehovah—had revealed himself first to the Jews, who by virtue of a covenant with him became in their own eyes his people. Thus from the very beginning Yahweh, though the Creator of the universe, had one people of his own to worship him. The Hebrew Scriptures—the Old Testament of the Bible, compiled over a millennium—embody this first phase of the national history of the Jews.

Jewish alliance with Yahweh had been a stupendous success—the liberation from Egypt, the conquest of Canaan, the great settlement, the conquering dynasties—but it had been followed by a steady decline as a result of the increasingly oppressive encroachments of great powers climaxed by the Babylonian exile in 582 B.C.E., in which, to be sure, only the upper classes were actually exiled.

These vicissitudes were hard to explain: the escalation of Yahweh, originally a local god, to the status of the all-powerful one God, Creator of the Universe, had created a special conundrum. How could his seeming helplessness be understood? If the covenant with his own people was eternal, what had gone wrong?

The classical Hebrew prophets had found the answer: Despite the malaise of the world and the disasters that had befallen the chosen people, the day of Yahweh would infallibly arrive. After a series of horrible calamities and an appalling upheaval on earth and in heaven, a new world, cleansed and regenerated, would be installed, with all the enemies of the Jews, including the great empires—Assyria, Babylonia—lying trampled in the dust by Yahweh's awful might.

But the prophets were also full of ethical feeling, generated by the notion that the Creator's will was being flouted. This was why they castigated their people; there had to be some explanation of Jewish suffering, and since the Creator could hardly be blamed, the Jews had to be.

The Jews were destined, said the prophets, to be severely punished, though without being wiped out. A remnant would survive, and from that remnant a new generation, pleasing to Yahweh, would arise and enter into a new covenant, modeled on Yahweh's old covenant with mankind after the Flood and later on with the Jews, through Abraham, Isaac, Jacob, and Moses. Yahweh would pour out his spirit on the newly chosen of the chosen people, the progeny of the remnant; Jerusalem would become a peerless city, worshipping Yahweh in total purity of heart with unheard-of splendor of ritual. Israelites would be united; old hatreds forgiven, the new Israel would be installed in matchless prosperity. And though all this basically concerned the Jews alone, the pagans, too—*en passant,* so to speak—would bask in the refulgence of Yahweh and of his Torah, the core of the the Hebrew Scriptures.

The Torah does not mention the resurrection of the dead, the ending of death, or the termination of ordinary history, with rewards and punishments being allocated in the world beyond. The World's End takes place in the natural world. This earthliness characterized the "classical" phase of the Jews' alienation from "ordinary" history. Though the hopes anchored in the World's End idea all included political and suprapolitical motifs, the World's End as a fact remained limited to this world both before and during the Babylonian Exile, which ended in 520 B.C.E. Thus the Kingdom of God, whose chief beneficiaries were to be the Jews, did not imply the end of history on earth: in this early, classical period the Kingdom of God was simple: Yahweh was to be king. That was all; from that all else flowed.

Still, though it is obvious that there is a natural tension in the contrast between the notion of Yahweh as the timeless Creator of the universe and the historic fact that this notion was cherished at the time by only one people—the Jews—it had never aroused them to action before.

For centuries the Jews, after their upper classes had been deported to Babylonia in 582 B.C.E., had been politically quiescent, and after the Persians, having shattered Babylonia, restored the Jewish elite to an enclave of some 1,200 square miles around Jerusalem a half century later and encouraged their religious autonomy for a couple of centuries, the Jews engaged in no political activity of any kind.

It was when Greek culture, after penetrating the Middle East for generations, finally achieved a political focus in the third century B.C.E. that the Jews once again began to play a political role, which lasted until the establishment of the Roman Empire, around the time Jesus was born.

The Greco-Macedonian conquests spearheaded by Alexander the Great changed the face of the Middle East, and of the world. Greek culture became a sort of epidemic: it undid the identities of all the nations the Greeks came across; it wiped out, as nations, Babylonians, Arameans, Egyptians, and the many smaller peoples scattered throughout the vast area. By converting the educated classes of all the conquered peoples, it created a new identity for educated people everywhere. Hellenism became a cultural commonwealth that transcended politics even though it was Hellenistic governments that underlay the cultural expansion. It wiped out the ancient Egyptians, for instance, in half a generation: as soon as they lost heart for teaching their offspring the ancient, complicated written language, the Egyptian people itself became culturally a rudderless peasantry.

Hellenization meant far more than a new government or the cultivation of the Greek language. In the area bounded by Egypt, India, and Central Asia Hellenist institutions became the very stuff of meaningful life, both public and private. Not only did it destroy Egypt as a society, it smashed the Persian state and transformed Persian society—though the Persians were to survive and retain their identity—and gave Rome itself its spiritual mold.

Aside from the Persians, the Jews and Romans were, indeed, the only other peoples to survive intact the epidemic of Hellenization—the Romans by swallowing Greek culture whole while conquering the Greeks militarily, the Jews by resisting it for a time spiritually and then, after digesting some of its elements, by integrating it with their own traditions.

Soon after Alexander the Great's conquests in the third century B.C.E. the Hebrew Scriptures were translated into Greek—a massive, unprecedented enterprise. The Jewish elite in Palestine, as well as Jews in general throughout the Diaspora, was steeped in Greek. In addition, the Jewish elite was for a time seduced away from Judaism altogether.

After the collision with Greek culture the Kingdom of God began to take on a novel, dynamic urgency. The seeds of future ferment were planted: There was an upsurge of visionary emotion that began to formulate a new perspective—the establishment of a real-life kingdom of God. And since it was difficult to imagine the vastness of Yahweh's power pinpointing specific changes in the world, people began to think of a human being as personifying the God-willed transition, as kings, priests, and leaders of all kinds have symbolized complex social processes. Just as Yahweh, during his ascension to the status of the one God, had had to be fitted out with earthly agencies—angels, the "Word," the "Presence" etc.—so it was felt that the Kingdom of God, too, required an agent of transformation, a herald.

The Messiah was that agent. Originally, to be sure, the word itself had meant no more than "anointed" (with oil): it was part of the ancient ceremony of enthroning a Hebrew monarch. It was also used for foreign rulers (like Cyrus of Persia); ultimately it became a metaphor for a human being who, like a true prophet, was doing God's will.

In common usage, accordingly, the Messiah had at first meant a flesh-and-blood descendant of the glorious King David, promised eternal dominion in the Hebrew Scriptures (2 Sam. 7:12ff), and was merely supposed to proclaim the Kingdom of God, a transformation of the present-day natural world. But with the Greek conquests that churned up the Middle East, including Jewry, earthly ideas came to seem inadequate to many Jews. The Kingdom of God heralded by a flesh-and-blood Messiah yielded to the idea of a supernatural world disclosed to the visionary imagination—an otherworldly Messiah from the heavenly heights was to terminate past History and initiate future history. The simplicity of monotheism was fitted out with a sort of auxiliary theory that included a battle between good and evil—conflicts, horrors, wars between angels and demons, heroes partly or wholly supernatural, the idea of a millennium to be followed by universal resurrection, general retribution, the Last Judgment.

Apocalypse, the visionary perception of all such rejections, was produced by the collision of the Jews with the Greeks; it flowered most influentially in Daniel, the final addition to the Hebrew Scriptures. It injected what may be called an element of vertical aspiration to the earthbound views of the Torah. The Apocalyptic concept of a stupendous cataclysm signalizing the destruction of the wicked workaday world and the installation of the Kingdom of God was to transform the spiritual life of mankind forever.

Specifically, it was the reaction to one of the successors of Alexander the Great (the Seleucid King of Syria-Palestine, Antiochus IV Epiphanes) that set the stage for Kingdom of God agitation on two levels—this-worldly and other-worldly.

In 166 B.C.E. Judaism for the first time was attacked root and branch by Antiochus IV, as part of a campaign to systematize the Hellenization of the Jews under his rule. He forbade observance of the Torah, circumcision, the dietary laws, and traditional sacrifices. He was, at first, successful: he had the whole-hearted collaboration of the Jewish aristocracy, enthralled by the charms of Greek culture and eager to adapt the stark simplicity of Judaism to the elegant cosmopolitanism of the Greek rulers. Antiochus IV was, in fact, a mere target of what was at bottom a Jewish civil war.

It was precisely this combination of pagan oppression and Jewish apostasy that brought about the resurgence of Jewry. The Maccabees, who totally rejected Hellenism and won out against Antiochus IV and the Jewish Hellenizers, founded a dynasty, the Hasmoneans, and a new Jewish state, the first in centuries. For three generations the Hasmoneans flourished: territorially their state came to exceed, in fact, the holdings of the Hebrew kings at the height of their power. Yet it was precisely the military triumph of the Maccabees that led to their undoing. They themselves, together with the vast Jewish Diaspora that had been growing since the Babylonian Exile and afterwards, were to collide with Rome, the greatest of all the exemplars of Hellenistic civilization.

The Roman Republic, which had been expanding throughout the Mediterranean and far beyond, was inevitably drawn into the byplay of rivalries and intrigues between various Jewish princes and their allies. Rome penetrated the entire area, gradually acquiring hegemony via a variety of client-rulers. In 63 B.C.E. Pompey forced his way into the Jerusalem Temple: for the first time an unauthorized person, and an idol-worshipper to boot, stood in the holy shrine of Judaism. Palestine was under a new regime.

The end of Jewish sovereignty, symbolized by the Roman conquest of Jerusalem in 63 B.C.E. and the extinction of the male Hasmonean line, turned the idea of the Kingdom of God from a mere vision into a seed-bed of action. It became a major factor in day-to-day politics—the "prehistory" of Jesus and John the Baptist.

For a time, to be sure, the starkness of Roman rule was camouflaged: during the conflict between Pompey and Julius Caesar a Jewish prince, Herod the Great, emerged as a favorite of the victorious faction: Herod, married to a Hasmonean princess, ruled the Jews on behalf of the Romans for thirty-three years. Thus a semblance of independence, or at least of insulation, was preserved: local life was more or less normal: foreign affairs were handled by Rome.

Herod the Great (reigned 37–4 B.C.E.) lived on a grand scale: vast sums were lavished on splendid buildings; taxation had to be very heavy. But the religious feelings of the populace were buffered by Herod's regime against the realities of Roman rule; Herod himself could be considered by the outside world, and also by the Jews of the Diaspora, as a real Jewish king, a faint, somewhat misshapen embodiment of the Hebrew monarchy.

At the same time the royal style he affected outside Palestine was wholly pagan, while he himself aggravated the mistrust felt for him by pious Jews because of his origins (he came from an Edomite [Idumean] family recently converted to Judaism), and because of his infatuation with the intellectual as well as the elegant aspects of Greek culture. His personal concerns were powerfully buttressed by his public extravagance, which exerted tremendous economic pressure on his subjects and kindled the first sparks of political agitation.

Herod the Great focused the bitterness of the Jews into an organized movement that was the most dynamic element in Jewish life until the Romans destroyed the Temple in 70. Thus even before its members became known as Zealots and also Sicarii ("Daggermen," because of their concealed daggers) an actual movement had been shaped that lasted several generations. Today the Zealots would be called diehards: extremists who refused to accept pagan rule. Their roots were in a passage in the Hebrew Apocrypha (1 Maccabees 2:27–30):

> Matthew cried out in the city with a loud voice, saying, "whosoever is zealous for the Torah and maintains the covenant, let him come forth after me." And he and his sons fled into the mountains and forsook all they had in the city. Then many that sought after justice and judgment went down into the wilderness to dwell there, they and their sons and their wives and their cattle.

Their inspiration was essentially religious: from their point of view submission to Rome meant lapsing from monotheism; thus it was a form of apostasy. Their attitude was ultimately based on the celebrated "royalty law" of Deuteronomy 17:14–15, which forbade Jews to submit to the domination of pagans. Because of their intransigence—compounded, of course, by their ultimate bloodstained defeat—they have gone down into conventional history with a bad name. They are generally referred to in writings concerning this period as "robbers," "highwaymen," "criminals," etc., words that, as indicated above, almost invariably signify militant insurgents against the foreign power of Rome and her vassals.

At the limit of the Jewish political spectrum, they came to the surface after the conquest of Judea by Pompey in 63 B.C.E. and for a long time they undoubtedly had the sympathy of the bulk of the population, including the popular religious party of the Pharisees; they were, in fact, the extremist wing of the Pharisees.

After the Roman conquest it was the Pharisee elders who went to the Romans and said that in view of the Mosaic injunction not to be ruled by anyone but the priests of their God Jews ought not to be ruled by a king. It is easy to imagine the Roman reaction to this: in any case no attention was paid to these requests put forth by the Jewish "moderates" the extremist opposition was inevitably strengthened.

It was Herod's idolatry and bloodshed that first engendered the public opposition of these diehards to the more general offensiveness of the introduction by the Romans into Judea of all the characteristic institutions of the Hellenistic world—the gymnasium, the arena and most outrageous of all, the trophies (images serving as objects of worship), which were an abomination to pious Jews. When the movement began to assume an organized form one of its first public acts was an attempt to assassinate Herod. Ten "Daggermen" in Jerusalem made futile use of their daggers, only to have their plot betrayed and to be tortured to death themselves.

Toward the end of Herod's life he ordered a large golden eagle to be set up over the great gate of the Temple, in such a way that it would gleam resplendently in the rays of the sun. This was violently opposed by two masters of the Torah, Judah ben Sarifai and Matthew ben Margaloth, who together with forty young men pulled the eagle down: they were all burnt to death. After Herod's death the country began to swarm with "robberbands." The Passover in 4 B.C.E. was celebrated by a vast slaughter of pilgrims in Jerusalem.

Herod's succession was uncertain for a decade. The Romans refused to let his oldest son (Archelaus) take office; they kept him on probation. He proved unsatisfactory to Romans and Jews alike; in 6 C.E. he was exiled. Judea-Samaria was reorganized as an annex of the province of Syria in charge of an imperial procurator with full financial and military powers, including the infliction of the death penalty. This procurator (Coponius) was the first of a line that was to include the most celebrated of all, Pontius Pilate, notorious for the sentencing and execution of Jesus.

When Judea-Samaria was absorbed directly into the Roman administration it was natural to have a census; Emperor Augustus ordered the legate of Syria to carry it out. A census of people was considered by all pious Jews to be contrary to Yahweh's will; even when Moses took a census it was only because Yahweh had specifically commanded him to. Centuries later, when David took a census, Yahweh sent a murderous plague (2 Sam 24); there were also prophecies, such as Hosea's (2:1) and unambiguous statements in the Torah (Gen 15:5; 22:17; 32:12) that there would be so many Israelites they would be "like the sands of the sea, which cannot be either measured or counted."

The census, furthermore, was an adjunct of the absorption of Judea-

Samaria into the direct administration of a pagan power: thus it was, according to Roman law, in essence confiscated. This totally contradicted the theory that Yahweh had promised the land to the Jews alone (Lev 25:23).

It was this census (the starting-point of Luke) that launched the movement of dynamic messianism that was to culminate in the Roman Jewish War of 66–70. The census, together with the absorption of Judea-Samaria into the Roman administration, initiated the career of Judah the Galilean, outstanding in the throng of Kingdom of God activists flung up after Herod's death and for much longer, until the war against the Romans and afterwards.

Until Herod's reign the visionary fermentation associated with apocalypse had been passive. Individuals were not supposed to do anything to help Yahweh. The aim of the Maccabees had been the defense of Judaism against the joint onslaught of the Greeks and the apostate Jews. The Maccabees had not intended, themselves, to install the Kingdom of God. Yahweh alone could transform the world and restore sovereignty to the Jewish people (Dan 7:14, 18, 27).

Not all Jews would benefit by it, to be sure: the appeal made by both Jesus and John the Baptist called for "repentance"—only the righteous and pious, from the past as well as from the current generation, could share in the Kingdom of God. The righteous who had already died would be resurrected to participate in the new order of the world. This concept was to be given a new relevance, and a sharp agitational point, toward the end of Herod the Great's reign; after his death it was to become the axis of insurrection against the Romans and their upper-class Jewish supporters.

It was no doubt Judah the Galilean who implemented, in a personal way, the theory and practice of the religious-political insurrection against Rome. Though a thinker, and for that matter learned, Judah the Galilean was essentially a man of action: his views were at bottom no different from those of the large grouping of Jews known as Pharisees, who differed from the aristocratic, priestly Sadducees primarily in their elastic attitude toward the Scriptures.

The Galilean was distinguished only by his determination to implement his views. What he did was to digest, as it were, the First Commandment—"Thou shalt have no other god before me"—and apply his interpretation in action. To him the commandment, in the circumstances of his time, had a peremptory simplicity about it: if no other God but Yahweh,

God of the universe, could be accepted, and if Yahweh was also sole ruler of the Jews, then no form of allegiance to anyone else whatever could be endured.

But if no alien government could be endured, and if the Romans were about to rule the country directly, without even the fig-leaf of a Jewish king, there was only one recourse—the rejection of Roman rule; not merely inner resistance to the Romans, but active revolt.

Active no doubt *outside* Galilee—whence his sobriquet—the Galilean modeled his tactics on David and the early Maccabees: he would hide in caves in the eastern Judean mountains, and from these and similar bolt-holes spring out to pounce on small Roman armed units and traveling functionaries and notables; he would also attack the property of rich Jews and harry non-Jewish territories, while sparing the basic Jewish population whose goodwill was vital for the movement. His fate is unknown; he was no doubt killed and his entourage, for a time, scattered (Acts 5:37).

Judah's whole family was celebrated for its intransigence. His father, Hezekiah, with a group of "bandits," had been executed by Herod, and Judah, his sons, and his grandsons spent their lives in stubborn opposition to the idolatrous Roman power. It was of course the political element in their activity that earned them their unfavorable reputation: most of what we know about them has percolated down to us in the writings of the Jewish historian Josephus, who as a professional client of the Romans takes every possible chance to denigrate them. Nevertheless, in one of his more neutral remarks he gives us the summary of their philosophy: "Others again (the Zealots) call no one Lord except God, even though one should torture or kill them."

Judah the Galilean's movement against the Romans was an aspect of the World's End crisis: his struggle against the census, against the Roman occupation of the land, against pagan rule in general, with its complex of afflictions, could convincingly be ascribed to the pangs of the Messiah that were to accompany the World's End. The census merely tested the faith of the faithful, their readiness for the Kingdom of God. From then on only those Jews who refused to obey the Roman Emperor could be thought of as true Jews.

Judah the Galilean's proclamation of Yahweh's exclusive reign was the first step to the World's End redemption of Israel. He had sharpened the interpretation of the First Commandment to the onset of the Kingdom of God, both by drawing out the implications of the Commandment as one of the Ten Commandments, and by giving a political focus to the "Hear, O Israel," breaking its routine aspect of a ritual formula repeated daily and forcing on the individual uttering it the awareness of those implications.

Judah the Galilean's attitude was by no means only a matter of faith; though crystallized out of the Hebrew Scriptures, it was, in practical terms, a novelty. (We shall see the implications of this view of the "Hear oh Israel" in the career of Jesus.)

The Galilean's innovation, to be sure, reached far into the ancient past preceding the Hebrew monarchy; Israel's "becoming like the other nations" by having a king had been objected to on the principle that Yahweh's people must be ruled by Yahweh alone (1 Sam 8;8:18 Ju 8;23). But applying an ancient attitude to the contemporary situation was to have explosive effects. By agitating the people and denouncing them for paying taxes to the Romans and thus for submitting to the rule of mortals—and pagans—instead of God, he had become a secular as well as a religious rebel. In the Gospels we see echoes of Judah the Galilean in the behavior of John the Baptist (Lk 3:7ff, Mt. 3:7) and in that of Jesus, who also "stirred up the people."

The eternal nature of God is not, of course, contradicted by his intervention in history; hence his transformation of the world into his Kingdom did not entail a reinterpretation of his will. Thus the admonition, "Hear oh Israel, the Lord our God is one God" need not call for activism on behalf of a temporal movement to collaborate with God's decision to install His Kingdom.

The question is one of temperament: Judaism, which requires the performance of certain duties, also obliges the pious to repeat the admonition "Hear, O Israel." This had been done for centuries before Judah the Galilean, and was still being done, of course, by pious Jews who did not agree with him, i.e., the "quietists." But if you had the Galilean's temperament, the admonition could also be considered a clarion call to action. Thus the Galilean's activism exposed the contrast otherwise only implicit between the timelessness of Yahweh and specific temporal action on his behalf. Abandoning the passivity associated with mere belief, he incited people to action through the conviction that the Kingdom of God and hence the dominion of his people, Israel, would be realized only if Israel implemented in real life the absolute sovereignty implied in "Hear, O Israel."

The broad concept underlying this was summed up in the phrase "forcing the end"; the activists' "zeal" for Yahweh implied that they would compel him, as it were, to bring about the consummation of his own handiwork. Thus it was natural to call such activists "Zealots"; the word itself implied the other-worldly dimension inherent in religious ardor. Phineas the son of Aaron had been "zealous" for his God (Num 25:13), and since Phineas was thought of as an incarnation of Elijah the prophet, who was meant to return one day as precursor of the Messiah (Mal 4:5), the concept of "zeal" for God in and for itself entailed a messianic thrust.

As the Torah gradually became more and more sacred, ever since the Babylonian Exile centuries before, what had been zeal for Yahweh was gradually transformed into zeal for Yahweh's word, the Torah. In this as in many other things, the Galilean's enterprise repeated many of the motifs of the Maccabean revolt.

Around this time the contrast between Israel and its neighbors was exacerbated by the expansion of the imperial cults throughout the eastern Mediterranean, especially in Rome where it was becoming more and more commonplace for emperors to be worshipped as gods. This imperial cult had itself arisen out of the decay of the ancient pagan gods. The Olympic pantheon had long since become a pale shadow, eliciting no emotion: thus the emergence of the emperors as objects of worship fused with traditional attitudes toward heroes, and after Alexander the Great's incredible military triumphs he himself had been apotheosized, as were his successors. The deification of rulers became endemic throughout the area. Thus the sharpening of the First Commandment into a political weapon heightened the contrast between Jews and pagans. It made the cleavage between them, in fact, unbridgeable. Against the background of deified local rulers of all kinds, Judah the Galilean's unwavering insistence on the implications of the First Commandment transformed politics. No compromise could be possible between the metaphysics of the Roman imperial cult and the imminent Kingdom of God. The simple insight that the First Commandment, broken by the Emperor's demand that he be worshipped as a god, *had* to entail a struggle for religious freedom, was moving *only to those who chose to act.*

It was, in fact, this notion of freedom that throughout this period of the early Roman Empire constituted the paramount thrust of Judah the Galilean's activism. But it would be anachronistic to imagine that the freedom sought by the activists was a political ambition of secular rebels. What the activists meant was not mere political freedom, it was really the redemption of Israel, associated with the World's End. To those involved in the struggle against Rome the concept required no analysis: religion and politics made a seamless web.

Judah the Galilean was not the only prominent rebel: in Peraea a man called Simon, a former slave of Herod, renowned for his good looks and physical strength, came to the fore, as well as a shepherd with the odd name of Athrongas, also celebrated for his gigantic stature and extraordinary strength. Both these men put forth their claims to the rule of Judea. They were both executed, but Judah the Galilean held out "on the outside," in the mountains and deserts, even after the revolt of 4 B.C.E. was crushed by the Roman general Varus and thousands of the insurgents crucified.

As Roman oppression increased one diehard after another presented himself as the promised Messiah. The Zealots, essentially Pharisees themselves, generally supported, explicitly or tacitly, by the Pharisee mainstream, as mentioned above, were eventually, through their mounting fanaticism, to intensify the opposition to Rome into the catastrophic war of 66–70.

Whether the Galilean's partisans called themselves "Zealots " at first or not, they were known as such later on. (The actual word first occurs as a description of one of Jesus' entourage, in Mt 10:4.)

In any case, the presence of an actual Zealot among the disciples of Jesus is illuminating. Nor was it a case of a random, former Zealot turning up among the disciples of Jesus. There were others.

Even if one disregards the temptation to look upon the otherwise mysterious nickname applied to James and John the sons of Zebedee, "surnamed Boanerges, that is, sons of thunder" as an obvious reference to their violent natures, the extraordinary name given to Simon the Rock himself, precisely at a moment when Jesus, on the eve of the decisive action in Jerusalem, is making him in effect his deputy, is intriguing.

In a celebrated passage (claimed by the Roman Catholic Church as its divine sanction) Jesus says this to Simon the Rock, when the latter acknowledges him for the first time as the Messiah:

> Blessed are you, Simon Bar-Yona! . . . I will give you the keys to the Kingdom of God, and whatever you bind on earth shall be bound in heaven, and whatever you loose on earth shall be loosed in heaven. (Mt. 16:17,19)

Aside from Jesus' plain meaning that in this ancient metaphor he was assigning the deputyship of his status, however conceived, to Simon the Rock, what is arresting is the curious name, Bar-Yona, usually translated as "Simon son of John."

Now, Judah the Galilean held out "on the outside," as mentioned above. This curious phrase is clarified by another remark in the Talmud, about a nephew of the famous Rabbi Yohanan ben Zakkai who was called "the Daggerman" and was the head of the *baryonim* of Jerusalem.

The word *baryonim* comes from an Aramaic word meaning "open country." They were those people living in the open country outside the towns; i.e., the outcasts, outlaws, and—extremists that the country was full of. Saul himself was mistaken for such a Daggerman by a Roman captain of a cohort:

> Are you not the Egyptian . . . who recently stirred up a revolt and led the four thousand daggermen out into the wilderness? (Acts 21:38)

It is plain from the context in which this word occurs that these *baryonim* were similar in all respects to the Zealots; they are doubtless to be thought of as a faction of the same opposition to Rome. Both Zealots and *baryonim* would thus be cognate with the so-called "fourth school of philosophy" mentioned by Josephus in addition to the Pharisees, Sadduccees and Essenes. Hence in the celebrated passage in Matthew, the word *bar* is not to be taken as the Aramaic for "son of;" the name Bar-Yona is in all likelihood to be understood as an echo of Simon the Rock's original calling, i.e., Simon the *Baryon,* Simon the extremist, the Daggerman, the outlaw, i.e., an adherent, like Simon the Zealot, of the ideas expressed by Judah the Galilean or someone like him.

This question of living "on the outside" is not to be understood as a mere matter of geography: the profound significance, from a devout Jewish point of view, of "leaving the town" was that it was conceived of as a method of avoiding the apostasy, or the sin, or at the very least the impurity of living under idol-worshippers. For in view of the power of Rome there were only two ways for such pious Jews to follow the Torah (i.e., the Deuteronomic "royalty law" mentioned above): vanquish the Romans or flee. Since the entire known world was Roman, subject to the rule of the "Prince of this world," the only way of eluding apostasy was to renounce all and go into the desert, to be purified there like the ancient Hebrews.

There was, to be sure, a third way, that of the quietists content to wait patiently until it suited God to liberate his people from the pagan yoke; this meant allowing oneself to be steeped in sin, with no excuse except that of weakness. This quietist course naturally had the advantage of not inflaming the authorities; individual quietists could be allowed to creep harmlessly about. From the Roman point of view they were ideal. Quietist Jews, although like other devout worshippers of Yahweh they too loathed the iniquity of their pagan overlordship, did not come to violent ends.

Political liberty was merely one aspect of the "freedom" the religious insurgents were willing to die for. From the Galilean's movement of resistance to the Roman census of 6 C.E. down to the suicide at Masada of the last survivors of the Roman-Jewish war of 66–70, the freedom sought for Yahweh's people meant the blanket elimination of all institutions imposed by pagan Rome. In 73 C.E., for instance, the leader of the Masada garrison was to repeat a motif of Judah the Galilean: "From the very beginning we were struggling to achieve liberty."[1] For him the dead are the happy ones: "They fell in the struggle for liberty."[2] Thus the theme embedded in the activists' appeal to the people over two generations was in fact their total freedom—under Yahweh.

The World's End redemption of Israel was patterned on the miracles performed by God during the Exodus from Egypt—this time, to be sure, on a much grander scale. When God gave signs of freedom to those who took to the desert in the Galilean's day, the "signs" really echo the "signs" given by God to the Israelites who have forgotten their reason for leaving Egypt and who reproach Moses for their distress in the desert. Thus, for Judah the Galilean, Yahweh could be provoked to "force the end" if the Jews showed their readiness for World's End redemption by collaborating with Yahweh in his grand design.

The Kingdom of God and the World's End redemption of the Jews had further implications. If Yahweh, while rectifying the inequities of the universe, also restored the fortunes of the Jews, it was only natural for Israel to rule the world on behalf of Yahweh. Thus both Israel and its God would rule the cosmos.

This notion of Israel's world dominion on behalf of Yahweh had come up under Alexander the Great's successors (ca. 165 B.C.E. in Daniel) and was ramified later on.[3]

Kingdom of God activists assumed that the role of Israel implied the Last Judgment on all idol-worshippers in general and on the oppressors of

Israel in particular. That was, in fact, the substance of the national hope held aloft by the Zealots. It is echoed unmistakably in the Gospels: Jesus [said], "In the world to come, when the Son of Man [the Messiah] is seated on his throne in heavenly splendor, you my followers will have thrones of your own, where you will sit as judges of the twelve tribes of Israel" (Mt 19:28, also Lk 22:28). But we [the pilgrims of Emmaus, after the execution of Jesus] had been hoping he was the man to liberate Israel (Lk 24:21). They asked (Jesus), "Lord, is this the time when you are to establish once again the sovereignty of Israel?" (Acts 1:6).

The details involved in the installation of the Kingdom of God were not, of course, agreed upon. Some believers thought the Kingdom of God was merely the natural world reformed and placed under the direct rule of Yahweh. Some believed in an other-worldly, etherealized Kingdom.

Saul of Tarsus, a contemporary of Jesus, believed in such an etherealized Kingdom, in which the national/religious opposition of the Jews to Rome had no place. As we shall see, Saul's influence was eventually to play a decisive role in the formation of Christianity, but that lay many decades in the future.

The Zealots concentrated on the old-fashioned, this-worldly, purely national theory of the World's End, centered in the restoration of Israel. Zealot activism revived the flesh-and-blood Messiah and, as Roman oppression grew intolerable, by the time of Jesus and Saul, the concept of the Messiah became concrete, *actual.*

Massively anchored in ardor, the Zealot movement naturally permeated the Temple milieu. From the very outset the lower strata of the priesthood seem to have been Zealots; it was they, indeed, who in the generation after Jesus were to trigger the war against the Romans by refusing to offer the daily sacrifices in the Temple on behalf of the Roman Emperor and the people of Rome, an institution maintained by the upper strata as a public demonstration of loyalty to the Empire. The lower priests were in a state of constant effervescence. Individual aristocrats, too, were inflamed by the messianic contagion.

Messiahship was in the nature of things disproved by failure. The posthumous career of Jesus was unique: the specific circumstances of his death launched, ultimately, a totally different type of movement, as we shall see, quite outside the orbit of traditional ideas.

There was a perennial crop of messiahs and prophets all with an assignment from the one God whose intervention was felt to be "at hand" and all of whom went down successively to defeat and death.

At the same time, the collapse of the innumerable messianic movements that proliferated throughout this period could never shake the pious conviction that no matter how things looked at the moment, all would be set right. Yahweh would prevail and redeem Israel in the wake of the *real* Messiah's appearance.

Throughout the Roman occupation of Palestine down to the war of 66–70 and afterwards, the expectation of a Messiah aroused the most powerful feelings, with a steady intensification of the fervor attached to the conviction that the Kingdom of God at the World's End called for action.

The emotions linked to this idea were intensified by another belief, rooted in contemporary chronology, that the Kingdom of God was "at hand" because the world was entering the fifth millennium (Jewish calendar). Even before the first century attempts had been made to pinpoint the advent of the World's End[4]; when Jesus said, in the wake of John the Baptist, that the "time was fulfilled" (Mk 1:14–15) and "the Kingdom of God was at hand," we can hear an echo of a prevalent belief that the year 5,000 in the calendar of creation according to the Torah was going to bring with it the sixth millennium—that of the Kingdom of God.

No doubt this prospect intensified the aversion to the Romans. There is some evidence that though the rapacities and inequities of the Roman administration were extensive, they were not much worse than before or elsewhere, but now, with the feverishness linked to the Kingdom of God agitation, inflamed still further by the calculations indicating the near advent of the millennium, it must have seemed to many that there was, at last, a way out. Thus it was not the Messiah who by his own action alone was to bring the Millennium, it was the scheduled millennium that was now escorted, as it were, by the Messiah.

Before the second quarter of the first century, the millennium might have seemed too remote to pin specific hopes to it in terms of action, but the appearance of Jesus (around 30 C.E.) might have coincided with the current of millenniarian speculation in which the year 30 was pinpointed as the beginning of the new millennium and hence of the Kingdom of God.

Judah the Galilean was himself considered a Messiah (as in the speech put in Gamaliel's mouth in Acts 5:36f); during the Roman War (66–70) his grandson, Menahem, behaved with matter-of-factness as King of the Jews, in this context the World's End Messiah.

The notion of a Messiah stemming from the house of David had deep historical resonance: a war Messiah was bound to be considered a scion of the ancient king, a notion that, even though sophisticates might have embroidered it metaphysically, was understood quite literally by ordinary people, as we shall see.

There were other factors in the Kingdom of God ferment.

The Romans, indifferent to the religion of their subjects, had one economic objective: to squeeze taxes out of them not only for the state but, more particularly, especially during the first century or so of the Empire, for the benefit of the various proconsuls, prefects, legates, and procurators who represented Rome in the provinces.

Oppressive as Herod the Great's taxation had been, it was overshadowed by the Roman procuratorial regime: a land tax had to be paid in kind, while a head tax was levied on every male child over fourteen and every female child over twelve: only the aged were exempt. In addition, revenue, cattle, and exports and imports were all taxed: there were market fees, bridge and harbor tolls, and town dues.

A special scourge was the ferocious system of tax-farming, abolished long before by Julius Caesar but reinstalled by the Romans when they moved into Palestine. Private contractors would buy concessions from the state authorizing them to collect the taxes; they were allowed to make as much personal profit as they could, and as government officials they could force extravagant amounts out of the helpless populace. Countless partisans of the religious activists came from various propertied groups made destitute by the tax-farming system.

In addition to the devastations of the tax collectors—the "publicans" of the King James Version—the Jews were subject to plundering by governors and procurators who had also acquired their positions by extensive bribery and had to make up for their losses. This was further aggravated by adventurers of all kinds who flocked to the provinces. When heavy new taxes had to be paid, usury at 50 percent was commonplace; if this was not paid, people would be sold into slavery.

The atrociousness, for the Jews, of having their Holy Land governed by idolaters was, in short, compounded by an entirely mundane factor—rapacious exploitation.

The tide of insurrection was sustained by all those without property or who had lost it—unemployed soldiers, slaves, shepherds, dispossessed farmers. An element of social upheaval ran through the religious activist movement from its inception. Just as at the outset the fury of the insurrectionists was aimed at the vast luxury buildings built in the Greek style and lavishly appointed by Herod the Great, so at the outbreak of the Roman war in 66 there were similar attacks on the great constructions of the aristocrats and the authorities.

Yet the religious motive was predominant: even if the economic oppression under Rome was only a trifle worse than the rule of the Hasmoneans or more recently of Herod the Great, as some think, the component of religious outrage gave it an entirely different dimension. Even though the upper classes accommodated themselves deftly to foreign rule, from which, because of their habits, training, and interests, they suffered far less or indeed not at all, the masses of the people were infuriated on two levels simultaneously.

At the same time, the very generality of the resistance made it difficult to organize. The fact that the religion, in and for itself, was not threatened, and its concomitant, that quietism was a real possibility for pietists, created a major stumbling block. It was hard to find a specific goal for would-be insurgents to unite around, harder still to establish the legitimacy of any given leader.

Judah the Galilean, after all, had simply put himself forward through his interpretation of the Torah, any pious Jew could do the same. Leaders had to vie with each other to establish their own legitimacy. Judah the Galilean emulated a principle laid down by the Maccabees, who claimed personal status as royalty because of their zeal on behalf of the religion. The Galilean and his descendants also took it for granted that as champions of Yahweh they had an inherent right to establish a World's End dynasty that would bridge the transition between the workaday world and the Kingdom of God.

In the event the Galilean founded a party with sharply formulated views and a firm organization, all anchored in a simple religious idea. His dynastic succession was to remain the core of the Jewish independence movement that was ultimately to sweep the bulk of the population into the war against Rome.

There were, of course, deep parallels between the Maccabees and Judah the Galilean. Both fought to preserve Judaism; the founder of the Maccabee movement, Matithyahu the priest, showed the same zeal as the Galilean by killing Jews who in their longing for Hellenization were flouting God's word, the Torah. The Maccabees, however, had fought against the attempt to *obliterate* Judaism; after success their religious motivation atrophied and they became conventional politicians.

The Galilean and his activists, on the other hand, had no need to defend their religion against the Romans, who, with the exception of the demented Caligula in the generation after Jesus, guaranteed Jews religious freedom. Yet it was just such a compromise that the Galilean could not accept. His extremist stance on the World's End crisis meant that Yahweh's omnipotence forbade any acceptance of pagan rule, tolerant or not and, for his partisans, the acceptance of Roman rule was *ipso facto* an acceptance of idol worship and apostasy. They were incapable of negotiating; the concept was meaningless for them. This in itself made them far more rigorous than the Maccabees.

Moreover, by the time the Romans placed Judea-Samaria under their direct administration in 6 C.E., the Hellenization, far deeper than mere politics, that had been pervasive throughout the Eastern Mediterranean had been digested by the Jewish elite as well as by countless ordinary Jews.

Jewish society, precisely by resisting the political straitjacketing attempted by Antiochus IV and his Jewish allies, was all the readier to absorb its cultural content. It managed to do this without abandoning its own traditions, by tucking various elements of Hellenism—literature, ideas, institutions—into the overarching embrace of monotheism.

A knowledge of Greek was *de rigueur* among the Jewish elite; in Alexandria and other Greek-speaking centers the Greek heritage was systematically adapted to Jewish traditions: pious Jews (like Philo of Alexandria), busily demonstrated the essential unity between the Torah—properly understood—and the monuments of Greek culture (Plato, Aristotle, Plotinus, Pythagoras, etc.).

Accordingly, by the time the Romans had installed themselves as political overlords without camouflage in 6 C.E., Judaism no longer faced the same threat as it had under Antiochus IV. For Judah the Galilean it was not the Romans' behavior that was offensive, it was the naked fact of their presence.

This itself was a decisive rupture with a tradition centuries old. From the first destruction of Jerusalem to the appearance of Antiochus IV four hundred years later the Jews had been docile; even later, when the initial upsurge of Maccabean independence had been eroded and a succession of Jewish princes had been subjugated by foreigners, the mere fact of alien rule had failed to provoke a Jewish resistance.

It cannot be overemphasized that Judah the Galilean's activist movement was wholly religious in character; it encompassed, in principle, all

Jewry, who as Yahweh's chosen people were obliged to live up to the demands of their election. This had nothing to do, of course, with kinship, though born Jews were by nature, as it were, identified with their religion. But Jewish backsliders—the "quietists" willing to live in peace with Rome—had to be cast out or killed, whereas pagans who accepted the Torah were welcome. For the Zealots the remnant of Israel who were to benefit from the redemption of the Kingdom of God were not only the survivors of the clash of arms with their enemies but also the resurrected individuals from among the righteous fallen in battle.

Many Jews, to be sure, notably the Sadducees, did not believe either in the afterlife or in personal resurrection.

Kingdom of God expectations had naturally been accompanied by an intensification of religious fervor; even in the older prophets (Isaiah 32:15, 44:3 and Ezekiel 11:19, 36:26), the gift of the "Spirit" had been promised as part of the transition to the paradise projected for the future. Thus, when religious fervor was intensified under the Romans and the World's End was felt to be "at hand," all Jews who now believed in it naturally claimed for themselves the possession of the "Spirit."

That is why in Acts 2:17ff much is made of Joel 2:28ff, which cites God as saying "I shall pour out my spirit upon all flesh" as a prelude to the great transition. (Also Rom. 5:5,8; Gal 3:2 and others). Judea, Samaria, and Galilee were in fact thronging with "prophets" of all kinds, all feeling "elected" by God for the World's End transition as their role required them to be imbued with the "Spirit."

The World's End fever also forced on believers a claim to a grasp of history—they had to be able to predict real-life events: in Acts, for instance, one of the "prophets" who came to Antioch from Jerusalem "stood up and foretold by the Spirit that there would be a great famine all over the world" (11:28).

There was, to be sure, nothing clear and unmistakable in the speculation concerning the events of the transitional period between the smashing of secular pagan dominion and the emergence into the messianic kingdom thought to precede the Kingdom of God proper. There was no limitation to the endless combinations of forces involved in Yahweh's direct intervention. This might include angels, different processes of dissolution among the enemies of Yahweh, various nations involved in a concerted attack from the East on the people of Israel, and so on.

Generally speaking, it was understood by Jewish visionaries that the actual redemption, taken for granted as inherent in the emergence of a herald of the Kingdom of God, would be preceded by a frightful era of "trial"—the "pangs of the Messiah."

Since there were no clear predictions, the shape and nature of this ordeal varied abundantly. Not only Israel would be affected, but all the nations on earth, and even the natural order itself. The stars in their courses would be shaken up; on earth justice would vanish, there would be natural convulsions, social upheavals, diseases, famine, etc.

In Judea specifically, the Jewish sanctuary, these various horrors would be brought about by a final onslaught of the pagan power. No doubt the historical model for such speculations was Antiochus IV's attack on Judaism two centuries before. This must have been in the minds of all those who had become inflamed by Pompey's conquest of Jerusalem in 63 B.C.E., during the riots following Herod's death in 4 B.C.E. (around the time of Jesus' birth) and also under the Roman procuratorial regime, when religious feelings were exacerbated by the Roman control over the Temple itself.

This was to be a continuous inflammation for two generations. Only a few years after Jesus' death, for instance, Caligula ordered a statue of himself to be set up in the Temple to be worshipped as a god: a general insurrection was forestalled only by his death.

The general idea of the redemption of Israel emanating from a cosmic superpower that was an enemy of God himself could, of course, be traced to Scripture (Ezekiel, Daniel). With the Roman occupation of Judea and Galilee, that enemy of God was naturally Rome, which came to stand for the "Fourth Kingdom" of Daniel. It was just this plausible, indeed, compelling identification, in which Rome gave body to the worst forebodings about the peril confronting Israel, that set its stamp on the World's End fever of the first century.

Rome was the natural current embodiment of the evil thought to have been embodied in the major historical enemies of Israel: Amaleq and Babylon, the destroyer of Jerusalem, symbolized by Esau, in the current age, Edom. Here the role of Herod the Great facilitated the transfer of the hatred from Edom to the Romans. Thus the cosmic role once ascribed to Antiochus IV could be shifted to the Romans, whose emperor assumed the features of the World's End tyrant. The evolving emperor cult naturally helped focus the hatred.

Since there was considerable variation of emphasis on the periphery of the central themes, different groups laid varying emphasis on the identity of the chief culprits in the cosmic drama: thus the Essenes, for instance, took the depravity of their own people (the corrupt priesthood) as meaning that the bulk of the Jews themselves were the chief enemy to be overcome at the World's End, while the major religious activists (the Zealots), though ferociously hostile to the Jewish aristocracy, concentrated on the Romans as their chief opponent.

This was given plausibility precisely by the behavior of the Roman governors, who were constantly threatening the sanctuary, and who as defenders of the state naturally took the lead in tracking down and killing all those who were "forcing the end." It was very easy and natural to identify Rome with the "Fourth Kingdom" mentioned in Daniel, especially in the discussion of the "days of wrath" that were conceived of as testing and purifying God's people through the onset of the redemptive crisis. Some natural external events, too, such as the persistent famine under Emperor Claudius (predicted by the prophet in Acts), must have lent plausibility to the notion that the World's End upheaval had finally erupted.

The activists interpreted these horrors so as to derive from them the lesson they were looking for. If the Jews went on docilely obeying the Roman pagans, the horrors could plainly be considered God's punishment for backsliding.

On the other hand, if the Jews saw the light and under the pressure of the steadily growing pagan oppression took to resistance, then the "pangs of the Messiah" would be transformed into a purification. The mere sufferings, afflictions, and so on of the resistance against Rome would then constitute no more than a test of the remnant to be spared. As long as most Jews accepted the pagan yoke, God's wrath was on them: if that was so the World's End could not be pinpointed. But if the lead of the activists was followed and the masses of the people, inflamed by zeal for Yahweh, launched a holy war against Rome, the crisis would be ended. Redemption would break forth.

The holy war itself was, of course, embedded in the Scriptures. Commanded originally by Yahweh himself, the Hebrew "volunteers" were also exhorted by a priest or by a charismatic leader. By definition, in fact, the holy war was a mere continuation of the worship of God. This ancient idea had merely been revived by the Maccabees under the goad of Antiochus IV's attack on Judaism. Matithyahu himself was of course a charismatic figure; his son Judah the Maccabee, after exhorting his troops by references to God's miracles in the past, would pray. He would divide the army (Exodus 18:21–26), eliminating cowards and cripples (Dt 20:5–8). Mere smallness of numbers would not necessarily mean anything, since, after all, "power came from Yahweh" (1 Macc 3:18ff).

Even the prophets after the Babylonian Exile conceived of Yahweh as personally intervening to help his people in the showdown with its enemies. The idea was to be absorbed into apocalyptic visions, where God moved not only against the enemies of Israel, on the human plane, but against the demonic powers sponsoring those enemies. Thus when the activists embarked on their long-drawn-out campaign against the Romans they had ready to hand the well-tried concept of a holy war that could easily be integrated with the World's End war against the pagan world power.

The concept of a holy war framed the movement that from Judah the Galilean on steadily gathered enough force to swing the bulk of the population into the bloodbath of 66–70. Many details that have come down to us from the conduct of the actual war imply that the army and its functioning were modeled on the Scriptures. In Galilee, for instance, Flavius Josephus, while still a commander on the Jewish side before deserting to the Romans, convoked a council of seventy notables, plainly patterned after the seventy elders of the desert (Ex 24:1; Nu 11:16).

The desert was the classical refuge of all enemies of the state; the partisans of Judah the Galilean left the desert for the settled areas only on guerrilla forays, before their success in swinging the masses of the population into the war against Rome. Except for such forays the activists might have seemed part of the ordinary population.

The desert, a place for testing and trial, where God had revealed himself to his people, was to be retreated to for the purpose of renewing the fight for Yahweh against the pagan powers. The recurrent theme of "going into the desert" must be understood politically. Since the Roman administration was too feeble to encompass the desert regions, withdrawal into the desert was not only a form of social protest, but a first-class political, economic, and military strategy. In an epoch of militant piety the desert, revered in tradition as a place for asceticism, for being tested (Dt 8:2), and for meeting God (Dt 32:10), was the natural ideal.

There was also, of course, a deeply rooted tradition of identifying primordial events with future events; the basic model was the Exodus out of Egypt, conducted by God. It was, after all, the desert where Israel, freed by miracles, had gazed for the first time on Yahweh. In a later period, accordingly, under renewed oppression by pagans, the desert inevitably had come to mean the World's End redemption of the Jews. Thus, Matithyahu, leader of the Maccabees, fleeing with his sons to the desert to prepare an attack on the pagan power, had set an example for all future activists: his basic appeal was an unconditional readiness to lose one's life for God (I Macc 2:27).

The Maccabees were to restore the Jews to political sovereignty for a short time; after the absorption of Palestine into the Roman orbit the desert was to play the same role for activists identified with the Kingdom of God agitation. This time, however, with the appearance of John the Baptist and Jesus, the results were to be entirely different.

2

John the Baptist and Jesus

In the Gospels Jesus is introduced in intimate connection, far from clear, with John the Baptist, a somber, enigmatic figure looming over the very threshold of Jesus' career, who is given practically the same formula as Jesus': "Repent, for the Kingdom of Heaven [God] is at hand. " (Mt 3:2).

The figure of the Baptist remains irremediably obscure. All we know about him is contained in the Gospels and in Josephus, our sole source for this whole period. (There are about fifteen references to the Baptist in the Gospels and one mention in Josephus.)

Josephus refers to the Baptist as a "good man," whose message to the Jews consisted only of some excellent advice concerning virtue, justice, and piety; he accounts for the Baptist's death, at the hands of the Tetrarch Herod Antipas, as being due merely to Herod's incomprehensible fears that John's ethical counsel might somehow have led to a movement to unseat Herod, which he forestalled by seizing, jailing and killing John. Josephus makes a special point of the Baptist's harmlessness: according to him all the Baptist wanted was to purify by baptism the bodies of those whose virtuous living had already purified their souls and thus make them welcome to God; it was the Baptist's eloquence, according to Josephus, that made the people flock to him and alarmed Herod.

In the Gospel of John, the Baptist's message is recorded only as the simple exhortation to "repent," given above, as well as the statement that a great purification by fire would precede the fulfillment of this promise (which like the Kingdom of God itself was part of Jewish belief). What he was urging his listeners to do was simply to have a change of heart that would enable them to live according to the will of God; this repentance would prepare both body and soul for the advent of the Messiah who was to herald the Kingdom of God.

Thus John's addition to the agitation about the Kingdom of God was the threat of punishment as well as the mere announcement of the Good News of its imminence (the original meaning of "Gospel").

There is a possibility that John's stark summons should be interpreted as meaning "repent so that the Kingdom of God may come," i.e., that his baptism was also a dynamic means of bringing the Kingdom about, as well as a way of securing access to the Kingdom for the individual penitent.

At various times the notion has became popular that the Baptist was connected with the Essenes, a monastic sect that believed in daily ritual ablutions, lived in seclusion, and had its chief monastery, as now seems likely, near the Dead Sea. Josephus for that matter clearly implies a connection with John, but there are some basic differences that make this doubtful. John's baptism seems to have been a rite that was undergone only once, as a permanent initiation of the converted, the "repentant," instead of a mere daily immersion like that of the Essenes. If he had any sectarian similarities with the monastery, or monasteries of Ein Gedi on Qumran, with their communal life and their ritual, then our Gospel text conceals them from us, a possibility, of course, that is altogether conceivable.

Otherwise John was not an unconventional phenomenon of the time. In those days the wilderness was a favorite rendezvous of the disaffected. It was not a mere wasteland: The wilderness referred to, for instance, in Mark is the lower valley of the Jordan near the Dead Sea. This has dense vegetation, including real trees, and at the very spot where Christian tradition locates Jesus' baptism by John, the Jordan River looks like a turbulent American or European river. "Wilderness" merely meant that it was largely uninhabited, except for a monastery, some pilgrims' stations, etc.

As for John's dress and diet, he "was clothed with camel's hair, and had a leather girdle around his waist, and ate locusts and wild honey" (Mk 1:6). This was traditional for prophets. Locusts and wild honey are perfectly good food, still eaten by many. Elijah, the Hebrew prophet, was a "hairy man, wearing a kin robe, and a leather belt around his loins" (2 Kings 1:8).

In short, as John appears in the Gospels and in Josephus's works, he seems to have been in the prophetic tradition of classical Judaism; he gave his message because God had inspired him.

As far as the rite of baptism itself was concerned, we can see from the Gospels that it had three qualities. It was a purification rite like other Jewish ablutions; it was a ritual of initiation, presumably into a real fraternity of penitents awaiting the Kingdom of God, and it was also a Jewish baptism of converts: just as baptism introduced non-Jews into the Jewish community, so John's baptism also restored the quality of a son of Abraham to those who had lapsed into sin.

Nothing is known about how John performed the ritual of baptism, or his personal role in it. Though Josephus and the Gospels agree on the fact of the baptism, they differ on everything else. Josephus writes as though it were no more than a symbol of a moral event, while the Gospel writers, doubtless thinking of Christian baptism in their own time, ascribed to it a practical efficacy against sin. The fact is, however, that such details elude us.

The Gospels are unanimous in linking Jesus' emergence as a prophet in his own right to his baptism by John. This association is not a mere chronological sequence; we are meant to believe that Jesus actually assumed his Messianic status as a consequence of John's baptism, though its meaning remains unclear.

It is obvious that though Jesus' career is somehow dependent on John, a systematic effort is made in the Gospels, wherever the question of John comes up, to harmonize all accounts in favor of Jesus' precedence, while at the same time respectfully according an honored status to John as Jesus' "forerunner." It is in fact just this contradiction—as we may now begin to expect—that guarantees its actuality, and also illuminates its historical— i.e., nonapologetic—meaning.

The problem of Jesus' baptism by John was obviously of the greatest delicacy in the formation of the most ancient tradition. For since the whole of Christian tradition was engaged in confirming John's validity only as a forerunner of Jesus, his baptizing of Jesus must have been a tremendous hurdle for the early chroniclers. It was a problem especially because John was survived by a sizable group of followers, whom it was evidently the intention of Christian propaganda to attract into the fold while keeping John subordinate to Jesus.

If Jesus was baptized by John, after all, by means of a baptism that was agreed to have been a "baptism of repentance for the forgiveness of sins" (Mk 1:4), it could only have implied either that Jesus was a sinner like everyone else, or else that he had become Messiah as a result of the baptism. Since both notions were of course incompatible with Christian thought, the attempt to circumvent the plain implications of John's baptism gave rise to many ambiguities, obscurities, and contradictions in the Gospels. Simply put, John's baptism of Jesus could not have been invented by Christians, who were interested not in heightening the Baptist's originality but in erasing it altogether, and in spite of all the attempts to veil this fact or tone it down it emerges in the Gospels with great clarity.

According to Mark and Luke it was not until the Baptist was arrested by Herod Antipas that Jesus actually began his own preaching. Mark reports the Baptist's arrest as taking place during the period of Jesus' withdrawal and meditation, when his consciousness of his mission presumably matured. Mark thus makes it clear that it was when the voice of the "one crying in the wilderness" had been put to a stop that Jesus launched himself on his own mission of proclaiming the Kingdom of God and his own role as herald, that is, of simply repeating John's theme. Thus, according to the Gospel account John was the triple cause of Jesus' career:

1. It was his fame that drew Jesus to the banks of the Jordan;
2. John's arrest propelled Jesus into a public career in order to carry on John's role;
3. Jesus became aware of his calling after being baptized by John.

In terms of the development in the Gospel account, the version in Mark is the simplest: Jesus was baptized by John in the Jordan (Mk 1:9b). This statement is so bald it defies adornment. The contortion of the narratives in the remainder of the Gospels is evidently due to the attempt to explain away this plain and simple fact.

The Matthew account, for instance, is far more complicated; since the chronicle makes Jesus' Messiahship dependent on nothing but his actual birth, Matthew is compelled to report Jesus' baptism as a mystery of God's will. In Matthew, John is reported as expressing surprise at being asked to baptize Jesus, saying Jesus ought to baptize *him*. Jesus merely replies, "Let it be so now; for thus is it fitting for us to fulfill all righteousness," i.e., carry out God's plan (Mt 3:15). Afterwards, it is implied, they can carry on as before, that is, Jesus can resume his inherent superiority.

The account of the Baptist in the fourth Gospel is revealingly obscure and contradictory. Jesus has more disciples than John (Jn 3:26; 4:1), yet no one receives his testimony (Jn 3:32); he baptizes (3:22, 4:1) and doesn't (4:2), etc. What these curious discrepancies imply is not, of course, mere awkwardness on the part of a writer or editor, but an actual difficulty with source-material; there must have been some document or recollection from a Baptist milieu, i.e., from the community that was still distinct from the Christians and doubtless being wooed by them.

In any case the attempt made in the Synoptic Gospels to pretend that Jesus' contact with the Baptist was brief is clearly artificial and collides with common sense. It is evident that the simple statement in *Mark,* after the report of Jesus' baptism by John, that "the spirit immediately drove him out into the wilderness" (Mk 1:12) implies with its "immediately" that there were no further personal relations between the two, and it is plainly at odds with every other indication in the Gospels. It is obvious that the Baptist and his followers were of great interest to the early Christians, who borrowed so many things from them, including baptism itself (see chapter 5) and probably fasting, common prayer, etc.

In the original tradition Jesus was simply baptized by John—that is, he was a follower, disciple, collaborator, or some other kind of subordinate, though possibly an intimate subordinate. This simple relationship was gradually both attenuated and distorted by the later doctrinal requirements that displaced Jesus' messianic status first to his birth (the Holy Spirit), then to his preexistence as the Word, etc. The fact that the fourth Gospel omits any specific mention of Jesus' actual baptism, while at the same time reporting other circumstances indicating Jesus' dependence on John, must be taken as a sort of doctrinal correction of the Synoptic accounts.

Looked at functionally, so to speak, the legend of the Baptist as fore-runner essentially implies that the Baptist tradition was simply absorbed by the Christian community; further, we must believe that in the oldest tradition Jesus was at first subordinate to John, and doubtless baptized by him. To be sure, the concession can be made that the actual act of baptism is per-haps to be understood as merely an indication, by means of a symbol taken from later Christian practice, when baptism was already solidly established, of the hierarchical relationship between John and Jesus.

The growth of doctrine in the evolving religion, long after John the Baptist and Jesus, led very naturally to the whittling down of nearly all veridical information about the Baptist. Just as he is mentioned by Jose-phus only in connection with something else (the reign of Herod Antipas), so the Gospels mention him only in connection with the baptism of Jesus. Because of the lopsidedness, for different reasons, of both these accounts, we remain in ignorance of the Baptist himself and of his movement.

In any case, the Baptist appears abruptly with a quotation from the Prophet Isaiah: "The voice of one who cries out in the desert, 'Prepare a way for the Lord, clear a straight path for him' " (Mk 1:3, from Isaiah 40:3). Jesus, too, repeatedly illustrates this theme: "Thereupon the Spirit sent him away into the desert, and there he remained for forty days" (Mk 1:12, and parallels). In short, anyone who, like John the Baptist, heeded Judah the Galilean's call and flouted the census had to follow the example of Matithyahu and his sons: abandon his property, flee to the desert, and stake his life on the outcome.

The activists' contempt for death was famous; the Romans, indeed, thought them out of their minds. Their fanaticism, their readiness to sacrifice all on behalf of their cause, prepared them as it were automatically for martyrdom. What was extraordinary was the number of people prepared to do likewise—that is, the dimensions of the mass movement. That readiness for death was summed up in a celebrated formula—"carrying the cross." Against the background of the resistance to the Romans this formula, used in the Gospels repeatedly, has peculiar poignancy, though very soon after the death of Jesus, as we shall see, it came to acquire a vastly different meaning.

The activists identified their current rebellion against the Romans with the premessianic "trial" that was to purify Israel and crystallize out the remnant that would survive the World's End. Their provisional task, accordingly, was to move the masses of Jewry into the holy war against the pagan power. From the activists' point of view the docile, peace-loving Jewish aristocrats and priests were their most dangerous enemies—apostates all, such quietists were standing in the way of the divine plan.

But the pro-Roman Jewish aristocrats were helpless in their turn to control the Roman machine for extortion. Though it took a couple of generations of constant agitation, eventually the activists did succeed, in the generation after Jesus, in launching a national uprising, after holding out in a guerrilla war against repeated attempts of the Romans to extinguish the countless foci of revolt throughout the country.

To summarize: two generations of religious activists made a potent fusion of two simple ideas: the national and the transcendental hope for the Kingdom of God.

Jews were not divided in the interpretation of this phrase. The religious activists were no different from other devout Jews, as far as their worldview was concerned. They differed only in the degree of personal activity. It was taken for granted that the outcome of all action was in any case wholly dependent on God's will. Of course, this implied a complete fusion between politics and religion. Among monotheists in those days a distinction between the two would have been senseless. The religious activists were distinguished by one quality alone—the total commitment of the individual based on zeal for God, with the concomitant assurance of victory and, in case of death, a reward in the world to come, the Kingdom of God.

It is because this basic concept, the Kingdom of God, is so profound that the pervasive silence of the Gospels about its true meaning, and especially the failure to link it to the crucifixion of Jesus, acquire a primordial importance.

It is, after all, bizarre that this powerful, activist idea, which led not only to Jesus' execution but to the war against Rome in the following generation and to the extinction of the Jewish state, should be mentioned only in the very brief and, in their present form, incomprehensible references in the first three Gospels. It would be quite possible to read and reread the Gospels and, if one did not already know the significance of the Kingdom of God movement, pay it no attention whatever. The Kingdom of God never took place, after all, and by the second century the very idea was extinct in Judaism.

This utterly transformed the perspective of the believers in Jesus; the original belief in the Kingdom of God as an upheaval of the world was transferred to a magnification of Jesus. And this dramatic shift can be pinpointed to an event that took place very shortly after the crucifixion—the vision of Simon the Rock on the Sea of Galilee.

We shall see that this vision, which gave rise to other visions, including the vision of Saul of Tarsus, globally transformed the perspective of the believers both in the Kingdom of God and in the special role of Jesus. All the various elements collected much later to form the New Testament were inspired by the vision of Jesus resurrected and glorified.

In the case of the four Gospels, three of which came into being many decades later, this led to a particularly puzzling situation. The recollections that began to be collected no doubt by the aging first generation were unconsciously organized in the light of the cosmic magnification of Jesus. There was no question of conscious falsifying; texts were merely selected and edited in terms of what was felt to be their relevance. Had there been a desire to falsify we would know even less than we do.

At the same time, the fundamental fact of Jesus' ascension gives us a criterion, indeed, our cardinal criterion, for the assessment of the histori-cal likelihood of various elements in the Gospels. Let us take the crucifix-ion of Jesus as our starting-point and go backward through the Gospels, to see whether we can arrive at an understanding of his death. We shall regard two facts as established:

1. The above-mentioned transformation of perspective of the earliest chroniclers, revolving around the resurrection and glorification of the Divine Savior.

2. The compilation and editing of the Gospels at a time when the newly evolving Christian sect was splitting off from the parent body of Judaism it had been identified with during the first generations of its exis-tence. The Christian community, while acquiring consciousness of its own separate identity, was at the same time colliding with the increasingly vir-ulent hostility of Jewry, especially in the form of the learned rabbis, who throughout the period of the formation of early Christianity were its chief opponents. What may be called the purely Jewish elements in the early faith were rooted out or swamped by the Greek elements, partly in conse-quence of the destruction of the Jewish state by the Romans in 70 C.E., which in its turn reinforced the rejection of the new sect by the Jews.

The Gospels, accordingly, were written in the light of this perspective, the basic focus of all Christian thought. The formula that may be taken as describing this process of literary transfiguration is summed up by Saul himself, whose sole concern was the "crucified and glorified Christ" (1 Cor 1:18, 23–24). This lapidary formula explains not merely the point of view of the first Christian generations, but also the rapidity with which the authentic recollections of Jesus' earthly career were subordinated and per-force accommodated to Saul's transcendental view of the Kingdom of God.

Taking this perspective into account, let us examine the Gospels from a dual point of view: the successive magnification of Jesus, consummated around this time, and the schism between Judaism and the new Christian religion. In examining the multiple, disparate elements woven into the Gospels by this perspective we shall have our cardinal criterion: *Anything that conflicts with this perspective is likely to be historical.* That is, any fragment that runs counter to the dominant Gospel tendency of exalting Jesus, preaching his universality as Savior of all mankind, and emphasiz-ing the differences between him and Judaism, will be regarded as *ipso facto* probable, other things of course being equal.

At present, the texts of all four Gospels constitute a puzzle—a puzzle that went unnoticed for centuries because tradition explained the Gospels in a way that was satisfactory for believers and that only in the modern period has became vulnerable to realistic analysis. The Gospel texts could be read without perplexity because the missing elements were not known to be missing, while the traditional explanation was quite convincing.

Since, as we know, the Kingdom of God in this era revolved around armed resistance to Rome, and since Jesus was executed by the Romans as a pretender to power, it is clear that the elimination of causal factors from the Gospel texts accounts for their unsatisfactory effect as a historical account and for the bewilderment, in a naive reading of the Gospels, arising out of an incomprehension of why Jesus was, in fact, executed by the Romans.

From that point of view, the Gospel texts, with their homey atmosphere, show a lack of coherence that only piety makes unnoticeable. But the desire, conscious or not, to reshape the meaning of Jesus' execution must have been paramount. The very nature of the Gospels, their charm, indeed, emerges from just this combination of homey detail and an ultimate bafflement that had to be compensated for by the tradition. Let us glance at the Gospels.

Looked at as it were naively, what an extraordinary impression the Gospels make! What a fascinating jumble of puzzles, contradictions, hints, and suggestions! The story is about a man, Jesus, but actually it tells nothing personal. Jesus seems to be moving in a vacuum, while the behavior of everyone else is scarcely reported at all. We never see what his everyday life was like, or what his relations with his companions were. In spite of the circumstantial atmosphere there is a pall of obscurity and timelessness about the events that blurs their connection; the rationale of Jesus' activities remains elusive. The anecdotes that actually make up the substance of the story all seem to hang in the air, as do Jesus' sayings and parables. The point of all these is symbolical in any case, but even when they can be understood they are so remote from real life that they illuminate neither his character nor the situation they might be relevant to. Motives are scarcely ever indicated, except with a childlike and obviously false simplicity. Jesus is always in some statuesque pose—healing, preaching, suffering. But as for what his inner thoughts and feelings were, or even his actual aims, there is not even a hint.

It would seem, in fact, that though the Gospels are intent on telling a story, that story is not meant to convey a notion of personality, but rather to build up a theme. And in the presentation of the theme there are so many discrepancies! Jesus is presented to us throughout as the quintessence of goodness, yet he comes to a cruel and violent end; he is called eternal and divine, yet detailed genealogies are given connecting him with the Jewish royal house; he even has a family, including a mother, four brothers, and at least two sisters, who so far from regarding him as divine think he is out of his mind; he is a devout Jew, yet seems to be intermittently both friendly with Jews and hostile to them; he has disciples who are supposed to teach, but the disciples themselves are taught in parables they not only find unintelligible, but are forbidden to communicate; at different points Jesus seems to be appealing to the Jews exclusively, then to the world at large; he seems to be meek, yet claims to be greater than Solomon, and for that matter to be at the right hand of God; he forbids the use of invective, yet is constantly excoriating his opponents; and so on.

The fundamental problem of Jesus' life is his death; but before discussing the reasons for his execution on a charge of sedition, let us glance at an essential question: To whom did he proclaim the Kingdom? Who was to benefit by it?

Put in another way, did he intend the announcement of the Kingdom of God for all mankind? Was he universalistic? This is of course a cardinal riddle for religion: let us try to clarify it here only within the framework of history.

We have seen that the very insistence with which he announced the advent of the Kingdom and the plain fact that, according to the Gospels themselves, this was his basic message, in and for itself places him squarely within the Jewish tradition. Not only is the Kingdom of God itself prayed for every day in the Jewish *Shemoneh Esreh,* mentioned above, but nearly all of Jesus' explicit statements are uncompromisingly, even extravagantly particularistic.

This is the more disturbing since, as indicated above, the Gospels took shape in the perspective of the religion that arose after Jesus, over his dead body, so to speak, and moreover betray a consistent strain of hostility to the Jews, running directly counter to Jesus' own statements and to the situation in Palestine during his lifetime.

It is true, oddly enough, that the Gospels, and especially Matthew, may actually exaggerate, if not Jesus' Jewishness as such at least his biblicism, i.e., his habit of referring authority to the Hebrew Scriptures (the Old Testament). This simply meant that the *very earliest* community, doubtless in a Jewish milieu and before the coagulation of a de-Judaized Christianity, was still intimately involved with historic Jewish religion as it was to be consummated by the arrival of a Messiah heralding the Kingdom of God.

In any case, what Jesus himself is reported as saying seems unmistakable. Not only does he proclaim the unique validity of the Torah, by quoting the focal prayer of Judaism:

> And one of the scribes came up and heard them disputing with one another, and . . . asked him, "Which commandment is the first of all?" Jesus answered, "The first is, 'Hear, O Israel: the Lord our God, the Lord is one: and you shall love the Lord our God with all your heart, and with all your soul, and with all your mind, and with all your strength.' The second is this, 'You shall love your neighbor as yourself.' There is no other commandment greater than these." (Mk 12:28–30)

Not only does he indicate his belief in the absolute, eternal immutability of the Jewish Torah:

> It is easier for heaven and earth to pass away, than for one dot of the Law to become void. (Lk 16:17)

> Think not that I have come to abolish the [Torah] and the Prophets; I have come not to abolish them but to fulfill them. For truly I say to you, till heaven and earth pass away, not an iota, not a dot, will pass from the [Torah] until all is accomplished. Whoever then relaxes one of the least of these commandments and teaches men so, shall be called least in the Kingdom of (God); but he who does them shall be called great in the Kingdom of (God). For I tell you, unless your righteousness exceeds that of the scribes and Pharisees, you will never enter the Kingdom of (God.) (Mt 5:17–20)

But he seems to make a point of his mission's being meant for the Jews alone: "I was sent only to the lost sheep of the house of Israel" (Mt 10:5–6). He actually goes so far as to maintain that his mission was reserved for no one *but* Jews:

> Now the woman was a Greek, a Syrophoenician by birth. And she begged him to cast the demon out of her daughter. And he said to her, "Let the children first be fed, for it is not right to take the children's bread and throw it to the dogs." (Mk 7:26–27)

This is paralleled by:

> But she came and knelt before him, saying "Lord, help me." And he answered "It is not fair to take the children's bread and throw it to the dogs." She said, "Yes, Lord, yet even the dogs eat the crumbs that fall from their master's table." (Mt 15:25–27)

The main point in all this is clearly not the question of Jesus' compassion, but the framework of his thought: he extends his personal compassion to a non-Jew by way of exception, since, as he says, his mission is exclusively for those who accept the Torah as the center of life, who are indeed the only ones for whom the very idea of the Kingdom of God would have any meaning. These are the only ones whose repentance would be significant, since they would be expressing it within a structure of thought, faith, and hope that would link it to its reward.

For the pagans of Jesus' day, the conception of a Kingdom to be materialized by the Jewish God and heralded by the Jewish Messiah would have been meaningless. This point is made very vividly by what must be a very ancient passage in Matthew, in which the chronicler, by reporting Jesus' reassurances to the Twelve Apostles that they would all be sitting on twelve thrones judging the twelve tribes of Israel, unmistakably implies that the Kingdom of God was only for the Jews (Mt 19:28). The same theme is unmistakable in a saying put in the Resurrected Jesus' mouth, from Acts: "So when they had come together, they asked him, 'Lord, will you at this time restore the Kingdom to Israel?' " (Acts 1:6). This, in its matter-of-fact assumption that the Kingdom of God was for Israel alone, must be very ancient too.

To be sure, the Jewish God was not merely one god among others, but the all-powerful God of the universe; hence nothing stood in the way of conversion. Once the Jewish God had expanded beyond a purely local setting, as the god of a particular people (such as Baal for the Canaanites, or Dagon for the Philistines, whom the ancient Hebrews had considered perfectly valid though inferior gods) and become not merely superior to other gods but God uniquely, anyone in the world might become a Jew, since it only meant accepting this simple belief and the rituals inherited from history as the one God's cult. But in any given historical setting that would mean finding one's way to this unique God through the vestibule, so to speak, of Judaism, and however universalistic the implications of Judaism, hence ultimately of Jesus' Judaism, too, it was the Torah alone that guided the way.

Even Jesus' miracles, which would have seemed to redound to his personal credit as at least a sign of his status, were merely ascribed in the normal way to his being favored by the divine power:

> And great crowds came to him, bringing with them the lame, the maimed, the blind, the dumb, and many others, and they put them at his feet, and he healed them, so that the throng wondered, when they saw the dumb speaking, the maimed whole, the lame walking, and the blind seeing; and they glorified the God of Israel. (Mt. 15:30–31)

It is not Jesus who is "glorified" by his ability to heal, but the God of Israel. Nor is it only a question of specific statements attributed to Jesus; traces of the original identity between his followers and other Jews are unmistakably recorded. We shall see later on (chapter 6) that Jesus' immediate followers, led by his brother, were proud of being pious Jews. "Held in high honor" by "the people;" they actually worship in the Temple (Acts 2:47, 5:13, etc.). This statement in itself, which was recorded at a moment when it lay in the interests of the new religion to disavow the particularistic Jewish connection, insofar as the missionary target was now the pagan masses of the Greco-Roman world, would be enough to indicate the essentially Jewish content of Jesus' own message. Yet throughout the Gospels he seems to be engaged in a perpetual debate with the Jews. If Jesus was in fact a devout Jew himself, what could they have been at loggerheads about?

The whole question has been deeply obscured by the singular role ascribed in the Gospels to the Pharisees, who seem to be Jesus' principal adversaries. Indeed, the New Testament has congealed the word itself into a synonym for pedantic hypocrisy.

This represents an extraordinary perversion of the circumstances of Jesus' lifetime.

The Pharisees and Sadducees were the two dominant tendencies in Jewish life until the destruction of the Temple in 70 (which only the Pharisees survived). They differed in their attitudes toward the Torah. Ever since Ezra (444 B.C.E.) the Torah had been the unchallenged religious source of religious authority for the whole of the Jewish people. Since it had been fixed in writing, however, it was obviously incapable of dealing with every specific problem that might arise in the course of time.

The Sadducees, as the aristocratic, priestly group, held the view that the Torah as written had to be supplemented by priestly decisions as the occasion arose. Thus the scope of the Torah tended to contract gradually with time.

The Pharisees, on the other hand, believed that the Torah was binding not merely by virtue of the collective oath taken by the representatives of the people in the time of Ezra but also because it was the direct expression of God's will. They enlarged the scope of the Torah, and made this socially feasible by evolving the concept of an oral Law, as ancient as the words of the written Torah itself and equally binding.

The Sadducees were conservative guardians of an ancient text; they considered the Pharisees innovators who acted as disturbers of the public order and as gadflies generally. They were simply aristocrats, high priests, men of affairs and so on—in short, the vested interests—who had an old-fashioned, literalistic view of religion that enabled them to carry on affairs of state and business generally without bothering about doctrine. For the Pharisees the oral Law, the living, ever-changing heart of the religion, was vital. The Sadducees denied its existence altogether.

The Sadducees were intimately associated with the government and especially with the Temple, which they ran until its destruction in 70. After the Temple was destroyed, in fact, the Sadducees as a group vanished altogether, though their views survived them for some time and found an echo or two in Jewish life later on.

The Pharisees, though not very numerous, were accepted as the representatives of the masses, even by those who did not submit to their discipline entirely. They developed both the synagogue and the schooling system into a powerful channel for the inculcation of religion in the lives of the people. They were never a political party as such, though events naturally made them take appropriate action in the pursuit of their aims. It was they who enabled Judaism to survive the fall of Jerusalem in 70 and even the total disruption of the Jewish people in 135. They are the fathers of Judaism as it has been practiced in the Jewish Diaspora down to our own day. In the time of Jesus the Pharisees, without being political, were essentially oppositionists; they found many sympathizers among these irked by the rule of the Sadducees.

In short, the historical role of the Pharisees in Jewish life was completely different from the impression given in the Gospels. Not only do we not see any general reason why Jesus should have been hostile to the Pharisees or they to him, but the very texts that labor this point reveal, in spite of themselves, a wholly different relationship. The impression is inescapable that the various Gospel accounts of disputes and controversies of one sort or another somehow do not ring true, or rather they ring true only in terms of the situation that we know developed in the environment of the Gospel writers themselves after Jesus' death. The problems faced by the early Church in its debates with the Jewish rabbis were translated into the circumstances of Jesus' life as transformed by the evolving tradition. They do not concern Jesus.

It is true that in some respects Jesus insisted on a more severe interpretation of the Torah (as in the case of marriage, where in contradistinction to Moses he regarded marriage as indissoluble (Mk 10:2–9), while in other respects he seems to have been more lenient (as in his observance of the Sabbath). In still other respects, and more generally, he seems to have extended current Jewish precepts in such a way as to emphasize the *ideal point* involved, as when he seems to relax the law of "an eye for an eye" by saying, "Do not resist one who is evil, but if any one strikes you on the right cheek, turn to him the other also" (Mt 5:39, etc.).

Here, however, the real oddity is not that the early tradition, written down so long after Jesus' death, emphasizes his differences with the Pharisees, as that in spite of the fact that the Jews were engaged in a virulent polemic against the claims of the new sect at the time the Gospels were written down, edited, and compiled, the early tradition nevertheless shows us Jesus carrying on his own discussion with the Pharisees of his own time in a purely Pharisaic way. He sees things in the perspective of the Pharisees, bolsters his interpretations by references to the Torah, is preoccupied by the same problems, and differs with them on their own ground. For instance, in defending his disciples for picking some grain on the Sabbath he refers to David and his famished soldiers eating the "show-bread" on the Sabbath (Mk 2:23): here the same authority is invoked by both the Pharisees and Jesus.

In insisting on the rigorousness of the marriage bond (Mk 10:6) he does so in the name of the divine spirit as revealed in the Torah, and excuses Moses for having been lax in the matter because of the hardness of the people's hearts. When he disregards davidic descent as being indispensable for the Messiah (Mk 12:35) he buttresses his case by a reference to David himself.

Even Jesus' attitude towards the burdensome dietary laws of the Jews, which we might reasonably expect him to have softened, was orthodox. Here is a celebrated passage generally taken to mean the opposite: "Hear me . . . and understand: there is nothing outside a man which by going into him can defile him, but the things which come out of a man are what defile him" (Mk 7:14–15).

This follows a passage that *sounds* as though Jesus were against many of the Jewish ritual acts, such as purifying oneself before eating, etc., as well as the washing of "cups and pots and vessels of bronze," etc. (Mk 7:4).

Now, if these instances were really to be interpreted as a systematic form of opposition to Jewish ceremonial, it would become inconceivable why the tradition in the early Church, which eventually swept away the entire Jewish ritual, did not refer this back to Jesus. For the contrary is the case. In Saul's struggle against the "Judaizers" in the early Church he could not base his relaxation of the Jewish ritual burden, including the cardinal Jewish rite of circumcision, on anything Jesus was reported to have said. Therefore, the above must be understood as having a specific reference that escapes us, as being, perhaps, part of his general understanding of the Jewish ritual in terms of its spiritual content rather than its letter, an attitude he shared with many later rabbis.

He was not opposed to any of the rituals of contemporary Judaism, nor did he institute any ritual reforms—the rite of circumcision is never mentioned, nor are any ritual innovations. He did not even baptize, as John did; even when dispatching the apostles on their mission, as we shall see, he gave them no instructions concerning baptism.

He never said anything against the veneration of the Temple. Though the Gospels are taciturn on this point, the few references they make seem unequivocal: the fourth Gospel mentions several visits to Jerusalem on the great holidays (2:13, 5:1, 7:2) and Mark, after reporting his healing of a leper (1:44) mentions his telling him to take his sacrifice to the Temple as prescribed by the Torah (i.e. Leviticus 14). Matthew also refers to the necessity of proper sacrifice at the Temple after making one's peace with one's brother, implying at least that it is a legitimate thing to do.

These few passages indicate that whatever else Jesus may have preached, he did not attack the Temple cult *as such*; if he had rejected the Temple Cult *as such* the writers and editors of the Gospels, writing at a time when the universalism of Christianity and its split with Judaism had become articles of faith, could scarcely have ignored such an opportunity to trace this view back to Jesus. It is impossible to explain these passages, as well as the passage in Acts mentioning the assiduity of the first disciples in the Temple, without assuming that no contradiction was felt in the early tradition between such actions and Jesus' views.

He even *approved* of the Pharisees: "Then Jesus said to the crowd and to his disciples, 'The scribes and the Pharisees sit on Moses' seat; so practice and observe whatever they tell you" (Mt 23:1–3).

This amounts to saying that he endorsed the religious authority of the Pharisees completely, in contradistinction to the Sadducaic priesthood. He goes on to rebuke them for their hypocrisy, it is true, but here again the point is that Jesus takes the authority of the Pharisees as his standpoint. He acts like a Pharisee himself, calling upon his fellow Pharisees to live up to their own virtues.

Even in Jesus' daily practice there are so many instances of his Pharisaic habits left in the Gospels that once again we see him framed within the general Jewish tradition. He broke bread, and carefully blessed the bread and the wine; he celebrated the Passover, and said the "Great *Hallel.*" When he said the "sabbath was made for man, not man for the sabbath" (Mk 2:27), he was evidently using a Pharisaic turn of argument to justify a specific action, or a specific category of actions, in terms of the Torah itself, just as the Pharisees themselves, as recorded in the Talmud, used the same *a fortiori* argument as Jesus did about the Temple and David's eating of the show-bread to prove the general point that the needs of life outweighed purely ritualistic restrictions. Even the wording of Jesus' remark is almost a duplicate of Rabbi Simon ben Menassiah's "The sabbath was given for you; you were not given for the sabbath." The same idea is expressed more pithily by Rabbi Jonathan, in the Babylonian Talmud: "Profane a sabbath in order to be able to observe many."

Hence, we see that what Jesus both said and did were substantially at one with the Pharisaic tradition; for that matter he taught in the synagogues and was invited to feasts, and when we recall once again that the tendency of the Gospels is to castigate the Pharisees, the general designation for the Jewish authorities at the time the Gospels were edited, that is, after the destruction of the Temple in 70 and the disappearance of any other organized Jewish authority, we can only be overwhelmed by this unequivocal identification of Jesus with Jewish tradition during his lifetime. Thus, without going into the nuances of the legalistic disputes current in the Jewish community so long ago, and quite apart from the fact that the existence of good scribes as well as bad scribes is mentioned in the Gospels themselves, Jesus' emphasis on the spirit rather than on the letter of the Torah in itself would have been entirely in accord with well-established Jewish ideas, most noteworthy of course in the prophets. This prophetic tradition, indeed, is just as old as or older than the legalistic tradition itself; it is a sort of organic parallel.

In short, all the instances in which Jesus seems to be going further than the normal observances of his time—concerning marriage, the sabbath, love of one's neighbor, etc.—do not constitute a new doctrine. They are simply extensions, within the framework of the accepted Torah, of basic principles to specific cases.

For that matter, despite the *general* atmosphere of conflict between Jesus and the Pharisees, generally summed up as his arch-enemies, the Gospels themselves are far from clear about the degree of this hostility. Mark, for instance, gives unmistakable indications of the initial adherence to Jesus of the Pharisees as well as the scribes, while in Luke various degrees of friendliness are shown (Lk 7:36, 11:37, 13:31–33, 14:1, 17:20).

Obviously, then, even though the basic mold of the Gospels was hostile to *official* Jewry by the time they received their final editing, they already contained these contradictory elements, which must have come from the earliest tradition. Either this tradition was unclear about the exact scope of the hostility between Jesus and the popular Jewish party, or else these contradictions survived the harmonizing influences of later editors. The extraordinary fact recorded in Luke (13:31–33), for instance, where the Pharisees actually give Jesus a friendly warning to escape from Herod, is enough to illustrate this dramatically. It is so contrary to the entire structure of the Gospel tradition that it is obviously authentic.

Once these points are made another question remains: Hebrew prophets before Jesus spoke of effecting a new alliance with Yahweh, an alliance that the Prophets gave a certain flexibility to as a sort of indefinitely renewable covenant with the Lord. Genesis 9:17, for instance, refers to the rainbow as an alliance between Yahweh and "all flesh on earth," concluded with Noah and his descendants; in Genesis 17:11 the rite of circumcision demonstrates the alliance between Yahweh and Abraham's descendants; in Exodus 24:8ff an alliance is renewed by blood between Yahweh and the people led by Moses after the handing down of the tablets of the Decalogue on Mount Sinai.

In the prophetic tradition itself, (Jeremiah 31:31ff) a new alliance is referred to as being about to be concluded between God and the houses of

Israel and Judah, which is to last much longer than the covenants made with the Hebrews upon their exodus from Egypt, since God will inscribe his Law in the hearts of his people and God and his people will be one. In the same vein Malachi 3:1 announces the near arrival of the "messenger of the covenant you are awaiting."

Thus there was a long tradition of covenant-making between the Jews and God; the covenants did not cancel each other out, but in some sense fortified each other along established lines; they reinvigorated and consolidated a basic covenant between God and the Jewish people. Hence there was no reason even from within the Jewish tradition why Jesus might not have regarded himself as authorized to conclude a new covenant with God. The question is whether he did. The most obvious support for this is to be found in the words ascribed to him in Mark: "This is my blood of the covenant, which is poured out for many" (Mk 14:24).

Now, even if we can believe that Jesus actually uttered these words, they could scarcely have referred to the abolition of the Torah—at most they would have been a rite similar to the ancient one recorded of Moses, of renewing in blood the covenant with God. This is surely demonstrated by the above mentioned passage in Acts (2:46, 47), where we are told of Jesus' disciples praying assiduously in the Temple. If anything, the disciples seem to have prided themselves on their legalistic correctness toward the Torah; therefore there can be no question of their having understood Jesus' words as meaning its abrogation.

There are a couple of other passages that call for comment:

> From the days of John the Baptist until now the Kingdom of God has suffered violence and men of violence take it by force. For all the prophets and the Torah prophesied until John. (Mt 11:12–13)

This is echoed in Luke:

> The Torah and the prophets were until John; since then the good news of the Kingdom of God is preached, and every one enters it violently. (Lk 16:16)

These two passages seem puzzling, since whatever the point they are making is, it seems to refer to John, not Jesus; if the Torah stops at John, it is not Jesus who is the innovator but John. In any case the mission of Jesus does not seem to be involved.

However, apart from the curious phraseology (see chapter 5), what is at issue here is in all probability not the abolition of the Torah at all, but a mere qualification intended to pinpoint the actual announcement of the Kingdom. This may be part of the explanation of the unusual inverted order of words in the passage from Matthew, where the prophets precede the Law. The meaning of both passages—insofar as they relate to the purely doctrinal aspects of the mission of both John and Jesus—may thus be quite simply that the Kingdom had previously been announced by the prophets and by the Torah until John, followed by Jesus, came to perform the same task. Thus the Torah is considered here simply from the point of view of its specific application to the announcement of the Kingdom; there is no question of abolishing it.

Our information about the details of his belief is so scarce that it is, of course, perfectly legitimate to suggest that while Jesus had no intention of abolishing the Torah he might have wished to extend it, by laying the emphasis on the subjective emotions of the individual and so on, again in accordance with the well-established prophetic tradition mentioned above. His own personal interest might have centered on the depth of personal emotion, rather than on external appearances. He clearly considered that the cardinal aspect of religion was that of the heart, as indicated by his quoting the Supreme Commandment (Mk 12:28–34), based on Deuteronomy and Leviticus, though even there he was in close accord with a strong tradition of Pharisaism itself. After the destruction of the temple in 70, Rabbi Yohanan, a disciple of the celebrated Rabbi Hillel, emphasized that works of loving kindness were worth more than sacrifices and the Temple.

Any supposition that goes beyond Jesus' emphasis on the religion of the heart is unfounded speculation. If there is a contrast between the two types of religion, it is not one that could have seemed relevant to Jesus and his generation, for whom the traditional structure of Judaism was capacious enough to encompass many differences of emphasis.

It is, in short, impossible to consider Jesus anything but an altogether devout Jew, however prophetic, i.e., non-legalistic he might have been.

It is true that there are a number of passages that seem to clash with Jesus' conduct in general. On closer examination, however, we shall see that we are confronted with examples of the patchwork effect of the Gospels, in which instances came down to us either out of context or overlaid by intrusions subsequent to the early tradition.

One of the most famous of Jesus' sayings, for instance, is sometimes claimed as proof of his determination to burst the bonds of particularistic Judaism:

> No one sews a piece of unshrunk cloth on an old garment; if he does, the patch tears away from it, the new from the old, and leaves a bigger hole. And no one puts a new wine into old wineskins; if he does, the wine will burst the skins, and the wine is lost, and so are the skins; but new wine is for fresh skins. (Mk 2:21–22)

A moment's reflection will indicate that this, like Jesus' remarks on the Sabbath and the dietary laws, must be an example of some reference to a specific incident long since lost: for if the broad interpretation of this were seriously possible, that is, if Jesus meant that the "old bottles" of Judaism were to be discarded, the situation would be irremediably enigmatic. Nowhere else, as indicated above, does Jesus indicate himself to be a Jewish schismatic, but as in the passage about the "children's bread" being "thrown to the dogs," or even more exuberantly in the passage about casting "pearls before swine" (Mt 7:6), which doubtless refers to the same thing, he puts his total identification with Israel in a singularly, indeed arrestingly gross form.

The greater likelihood is that since the passage concerns fasting, where Jesus is defending his disciples for not fasting in the manner of the Pharisees, what he is concerned with is not the practice of fasting itself, but with what he may have regarded as an excess of pietistic vanity. The Torah proper did not insist on any fast except that of the Day of Atonement (after sending the scapegoat out into the desert on the tenth day of the seventh month: Leviticus 16:29, 23:27). Everything else observed by pious Jews to deprive themselves of food according to a few recommendations made in the prophets and in the historical Scriptures (such as 2 Samuel 12:16, Isaiah 58, Jeremiah 14:2, etc.) was no more than custom by Jesus' time. Thus he might have differed with other Jews in respect to fasting and still have said nothing against the Torah. This is why the above-mentioned passage must be seen in some larger context before its implications can be understood, and since it is just this larger context that is missing, we are bound to see it as a specific debating point, wrenched out of context. In any case Mark gives us neither the specific occasion on which Jesus uttered the phrase, nor the general framework in which it is to be understood; consequently we must interpret it, on the one hand in terms of its specific content (i.e., the assessment of fasting), and on the other as a complement of Jesus' other sayings, which are unquestionably framed by his acceptance of the Torah.

Here is another passage, recording what Jesus is supposed to have said to some Pharisees, that at first sight seems to imply a revolutionary attitude toward Judaism: "I tell you, something greater than the Temple is here" (Mt 12:6).

If this "something" actually refers to Jesus, and not to God, it must be ignored: it would be inconceivable for Jesus actually to have said this without being instantly accused of blasphemy. The statement is actually made only in Matthew. The passage as a whole, about the breaking of the Sabbath, which is paralleled in Mark (2:25–28), contradicts the point in the Markan passage, which scholars agree was taken from the same primitive source (i.e., the Logia, or "Sayings" of Jesus). The particular point about the Temple must be part of the subsequent christological magnification of Jesus.

There is also Jesus' prediction of the destruction of the Temple (Mk 13:1–2, 14:58), but this clearly does not imply contempt for the Temple as such; it merely resumes a familiar prophetic theme (Micah 3:13, Jeremiah 26:18; also the Apocryphal Enoch 90:28).

Still another passage definitely sounds like an act of schism with respect to the Torah:

> Jesus said to her: "Woman, believe me, the hour is coming when neither on this mountain nor in Jerusalem will you worship the Father. You worship what you do not know; we worship what we know, for salvation is from the Jews. But the hour is coming, and now is, when the true worshippers will worship the Father in spirit and truth, for such the Father seeks to worship him. God is spirit, and those who worship him must worship him in spirit and truth." (Jn 4:21–24)

Here, though Jesus says salvation comes from the Jews, he also indicates that the Torah is obsolete. But all independent critics agree that this passage is a manifest echo of the religion that arose *after* Jesus. Hence, it could not have been Jesus but the editor or writer of the Gospel who expressed this thought as it has come down to us.

In short, Jesus had the same attitude toward practices, rites, and the Holy Temple as he had toward the Torah. He did not condemn *in princi-*

ple any of the things accepted by contemporary Judaism, though his general tendency was to emphasize the spiritual content rather than the letter of the Torah, following in this too a well-defined strand of Jewish thought.

This is why the whole classic debate among liberal scholars about whether or not Jesus was "universalistic" or "particularistic" is *quite unhistorical.* He never had any occasion for a choice between these two types of Judaism. As far as the permanent validity of the Torah was concerned Jesus remained entirely within the Jewish enclosure, regardless of the emphasis he may have laid on one attitude or another within his matter-of-fact acceptance of the Torah.

It is indeed his wholehearted identification with the Torah that gives us the only possible perspective for his innovations or reforms within it. The very manner in which he expresses his criticisms of contemporary practice is really meaningful only if the framework of the Torah as such is taken for granted. His so-called innovations actually demonstrate more cogently than anything else the unquestioning steadfastness with which he stood on Jewish terrain and preached to Jews alone. The exceptions in his behavior are evidently recorded either because they are exceptions intended to illustrate Jesus' compassion, as in the cases of the Syrophoenician woman and the Roman centurion (whose servant Jesus heals while marveling at the centurion's faith, which Jesus has not found "even in Israel" [Mt 8:10]), or because they embody later editorial emendations interpolated at a time when the newly evolving religion, rejected by most of the Jews, had already struck root in pagan soil.

An endearingly naive example of this bow in the direction of the pagan world is the episode of another centurion, who as witness to Jesus' crucifixion is summoned by the Gospel-writer to endorse Jesus' status as "son of God" and duly exclaim, "Truly this man was a son of God!" (Mk 15:39).

This sort of thing is clearly *post facto* propaganda. The real point is that Jewish Messianism as such would have been quite simply unintelligible to non-Jews; the question of "saving" the pagans could arise at all only if the pagans were to become Jews and participate in the promise made to the chosen people. As long as they remained outside the barrier of Judaism, the question of bringing them a message was simply nonsense. In short, Jesus came for Israel alone, nor in his day could it have been otherwise.

3

The Collision with Rome

Accordingly, instead of discussing the meaning of Jesus' message from the viewpoint of later centuries, we shall simply deal with it in terms of his own day and his own people. Taking as starting-point his unquestioning attachment to his religion, let us see what that might have meant in the turbulent, oppressed, divided society of his time.

In this broader sense, it is possible to establish a contrast between him and the Jewish authorities on what we could call today a socioeconomic basis. As a man of action he could not have been preoccupied either by the exegesis of the sacred texts or the observance of the 613 written commandments of the Torah and its 1,000 unwritten recommendations—the sort of thing that absorbed the attention of religious scholars, scribes, etc. The bureaucratic encrustations of the religious schools might have seemed in some sense repugnant to him, especially since they were doubtless associated with the arrogance characteristic of any vested interest.

There may be an echo of this in a sentence from Matthew already referred to: "For I tell you, unless your righteousness exceeds that of the scribes and Pharisees, you will never enter the Kingdom of Heaven" (Mt 5:20).

The word translated here as righteousness (*dikaiosyne)* is used in the Greek of the New Testament in contrast to a word for sin (*hamartia*) and another implying ignorance of or contempt for the Torah (*anomia*), as well as impurity (*akatharsia*). The Gospel-writer is telling us that Jesus did not consider the pedantry of the religious experts either a necessary or a sufficient guarantee of acceptance in the Kingdom of God. It is in a way an echo of John the Baptist, who seems to have thought the Messiah could not come until the Jews had fulfilled the Torah in every detail, and modified this in his own fashion to allow the new elect, the new Israel, rebaptized in purity, to inherit the Kingdom.

Jesus' celebrated phrase, "Come to me, all who labor and are heavy-laden, and I will give you rest. . . . For my yoke is easy, and my burden is light" (Mt 11:28,30), can be understood when we remember that he intended to fulfill, to the last jot and tittle, the Torah *and the prophets,* too— i.e., it is another way of referring to the spirit of the Torah that underlay its numerous legal specifications.

This was doubtless the axis of the distinction between Jesus and his contemporaries *within* Judaism. He thought the complex analysis that went into the contemplation of the Torah was a very tortuous pathway toward virtue. Hence he emphasized, or even overemphasized, simplicity of heart and wholehearted allegiance to the principles underlying the Torah as the prerequisites for the Kingdom.

This insight leads us still further. For while Jesus plainly had an aversion for the bad scribe, arrogant in his knowledge of legalistic punctilio while indifferent to the spirit of the Torah, an attentive reading of the Gospels seems to indicate that Jesus was in some sense opposed to the good scribe, too. If he identified himself with the so-called *am ha-ares,* i.e., the "people of the land," the common people of Israel who would have been too absorbed in their daily tasks to devote the attention to the Torah thought appropriate by the religious doctors, he might have been against the learned classes generally.

On this question of observance, for instance, even the good scribe, as represented, say, by Rabbi Hillel, celebrated for his indulgence, was hostile on principle to the inherent laxity of the working population. Hillel said: "No *am ha-ares* can be pious," which sounds like an echo of "This crowd, who do not know the Torah, are accursed" (Jn 7:49) put in the mouth of anonymous Pharisees.

Indeed, it was part of a pietistic convention to contrast these "people of the land" with the children of God, i.e., the scholars of the Torah.

Thus, even in the Gospels we perceive that while Jesus, Jewishly speaking, was essentially at one with the Pharisees, he may have been, *socially* speaking, against the institutional authorities of contemporary society. Hence it may be possible to classify Jesus in the Jewish social spectrum of his day, using our own terminology, as being on the side of the simple people against the "upper classes"—the wealthy and educated.

This may be the ultimate significance of the celebrated remark in Matthew: "Those who are well have no need of a physician, but those who are sick. . . . For I came not to call the righteous, but sinners" (Mt 9:12,13), which is echoed in Luke: "For the Son of Man came to seek and to save the lost" (Lk 19:10). It may also, of course, be the ultimate, though distorted significance of the phrase in the Sermon on the Mount: "Blessed are the poor in spirit, for theirs is the Kingdom of [God]" (Mt 5:3). This sentence is even simpler in Luke: "Blessed are you poor, for yours is the Kingdom of God" (Lk 6:20). Thus we may be given a glimpse into the social turmoil that will bring the execution of Jesus down to earth and make it understandable.

Now, everything we have said above about the essentially Jewish nature of Jesus' message and the audience it was intended for plants Jesus squarely within the Jewish intellectual world of his time. This world was, to be sure, far less monolithic than has often been thought; it had far more tendencies, varying emphases, and differences of individual aims. Above all, it was the intellectual world of a community oppressed by an alien and odious power, which was in the last analysis, as we have seen, instrumental in Jesus' undoing.

It is that alien power that must retain our attention. The Romans were indifferent to the religious affairs of their subjects, and while they disliked the Jews for a variety of reasons—a turbulent subject people in a crucial outpost of empire, incomprehensibly devoted to a bodiless god—there is no reason to think they would have been disturbed by a purely religious movement among their subjects.

In the Gospel account, on the other hand, Jesus *seems* to have been preoccupied exclusively with abstract ethics and religion. His celebrated overt reference to the state power, "Render to Caesar the things that are Caesar's, and to God the things that are God's" (Mk 12:17), clearly sound as though it was designed to endorse the status quo. Thus, it is difficult, on the basis of the Gospels, to grasp the Roman role in Jesus' execution.

The same may be said about the Temple authorities. Though there are indications that Jesus might have been opposed to the Jewish upper classes generally, it is just this that eludes us. His sayings seem well contained within the bounds of normative Judaism, and if his message is really summed up by what has come down to us in the Gospels we cannot see why the Temple authorities, or the Jewish aristocracy generally, should have bothered implicating themselves in a plot actually to kill him.

Now the Gospels, despite their failure to report motivation, indicate a turning-point in Jesus' career that, however puzzling, is unmistakable. After he dispatches his disciples on their mission (Mt 10:5ff), giving them instructions that seem to radiate optimism and the hope of the imminent Kingdom, there is an abrupt break in the narrative. Jesus' wanderings back and forth in Galilee, which in any case have no discernible rationale, are suddenly cut short: his whole career refocuses in a decision to go up to Jerusalem.

The entry of the Holy City is obviously heavy with meaning. Jesus' reasons for going there have exercised the ingenuity of countless students. The account of what he does there is so arid and obscure that a variety of hypotheses have seemed persuasive.

There is no need to discuss them here. The Gospels are fundamentally indifferent to Jesus' real, that is, historical motives; from their point of view it is obvious that his entry into Jerusalem introduces the drama of the crucifixion, resurrection, and glorification. This vantage-point, as we shall see, dominates the whole of the New Testament.

In Mark, the earliest version of Jesus' activity, the entry into Jerusalem is not only the climax of Jesus' career, it is its crux. The change of mind leading up to it is summed up in the following passage:

> And Jesus went on with his disciples to the villages of Caesarea Philippi; and on the way he asked his disciples, "Who do men say that I am?" And they told him, "John the Baptist; and others say, Elijah; and others, one of the prophets." And he asked them, "But who do you say that I am? Simon the Rock answered him, "You are the Christ." And he charged them to tell no one about him. And he began to teach them that the Son of Man must suffer many things, and be rejected by the elders and Chief Priests and the scribes, and be killed, and after three days rise again. And he said this plainly. And [Simon the Rock] took him, and began to rebuke him. But turning and seeing his disciples, he rebuked Simon the Rock, and said "Get behind me, Satan! For you are not on the side of God, but of men." (Mk 8:27–33)

Everything in Mark seems to be a prologue to the confession in this passage. Before this, Jesus' messiahship was presumably hidden; afterwards, in the plan of the Gospel writer, he is portrayed as the suffering Messiah moving on to glory via his crucifixion.

But it is this plan of the Gospel writer that belongs most evidently to later doctrine. A later generation, which *knew* the transcendental purpose of the crucifixion and glorification, and *knew* Jesus to be the Messiah, was bound to interpret the whole final act of the tragedy, as well as the Savior's whole life, in such a way as to make it possible to swallow what Saul called the "stumbling-block of the cross," which without some esoteric interpretation could only impress the Jews of Jesus' own time as peculiarly ignominious and repellent.

The fact that this exalted interpretation of the crucifixion is a subsequent, doctrinal rectification of the events, so to speak, can be demonstrated by some otherwise inexplicable passages:

> He was near to Jerusalem, and . . . they supposed that the Kingdom of God was to appear immediately; (Lk 19:11)

and

> Jesus said to them, "Truly, I say to you, in the new world, when the Son of Man shall sit on his glorious throne, you who have followed me will also sit on twelve thrones, judging the twelve tribes of Israel." (Mk 19:23)

These words indicate that the group was filled with enthusiastic anticipation of the longed-for event as they drew near Jerusalem, and consequently that Jesus' predictions to his disciples of his suffering and death must have been put in later on (Mk 10:33ff, 8:31,9:31).

The same theme is given, in reverse, by a bald statement recording the plain fact that Jesus' followers were so disconcerted by the frustration of the hopes just mentioned that they took to their heels: "They all forsook him, and fled" (Mk 14:50). Considering the piety of the time this was written it must surely be regarded as a masterpiece of reserve. Though the Gospels' attempt to mitigate the behavior of the disciples in various obviously apologetic ways, all implying that since Jesus had in any case foreseen everything they were bound to conform with the inevitability of the whole event, the fact of the disarray and abandonment remains. Historically speaking, it contradicts Jesus' composed, serene prediction of his own suffering and end.

Accordingly, since Jesus' activities as recorded in the Gospel account do not really explain his death, he must have been undone for other reasons, which have been obliterated. Let us try to look behind the doctrinal embroidery overlaying the Gospels. Disregarding for the moment the later interpretation of the meaning of the Crucifixion, what might have been Jesus' practical object in coming to Jerusalem?

We must suppose that he decided to seek a decision in Jerusalem as a result of his failure in Galilee; despite some Gospel references to Jesus' popularity there the overriding impression remains that he did not meet with sufficient popular acclaim. Indeed, there is a peculiarly savage indictment of the cities of Chorasin, Bethsaida, and Capernaum that must surely be a recollection of his disappointment, if it is not simply another editorial embellishment.

Now, if we look on the showdown in Jerusalem from a purely spiritual point of view, what success could Jesus have hoped to have in the sophisticated, institutional, governmental milieu of Jerusalem, if he had not made enough of an impression on the simple folk of Galilee to make it worth his while to stay on there? The Jerusalem aristocracy—to say nothing of the Romans!—would presumably have considered him a provincial upstart, and ignored or rejected him entirely.

To recapitulate: On the basis of everything reported in the Gospels—Jesus' spiritual teaching, his proclamation of the Kingdom of God, his limited popular success—we cannot perceive either why Jesus decided to make a solemn entry into Jerusalem, or why once he did so he came to such a cruel and ignominious end.

The more all this is looked at, the more puzzling it becomes. With information so scanty it is difficult to establish a scale of plausibilities. We seem to be lost without a compass. But in fact a compass can be found. At the very core of the entire Gospel narrative, its climax, there is a conundrum—the crucifixion and its causes. This conundrum is itself the result of the unconscious camouflage to which the early tradition was subjected.

It is the very enigma embedded in the crucifixion itself—its motivation—that will indicate the flux of forces that were to bring about a radical transformation of the actual facts and give them an order in a different sequence of ideas. That were, in fact, to provide a meaning for the Roman execution of Jesus that was to have a permanent effect on history.

The puzzle itself is a simple one. It is this: Jesus, a pious Jew, falls out with other Jews, who are declared to be hostile to him and intent on his undoing, whereupon he is finally executed, though not, as we might expect, by the Jews, but by the Romans. What happens is that a Roman governor crucifies a politically inoffensive Jew for what is, at one point, said to be an offense against the Jewish religion, while, at another point, the offense against Rome itself, which is also mentioned, is expressly declared to be imaginary. Yet it is this offense against Rome that is ultimately the reason Jesus is crucified.

Now, the very first Gospel, Mark, was not written down, even in its most primitive form, until a generation after Jesus' death, and the others somewhat later, while the final harmonizing (highly defective, as we shall see) and editing of the earliest traditional elements incorporated in our present Gospels did not take place until this much later time. Jewish hostility was to force the universal mission of Christianity to find its arena not among the Jews, but throughout the Roman Empire.

Keeping in mind, accordingly, the positive factor of the new perspective of the divine Jesus, and the negative factor of the hostility between the Jews and the newly evolving Christian Church, we shall be able to see to what an extent the clear-cut expression of this anti-Jewish feeling, especially in Matthew and John, lies behind the enigmatic character of the crucifixion.

It is because of this rancor, embedded in the Gospels, that an impression has become fashionable that the Jews were primarily responsible for Jesus' undoing. For that matter this has been a leitmotif of Christianity, with varying degrees of intensity, ever since its inception. The impression is unmistakable that the rancor of the Gospel writers was directed at the Jews, while the Romans are referred to in quite an innocuous way. Indeed, it is obvious that an attempt is occasionally made, before our eyes, so to speak, to whitewash the Romans and exonerate them as far as possible of any active role in the execution of Jesus. The Gospels put the Roman authorities in the position of being innocent tools of a Jewish plot. We are actually told in so many words that the Roman procurator, Pontius Pilate, was really opposed to Jesus' condemnation, but was forced to consent to it by Jewish pressure. In the climate of the Gospels, this is surely the prevailing wind.

Now, why should Pilate, a notoriously hard-bitten Roman functionary, intervene to save some Jewish visionary? Or conversely, why should Jesus' fellow-Jews insist on having him killed by the Romans? We shall see that there is a more or less conscious desire to blame the Jews and exculpate the Romans, and it is this anti-Jewish rancor of the Gospel writer that, while partially explaining the friendliness to the Romans, makes it all the more significant that in the last analysis the actual execution of Jesus nevertheless inculpates the Romans.

That is, if the Gospel writers were so hostile to the Jews, and took such pains to blame them for the crucifixion of Jesus, why is it that in spite of the absence of detail in the narrative, which would obviously make all sorts of inventive fancies possible, all four Gospels report that it was the Romans who in fact sentenced Jesus to crucifixion and carried out the sentence themselves?

The crucifixion is in itself decisive. It was a characteristic Roman execution of the time; it was not used as a capital punishment by Jews. The capital sentences that the Jewish authorities were authorized to carry out were strangulation, stoning, burning at the stake, and decapitation. The mere fact, accordingly, that Jesus was crucified directly involves the Romans.

Crucifixion was, furthermore, while apparently of Oriental origin, the ignominious death *par excellence* by the time it came to the Romans, who learned it from the Carthaginians as the Greeks had learned it from the Persians: it was originally reserved for slaves and later on extended to thieves, criminals in the provinces, political offenders, etc.

But it was not merely the mode of execution that was Roman; the charge itself that justified Jesus' crucifixion was a charge that was of interest primarily to the Romans: he was executed as *King* of the Jews, that is, as a contender for power, not a religious matter at all, one of great concern to the Roman state.

It is true that at the trial the Gospels record as having been given Jesus by the Jewish tribunal, the Sanhedrin, the charge was made of his being the Messiah, that is, the (anointed) one who was to come—i.e., the herald of the Kingdom of God. But if we look at the account more closely we are struck by the singular coincidence that of the various charges supposed to be laid against Jesus by the Jewish authorities (perplexingly obscure and contradictory, as we shall see) the charge of claiming messiahship was the *only* one that would have appeared to the Romans to have had any political significance, while at the same time it was *not* a religious offense within Judaism.

The Roman authorities would inevitably have disregarded the otherworldly trappings of the Jewish Messiah and have interpreted the words as a mere circumlocution or euphemism for king. The identity in the Jewish mind of these spiritual and material functions would have interested the Romans only in respect of the material claim to power, since the purely religious views of the Jews had no interest for them at all. In any case, even if a claim to messiahship was a charge laid against Jesus by the Jewish authorities, and even if claiming to be the Messiah was blasphemy in the eyes of the Jews, the actual sentence was handed down and carried out by the Romans, on a Roman charge (kingship), and by a Roman execution.

Thus, while there is no doubt that a systematic effort has been made in the Gospels to create an entire framework of *Jewish* judicial procedure around the capture, trial, and execution of Jesus, and at first sight this framework gives an impression of coherence, this impression lasts only a moment: the most cursory examination indicates that the entire structure of Jesus' trial is highly insubstantial, contradictory, and above all *tendentious.* Let us look at the events leading up to the arrest and trial of Jesus, and see what may be made of their broad outline.

The general impression that emerges from the Gospel account is that Jesus' career was put to an end by the Jewish religious authorities, who at a crucial moment were aided by the treachery of Judas. Since we know from Josephus that the Temple summits did not oppose the Romans to the point of violence, there is no reason to question the probability that Jesus was at odds with the conservative individuals who controlled the Temple. It is not the *general* disharmony between Jesus and the Temple authorities that seems implausible, but the specific objectives and methods described in pseudodetail in the Gospels.

We are told that the Temple authorities were chary of arresting Jesus in the midst of the Passover feast, when Jerusalem was filled with great multitudes of people, "lest there be an uproar of the people" (Mk 14:2). The reason for the Temple authorities' hesitation was thus fear; Jesus' enemies were afraid of simply stopping his agitation.

But this is inadequate: If there was really enough public sentiment in favor of Jesus to intimidate such an immensely powerful institution as the Temple, the second seat of authority in Palestine after the Roman power, what was there to be gained by this in the long run? It is presumably the actual arrest of Jesus that would have annoyed his followers, and not its circumstances. And why, in fact, should they have been afraid of Jesus and his popularity? Was his agitation directed at them? If so, why didn't they make specifically Jewish charges against him?

Above all, why are the Romans not reported as also having been alarmed, since their regime depended on the docile local institutions? Why doesn't Pilate make his appearance at once?

If the Jewish plotters were unable to use their own police against Jesus, why haven't they involved the Roman authorities immediately? If what they were afraid of was Jesus' popularity among the Jews, nothing could have been simpler than shifting the entire blame onto the Romans, who were sufficiently hated in any case.

Perhaps the real problem is simple: How could a provincial Jew have aroused the fury of the wealthy, conservative, and powerful Jewish aristocracy? If, on the other hand, Jesus' popularity was not so great, and granted their lack of sympathy with whatever his teaching was, why should they have hesitated so long, clutching at various ruses to avoid appearing in a disagreeable role?

All this is curious and enigmatic. The contradictions in detail are made still hazier by the style of narration, which while psychologically arid seems grounded on the most intimate and unknowable thoughts, feelings, and intentions of the conspirators. In the first three Gospels especially the narrator sounds as though he were wholly in their confidence; how else could he know what he appears to know?

Jesus' arrest itself is very strange. Its actual mechanism is described as being set in motion by the defection and treachery of Judas Iscariot.

This presents a curious problem. For generations attempts have been made to penetrate the meaning of Judas's treachery; the moral problem it poses, considered beyond comprehension, has generated a vast amount of pseudopsychological speculation. We are bound to believe it actually took place, for it was an extraordinary embarrassment for Christianity both in the beginning and afterwards. How could the Lord's prescience be reconciled with his accepting a traitor as an intimate?

The Gospels themselves, which contain all we know about it, tell us practically nothing. Mark attempts no explanation at all, while Matthew simply advances as the motive Judas's greed (Mt. 26:15): he is recorded as bargaining for thirty pieces of silver, an amount that, as such, is of course absurd, and is doubtless to be taken as nothing more than an emendation of a parallel passage to give a greater show of accuracy. But if Judas were interested in money only it would obviously have been far easier for him simply to have absconded with the treasury of Jesus' followers than actually to sell his Lord. For that matter the actual figure of thirty is doubtless taken from Zechariah 11:12, and is in line with Matthew's general preoccupation with the Hebrew Scriptures.

The fantasy of scholars has run riot in the attempt to extract a believable motive from the meagerness of the Gospel narrative. The most extravagant, ingenious, and subtle theories have been elaborated to make Judas's betrayal intelligible. Goethe, for instance, developed a theory based on the assumption that Judas was determined to push Jesus into action, to have his claims put to the test *because* he believed in him; he wanted to trap him into realizing his aims. Judas's deed was, that is, tantamount to an act of faith: after realizing his mistake he felt obliged to commit suicide.

Ambition and jealously have also been advanced as explanations for the betrayal. But it is impossible to say what Judas could have been ambitious for, or whom he could have been jealous of, or how could his jealousy be satisfied by betraying his Lord?

All these theories are mere speculation, and with no facts to go on quite implausible to boot. Perhaps the most plausible of the nonfactual explanations is that which takes Judas's act, incomprehensible on the human plane, as a mere personification of a legend that sprang up later, and which is indeed the leitmotif of the Gospels taken as a whole. The name Judas is understood by this interpretation to be simply the Jew *par excellence,* and hence the whole story is a legendary way of expressing the Christian tradition as it became embodied in the New Testament, i.e., that Jesus was undone by the Jews, who delivered him over to Pilate.

There is another, ingenious explanation , considered plausible by some scholars, to the effect that the word Iscariot is actually a sort of sobriquet meaning the Deliverer: taken from a Hebrew root (*skr*) meaning "to deliver," it in reality represents the sentence of Isaiah (19:4) "I shall deliver Egypt into the hands of a cruel taskmaster." This same word is supposed to have been used by Judas himself in his offer to the priests: "What will you give me if I deliver him to you?" (Mt 26:15), and is also mentioned by Saul (I Cor 2:23). Of course, for such a word to have been used by the writers of our Gospels without their understanding it must mean that it goes all the way back to Jesus' original Aramaic-speaking background. It is, therefore, actually the best argument for the historicity of the event.

But all such explanations are bound to sound far-fetched: they founder primarily on the sheer absence of data, and also on the unintelligible element of baseness that clings to the deed. No theory, to be sure,however plausible, can actually persuade us to believe in the Judas story as it now stands: it is inherently senseless, for the simple reason that aside from Judas's motivation the betrayal had no objective purpose.

The Gospels tell us that the Temple authorities were alarmed by the simple fact of Jesus' popularity, that is, by the dimensions of a popular movement they disliked. This obviously implies that Jesus was a celebrity whom multitudes must have known about. He was a well-known figure who had preached to crowds in the enormous Temple courtyard and the leader of a movement large enough to arouse the hostility of the authorities, both Jewish and Roman—so why did Judas have to point him out to his captors? Quite apart, that is, from Judas's inexplicable baseness, just what information was he supposed to be selling? What was it worth?

Thus, with respect to Judas, there is a curious incoherence and a tendency toward contradiction in the present Gospel account that has, in fact, led many scholars to deny any historicity at all to the episode and to regard it as either quite unintelligible or a reflection of some later legend. I shall try to show later on that there is another, and to my mind more plausible, reason both for Judas's defection and for the later suppression of the underlying facts.

Now, going on from Judas's "delivery" of Jesus to his captors, the next question is: Who carried out the arrest?

The Synoptic Gospels give the impression that Jesus was arrested by a disorderly throng at the behest of the "Chief Priests and the scribes and the elders" (Mk 14:43), that is, in the service of the Jewish authorities, who had been informed by Judas.

Perhaps the point about the Synoptic account that is so striking at first glance is just this fact of the disorderliness of the arrest. Although Jesus was later, presumably, taken to the Jewish Sanhedrin and put on trial, the Synoptic narrative does not give the impression of a regular act but of something impromptu. Yet if the Temple authorities were going to try him on a relevant charge why did they not have him arrested normally and brought before their tribunal? Roman soldiers would never have arrested him merely to bring him before a Jewish court competent only in religious affairs.

The fourth Gospel's divergence from the Synoptic account is of special significance. In John Judas is reported to have procured a band of men and officers from the chief priests and Pharisees (Jn 18:3) and then brought them to where Jesus was staying. The colorless or misleading word used here, "band" is significant, since the word in Greek (*speira*) means a "cohort" and refers to the Roman force garrisoned in the Antonia tower of the Temple: a little later (Jn 18:12) its commander is called *chiliarchos,* translated in Latin and English by the word *tribunus* (tribune) or captain, and making it unmistakable that if the "band" of people was disorderly they were in any case accompanied by a force of Roman police. In short, it was the Roman police who in fact arrested Jesus, and the mention of it here is the most convincing proof of the Roman responsibility for the arrest of Jesus. Since the whole tendency of the early Christian tradition was to take the blame away from the Romans it is a detail that could never have been invented after the event.

But how could Judas possibly have had the authority to summon a Roman cohort? Obviously he could not have. Thus the relationship between the Jewish and the Roman authorities remains obscure.

Like all the other obscure points in this account it has received an enormous amount of critical attention. Most scholars have agreed that since the fourth Gospel goes farthest, generally speaking, in exculpating the Romans and blaming the Jews, it must represent a fact.

On the other hand, it must be admitted that since the point of all four Gospels is not only the allocation of blame but even more the magnification of the Savior in the face of his persecutors, both Jewish and Roman, it is conceivable that the fourth Gospel simply built up its story from a dramatic point of view, and included the detail about the Roman police to heighten the effect.

But this is improbable. Primarily because in its net effect the fourth Gospel, in its present state, does not emphasize in any way the presence of the Romans; they seem to have slipped as it were into the stream of the narrative almost unconsciously. The dramatic effect of the mere word "chilarchos" etc. is negligible. While vital as historical evidence, once it is looked for, it contributes nothing to the exaltation of Jesus at this crucial moment.

It is far more sensible to take it at its face value, as a detail ultimately founded on fact that somehow remained firmly interwoven with an early strand of the tradition that was busily engaged for the most part in cutting out all hostile references to the Romans wherever possible. Let us leave this point for a moment and look at the actual trial, which is, of course, the crucial point.

4

The Trial of Jesus, Dissected

Now, at Jesus' trial, what were the charges and who were the judges? The Gospel account implicates both the Jews and the Romans in Jesus' trial, though in contradictory and ambiguous ways; both the procedure and the content of the trial are deeply confused. The charges laid against Jesus are not those he is condemned on; we are told that the Romans, who actually condemn him, consider him innocent, while the Jews, who do not carry out the sentence, seem determined to undo him for reasons that either don't concern them or from their point of view have no validity.

This is the general outline of the Synoptic account of the trial.

Jesus is supposed to be taken to the High Priest's house by the band that has arrested him. The Sanhedrin assembles there at once, in the middle of the night. Jesus is interrogated by the High Priest, confronted by witnesses, ill-treated, and finally condemned to death for blasphemy.

The following morning there is another meeting of the Sanhedrin, which decides to take Jesus to Pilate: we are now shifted to the Romans.

The trial is reopened before Pilate. The charge, given only in Lk 23:2,4, is that of inciting the people to revolt, forbidding them to pay tribute to the Caesar, and putting himself forth as the Messiah.

This charge is incontestably of Roman concern; it is also completely different from the charges of blasphemy etc. that are supposed to have been heard during the Sanhedrin trial.

The purely judicial portion of the trial before Pilate boils down to nothing but a brief interrogation, the showing of both Jesus and a certain Barabbas to the multitude, the sentence of death extracted from Pilate by Jewish pressure, and the scourging of Jesus prior to crucifixion. With the exception of the transformation of the charges this general outline hangs together, but only at first glance. It is, so to speak, a global impression convincing only to an uncritical reader. The impression depends on disregarding the manifest disagreement in fundamental details between the various Synoptic accounts. In fact, it reflects only Mark (which is followed by Matthew): Luke is ignored.

Luke not only gives a different order of events, but makes a different impression altogether. It speaks of only one meeting of the Sanhedrin (the morning one), mentions no witnesses, and refers only to Jesus' messianic claims. In addition, no judgement is actually expressed; Jesus' confession is sufficient. The Sanhedrin is curiously passive; it does no more than take Jesus before Pilate, without having either judged or condemned him. Generally speaking, Luke, far more than Matthew or Mark, gives the impression of a case that involves the Romans only, or at any rate has only been tried by them, though no sentence is actually indicated as having been passed by Pilate. Jesus seems to have been left for the Jews to deal with (despite, as we shall see, the plain fact of the crucifixion itself).

When we look at John still another impression is given. Despite its greater antipathy to the Jews there is never really a question of the Sanhedrin at all. According to John Jesus is simply "led to Annas; for he was the father-in-law of Caiaphas, who was high priest that year." (Jn 18:13)

This is puzzling. It seems to indicate that the early tradition was unsure of the actual name of the high priest who was supposed to have presided at Jesus' Jewish trial. Caiaphas is not mentioned in Mark at all, though the name occurs in Luke (3:2) as well as in Acts (4:6). The awkwardness of the passage in John seems to imply that the original text incorporated into our present Gospel may have read simply "to Annas," and that the name of Caiaphas was inserted later in order to harmonize with Matthew (26:57). In any case, Annas simply asks Jesus "about his disciples and about his doctrine"(Jn 18:19), surely the vaguest of formulae, and upon a quite unincriminating reply from Jesus sends him off to Caiaphas, where oddly enough nothing actually happens either. Jesus is simply taken from Caiaphas to Pilate in the early morning; thus, it is Pilate who is to try Jesus after all and, by implication (Jn 19:16), to condemn him. The Sanhedrin itself is not referred to as playing a positive role.

Of the two charges that are made against Jesus in the fourth Gospel—that Jesus is King of the Jews and that he claims to be the Son of God—the first is obviously of moment to the Romans, while the second is a matter of indifference, implying as it does some parochial conflict within Judaism. Yet when Pilate refuses to deal with the matter, the Jews parade Jesus' messianic pretensions (Jn 18:29–31) (a version of his being "King of the Jews"), but then unaccountably insist on his being an "evil-doer"—and it is on *this* point that Pilate yields.

And when Pilate asks Jesus whether he is king, and Jesus admits that he is, Pilate thereupon goes out to the Jews and tells them he finds him guilty of nothing. Then Pilate proposes, as a compromise, releasing Jesus for Passover. The Jews refuse: they demand Barabbas. Pilate goes further by way of concession: he suggests flogging Jesus, which would at least presumably save his life while at the same time giving the Jews satisfaction in principle. But this fails: The Jews persist in demanding Jesus' death because he had made himself Son of God (Jn 19:5–7). Pilate interrogates Jesus on this new accusation and again finds him innocent (19:8–11), though it is obviously outside his competence or interest. Then the *Jews* take up the political charge again and by threatening Pilate with a denunciation at Rome as no friend of Caesar's manage to persuade him to take his place at the tribunal and pronounce sentence. Although the verse "then [Pilate] handed him over to them to be crucified" (Jn 19:16) seems to indicate that Pilate gave Jesus back to the Jews for crucifixion (quite impossibly, as we have seen) the statement is contradicted by a remark that follows immediately: "Pilate also wrote a title and put it on the cross: it read, 'Jesus of Nazareth, the King of the Jews' " (Jn19:19). In the fourth Gospel, accordingly, Pilate is plainly the focus of the essential action.

If we compare the account of the Sanhedrin trial in the fourth Gospel with the evidence of the Synoptic Gospels, we see that the Sanhedrin trial in John basically tells us nothing. The two elements emphasized in the Synoptic account are Jesus' remark about the destruction and rebuilding of the Temple, and then his statement about the Son of Man (generally taken to be a synonym of the Messiah) coming on the clouds of the skies. In John the first element is transposed to the beginning of Jesus' career, where it is unintelligible in terms of the Sanhedrin trial, while the second is altogether omitted. The omission is probably to be explained by the subsequent development of the purely theological aspects of Jesus' life in a way that conflicted with the notion of the Son of Man coming on the clouds, a very ancient formula that, since it makes no reference to the resurrection or the glorification of Jesus, evidently precedes this subsequent hub of the new cult. Parenthetically, it is also likely to be an authentic remark of Jesus' for the same reason; it may be a recollection of Jesus' essential belief about the Kingdom of God he was herald of. Now let us look at the trial in greater detail.

In all four Gospels the manner in which the Jews simply convoke Pilate to deal with a case presumably of interest only to themselves is bound to make us restive. In Mark, for instance, we are told:

> And as soon as it was morning the chief priests, with the elders and scribes, and the whole council held a consultation; and they bound Jesus and led him away and delivered him to Pilate. And Pilate asked him "Are you the King of the Jews?" and he answered him "You have said so," and the Chief Priests accused him of many things, and Pilate again asked him, "Have you no answer to make? See how many charges they bring against you." But Jesus made no further answer, so that Pilate wondered. (Mk 15:1–5)

The presumption, accordingly, is that Pilate held himself at the disposition of the Jews, on a feast day, moreover, when he must have known there could have been no trial. He then simply asks Jesus a straightforward question involving the capital charge—whether he has claimed to be the Messiah. Roman justice must certainly have had more protocol. The absurdity of it is capped by Jesus' straightforward reply to the question, in the affirmative—"You have said so." Since Jesus, in our texts, had always forbidden his disciples to put it about that he was the Messiah his own admission of it, at this moment, is surely very strange.

There has, naturally, been a great deal of discussion about the nature of the statement—"You have said so," or, more colloquially, "You're the one who says so." But as far as the Gospel writers are concerned the sense can only be affirmative, for we have been prepared for it by the same unequivocal answer Jesus has already given at his supposed trial before the Sanhedrin, when the high priest asks him whether he is the Messiah: "And Jesus said, 'I am; and you will see the Son of Man sitting at the right hand of power, and coming with the clouds of heaven' " (Mk 14:62). Thus it is clear that Jesus has acknowledged *in advance* the charge made against him before Pilate as well as before the Sanhedrin.

In fact, the curious parallelism between the two appearances before the Sanhedrin and Pilate is deeply suspect. We cannot help feeling that the same data are being unrealistically duplicated. For instance, in the account of the trial before the Sanhedrin, what is stressed by the Synoptic Gospels is the crime of claiming to be the Messiah, which while no religious crime *per se* as we have seen, is the only crime that could have interested Pilate. "The High Priest . . . asked [him], 'Are you the Christ [i.e., the Messiah], the Son of the Blessed?' " (Mk 14:61). The last is, of course, a very peculiar phrase for a Jew.

The Trial section in Mark is organized so as to emphasize the following three episodes:

- the deposition of the witnesses (14:55ff);
- the interrogation of Jesus (14:60ff);
- the abusive treatment of Jesus by the audience and the servants (14:65ff).

Now, the identical episodes are merely *repeated* in the account of the trial before Pilate, in the form of

- the testimony of the Jews,
- the questioning by Pilate, and
- the insults of the soldiers.

It is obvious that the account represents a duplication of the same facts, whatever they were, and since the actual core of the matter is evidently Jesus' condemnation and execution by the Romans on a political charge, we are bound to believe that the arbitrary parallelism is due to the redundancy of the Sanhedrin trial. The trial before the Sanhedrin, in fact, appears to be nothing but an artificial device; it was introduced to lay the death of Jesus at the door of the Jews, just as the celebrated episode of Barabbas, which we shall now glance at, was put in for the purpose of making the Roman Procurator the guarantor of Jesus' innocence.

It is a minor, though perhaps intriguing question how the original narrator could have known what had been going on in the presumed nocturnal session of the Sanhedrin, since Simon the Rock, the only disciple physically close enough to the scene to have learned something of this, was busy denying his Lord at cockcrow (Mk 14:53–72). One can, of course speculate on the possibility of the informant having been Joseph of Arimathaea, or some other member of the Sanhedrin who was converted after the resurrection, but this never occurred to the Gospel writers themselves.

A mere juxtaposition of Matthew, Luke, and John is quite enough to make the progressive tendency toward the inculpation of the Jews apparent at once.

Matthew (27:11–19, 24–26)	Luke (23:6–16, 21–25)	John (18:38, 19:4,19:6,12–16)
Pilate insists on freeing Jesus, asserts the Jews are acting out of envy; his wife's dream; washes his hands of it; the Jews accept their responsibility.	Pilate sends Jesus off to Herod, and it is Herod and his soldiers who insult Jesus, not Pilate's; Pilate says unequivocally that Jesus is innocent; he does not condemn him, and even on the insistence of the Jews does not, in fact, condemn him formally.	Pilate proclaims Jesus' innocence three times over, and out of personal fear of his own of a denunciation to the emperor abandons Jesus, but does not, in fact, condemn him formally.

We are obliged to conclude that there is a progressive development to the Gospel texts in the direction of placing the blame for Jesus' death on the Jews; if we take this development in the inverse sense our opinion is bound to be fortified, as we survey the building up of the case against the Jews that took place between Mark and the fourth Gospel, that the earliest Christian records must have laid all the responsibility for Jesus' execution on the Romans, *not* on the Jews.

This general theme of Jewish guilt is further emphasized by the celebrated episode of Barabbas. This whole episode is very peculiar. Here it is, as given in Mark:

> Now at the feast he used to release for them any one prisoner whom they asked. And among the rebels in prison, who had committed murder in the insurrection, there was a man called Barabbas. And the crowd began to ask Pilate to do as he was wont to do for them. And he answered them, "Do you want me to release for you the King of the Jews?" For he perceived that it was out of envy that the chief priests had delivered him up. But the chief priests stirred up the crowd to have him release for them Barabbas instead. And Pilate again said to them, "Then what shall we do with the man you call King of the Jews?" And they cried out again, "Crucify him." And Pilate said to them, "Why, what evil has he done?" But they shouted all the more, "Crucify him." So Pilate, wishing to satisfy the crowd, released for them Barabbas; and having scourged Jesus, he delivered him to be crucified. (Mk 15:6–15)

The first thing that arrests the eye is the idea of the custom itself, that is of the Roman authorities' being *compelled* to release a convicted criminal at the mere command of a Jewish mob. Not only is there no other evidence for this in any classical record, but inherently it is most improbable; it must be classified as either entirely legendary, or reflecting some otherwise vanished state of affairs.

Lawyers have of course exercised their talents on this as on all the other aspects of Roman judicial procedure, but though instances of clemency have been found they do not apply to the case of Barabbas. A free pardon might have been thinkable, but that would presumably have been dependent on the senate, and even if Caesar himself would have had the right to exercise it independently of the senate it is far from likely that his procurator would have exercised it in his place. Even if that were possible, why on earth should Pilate have wished to do so, in favor of a convicted rebel against the Roman power?

In all probability the formation of the belief in the Roman custom of releasing a prisoner to a mob on demand was purely literary, as the juxtaposition in sequence of the relevant passages will show:

Mk 15:6–8	Mt 27:15–16	Lk 23:17	Jn 18:39
Now at the feast he used to release for them any prisoner whom they asked. And among the rebels in prison who had committed murder in the insurrection, there was a man called Barabbas. And the crowd came up and began to ask Pilate to do as he was wont to do for them.	Now at the feast the governor was accustomed to release for the crowd any one prisoner whom they wanted. And they had a notorious prisoner, called Barabbas.	(absent in best mss.) Now he was obliged to release one man to them at the festival.	"But you have a custom that I should release one man for you at the Passover; will you have me release for you the King of the Jews?"

The absurdity of such a Jewish privilege is heightened still further by the abrupt reversal of the mood of the populace, which the Gospels elsewhere indicate to have been enthusiastically in favor of Jesus.

The Barabbas episode in its present setting, in short, has an artificial, histrionic, and tendentious effect, well in line with the general anti-Jewish and pro-Roman tendency of the Gospels but flagrantly contrary to all probability. But "probability" here simply means historical probability or fact, a notion alien to the writers and editors of the Gospels, who were interested solely in discovering occasions for edification. The Barabbas episode fits admirably into the moralizing tendency of the Gospels in yet another way. It symbolizes the choice offered the Jews between the Way of God and the Way of Satan—they *chose* Barabbas, the son of their father Satan, and not the Son of God: "You are of your father the devil, and your will is to do your father's desire" (Jn 8:44).

Perhaps the most interesting substantive element in the whole Barabbas episode is the use of the word "insurrection" in the above-mentioned passage from Mark; it must surely be of great significance. In the parallel account in Luke it has been softened to "a certain insurrection made in the city" (Lk 23:19); this also makes an odd impression, since no further mention of such an insurrection is made and Barabbas is otherwise referred to as a mere "murderer." (I shall return to this in chapter 7).

The casual reference in Mt. 27:19, mentioned above, to Pilate's wife, scarcely calls for comment. If not much is known about Pilate, nothing at all is known about his wife; the only other references to her are in countless apocryphal legends.

Perhaps the most revealing detail in this whole strangely contorted caricature of Roman judicial procedure is the language ascribed to Pilate in Mt 27:24 above. His unaccountably favorable attitude toward Jesus is expressed here in an unmistakably Jewish manner, in the symbolical gesture of "washing one's hands of something." Not only is the gesture Jewish, as well as what it symbolizes (Deut. 21:6; Ps. 26:6), but Pilate's answer to the mob, in fact, as he "washes his hands" of Jesus' blood, actually contains a quotation from the Hebrew Bible, where David is supposed to have said: "I as well as my kingdom am guiltless before the Lord for ever from the blood of Abner the son of Ner;" adding, "Let it be on the head of Joab, and on all the house of his father" (2 Sam 3:28,9).

It need hardly be said that the traditional Gospel account is not concerned with reporting Pilate's cowardice, but with condemning the Jews for

Jesus' execution. It is perhaps ironical to reflect that this sentence, which has wrought so much havoc through the ages, is due to nothing more than a late editorial insertion. The Gospel writer is so indifferent to mundane history that he actually has a Roman Governor express himself in a purely Jewish manner, with what amounts to a quotation from the Jewish scriptures, and in a version that in fact comes from the Greek translation of those Scriptures (the Septuagint) since that was the version the writers and editors of the Gospels themselves were familiar with. The mob naturally gives the counterpoint in its own fashion by completing the Hebrew reference: "His blood be on us and on all our children" (Mt 27:25).

None of these above-mentioned oddities can be reconciled except by dint of painful contortions; hundreds of scholars have broken their teeth on various rearrangements or violations of the text, generally chronological, in an attempt to restore a logical sequence. Aside from general questions of plausibility the specific difficulties are too great. I shall outline the principal ones.

It was against Jewish custom to begin a trial on Passover day. The arrest of Jesus and his appearance before the Sanhedrin are recorded in Mark as having taken place on the Passover night, so that we are to presume that instead of celebrating the great Passover festival in a normal way all the authoritative people were rushing about the streets involved in a criminal case.

John, it is true, has a different chronology, but if anything it makes this difficulty insurmountable. In John the Sanhedrin sits in judgment at night, but Jewish custom did not allow nocturnal judgments, nor could a judgment be handed down on the same day as the interrogation itself.

Further, there is some question about the Sanhedrin's having had the right in general to pronounce a capital sentence. This has naturally been much debated, but the real point in any case lies elsewhere. Even if it is true that the Sanhedrin could inflict capital punishment in religious crimes (now the scholarly consensus), Jesus is not in fact condemned on a religious charge anyhow.

When he is handed over to Pilate a completely fresh trial begins, as though it were entirely outside the competence of the Sanhedrin, as though, in any case, the Sanhedrin had neither tried the case nor decided it. Also, the charges themselves, as well as the character of the sentence, make the whole procedure quite different from the mere transfer of a heretic by a religious tribunal to the secular authority. As I shall show later on, Jesus was not in any sense of the word a heretic from the point of view of the Torah: nor were the charges leveled at him in different parts of the Gospel narrative relevant to the Torah. He did not, in fact, blaspheme, even if it were true that he declared to the Jews that he was the Messiah. Announcing oneself as the Messiah might have been a criminal matter, as part of raising an insurrection, but it was not blasphemy, since the Messiah was expected to be a perfectly normal man inspired by God; thus, it had nothing to do with the religious arm of the state. It was, of course, very much the concern of the secular arm—the Roman procurator.

Also, if Pilate were merely to be taken as being in the position of confirming a decision laid down by a Jewish tribunal, the punishment would in all consistency have been Jewish too, that is, stoning, the stake, strangling, or decapitation, as mentioned above. But Matthew and Mark indicate unmistakably that the *real* condemnation, i.e., that followed by execution, was pronounced by Pilate and was, in fact, crucifixion, the characteristic Roman punishment.

The bringing in of Herod (an episode peculiar to Luke) is quite preposterous from a historical point of view; it must be taken to be an alternative way of dissipating the culpability of the Romans in Jesus' undoing and establishing the blameworthiness of the Jews. Herod simply represents the Jewish authorities. Historically, it is silly to imagine that Pilate would have renounced his own jurisdiction in a matter affecting the security of the state.

There is also, to be sure, a reference to Herod not only in Acts (4:27), which is not surprising in view of the identity of authorship between Acts and Luke, but in the apocryphal Gospel of Peter where Herod is represented as one of Jesus' judges, who actually orders Jesus to be removed for execution. Without going into the usual questions of scholarship concerning the authorship, date, etc. of the Gospel of Peter, we may simply take it for granted that there was an early legend somehow implicating Herod in the crime and finally putting the entire blame on him. It corresponds to the fiction of the trial before the Sanhedrin and is another way of rearranging the historical recollections in the light of the much later perspective of the Gospel writers.

The lack of precision in Pilate's interrogation is preposterous as a record of a genuine interrogation. Those who maintain that the Roman trial was a parody of justice fall into an absurdity: Why should a Roman official have parodied his own justice? Perhaps the chief point that leaps to the eye is that if Jesus had been proscribed and sought, before being arrested, he must have been charged with something perfectly definite. Why then should there have been any hesitation about the charge when he appeared before Pilate?

The whole portrait of Pilate, indeed, is completely out of touch with reality. Even if we did not have accounts of him from other sources depicting him as a man exceptionally cruel even by Roman standards and full of antipathy to the Jews, whose intractability he found incomprehensible, the futile leniency and passivity ascribed to him by the Gospels is obviously grotesque. Even though he doubtless would not have been moved by the plight of some visionary or religious reformer (as the Gospels present Jesus) it is even less likely that he would have been moved to make a legal decision under the pressure of a Jewish mob.

Taking the Gospel accounts of the trial at their face value, we are bound to come to the conclusion that if Pilate had thought Jesus innocent he would simply have acquitted him; if he had thought him guilty, he would have condemned him. But for reasons peculiar to the Gospel writers, they would not admit that Jesus was a genuine danger from the Roman point of view, and at the same time were equally incapable of saying, in the teeth of a firmly established fact, that Pilate had freed him.

Perhaps the most striking thing about the trial in all four Gospels is the barrenness of the information given. On examination all we can say with any assurance is that Jesus was arrested, tried, and condemned by the Romans, perhaps with the support of the Jewish Temple authorities, and crucified by the Romans on a capital charge of sedition. It is evident that the writers and editors of the present Gospels in all probability did not know anything beyond this. When the Synoptics tell us, for instance, that the Jews made a great many accusations against Jesus, the vagueness of this remark makes it clear that the chroniclers had no idea what those accusations were.

One thing is obvious from the stylized, fragmentary way the trial is reported in the Gospels: The last thing that was in the minds of the chroniclers was the idea of reproducing an actual Roman, or for that matter Jewish trial, with any accuracy. Their perspective was altogether different.

It was not a mere matter of either forgetting or suppressing facts; by the time the Gospels achieved their present form the Christian community had already taken shape, with all that this implies. The ritual and cult were established; the process of dogmatizing the religion had begun. Jesus' earthly career was only understood in the light of transcendental factors. In the eyes of the Gospel writers their Savior had been crucified as the result of an utterly appalling sacrilege that was simultaneously, however, no more than the mysterious working out of God's will. The Gospel writers could not, after all, have been interested in a mere historical account. Since their whole perspective was that of the resurrection and glorification of their Savior, the historical elements of his actual life on earth were of interest to them only in so far as they conformed not only with this perspective, but doubtless even more with the ritualistic forms of the cult that was already established by the time the Gospels were being reduced to writing and editorially harmonized.

By this time the quarrel with Judaism had long since become embittered. Regarded in the first century or two after Jesus as mere Jewish sectarians, the early Christians had the burden on the one hand of differentiating their cult from that of Judaism, and on the other of making it perfectly clear to the Hellenistic world that they had nothing in common with the Jewish trouble-makers who had in any case been crushed by Titus, Vespasian's son, in 70. Hadrian, who crushed the second Jewish insurrection of 133, merely put the finishing touches to the Roman campaign of national liquidation.

The entire inculpation of the Jews, accordingly, must be viewed in the light of this much later perspective. The trial of Jesus by the Sanhedrin, as recorded in the Gospels in its present form, was obviously the most demonstrative available evidence of the dynamically pernicious role of the Jews in furthering Satan's intention of undoing the Savior in the acting out of the divine drama of the redemptive crucifixion.

In chapter 12 I shall discuss the possibility of a historical explanation of a Jewish role in the undoing of Jesus. At this point I should like to indicate merely that on the basis of the present Gospel account the role of the Jewish authorities is unintelligible, and that in its present form it can only represent a much later editorial manipulation of whatever the facts might have been.

The present Gospel narrative, in short, is so full of irreconcilable discrepancies that any attempt to stitch them together by subjective projections of one kind or another is bound to be frustrated. The present texts have of course been studied from a legal point of view any number of times; the most these quasi-juridical studies have produced is the unintelligible claim that every form of justice was violated, that Jesus was the victim of a judicial murder.

Such explanations, which ultimately revolve around the notion of a "misunderstanding," might have some weight if they provided us with some theory of *why* he was murdered, *why* justice was travestied, *why* his message was misunderstood, etc, but that is where they fail us. If there was a misunderstanding our present texts were the first victims of it. For there must, after all, have been some kind of trial. The only question is whether Jesus, aside from the charges against him, was important enough, from the Roman point of view, to warrant one.

It is, perhaps, the very silence on Jesus' culpability, so resolutely but unsuccessfully cloaked by the Gospel account, that may give us a hint. If Jesus was tried he must have been tried for something; he must even have defended himself, or had a defense of some kind; consequently our present tradition, by obscuring his real defense and replacing it with nothing but vagueness, contradiction, and stylized moralization, must be a later, secondary growth. Jesus' authentic defense, whether in court or in life, must have been repugnant to the earliest Christian tradition, and it must be this that led to the suppression or omission, whether conscious or not, of the factual side of the events and to the creation of the present, essentially theological account of Jesus' behavior.

Beginning with the perception that the Jews did not have any reason for executing Jesus, and in fact did not do so, we must ask: Why did the Romans kill Jesus?

5

The Insurrection—The Crucifixion

We have seen some of the oddities in the Gospel accounts of the Roman trial of Jesus. They make up part of the jigsaw puzzle I have referred to. Is it possible to fill in the rest of the jigsaw puzzle with other elements hinted at in the Gospels, or legitimately to be deduced from them? Let us see whether there is some way of bridging the gaps in the traditional story.

What are the bare bones of Jesus' activity in Jerusalem?

The core of the Gospel narrative is this: Jesus entered Jerusalem at the head of a group of men; he occupied the Temple for a while; he was betrayed; he was then tried, condemned, and executed on a charge of sedition.

Now, if we take Jesus' crucifixion once again as our starting-point, our attention is bound to be arrested by one other element in this skeleton summary of Jesus' downfall that in its implications is far more startling than even the crucifixion. *Jesus held the Temple.* How could this have been possible?

The Jewish Temple, celebrated in antiquity as the most splendid shrine in the world, was a vast edifice. Destroyed by Nebuchadnezzar in 586 B.C.E., it had been rebuilt in 518–516 B.C.E. upon the return of the Jews from their first exile. It was restored on a still more magnificent scale by Herod the Great; more than 200 yards wide and 450 yards long, its rebuilding began in 20–19 B.C.E. The work was so extensive that by the time of Jesus—forty-six years later, according to John (2:20)—it was not yet completed. The work on the outbuildings and the courts was actually to go on for eighty years altogether; it was not finished until 62–64 C.E.; it was burned to the ground in 70 during the siege of Jerusalem.

The Temple was the nerve center of Jewish national life. It had a gigantic staff of attendants, as many as twenty thousand people, for a wide variety of functions.

It was also a great public treasury. Like other shrines in the Oriental world of the time, and even more so, it was in effect the national bank. There was immense wealth in the form of "raiment money," mentioned in Matthew (6:19), and wrought precious metal, as well as great sums of coins and vast deposits made by individual creditors, not only by widows and orphans, but also by the rich. These deposits were not allowed to remain idle. The Temple was not a hoard; the money was continuously being worked. The Jews, like the rest of the Hellenistic world, had inherited from Babylon the whole system of bills of exchange, bonds, and personal checks invented there long before, and the vast wealth of the Temple was constantly being deployed in money transfers all over the world. Though it is true that Jews were prevented from taking any interest in transactions between Jews, they were not forbidden to benefit by the profits of Jewish commercial enterprises, and the prohibition of interest did not extend to dealings between Jews and non-Jews. For that matter, in view of the complex network of business relations that prevailed throughout the empire, there must have been methods of getting around this prohibition of interest even between Jews.

The Temple was, in short, the most important and most massive institution in the country, both physically and functionally. It was, accordingly, protected. Its chief protection was the Roman garrison of Jerusalem, consisting of a cohort of some five to six hundred men, with the usual auxiliaries in camp-followers and troops. There was also a Temple police guard, obviously of considerable strength, in view of the size of the establishment and the throngs of people continually passing through even at ordinary times. The pressure reached a tremendous pitch of concentration at the great annual festival of Passover, when tens of thousands of pilgrims came not only from Judea and Galilee but from all over the known world. It is also likely that on the occasion of Passover the Romans would have reinforced their standard cohort considerably by bringing in even more troops to Jerusalem. Though this is not quite certain, there is no doubt that the Romans kept a substantial force in Fort Antonia, at the edge of the Temple area, some years later, when Saul was arrested (Acts 21) for bringing an uncircumcised Greek into the Temple in defiance of the Jewish purity law; hence it is likely that Fort Antonia was occupied even earlier, when Jesus came up to Jerusalem.

The very nature of the Passover festival, with its throngs of unknown pilgrims streaming through the precincts of the vast sanctuary, made reinforcement indispensable. A conventional military custom of the time was to conceal daggers or short swords beneath the voluminous Oriental robes, then to snatch them out by signal and attack anyone at hand. In the circumstances of the Passover festival this practice naturally called for special vigilance.

But even if there was no substantial Roman force in the Temple area proper at this time, Roman troops were certainly stationed west of the city; in any case, the seizure of the Temple could clearly have been accomplished only by an act of violence, by armed force. Jesus could scarcely have dropped in at the Temple, bandied remarks with the Temple police and priests, to say nothing of the Roman soldiers on duty there, and purely as a result of his personal, *spiritual* authority, have actually *held* the Temple.

Most theological interpretations of this episode accept the account of Jesus' occupation of the Temple as historical (which is natural since believers regard the whole Gospel account as literally true), but they make the event spiritual or symbolical. Liberal students of the New Testament, on the other hand, generally doubt the historicity of the event, but their reasons are essentially naive; they all agree that it would have been a major enterprise requiring force, and therefore say it never took place. But the relationship of Jesus to the Temple is so central a theme in the Gospel story, it is so obviously the springboard for his arrest and trial, that its historicity must be accepted.

Let us weigh its implications. A passage in the fourth Gospel gives us a material hint:

In the Temple [Jesus] found those who were selling oxen and sheep and pigeons, and the money-changers at their business. And making a whip of cords, he drove them all, with the sheep and oxen, out of the Temple; and he poured out the coins of the money-changers and overturned their tables. (Jn 2:14–15)

Here the words "whip of cords," though they unmistakably imply violence, equally unmistakably represent a minimal toning down of what actually must have been a massive undertaking. If we simply imagine the size of the Temple, the tens of thousands of pilgrims thronging into and through it, the numerous attendants, the huge police force, the Roman soldiers, as well as the normal reaction of the ox-drivers themselves, to say nothing of the money-changers, we see that it must have taken much more than simple peremptoriness to accomplish it. The scene behind this fragmentary recollection in the fourth Gospel *must* have been vastly different; the chronicler has softened it by "spiritualizing" it out of all reality.

This spiritualizing tendency has gone even further in the other Gospels; in Matthew it simply says:

> Jesus . . . drove out all who sold and bought in the Temple, and he overturned the tables of the money-changers and the seats of those who sold pigeons. (Mt 21:12)

In Mark the chronicler reports a seemingly innocuous visit by Jesus to the Temple:

> [Jesus] entered Jerusalem, and went into the Temple and when he had looked round at everything, as it was already late, he went out to Bethany with the twelve. (Mk 11:11)

This sounds as though the final remnant of incriminatory evidence had been removed; it is followed by the equally colorless "[Jesus] began to drive out" etc., though the sentence immediately after this phrase, usually translated as "he would not allow anyone to carry anything through the Temple" (Mk 11:16) is thought by some to require "armor" instead of "anything."

Jesus must have had an armed force powerful enough for him to seize this vast edifice and hold it for some time, judging by his reference to the "day after day" he had spent "teaching" in the Temple (Mk 14:49 and parallels). He must have had a force large enough to withstand the opposition not only of the Roman soldiery or the Temple police alone, but presumably also of the many other Jews who were doubtless out of sympathy with the Galilean upstart (if we are to take seriously the hostility of the Jewish mob after Jesus' condemnation, as reported in the Gospels). In short, to overcome armed forces Jesus' followers must have been armed.

In addition to evidence of this throughout the Gospels—attenuated but unmistakable—ancient authorities refer to the armed character of Jesus' enterprise in the most matter-of-fact way. Tacitus, for instance, the Roman historian, simply takes it for granted that from the Roman point of view Jesus was an enemy; in discussing the attempt made by Nero to blame the burning of Rome, which slanderous rumors had attributed to him, on "those whom the common people called Christians," he adds that this name came from one Christ, "who was executed by Procurator Pontius Pilate under Tiberius."

The insurgents against Rome, both before and after Jesus, were commonly designated by the word for highway robber, this was in fact the equivalent in modern terminology of rebel; it occurs even in the Gospels, for instance in Lk 23:40, where it is used concerning the "companions" crucified together with Jesus.

The conventional translation in all editions of the Gospels obscures the historic significance of this basic word, which for that matter was applied to Jesus also:

> One of the criminals who were hanged railed at him saying, "Are you not the Christ? Save yourself and us." But the other rebuked him, saying, "Do you not fear God, since you are under the same sentence of condemnation? And we indeed justly; for we are receiving the due reward of our deeds; but this man has done nothing wrong." And he said, "Jesus, remember me when you come in your kingly power." (Lk 23:39–42)

Here the notion of their "companionship" is expressed in unmistakably concrete terms: the "same condemnation" is simply reported. It is the only thing that makes sense of the "criminal" exhorting Jesus to save him because he is the Messiah: why should the Messiah save a random criminal? The phrase, "This man has done nothing wrong," is clearly incomprehensible in this context, since Jesus, according to the same Gospel, had acknowledged the charge of being King of the Jews; accordingly, it can only be understood as an interpolation by some later scribe or editor.

But there is also direct evidence in the Gospels of actual arms being carried by Jesus' followers. Here are the Synoptic accounts of their arrest:

> But one of those who stood by drew his sword, and struck the slave of the high priest and cut off his ear. And Jesus said to them, "Have you

> come out as against a robber, with swords and clubs to capture me?" (Mk 14:47–48)

> And when those who were about him saw what would follow they said, "Lord, shall we strike with the sword?" And one of them struck the slave of the high priest and cut off his right ear. (Lk 22:49–50)

> Then Jesus said to the chief priests and captains of the Temple and elders who had come out against him, "Have you come out as against a robber, with swords and clubs? (Lk 22:52)

> One of those who were with Jesus stretched out his hand and drew his sword, and struck the slave of the high priest, and cut off his ear. Then Jesus said to him, "Put your sword back into its place; for all who take the sword will perish by the sword." (Mt 26:51–52)

In the last passage, it is true, Matthew has Jesus say, "Put your sword back into its place," etc. This is clearly a later addition; not only is it contradicted by the logic of the situation involved, but in still another of Jesus' sayings that survived the "pacifying" attempts of later editors and scribes, a background of violence is clearly implied:

> [Jesus] said to them, "But now, let him who has a purse take it, and likewise a bag. And let him who has no sword sell his mantle and buy one. For I tell you that this scripture must be fulfilled in me, "and he was reckoned with transgressors." And they said, "Look, Lord, here are two swords." And he said to them "It is enough." (Lk 22:36–38)

Attempts to explain this "symbolically" or "allegorically" cannot overcome the textual evidence, combined with the actual course of events as dimly perceived beyond the texts. In point of fact the "fire and sword" passages in Matthew and Luke, though not so specific as the above-mentioned references to actual weapons being held by Jesus' band, are clearly genuine: like the others they too have survived all conciliationist attempts to smooth them over:

> I came to cast fire upon the earth; and would that it were already kindled! . . . Do you think that I have come to give peace on earth? No, I tell you, but rather division: for henceforth in one house there will be five divided, three against two and two against three: they will be divided, father against son and son against father, mother against daughter and daugh-

ter against her mother, mother-in-law against her daughter-in-law and daughter-in-law against her mother-in-law. (Lk 12:49–53)

Do you think that I have come to bring peace on earth? I have not come to bring peace, but a sword. For I have come to set a man against his father, and a daughter against her mother, and a daughter-in-law against her mother-in-law; and a man's foes will be those of his own household. (Mt 10:34–37)

There is a curious reference, in Luke (13:4), about eighteen people killed by a fall of the tower of Siloam; this tower of Siloam is considered to have been one of the towers of the city wall of Jerusalem that was redis-covered during the course of excavation carried on in Jerusalem during 1913–1914. This conclusion had already been reached by other scholars as a result of the examination and comparison of various statements made in Josephus concerning the city wall in the neighborhood of the pool of Siloam.

Now, it is unlikely that in these fortifications, which had only recently been restored by Herod the Great after the storming of the city by Pompey, a tower would simply have fallen by itself. An earthquake, on the other hand, would surely have been mentioned if only as a profound portent. Also, there is a rabbinic tradition that no building had ever fallen in Jerusalem, one of the "ten wonders granted to our fathers in the sacred place," doubtless to be understood more prosaically as a result of the fact that the whole of Jerusalem is constructed on solid rock. Thus, the likeli-hood is that this curious phrase about the "eighteen killed by a fall of the tower of Siloam" is an echo of the siege operation that must doubtless have been executed by the Romans in order to recover control of the city after it had been taken by Jesus and his insurgents. It would have been a siege carried out by the conventional battering-ram and *testudo* of the Romans; why would they have done something like it against their own garrison town unless they had been forced to?

This suggestion of a siege is doubtless paralleled by the "Galileans" mentioned in the same passage (Lk 13:1) as having had their blood min-gled by Pilate with their sacrifices. They may very well have been the group who took and held the Temple, in conjunction with the other oper-ation directed against the Tower of Siloam; the two "criminals" crucified together with Jesus may have been the insurgents in command of these two points: this not only explains the plea of Jesus' fellow-rebel to him to save himself and them but also provides an understandable background for the other "criminal" who accepts the will of God; he is prepared to "share the cup" with Jesus, his leader and king, and thus is given Jesus' promise to be with him in paradise.

Even if this phrase has been embellished by Luke with the moralizing tendency that has produced the pious legend of the "good" and the "bad" thief, it is clear that here again there is a murky recollection of deeds of violence.

There is another passage that is even more persuasive in its utter—and inexplicable—simplicity: the casual way this whole operation is simply referred to, without explanation, in Mark:

> And among the rebels in prison, who had committed murder *in the insurrection,* there was a man called Barabbas. (Mk 15:7)

The words "in the insurrection" are left without comment. No commentator has as yet ventured to explain this simple phrase in an intelligible, nonpolitical way. It recurs in a parallel passage in Luke, where Barabbas is said to have been thrown into prison "for an insurrection started in the city" (Lk 23:19). This is evidently an attempt to slur over in a plausible way some mutilation or omission in an earlier account that must have been nearer the authentic events.

The above quotation from Mark (15:7), to be sure, does not explicitly say that Barabbas was a rebel himself, but was simply "among" them. This reticence may contain a hint for us, since the name implies the possibility that Barabbas (the Greek spelling of Bar Abba, "son of the father," or possibly, *Bar Rabba,* "son of the rabbi") may have been arrested by the Romans in error, and in fact was one of the Temple hierarchy. It may of course convey the further hint that some of the Temple hierarchy (the younger men) collaborated with Jesus.

In any case, if Barabbas, whose other name, by what sounds like a *very* strange and perplexing coincidence, was *Jesus* Barabbas, was actually one of the Temple hierarchy, we have here an insight into the origin of the so-called Roman custom of releasing a prisoner on the mob's request that is otherwise so baffling. If it was merely a single instance grounded in the mistaken arrest of some Temple dignitary, or his son, who was liberated "for the feast"—i.e., in time to participate in the holiday,—this may have been the germ of the custom that was then gradually built up in the literary way mentioned above.

If this is so then Pilate's question in Mark 15:9, asking whether he should release the King of the Jews, may be based on a mere mistake in names; hearing some people—those Jews opposed to the insurrection, or probably the Temple coterie itself—call for "Jesus Barabbas," he at first thinks they mean Jesus, and is ruffled by their presumption. Then, on learning that they mean Barabbas, a member of the ostensibly pro-Roman party who had been arrested by mistake, he releases him. To be sure, the Gospels contain nothing more substantial to justify this speculation, intriguing as it is.

Now, once we accustom ourselves to the idea of the violence that must have been involved in the culmination of Jesus' career, we shall be better prepared to cope with further hints at the real nature of his entire enterprise. Of these hints there is an abundance.

First, let us consider the whole point of Jesus' having disciples at all. What were they supposed to do? His purpose in selecting them is never intelligibly explained. The only things he calls on them to do are to cast out devils (i.e., heal the sick), understand his parables, and presumably to spread them. But it is expressly stated that these parables were incomprehensible to them; when they ask for an explanation they are told that the parables are *meant* to be baffling to the multitudes, though an explanation has been accorded to *them.*

> To you has been given the secret of the Kingdom of God, but for those outside everything is in parables; so that they may indeed see but not perceive, and may indeed hear but not understand; lest they should turn again, and be forgiven. (Mk 4:11,12)

Unfortunately, however (disregarding this curiously sadistic explanation of the Jewish failure to accept Jesus, or rather to accept the Church's traditional claims), it is not only those "outside" who don't understand these parables, the disciples themselves are evidently baffled.

> And [Jesus] said to them, "Do you not understand this parable? How then will you understand all the parables?" (Mk 4:13)

These mystical allegories are the sole explanation offered of the Kingdom of God in the Gospels. Devised, according to Jesus' words, to elude the understanding of the masses, they also puzzle the disciples who are supposed to enlighten them.

The disciples are curiously ineffective altogether: full of vacillation, with no understanding for their leader or his mission (Mk 9:6,10; 10:13–16, 28–31,32) who lack his power (Mk 9:18) and quarrel about precedence (Mk 9:34; 10:35–45), one of them, Judas, actually betrays him, and after his arrest they all desert him and flee (Mk 14:50). Even Simon the Rock, who seems to be Jesus' favorite, is treated rather cavalierly by the chronicler. Though he is acknowledged as the first to understand that Jesus was the Messiah, he fails to see the necessity of the passion (Mk 8:27–34); he caps his shortcomings by actually denying Jesus through fear (Mk 14:66–72).

It is easy to say that the disciples were all too human: so they were, but this curiously denigratory, yet evasive treatment of them in the earliest tradition suggests precisely that—a purely human situation that existed before the institutional, "official" myth about them had taken shape. There is something incoherent in the very conception of the "discipleship" in terms of the Gospel narrative. The institution itself seems to hang in the air, with no understandable function. Indeed, the fact that the word "apostles," a synonym for "disciples," is used so rarely in the Gospels casts great doubt on the historicity of Jesus' institution of the apostolate, especially since, as we have seen, it is impossible to grasp its point. It is possible, of course, that the number twelve came about somewhat later as a way of symbolically encompassing Jewry (the twelve tribes); it is also possible that Jesus happened to be left with twelve principal followers at his death.

But even if Jesus did not institute the apostolate himself, it is clearly ancient, since the above-mentioned passage in Matthew (19:28), about the twelve apostles judging the twelve tribes of Israel obviously belongs to the very earliest stage of the tradition, implying, as it does, the existence of only Jews in the Kingdom of God.

But once again that is only in terms of the present account. If we imagine that the disciples were not mere preachers of a word that was as incomprehensible to them as it was to the people they were preaching to, but were in fact Jesus' lieutenants, the picture is restored to its proper perspective. They may not, of course, have been lieutenants in a military sense, but were in charge of an organized enterprise that contained a military factor.

It was only later, after Jesus' worldly enterprise had to be excised from the tradition as a fiasco, that the authentic function of his disciples was subtracted from the traditional accounts, leaving an unintelligible void.

It is, in fact, only within the framework of this insight into the organized-cum-military character of Jesus' movement that we can understand what might have been the role of his protodisciples. This perspective will also enable us to understand the sole intelligible reason for Judas's betrayal. If we try to explain his treachery, either psychologically or functionally, on the basis of the present Gospel account it remains altogether enigmatic, as we have seen above, while if we take as our starting-point the existence of an armed contest between an insurrectionary group and the powerful institutions it was assaulting we begin to see its purpose.

Judas *did* have something to betray—i.e., the hiding-place, not merely of a popular preacher lecturing to multitudes in a vast public square, but of the leader of an armed revolt. If the story of Jesus' coming to Jerusalem only during the day and spending his nights in Bethany (about a mile and a half away from Jerusalem on the road to Jericho) conserves an element of actuality, then perhaps this is to be taken as a somewhat denatured remnant of another recollection—that after the collapse of the insurrection, after the Roman cohort and the Temple police had broken the back of the revolt and restored order, Jesus took refuge in some hiding-place, and it was this that Judas betrayed to the authorities.

To be sure, this leads us no further into the psychological tangle; nothing could, since in the total absence of information there is no limit to the number of possible psychological explanations, but it does provide us with a point of view that makes the betrayal at any rate functionally meaningful.

Judas is not the only eccentric follower of Jesus; even to the unaided eye there is something odd about a number of them. These oddities not only conform with the impression that the seizure of the Temple must have been accomplished by means of an armed coup, but give a hint of the social background of Jesus' movement.

This is the account of their selection:

> [Jesus] called his disciples, and chose from them twelve, whom he named apostles; Simon, whom he named Peter [the Rock], and Andrew, his brother, and James and John, and Philip, and Bartholomew, and Matthew, and Thomas, and James the son of Alphaeus, and Simon who was called the Zealot, and Judas the son of James, and Judas Iscariot, who became a traitor. (Lk 6:13–16)

> He appointed twelve to be with him, and to be sent out to preach and have authority to cast out demons: Simon whom he surnamed Peter [the

Rock]; James the son of Zebedee and John the brother of James, whom
he surnamed Boanerges, that is, sons of thunder; Andrew and Philip, and
Bartholomew, and Matthew, and Thomas, and James the son of Alphaeus,
and Thaddeus, and Simon, of the Zealot party, and Judas Iscariot, who
betrayed him. (Mk 3:14)

We have already seen (chapter 1) the meaning of the word "Zealot" (mentioned again in Acts 1:13). It places us once again at the stark fact of Jesus' violent death; the savagery of the sentence is explained.

We are forced to the conclusion that Jesus came to his cruel and humiliating death for reasons that in Roman eyes were eminently compelling. Even the sketchiest attempt to fill in the social background against which Jesus was executed highlights the hollowness of the "misunderstanding" conventionally put forth to explain the crucifixion—that is , that ignorant, blind men were bent on destroying a paragon of abstract and timeless virtue merely because he had a message beyond their comprehension.

Jesus and his followers were engaged in an organized enterprise that had its roots in the circumstances of his own specific society. He had placed himself squarely in the long line of religious Jewish insurgents against the idolatrous Roman state.

We can now see the climax of Jesus' career in an unexpected light; by entering Jerusalem with a group of armed men large enough, or with enough popular support to overcome the defenses of its headquarters, he arrogated sovereign power to himself. Whatever his own interpretation of this, whatever his specific motivation, whatever his ultimate purpose, this act of armed and organized violence was obviously bound to bring down on his head the swift retaliation of the Roman authorities.

Consequently his being described on the cross as "King of the Jews" was from the Roman point of view a simple statement of fact; for them there was nothing other-worldly about it at all—it referred to a basic act of insurrection that was punished as such.

Nor was it only the Roman power that was threatened by Jesus' enterprise. The seizure of the Temple was directed just as much or more at the actual priesthood in charge of it, and in a larger sense doubtless at the entire Jewish aristocracy, which, however unwillingly, had become an outpost of the Roman state in Judea.

Hence, when Jesus' forces seized and held the Temple he also fell foul of the Jewish aristocracy and the priesthood. For while as indicated above he did not disapprove of the Temple cult in principle, and had no theory of reform, there was undoubtedly an element of social protest in his otherwise stark, simple message of "repentance."

There is an undeniable note of indignation throughout the Gospels at the condition of the poor. It seems evident that Jesus was a prophet of the people; he represented the "humble of Israel" and the "people of the Land." Within the framework of Judaism he was on the side of the downtrodden.

Thus, it is more than likely that his attack on the Temple had the additional motivation of protest against social unrighteousness, as well as of a prophetically inspired aversion to the element of idolatrousness in the images of the Roman and other coins kept in the Temple. There is a revealing passage in Josephus that gives a startling picture of the oppression of the poor of the time by the rich via the Temple: he reports that the insurgents wanted "to destroy the money-lenders' tallies and to prevent the exaction of debts, in order to win over a host of grateful debtors and to rouse the poor against the wealthy with impunity."

Indeed, the passage in Mark (6:8) expressly forbidding his disciples to carry money, and enjoining them to take nothing for their journey but a staff, with no bread, no bag, and no money in their belts, may even be a distorted recollection of Jesus' aversion to money as such.

In the traditional Gospel account the genuine, compelling motives for the attack on the Temple have been blurred beyond recognition. The only things left are the banal slogans about the turning of the "universal house of prayer" into a "den of robbers," as though it were a mere question of ethical theory divorced from the turbulence of the times. In the Synoptics generally, as a matter of fact, the chief motive underlying the resentment of the Temple authorities is given as Jesus' lack of a rabbinical education; the very simplemindedness of this explanation clearly suppresses the true background of the Temple occupation.

In view of the violence involved there must have been a factor in the seizure of the Temple that was deeply rooted in the social conflicts of the time, ideologized by religion as of course they were, The squeezing of the poorest classes by the middlemen who were interposed between them and the Temple hierarchy must have contributed to the explosive character of a movement that was bound to involve Jesus in a clash not only with the Romans but with the Jewish aristocracy. The populace was exploited in the Temple, for instance, not only by the exactions of interest, etc, but doubtless by a sliding scale of payments, in which the beasts purchased by the pilgrims were assessed at a maximum price, while those who were selling animals for Temple disposition would always be told that their animals had blemishes that made them unfit for sacrificial use, etc.

The Temple, the unassailable and impregnable seat of socioreligious authority, must have provided the parasitic priests and middlemen with an effective shield against any nonviolent popular protests; it was Jesus' attempt to smash this shield, as part of his larger enterprise of presiding over the installation of the Kingdom of God in the teeth of the Roman power, that brought about his downfall.

Moreover, as we have seen, Jesus was, theoretically too, entirely in harmony with that prophetic tradition, still alive in Israel, which had already completely spiritualized the relations of the Jews with their God; thus the entire Temple traffic in wine, oil, incense, wood, and animals for sacrifice, might have seemed odious to him, at least in its exaggerated forms, whatever his acceptance of the Temple cult in principle. Thus, however pious a Jew Jesus thought himself, his enterprise was bound to collide with the Roman and the Jewish authorities simultaneously.

I have resisted the temptation of filling in this shadowy picture with persuasive, imaginatively elaborated details. As indicated above there is actually no source material for a full biography of Jesus the man. Even his specific actions are hidden from us by the dearth of information, in which random fragments are disclosed only through the distorting mirror of the earliest tradition. The nuggets of historic actuality, or probability, that have been recovered are completely silted over by layers of later tradition; they remain isolated oddments with few interconnections.

Since a connected narrative is impossible, it seems best to be content with those salient points that in accordance with our cardinal criterion of authenticity are most plausible. We thus return to Jesus' death as the one most unquestionable, most solid, and most significant event of his otherwise obscure life; perhaps we can now retrace our steps once again to see whether our criterion can help assemble still other probabilities.

We have seen that the presence of at least two, and more probably four Zealots, or men sympathetic with the Zealots in the small group of Jesus' followers must be revealing. Now, in considering this question of violence as a factor in Jesus' movement, the violence that also ended John the Baptist's career cannot be overlooked; it leads us to the consideration of an important fact—a fact that leads to the rounding off of what was said about the Baptist in chapter 2. The likelihood is that the Baptist was also a *baryon*—an extremist living "on the outside." This is probably the real significance of the passage "And there *went out* to him all the country of Judea" (Mk 1:5, also Mt 3:5). This sounds innocuous, but of course it refers to a form of sedition, perhaps echoed, as we shall see, in Jesus' own command to "renounce all and follow" him.

In view of the Baptist's violent end it is inherently improbable that his message could have been construed at the time as a mere exhortation to personal virtue, an admonition to wait for a divine miracle. This would doubtless have been welcomed by the hated authorities as a form of pious quietism. John was no doubt regarded as a dangerous agitator, i.e., the end he came to was appropriate. This is perhaps demonstrated most clearly by the celebrated passage from Matthew and Luke:

> Among those born of women there has risen no one greater than John the Baptist. . . . From the days of John the Baptist until now the Kingdom of God has suffered violence, and men of violence take it by force. For all the prophets and the Torahs prophesied until John. (Mt 11:11–13)

> The Torah and prophets were until John; since then the good news of the Kingdom of God is preached, and every one enters it violently. (Lk 16:16)

Once the idea is accepted that John the Baptist met his end for a very good reason, from the point of view of his executioners, it is possible to grasp the meaning of these otherwise cryptic words. The implication is clear that before the Baptist people were satisfied with talk; he was the first to *do* something.

We can see now who the "men of violence" are: Jesus is thinking of the agitation that began to intensify under Herod and reached a high pitch under his successor Archelaus (4 B.C.E.–6 C.E.) and afterwards; he is referring to the Zealots, the guerrilla fighters for Jewish independence. The Kingdom of God that they tried to "take by force" was the attempt to restore a national kingdom by the grace of God—in other words, a messianic theocracy.

Now we can appreciate the inwardness of Josephus's singularly reserved reference to the Baptist as being no more than a "good man." Josephus emphatically implies that the Baptist was perfectly innocuous politically; there is no suggestion in his account that John was animated by any nationalistic aims or in general by any political designs. What Josephus is saying, for the benefit of his Roman and Greek-speaking readers, who were doubtless aware to some extent of the prevalence of these messianic Zealots in Judea, is that John the Baptist was not one of them. Since Josephus himself was violently opposed to all forms of Messianism, in which he foresaw the doom of his people—quite accurately!—he is systematically unreliable whenever he refers to them. He is famous for his apologetic, "harmless" explanations of Jewish behavior in such a way as not to arouse in the minds of his pagan readers any suspicion of Jewish intransigence.

Consequently his portrait of John as an abstract moralist is inherently suspect. In a milieu where everyone was expecting cataclysmic events, and the authorities were on the watch for sedition, it is scarcely conceivable that a purely abstract preacher such as Josephus tries to present us with in his picture of the Baptist could have arisen at all, in the first place, or that if he had the authorities would not have been overjoyed by the addition of a soothing ingredient to the turbulent brew they were trying to control. If his abstractions had been as harmless as they sound he would doubtless have been welcomed.

But Josephus gives himself away: the phrase he uses about John is unintentionally revealing. He says John exhorted the Jews to apply themselves to the practice of virtue and justice between themselves and of piety toward God, and called upon them to "be united by a baptism." Now, the Greek equivalent of "to be united" unmistakably implies a ritual of initiation, which in its turn implies an association of some kind. In this case, since despite his reluctance Josephus is also compelled to report that Herod felt obliged to intervene, this association must obviously be considered a seditious group of some sort, and it is John's influence over the people that is explained as having led Herod to jail and execute him.

Now, the framework of the Baptist's activity must have been the wilderness, i.e., "the outside"; the reason for his followers flocking to him there was the religious impulse referred to above: their desire to avoid pollution by idol-worshippers, in accordance with the "royalty law," and to adopt a "good life." There is an ancient life of the Baptist which reports that he advised his followers to "leave the towns," a program that would of course have alarmed the authorities if the abandonment of the towns assumed sizable proportions. This would have been a "popular secession"; they would naturally have intervened with violence.

This circumstance, together with the fact that the apparently general exhortation to purity was in fact an initiation rite into a disaffected group, as unintentionally revealed by Josephus, clarifies a passage in Luke:

> [John] said therefore to the multitudes that came out to be baptized by him, "You brood of vipers! Who warned you to flee from the wrath to come? Bear fruits that befit repentance, and do not begin to say to yourselves, 'We have Abraham as our father'; for I tell you, God is able from these stones to raise up children to Abraham. Even now the ax is laid to the root of the trees; every tree therefore that does not bear good fruit is cut down and thrown into the fire."
>
> And the multitudes asked him, "What then shall we do?" And he answered them, "He who has two coats, let him share with him who has none; and he who has food, let him do likewise." Tax collectors also came to be baptized, and said to him, "Teacher, what shall we do?" And he said to them, "Collect no more than is appointed you." Soldiers also asked him " And we, what shall we do?" And he said to them, "Rob no one by violence or by false accusation, and be content with your wages." (Lk 3:7–14)

The speech, which has always been interpreted conventionally as a mere homily of a general nature, an exhortation to the good life, is plainly rather watery and banal, but it has some point if we note that the word translated here as "soldiers" in reality means "combatants." If we assume that John was not merely exhorting some anonymous multitudes to live better, but was actually giving specific instructions for the conduct of a national guerrilla campaign against a hated oppressor, we may perceive its point. The "multitudes" reported as asking John for advice thus represent the swarms of adherents who had followed him to "the outside," and were being instructed by him how to repair their sins, i.e. how to resist the idol-worshippers. This would also explain the curious inclusion of tax-collectors, singled out as a category of those seeking advice: the word translated as "tax-collector" is to be understood as indicating approval of taxes in a worthy cause: only the Roman supertaxation, for inherently impure purposes, was execrated.

John's baptism, in short, was an instance of what has been referred to above; for the followers of the diehard anti-Roman movements among the Jews the baptism was intended to be the rite of initiation into a new Israel. That is why, when the "multitudes" came to him for baptism and purification, claiming a special privilege as children of Abraham, he specifically discounted their old-fashioned Jewish status as giving them any priority whatsoever in the Kingdom of God. The sin of serving the Roman idol-worshippers had reduced them to the level of the heathen, and John's baptism was meant to purify them of the cardinal sin and establish them in the *new* Israel. This is the basic and particular—not general—meaning of the phrase, baptism in "the name of the Lord." John meant recognition of God as the true and sole ruler of the world, and of the national king, i.e., the Messiah, while at the same time he called for the false gods of this world to be abjured. As John put it, according to Josephus, the Jews could be governed only by the Almighty who had sent him.

This is clearly the logical deduction from the Deuteronomic "royalty law" mentioned above; it clarified John's baptism as being in effect an oath of allegiance to the one true God and his Messiah, and it forms the "way of the law" that was practiced by John the Baptist and by Judah the Galilean.

Thus, John's admonition to the "soldiers" in Lk 3:14 must be a vestige of the sort of peptalk made by an army chaplain. The baptism in the new army of God was actually a soldier's oath. This is the origin of the use of the word "sacrament" in the later Christian Church: sacrament meant a soldier's oath of allegiance, and John's baptismal confession was the oath of the soldiers entering the army of the fighters for the Messiah.

Consequently the new Israel, as foreshadowed by both John the Baptist and the Zealots, was to be regenerated by John's baptism into a new covenant with the ancient national, now universal God of the Jews. Those "children of Abraham" who did not take the oath and thus undergo the rite of lustration for the army of the Messiah were to be regarded as backsliders into paganism.

Incidentally, the ancient origin of the fragment about God being "able from these stones to raise up children to Abraham," is demonstrated by the Hebrew pun concealed in the Greek translation: "stones" are *abanim* in Hebrew, "children" are *banim.*

This is the significance of John's baptism as an instance of the old Jewish baptism prescribed for all converts. Since the unregenerate Jews still serving the Roman idol-worshippers were considered apostates they had to be treated in the same way as pagans seeking conversion to Judaism.

In terms of the epoch, this baptism was thus the first outward sign of the desire for "liberty" that John was accused of inciting the people to. This "liberty" was actually the Kingdom of God, against the kingdom of this world, i.e., heathenism, idolatry, temporal power, and wickedness.

At the same time, to be sure, since doubtless John, like his follower Jesus, also believed in the imminence of the material transformation of the universe involved in the installation of the Kingdom of God, he meant his baptism, by virtue of this reinitiation, to be a way of escape from the "wrath to come" as well—the Last Judgment. It was a "washing for salvation"—salvation as understood in the pre-Christian concrete sense of being saved from the destruction that was about to be visited on "this world" of sin and violence.

Consequently, Jesus' eulogy of John the Baptist as the greatest man who ever lived is profoundly significant. He could hardly have been referred to so extravagantly simply for heralding the coming of someone else; it must mean that Jesus regarded him as the father of the movement exemplified by the Zealots—the first effective leader to rise in the campaign to restore the Jews to their ancient independence. In other words, looking back on this from our own vantage point, John is to be considered as having represented the same form of politico-religious dissidence as Judah the Galilean; he was a rival or possibly a successor.

A different picture is beginning to emerge of the relationship between Jesus and John, both preachers of the imminent advent of the Kingdom of God, both at loggerheads with the powers that be, and both executed by the authorities.

But their methods seem to have been different. If it is true that John met his death for involving his followers in a massive secession from the state, while Jesus was crucified for storming the Kingdom of God in Jerusalem itself, the sacred citadel of his religion as well as the capital city of the secular regime, the implication would seem plain that Jesus, after following John or collaborating with him for some time, later fell out with him about strategy. The relationship between Jesus and John, established by Jesus' baptism at John's hands, must have *ended in a rupture.*

Let us consider this curious question of baptism, of cardinal significance to the Christian religion that was to develop after Jesus' death, but that Jesus himself never seems to have used. I have mentioned the curious discrepancy in the fourth Gospel concerning Jesus' attitude toward baptism: i.e., Jesus baptizes (Jn 3:22; 4:1) but doesn't (Jn 4:2). It must be recalled that there is not a single instance throughout the first three Gospels that shows Jesus either baptizing or preaching baptism, with the exception of the famous verse: "Go therefore and make disciples of all nations, baptizing them in the name of the Father and of the Son and of the Holy

Spirit" (Mt 28:19). This is put into the mouth of the risen Christ, and all independent critics agree that this verse cannot be attributed to Jesus. Consequently the passage in the fourth Gospel is decisive:

> Now when the Lord knew (learned) that the Pharisees had heard that Jesus was making and baptizing more disciples than John (although Jesus himself did not baptize, but only his disciples), he left Judea and departed again to Galilee. (Jn 4:1–3)

Here the immediate disclaimer of baptism—"Jesus himself did not baptize, but only his disciples"—is bound to carry conviction. By the time this was written down baptism had already become a basic rite of initiation into the Christian community, and both the original author of the fourth Gospel and its later editor could never have failed to attribute this basic institution to the Savior unless the weight of the tradition they were guided by could not be gainsaid.

The simple phrase is all the more significant since it appears in the form of a correction of a prior statement (Jn 3:22) that Jesus *had* baptized, and in fact had baptized more disciples than John ever had (Jn 4:1).

In view of this contradiction it seems sensible to assume that by Jesus' having baptized more disciples than John the pious writer was symbolically referring to the results of Jesus' preaching, i.e., the size of the Christian community of his day. The moment he is recalled to Jesus' personal practice he enters the correction directly into the text. There can thus be little doubt that whatever may have been Jesus' practice when he was a disciple of the Baptist, when he embarked on his own campaign he did not use baptism.

Now, there is a reference in the fourth Gospel to a dispute between John's followers and a "Jew" over purifying:

> Now a discussion arose between John's disciples and a Jew over purifying. And they came to John, and said to him, "Rabbi, he who was with you beyond the Jordan, to whom you bore witness, here he is, baptizing, and all are going to him." John answered, "No one can receive anything except what is given him from heaven. You yourselves bear me witness, that I said, I am not the Christ, but I have been sent before him. . . . He must increase, but I must decrease. (Jn 3:25–28,30)

Scholars have long thought that the original of this curious passage must have read, not "a Jew," but "the followers of Jesus." It is hardly likely that the change was made as the result of a mere copyist's error: the whole passage is clearly one of those designed to establish a hierarchical relationship between Jesus and John in favor of Jesus. But the relationship between the two groups seems incoherently recorded, even if we disregard the singular disclaimer of Jesus' use of baptism mentioned above, in the passage about Jesus leaving Judea. It must be assumed that the unintelligible, unexplained, unmotivated, and obviously superfluous mention of the "Pharisees" in the above quotation (Jn 4:1) is to give Jesus a plausible reason for leaving Judea without involving John's disciples. Accordingly, the original must have read: "When the Lord learned that . . . he left Judea." Now, what Jesus learned could not have been the dispute itself, since he would have been a party to it; the passage must refer to his having learned that John himself had found out about it.

That is, there are only two reasons why Jesus would have left Judea upon learning that John had heard of his making more disciples than he. Either:

a. he wanted to avoid competing with John, or appearing to, or

b. John's declaration as given in the original source must have been altogether different. John could not have sponsored him, as the present text reads: He must have disavowed him. He did not say, "He must increase, but I must decrease" (Jn 3:30) but *the opposite*; Jesus, hearing this, naturally decided to leave.

This tells us the significance of the dispute about "purification," which otherwise sounds like a fine point in homiletics.

The reason Jesus split with John, after having been in close collaboration with him for some time, was that he no longer shared his views as to what was to be the manner, or the function, of baptism, which as we have seen was a rite of initiation into a group organized along religious lines to oppose the authorities. The dispute was either between John's followers, or John himself, and Jesus personally, since it was Jesus who departed.

It is impossible to conceive of this departure except as a rupture. If Jesus actually left John because he no longer shared his views on baptism, we must assume, if we agree that this baptism was not merely a piece of abstract theology but a practical matter between determined men, that his activity alongside John in the beginning had been a genuine collaboration.

Thus, when Jesus preached and baptized in Peraea it was as a disciple of John's; it was not his own baptism he was giving, i.e., he was not launching his own movement. When he left John he ceased being his follower and started a new enterprise, which has come down to us, at least in terms of this aspect of its ritual—i.e., its organizational form—as characterized by nonbaptism.

In short, the purification mentioned is baptism, and the disagreement between John and Jesus concerning it, in view of their basic accord on the imminence of the Kingdom of God, must have been due to a difference in program. Whereas the Baptist stayed "on the outside," in the wilderness, preaching his own type of sedition, Jesus went back to the towns, back to civilization, consorted with "tax collectors and sinners" and tried to spread his message, to "stir up the people" (Lk 23:5), among the settled population of Galilee and Judea.

The rupture between Jesus and John so blurrily implied in the fourth Gospel is thus a historic fact of great importance. Its retention in the text of the Gospels, despite its conflict with the whole evolution of the official view of Christianity concerning the relations between the two men, vouches for its historicity.

Still other signs of divergence between the two movements have been preserved in our Gospels: The Baptist is described as having been an ascetic, while the point is made repeatedly that Jesus' life was in complete contrast.

> John came neither eating nor drinking, and they say, "He has a demon:" [*sic*] the Son of Man came eating and drinking, and they say, "Behold, a glutton and a drunkard, a friend of tax-collectors and sinners." (Mt 11:18, also Lk 7:33)

Another passage:

> Now John's disciples and the Pharisees were fasting; and people came and said to (Jesus), "Why do John's disciples and the disciples of the Pharisees fast, but your disciples do not fast?"(Mk 2:18)

This would seem to indicate a clear-cut awareness of the separateness of these three groups, or rather, the singling out of John's followers and Jesus' from the broad body of Pharisees, as well as an awareness of a basic difference of ritual, in addition to the disagreement on baptism.

There is a point of added interest in the omission of John's name in this account; it seems to imply that John had already disappeared from the scene either after his death or his imprisonment, leaving his followers behind to carry on his movement.

Another revealing hint of this split between the two men is preserved in Matthew (11:2–6), where John, while in prison, is supposed to send messengers to ask Jesus whether he is in fact the awaited Messiah. Jesus refers to his deeds, presumably as "signs" of his status; the episode ends with his saying, "Blessed is he who takes no offense at me."

The chronicler's failure to report the reaction here either of John or of his disciples must be considered of paramount importance. It can only mean that the response to Jesus' claims, however interpreted—i.e., as a sort of code referring to Messianic status—was reserved, not to say downright negative. Otherwise the pious chronicler would obviously have been delighted to reiterate this point, already made elsewhere, that John was in fact Jesus' Forerunner and acknowledged himself as such.

Probably the chief reason our present text is in such confusion is that one of the original documents originated in a Baptist milieu, and thus had to be docked and mutilated in order to make it fit the aim of the Christian writer. The object of this conflation, as indicated above, was to retain the advantage of John's authority over his still-existent movement while subordinating it to that of Jesus. Thus, in accordance with the interest of the later Christian community in harmonizing the claims of the two leaders in this way, pains are taken to indicate that John's mission was also divine:

> The chief priests and the scribes and the elders . . . said to [Jesus], "By what authority are you doing these things, or who gave you this authority to do them?" Jesus said to them, "I will ask you a question; answer me, and I will tell you by what authority I do these things. Was the baptism of John from heaven or from man? Answer me." And they argued with one another, "If we say, 'From heaven' he will say, 'Why then did you not believe him?' But shall we say, 'From men'?"—they were afraid of the people, for all held that John was a real prophet. So they answered Jesus, "We do not know." And Jesus said to them, "Neither will I tell you by what authority I do these things." (Mk 11:29–33, also Mt 21:24–27 and Lk 20:3–7)

Aside from the wily casuistry shown here by Jesus, perhaps the most important point is not only that Jesus thought John had divine authority, but that the chief priests themselves had to adopt a defensive position because of the Baptist's popularity. It is an indication of the strength of his movement, also a further hint that Jesus himself was in a strong current of popular favor.

The link between the two, on the other hand, is kept under careful control: while it is reported that Jesus is sometimes thought to be John resuscitated, the point is made elsewhere that John "was not the light, but came to bear witness to the light" (Jn 1:8). Because of its insistent tone we must assume this remark to be a shaft aimed specifically at the surviving disciples of the Baptist. We have here a hint, accordingly, not perhaps about the Baptist himself, but about the followers he left behind whom the early Christians were intent on absorbing, naturally on their own terms.

Perhaps another indication of their relationship is to be seen in the curious remark Jesus makes about the Baptist, after eulogizing him as the greatest man ever born: "Yet he who is least in the Kingdom of God is greater than he" (Mt 11:11). This, which sounds like a rather peculiar compliment, may be more intelligible if it is translated, as some scholars have suggested, as "Yet his junior in heaven is greater than he," and it is assumed that his "junior" is Jesus himself. I. e., Having followed John in heralding the Kingdom of God, Jesus now regarded himself as the leader.

We begin to discern the outline of some sort of movement, characterized by opposition to the secular order of the time, the idolatrous Roman Empire and its vassals, but perhaps differing in approach. Since we can only get at the substance of Jesus' activity from the utterly different perspective of the chronicles set down after his deification, it is impossible to arrive at a view of details that weren't either falsified or forgotten.

If it is true that John the Baptist called on Jews to renounce life under a pagan overlord and be baptized into the new Israel of those awaiting the Messiah, and if it is true that Jesus, after being associated with him in this enterprise for some time, finally changed his mind and went to seek a decision in the sacred city that was the only place such a decision could manifest itself, we have here a comprehensible program for action.

It seems likely that the contrast between Jesus' apparently quietist— "meek and mild"—statements, and his "fire and sword" statements must somehow be linked with this.

Jesus might simply have abandoned John's movement, for instance, and started one of his own, more dynamic and aimed directly at the center of secular and religious power in Jerusalem. In that case we should have to ascribe his "quietist" statements, as they are preserved in the Gospels, to the period when he might still have been gathering support for his new enterprise. This would also explain the curious ambiguity or secrecy about his intentions—his admonition to his disciples to say nothing about his special status, his speaking in parables, i.e., innuendoes, and his going about the country as though in flight, all of which seems to describe someone avoiding attention.

His attitude seems to have changed abruptly:

> What I tell you in the dark, utter in the light; and what you hear whispered, proclaim upon the housetops. . . . Whoever denies me before men, I also will deny before my Father who is in heaven. (Mt 10:27–33)

> Is a lamp brought in to be put under a bushel, or under a bed? . . . For there is nothing hid, except to be made manifest. (Mk 4:21, 22, also Lk 8:16ff; Mt 5:14ff)

This sounds as though it meant that the whole project was out in the open, and that Jesus was now a publicly proclaimed leader of a movement of rebellion. Having begun by preaching the "better righteousness," at some point he changed his mind and moved on to Jerusalem and death.

A passage that seems to sum up the transition is the following:

> [Jesus] said to [the disciples], "When I sent you out with no purse or bag or sandals, did you lack anything?" They said, "Nothing." He said to them, "*But now,* let him . . . who has no sword take his mantle and buy one." (Lk 22:35–36)

The "but now" seems pregnant with reversal.

The difficulty is that it is impossible to tell the sequence of stratification in the various layers that make up the Gospels; some of the elements in them, after all, come from the time Jesus was actually associated with the Baptist, and thus may be an echo of the Baptist's own summons with respect to the central slogan they had in common—"Repent, for the Kingdom of God is at hand."

One of Jesus' most celebrated exhortations is the following:

> Therefore I tell you, do not be anxious about your life, what you shall eat or what you shall drink, nor about your body, what you shall put on. Is not life more than food, and the body more than clothing? Look at the birds of the air: they neither sow nor reap nor gather into barns, and yet

your heavenly Father feeds them. Are you not of more value then they? And which of you by being anxious can add one cubit to his span of life? And why are you anxious about clothing? Consider the lilies of the field, how they grow; they neither toil nor spin; yet I tell you, even Solomon in all his glory was not arrayed like one of these. But if God so clothes the grass of the field, which today is alive and tomorrow is thrown onto the oven, will he not much more clothe you, O men of little faith? Therefore do not be anxious, saying, "What shall we eat, or what shall we drink?" or "What shall we wear?" For the Gentiles seek all these things; and your heavenly Father knows that you need them all. But seek first his Kingdom and his righteousness, and all these things shall be yours as well. Therefore do not be anxious about tomorrow, for tomorrow will be anxious for itself. Let the day's own trouble be sufficient for the day. (Mt 6:25–34)

This sounds like a clear echo of the renunciation of the temporal order that also characterized John. To conceive of it as a timeless rule of conduct is to misunderstand Jesus' activity. Since he thought the Kingdom of God was about to be installed he may have thought this particular type of renunciation a means of heralding or, possibly, of accelerating the installation. He trusted in God in a specific context of space and time—as part of a movement bound up with a program, which he necessarily changed upon realizing that a timeless aversion to money as such could no longer accomplish his purpose.

In any case, however, whether Jesus was a quietist before joining the Baptist, or whether he became one after leaving the Baptist, and then abandoned that too in favor of his final onslaught on the Temple in Jerusalem, he made his decision and went on to Jerusalem not only like the herald of the Kingdom, but like the herald of the Kingdom bringing it about *in power.* He could be thought at least a messianic Herald, if not the Messiah himself. (See below.)

We have indicated above why his entry into the city and his occupation of the Temple were messianic, from the point of view of the Romans: Jesus came into the city and actually exercised sovereignty, as "King of the Jews," by seizing and holding sway within the Temple.

Now let us consider whether it was a messianic entry from the Jewish point of view as well.

There is of course no doubt that the Gospel writers intended to describe a messianic entry: the beginning of Mark 11 (1–11) is obviously intended as such, in terms taken from the Hebrew prophet Zechariah (9:9), who is also the prophet referred to in this passage:

> This took place to fulfill what was spoken by the prophet, saying, "Tell the daughter of Zion, Behold, your king is coming to you, humble, and mounted on an ass, and on a colt, the foal of an ass." (Mt 21:4,5)

There is also evidence, if the Gospels are acceptable here, that Jesus was actually acclaimed by the people as Messiah. The "Hosanna" passages are illuminating:

> Many spread their garments on the road, and others spread leafy branches which they had cut from the fields. And those who went before and those who followed cried out, "Hosanna! Blesed be he who comes in the name of the Lord! Blessed be the kingdom of our father David that is coming! Hosanna in the highest!" (Mk 11:8–10)

> The crowds that went before him and that followed him shouted, "Hosanna to the Son of David! Blessed be he who comes in the name of the Lord! Hosanna in the highest!" (Mt 21:9)

> ... the whole multitude ... began to praise God ... saying, "Blessed be the King who comes in the name of the Lord! Peace in heaven and glory in the highest!" (Lk 19:38)

Now, while the meaning of all this is clear and most revealing, the actual phrase that is repeated, "Hosanna in the highest," is nonsensical. As a rule the word "hosanna" is taken to be a transliteration of a Hebrew word meaning "save us," and is assumed to be a reference to Psalm 118:25, "Save us, Yahweh, save us!" But it can also be taken to be a similar Aramaic word that means "free us," appearing in all Syriac versions as the equivalent of "free us!" in the current Aramaic speech of Jesus' time.

Yet no matter how it is translated, the idea of either being "saved" or "freed" in the heights, or in the highest, is clearly absurd. Both notions have a value only on earth; they are a mundane outcry on the part of the "multitude" who followed Jesus and went on before him. The absurdity of the above passage from Luke is highlighted by contrasting it with another sentence from the same Gospel, where the kink has been ironed out: "Glory to God in the highest, and on earth peace, good will among men" (Lk 2:14).

In Mark, quoted above, the word "in the highest" must be assumed to be some kind of insertion on the part of an editor or scribe to whitewash Jesus of the suspicion of Messianism. The intent was thus to dilute the passage by inserting "in the highest" as follows:

> Blessed—in the highest—be he who comes in the name of the Lord!
> Blessed—in the highest—be the Kingdom of our father David!

The sense is completely restored when we remove this apologetic intrusion intended to convey the impression that some pious pilgrims were simply saying that the Messiah and his kingdom were blessed in the heights above, and had nothing to do with anything the authorities found objectionable.

The same thing applies to the quotation from Matthew above: "Hosanna to the Son of David!" is senseless. The expression "to the Son of David" must have been taken from the preceding verse. When corrected the whole thing would read: "The crowds . . . shouted to the Son of David, 'Free us!' "

Here the intent of the copyist is even more obvious: he was trying to obscure the Messianic outcry of the mob, addressed to Jesus, by displacing the meaning "free us!" of Jesus' colloquial Aramaic to the "save us!" of the Hebrew Psalm 118:25; i.e., he was trying to interpret it as an appeal by the crowd to God to "Help the Son of David!," which would sound as harmless as possible.

In Luke 19:38 (above) the "hosanna" vanished altogether; it was simply omitted, and in order to make the correction plausible the words "the whole multitude . . . began to praise God" were inserted in the preceding verses.

It is illuminating to recall that it is because of this artificial alteration of the Aramaic *osha'na*—"free us"—into the Psalmist's Hebrew *hoshi-a'na*—"save us"—that the fourth Gospel had brought down to us a record of "palm branches" being carried in this Messianic procession. The festal bouquets of the Feast of Tabernacles were colloquially known as "hoshannas": their principal item was a palm branch. As indicated in Mark above, none of the pilgrims carried the "palm branches" in their hands; they strewed the ground with the leafy branches they had cut from the fields. The notion of their carrying them in their hands is a revealing instance of later Greek ignorance of Jewish affairs, since the only text we have of John was translated and edited in Greek.

As a result of this repeated apologetic manipulation the words of the actual acclamation have been thrown into a confusion that passes unnoticed by people who may have repeated them by rote since childhood. It is one of the numerous ways in which the events leading up to the climax of Jesus' career were obliterated to such an extent that the climax itself has become grotesque, as well as obscure.

Jesus' teaching, in short, was not addressed to a circle of mystics, but to a people longing for liberation from an alien yoke. His Jewish partisans did not mean what Saul later came to mean by "liberation from bondage" i.e., from sin and wicked spirits, but quite literally liberation from worldly oppression. Looked at in our own terms, Jesus was playing the part of a national leader, one of the many, as we have seen, who sprang up among the Jews during their long-drawn-out subjugation by Rome.

None of the above, of course, can settle the question of what Jesus himself thought about all this—whether he considered himself the Messiah or simply the herald of the Kingdom, inspired by God and performing a messianic function, but not actually the Messiah himself.

The fact that according to current Jewish conceptions, the Messiah was indubitably a man like another, does not, perhaps, make that question one of cardinal importance. Bar Kochba, the leader of the second Jewish Revolt against Rome, in 133, was acclaimed as Messiah by Rabbi Aqiba; the question of Bar Kochba's unique status in any other sense was never raised.

The question is simply one of fact. Did Jesus think himself the Messiah or not? Unfortunately, the tendentious perspective of the Gospels veils his thought on this, too.

Since the Gospel writers took Jesus' resurrection as their starting point, as indeed his earliest disciples did too, they were obviously bound to retroject this assumption to Jesus' lifetime, and naturally make the further assumption that he could scarcely have failed to be aware of his own mission.

But on this point the evidence of the Gospels as a whole is baffling. The celebrated "messianic secret"—i.e., Jesus' constant admonition to his disciples for at least part of his campaign to keep quiet about his status—cannot really be understood except as a makeshift device for reconciling the attitude of the resurrected and glorified Jesus' subsequent worshippers with the historical fact that Jesus never actually claimed to be the Messiah. He is never actually reported as having simply said, "I am the Messiah," and despite the torrents of argumentation engendered by this omission there seems to be no good reason why if he thought so he shouldn't have said as much.

There are some individual passages that buttress this impression substantially. Here is one from Mark, quoted above as one of the varying estimates of the imminence of the Kingdom: "[Jesus said], 'Truly, I say to you, I shall not drink again of the fruit of the vine until that day when I drink it new in the Kingdom of God' " (Mk 14:25).

In this announcement of the Messianic feast Jesus says nothing whatever about a special place being reserved at it for himself, and if there had been any recollection of such a portentous utterance among his followers the chronicler would surely have made a point of it.

There is another passage, somewhat obscure, that is most convincing here. I have quoted it before as an indication of the dramatic change of mind that deflected Jesus' career into a fatefully different direction, but it is also of great significance with respect to Jesus' view of his own person. It is almost certainly to be interpreted as a disclaimer of Messiahship:

> Jesus went on with his disciples . . . and . . . asked [them], "Who do men say I am?" And they told him, "John the Baptist; others say, Elijah; others one of the prophets." And he asked them, "But who do you say I am?" [Simon the Rock] answered him, 'You are the Christ.' And he charged them to tell no one about him. And he began to teach them that the Son of Man must suffer many things, and be rejected by the elders and the chief priests and the scribes, and be killed, and after three days rise again. And he said this plainly. [Simon the Rock] took him and began to rebuke him. But turning and seeing his disciples, he rebuked Simon, and said, "Get behind me, Satan! For you are not on the side of God, but of men." (Mk 8:27–33)

Now, the structure of this passage indicates the desire of the chronicler to situate this incident, which in Mark is the crux of Jesus' whole career, in the light of the divine plan of early Christianity, in which Jesus foresees everything.

Historically, however, the fact that Jesus actually forbade Simon the Rock, incomprehensibly, to disclose his messiahship to anyone, and then rebuked him so sharply afterward for having clung to his own opinion nevertheless, must mean that while some of Jesus' disciples might have believed he was the Messiah there was no firm recollection of his ever having made this claim himself.

In short, what the Gospel editors were trying to do was to reconcile their own conviction of Jesus' messiahship with the facts of his career. Since they could not believe he himself hadn't shared their own certainty they had to invent the otherwise baffling secrecy of his whole mission, and to imagine that he intimated his status by means of signs meant to be misunderstood.

The traditional—i.e., apologetic—explanation of this is that Jesus was unquestionably the Messiah and naturally knew it, but since his messiahship was of a type that was completely novel in Israel it could not be given out as such for fear of arousing the contempt or opposition of his listeners.

This seems incredible. In the first place, there is no record in Jewish messianic belief of a suffering Messiah. To circumvent this there has been speculation (chiefly among scholars who disbelieve in Jesus' historical existence altogether) on the possibility of there having been certain Jewish sects whose messianic conceptions had been distorted by the dying and rising gods of the pagan mystery cults.

The difficulty here is that there is absolutely no evidence of such sects. The mythologists who do not believe Jesus existed have been obliged to imagine a Jewish background for what they regard as the "myth" of his agony, while apologetic scholars, on the other hand, feel obliged to harmonize in their own way later Christian theology with the facts of Jesus' life.

In any case, aside from the mere unlikelihood of one individual's originating the novel conception of the Messiah that apologetic scholars attribute to Jesus himself, the real point is that if the novelty of Jesus' conception could actually be considered historically possible it would have to be explained at some length in the Gospels themselves, which is never the case. There would have to have been some attempt on Jesus' part to explain just what his view of the Messiah was, precisely if it was novel—How could his followers have understood him otherwise?

Consequently, during the lifetime of Jesus, before the formation of his followers' later views, Jesus could only have been expressing ideas that at least his intimates would have understood.

Besides, as we have seen, Jesus *did* try to take the Kingdom of God by storm. Hence, even if he did not think himself the actual Messiah his role was certainly martial. It would have corresponded with the current Jewish conception of the warlike Messiah and, since in any case there was no room in Jewish messianic belief for a pacific Messiah, an apologia was bound to be called for in the evolution of Christian belief as soon as it became necessary to tone down the political elements of Jesus' career.

It is the extraction of this whole element of violence from the Gospel accounts that has left the "messianic secret" hanging in the air, to provide one more hurdle for the apologists who were later obliged to retain a pacific version of Jesus' activity while at the same time laying claim to his messiahship.

To be sure, this particular stage in the development of the theory was relatively brief, of course, since it had a point only while the belief in Jesus was confined to his immediate Jewish followers, who in any case compensated for the failure of his enterprise by an ardent belief in the imminence of his return together with the Kingdom of God. Once the belief in his messiahship was transposed to a Hellenistic terrain it was quickly overlaid by his rapid deification and thus lost its importance.

But there are other, even more unmistakable indications, both in Acts and in Luke (by the same author, as mentioned above), which clearly imply that Jesus was not thought to be the Messiah during his own lifetime. They are all the more significant since Luke and Acts were written in fairly close connection with the events of Jesus' career, and by someone entirely persuaded of Jesus' messianic status, or elevation, *after* the Resurrection. In Luke, for instance, we read:

> And he said to them, "What things?" And they said to him, "Concerning Jesus of Nazareth, who was a prophet mighty in deed and word before God and all the people." (Lk 24:19)

While in Acts there is the following:

> Men of Israel, hear these words: Jesus of Nazareth, a man attested to you by God with mighty words and wonders and signs which God did through him in your midst, as you yourselves know—This Jesus God raised up, and of that we all are witnesses. Being therefore exalted at the right hand of God, and having received from the Father the promise of the Holy Spirit, he has poured out this which you see and hear. Let all the house of Israel therefore know assuredly that God had made him both Lord and Christ, this Jesus whom you crucified. (Acts 2:22, 32, 33, 36)

Also:

> You know . . . the word proclaimed throughout all Judea . . . how God
> anointed Jesus of Nazareth with the Holy Spirit and with power; how he
> went about doing good and healing all that were oppressed by the devil,
> for God was with him. (Acts 10:36–38)

All these passages, by omitting the mention of Jesus' messiahship during his lifetime, give us the vivid impression that the chronicler did not
extend this claim of messiahship to Jesus' own life, and that Jesus himself
did not, consequently, present himself to Israel as the Messiah. In fact,
these passages from Luke and Acts merely confirm the conclusion we
came to above, to the effect that Jesus had presented himself to his people
basically as the herald of the Kingdom, "The time is fulfilled, and the
Kingdom of God is at hand; repent, and believe in the Gospel" (Mk 1:14).

We are back once again to the portrait of Jesus as recorded in the
Gospels. It is that of an old-fashioned prophet, inspired by God and exhort-
ing his people to follow God's ways to facilitate the establishment of the
Kingdom of God. He did not claim messiahship.

We have seen that events have been piously retouched to smooth away
these aspects of Jesus' enterprise that were to prove indigestible to later
Christian theory. The violence that attended Jesus' movement, its anti-
Roman political implications, and above all, perhaps, its material failure,
were all either forgotten or obliterated in the new perspective of Jesus'
devotional glorification. This is why, as I have pointed out so often, the
nuggets of historic probability embedded in the text are indispensable.
Even in the present text we can dimly perceive that something happened
to make Jesus change his mind, as we have seen, and embark on an effort
to bring about the establishment of the Kingdom by means of a massive
insurrection against the power of Rome and her local vassals, and that this
led to his undoing. It is tempting to look for the occasion that led to his
change of mind; we may find it outside the Gospels.

Josephus tells us that Pontius Pilate attempted to set up the standards
of the Roman legions inside the Temple area. Now, these standards bore
medallions with exchangeable portrait heads of Caesar. The Roman forces
were stationed principally in the city; there was only one cohort stationed
in Fort Antonia, but since the Jews regarded this as part of the Temple area,
which they took to embrace the whole Temple elevation, they reacted vio-

lently to the setting up of these profane images. Josephus gives us an impressive account of their consternation and fury. They were determined to make Pilate slaughter them unless he removed the standards bearing Caesar's image. Pilate, baffled by what he must have considered senseless fanaticism, finally gave way.

The point is that the Jews regarded the setting up in the Temple area of images to be worshiped as the fulfillment of a prophecy to be found in Daniel (11:31), that of the "abomination of desolation" (or the "desolating sacrilege") being "set up where it ought not to be" (Mk 13:14). In Daniel (12:11) this desecration of the sanctuary was to usher in the last times, which the author of Daniel calculated would extend over a period of about three and a half years, more then 1290 days; at the end of this period the death of the Messiah was to be expected, as well as the devastation of the Holy City in the messianic war that would continue until the World's End and terminate with the annihilation of the prince of this world, the adversary of God, and of the godless in general, by means of another flood like the one that wiped out the human race at the time of Noah.

In any case, many Jews interpreted Pilate's action as the defilement of the sanctuary foreseen in Daniel. This is Jesus' apocalyptic speech:

> But when you see the desolating sacrilege set up where it ought not to be [let the reader understand], then let those who are in Judea flee to the mountains; let him who is on the housetop not go down, nor enter his house, to take anything away; and let him who is in the field not turn back to take his mantle. And alas for those who are with child and for these who give suck in those days! (Mk 13:14–17, also Mt 24:15)

This seems to indicate that Jesus and many of his contemporaries expected the destructive flood to follow this desecration, in accordance with the prophecy in Daniel.

This is suggestive; it may actually give us the specific occasion that set Jesus off on his career, and by pinpointing his change of mind within the framework of his general opposition to the social and political order shed some light on his reasons for taking to the road of violence in quest of his "other-worldly" aims.

We have seen the curious insubstantiality of the Gospel accounts of Jesus' trial, both Jewish and Roman, though at the same time they disclose a hard core of truth, namely that the charge was sedition and the punishment crucifixion, both of them Roman. I say "hard core," but it would be better to call it an oasis in a desert, for the entire Synoptic narrative of Jesus' entry into Jerusalem gives us an overriding impression of almost complete emptiness. The verbosity and repetitions in the discourses do not lessen the effect of this emptiness; they increase it. If we were to go by Gospel tradition we would be obliged to believe that it retained practically nothing solid at all of what must have taken place. Events that must have caused a vast commotion and led to such an agonizing death for Jesus personally and to the bitter frustration of all his followers, have come down to us as glimpses of shadows.

It is scarcely conceivable that the memories of Jesus' followers, whose devotion to him was, after all, enough to give rise to their faith in his resurrection and messiahship, failed to retain a vivid, though no doubt painful memory of the crucial week in his career. It is just this gap in recollection that is the most dramatic proof of the process we have referred to so often, that of the transformation of the entire view of Jesus' career by the perspective of his triumphant glorification, which led to the obliteration of essential facts relating to his activity in Jerusalem, including his reasons for going there.

In fact, as we have seen, the inscription on Jesus' cross gives us as succinctly as possible the explanation of his death. Not only was the charge of setting himself up as "King of the Jews" an entirely adequate reason for executing him from the Roman point of view, it was perfectly intelligible and cogent from the Jewish point of view as well, considering the secular as well as religious content of the status that would automatically have been assumed by anyone doing what Jesus tried to do, even without claiming to be the Messiah.

The significance of this title is revealingly emphasized in a little byplay between Pilate and the "chief priests of the Jews" reported in the fourth Gospel:

> Pilate also wrote a title and put it on the cross; it read "Jesus of Nazareth, the King of the Jews." ... The Chief Priests of the Jews then said to Pilate, "Do not write, 'The King of the Jews,' but 'This man said, "I am King of the Jews." ' " Pilate answered, "What I have written I have written." (Jn 19:19, 21,22)

Pilate's point is clear. When the Jewish authorities tried to exculpate the Jews of disaffection toward the Romans by putting the whole blame for the insurrection on Jesus alone, Pilate reminded them that from his point of view Jesus' seizure of power had not been a mere outburst of individual fanaticism, but had had a collective character. Jesus had been *acclaimed* king, and for a time had, in fact, exercised sovereignty with the consent of a sizable portion of the community. The brevity of his reign meant nothing; the mere notion of a self-appointed Jewish king was reason enough for Roman intervention.

The above passage from the fourth Gospel sounds like an echo of some other deliberations between the "chief priests," in another curious passage, where Jesus' appeal for a substantial part of the population is confirmed in an inverted way:

> So the chief priests and the Pharisees gathered the council, and said, "What are we to do? For this man performs many signs. If we let him go on thus, everyone will believe in him, and the Romans will come and destroy both our holy place and our nation." But one of them, Caiaphas, who was High Priest that year, said to them. "You know nothing at all; you do not understand that it is expedient for you that one man should die for the people, and that the whole nation should not perish." (Jn 11:47–50)

This has a genuine ring to it. Of course, it is difficult to see just how the discussion taking place in this privy council could have been transmitted to a follower of Jesus, but historically it is at least a common sense attitude to imagine the Temple party as having taken.

Indeed, in spite of the chronicler's manifest intention of exploiting the incident as another way of inculpating the Jews, as we have discussed above, it may not even imply real hostility to Jesus. Caiaphas's plea is the choice of a lesser evil; it sounds like a man of the world's attempt to save the nation from the consequences of its own hot-headedness.

Jesus' role as a national Jewish prophet, epitomizing his people as against the Romans, is poignantly conveyed in Luke:

> And there followed him a great multitude of the people, and of women who bewailed and lamented him. But Jesus turning to them said, "Daughters of Jerusalem, do not weep for me, but weep for yourselves and for your children. For behold, the days are coming when they will say, 'Blessed are the barren, and the womb that never bore, and the breasts that never gave suck!' Then they will begin to say to the mountains, 'Fall on us;' and to the hills, 'Cover us.' " (Lk 23:27–31)

> And all the multitudes who assembled to see the sight, when they saw what had taken place, returned home beating their breasts. (Lk 23:48)

The Romans appear here as the enemies of both Jesus and the Jewish people simultaneously. The identity of Jesus and the Jews is here confirmed, in contradistinction to the other, doubtless later tradition which had the Jewish mob calling out—incomprehensibly—for Jesus' blood when he is about to be crucified on Pilate's orders. Jesus is speaking here, as it were *ex cathedra,* as a national leader. In addition, this passage provides us with some positive evidence that despite the indications of Jesus' failure to carry the whole Jewish people with him in his assault on Rome, he nevertheless had a substantial popular following.

The above-mentioned passage is scarcely likely to be an invention of the author of Luke, which, like the other three Gospels, also reports a Jewish mob as forcing Pilate's hand; consequently the retention of this fragment seems to favor its historicity. Indeed, though it might be thought to be a sentimental adornment, if it was an invention, it is not. The whole point of early Christianity was that the Christ had been despised and rejected by all; hence this is not a mere edifying detail, and must be authentic.

There are other instances of the deep and entirely mundane gloom that must have been recalled by the very earliest witnesses to the catastrophe of the cross:

> And taking with him Simon the Rock and the two sons of Zebedee, [Jesus] began to be sorrowful and troubled. Then he said to them, "My soul is very sorrowful, even unto death." . . . Going a little farther he fell on his face and prayed, "My Father, if it be possible, let this cup pass from me. . . ." (Mt 26:37–39)

> And being in an agony he prayed more earnestly; and his sweat became like great drops of blood falling down upon the ground. (Lk 22:44)

There is a suggestion of melancholy in these and parallel passages that must embody a lingering recollection of the state of mind of Jesus' company at the time of the tragic climax. The details, to be sure, cannot claim to be well attested: Who could have overheard Jesus? Nevertheless this slightly embroidered form no doubt conceals something substantial.

The same applies to a curious incident recorded in Luke, when Jesus, after his resurrection, approaches two of the apostles, who are going to Emmaus (some seven miles from Jerusalem) and chatting on the way:

> [Jesus] said to them, "What is this conversation which you are holding with each other as you walk?" And they stood still, looking sad. Then one of them . . . answered him, "Are you the only visitor to Jerusalem who does not know the things that have happened here in these days?" And he said to them, "What things?" And they said to him, "Concerning Jesus of Nazareth, who was a prophet mighty in deed and word before God and all the people, and how our rulers delivered him up to be condemned to death, and crucified him. But we had hoped that he was the one to redeem Israel." (Lk 24:17–21)

This incident, seemingly so trivial, is striking because it contains a recollection of the disheartenment of his immediate followers after the crucifixion, and gives us further confirmation of what they had been hoping for, namely, the redemption of Israel; also, it indicates their shaken faith in Jesus as the one to effect it.

It is thus an ancient fragment that must go back to the period immediately following the crucifixion, before his scattered band of followers had had time to become firmly anchored in their faith in his resurrection: "Jesus said to them: 'You will all fall away, for it is written, "I will strike the shepherd, and the sheep will be scattered" ' " (Mk 14:27 and parallels).

As we have seen, for such a detail to have survived the steamrollering process of the whole early tradition, which lay in the direction of emphasizing Jesus' masterful serenity, implies that it was unshakably rooted in some early tradition too well attested to be tampered with.

But of course the tragic climax of Jesus' career could not be summed up more poignantly than in the first two Gospels, where the despair of Jesus' followers is put directly and unequivocally into Jesus' own mouth: "My God, my God, why hast thou forsaken me?" (Mk 15:34, Mt 27:46).

This cry of despair must be historical; it is given in both Gospels in Jesus' native Aramaic speech, which must be the earliest layer of the Palestinian tradition and is presumably used whenever actual words or fragments of speeches had become hallowed enough to be recalled in their original form. It is in flagrant and irremediable contradiction with the systematic tendency of the Gospel writers to present Jesus as invariably in serene communion at all times with the divine will in the face of suffering.

Nor is it conceivable that the first generations of Christians could have devised this despairing outcry as a sort of edifying detail in the process of enveloping their Savior with a variety of legends. Hence its mention in Mark and Matthew testifies to an absolutely impregnable chunk of tradition that withstood all apologias. If anything, it is further strengthened by the obvious fact that the oldest tradition does not harp on any of the actual physical torments of Jesus on the cross; therefore its recollection of his moral agony is all the more significant in view of the perfect communion with God that was naturally attributed to him.

The wording of the outcry comes from Psalm 22, to be sure, which goes on to conclude on a more reassuring note. Because of this some students have attempted to explain the note of despair in the phrase itself, which sounds heart-rending, as in reality a mere hint to the wise, to raise their spirits. This explanation gives the outcry the character of a library reference. If it were conceivable it would then become impossible to explain why the authors of Luke and John, who were, after all, fairly close to the original situation, would have failed to report it. Its mere origin in a Psalm tells us nothing. Both Jesus and his earliest chroniclers were imbued with the Hebrew Scriptures in general and doubtless with the Psalms in particular. Thus we are obliged to regard Jesus' cry of despair on the cross as in essence authentic.

The author of Luke, of course, had already progressed to the point of sentimentalizing the final scene by putting in Jesus' mouth an appropriately phrased statement of trusting communion, "Father, into thy hands I commit my spirit!" (Lk 23:46) and in the fourth Gospel the Christological process has gone so far that the cross has become a sort of throne from which Jesus sets the seal on the consummation of the Divine Plan (in accordance with the Johannine view): "[Jesus] said, 'It is finished,' and he bowed his head and gave up his spirit" (Jn 19:30). But it is just these other-worldly preoccupations of Luke and John that confirm all the more graphically the genuineness of the bitter cry borne witness to by the other two Gospels.

Now, once Jesus is seen to have played a role in real-life that gave practical justification to the Romans' insistence on calling him "King of the Jews," it becomes evident that the importance, in a purely secular sense, of the insurrectionist movement he led must be radically reassessed. It is a remarkable fact that generations after Jesus' execution a police writ ordered by Vespasian against "Davidides" was still in effect. Two of Jesus' grand-nephews (sons of his brother Judah) were denounced to the authorities in Palestine and brought to a hearing conducted by Caesar Domitian himself, Vespasian's second son.

Now there still survived of the family of the Lord grandsons of Judas, his brother according to the flesh, and they were informed against as being of the family of David. These the officer brought to Domitian Caesar, for, like Herod, he was afraid of the coming of the Christ. He asked them if they were of the house of David and they admitted it. Then he asked them how much property they had, or how much money they controlled, and they said that all they possessed was nine thousand denarii [about $100] between them, the half belonging to each, and they stated that they did not possess this in money but that it was the valuation of only thirty-nine plethra [about 25 acres] of ground on which they paid taxes and lived on it by their own work. They then showed him their hands, adducing as testimony of their labor the hardness of their bodies and the tough skin embossed on their hands from their incessant work. They were asked concerning the Christ and his kingdom, its nature, origin, and time of appearance, and explained that it was neither of the world nor earthly, but heavenly and angelic, and it would be at the end of the world, when he would come in glory to judge the living and the dead and to reward every man according to his deeds. At this Domitian did not condemn them at all, but despised them as simple folk, released them and decreed an end to the persecution against the church. (Eusebius, Hist. Eccl. 111.18.4–20.7, quoting Hegesippus, about 180)

The "Davidides" were still under a police writ into the reign of Domitian's successor, Trajan.

We can now situate the question of Jesus' importance, from a secular, i.e., Roman point of view.

Since the Romans could scarcely have bothered giving actual trials to the multitude of Kingdom of God activists they crucified, it is clear that "trying" Jesus—if they did—and identifying him as "King of Jews" was a natural way of explaining the point of Jesus' execution; it represented the crushing of a national rebellion. Hence the report of the police writ against Davidides has a commonsense rationale.

On the other hand, from the point of view of the burgeoning of the group of Jesus' followers, more and more under the influence of Saul's ideas, the royal claim made on behalf of Jesus, as a descendant of King David linked to a messianic program, would have been senseless once he was thought to be the Son of God and Savior of the World. Thus it was only natural for the inscription on the cross to have remained a puzzle for Christian doctrine down to the present. Its appearance in all four Gospels no doubt means it was universally known and despite its meaninglessness for the new religion could not be dropped.

To recapitulate:

In the blurred and mutilated recollections of Jesus' earthly career we can dimly discern the outlines of a visionary who was a man of action, too, and who attempted to set in motion, by his own authority, the machinery of God's will.

He was squarely in the tradition of the religious patriots who sprang up in the Jewish provinces of Rome, to contend with the crushing weight of the Empire. We see his enterprise frustrated and himself undone; his followers scattered, and his movement, doubtless, drowned in bloodshed.

But of course this was not the end of it; his name was to become enshrined as the focus of a completely different religion among nations he had never known. The idea of this new religion, with himself as its deity, was something he could never have had the slightest inkling of.

How was the gulf bridged between his life and the religion that sprang up in his name?

Part Two

Christ after Jesus

Introduction

How did it come about that Jesus' enterprise, enclosed by Judaism and by Jewish national interests, diverged so radically from its origins?

How was the gulf bridged between Jesus' life and the religion named after his best-known title, the Greek translation of a word and concept that had previously been meaningful only for Jews?

If Jesus died a Jew, why are his followers not Jews?

I shall try to answer these questions by discussing, first, traditional accounts (the Gospels, Acts, and Saul), all of them composed some time after the death of Jesus, and then concentrate in particular on Saul's Epistles, which were to create not merely the very core of Christianity, but its framework.

The bridge between Jesus and the religion named after one of his titles was independent of his activity. It was his death, or rather his crucifixion that initiated the process or, more precisely, it was not the mere fact of his death but the conviction of his resurrection that became the cardinal element of the new religion.

Still more precisely, it was not the conviction of Jesus' physical resurrection that initiated that process; it was not, that is to say, the resurrections attributed to Jesus the man (like that of Lazarus) but his deification. Through the murkiness of detail the outline of this evolution may be clearly discerned.

The deification of Jesus, the clearest element of this evolution that can be pinpointed, was the direct result of the vision of an individual, Simon the Rock (Peter), which was shared by others.

6

The "Mother Church"

The Gospel of Luke ends on a simple view of Jesus resurrected: "While he blessed [the disciples] he parted from them. And they returned to Jerusalem with great joy" (24:51, 52). That is all. Presumably Jesus' followers in Jerusalem established the small community of those who believed him to be the Messiah and were remaining in the Holy City to await his return. To them, it is clear, this implied the establishment of the Kingdom of God.

The bridge between these events is missing. When we read in Acts, to our amazement, that one of Jesus' brothers, Upright Jacob (the Greek name *Jacobos* is usually translated *James*; in this book we shall use *Jacob*), was one of the same brothers who according to John (7:5) "did not believe in him," we have no idea how this came about.

What is particularly puzzling is the fate of the disciples. As we have seen above, the account of their mission itself seems to have been curiously inane; whether or not this emptiness of function points to the suppression of their partly military role, their conduct at Jesus' execution and afterwards is never mentioned; their behavior during the crisis was altogether forgotten by the earliest tradition. Not only do they "all forsake" Jesus and flee, they do not—even more surprisingly—reappear during Jesus' trial (surely another indication of the fictitiousness of the present account), nor are they present at his execution, nor do they bury him.

Where could they have been? More particularly, how is it they were not directly involved in the final denouement? Why were they not arrested?

Is there some special significance to be attached to Simon the Rock's denial of his Lord? Some doubt has been cast on the historicity of this episode; if it is a later invention, or perhaps a symbolic fiction of some kind, that of course makes it all the more revealing as a development of the later tradition, and possibly of the doctrinal disputes that doubtless played a role in the post-apostolic community.

We next see the little band of Jesus' followers peacefully worshipping at the Jewish Temple (Acts); they seem to have come back from Galilee to Jerusalem fairly soon. It is clear that a veil has been drawn over the climax of Jesus' activity; perhaps the only way to explain Simon the Rock's denial at cockcrow is to assume that it symbolizes a recollection of the manner in which Jesus' followers escaped the punishment meted out to him. They had managed to survive Roman justice by disavowing complicity and fleeing.

Let us try to see how they recovered from the bitter discouragement that must have befallen them after Jesus' crucifixion, which made still more poignant the failure of the Kingdom of God to appear. That is the fundamental question. How did the belief in Jesus' Resurrection evolve into Christianity?

I shall give only the broadest outline of some salient points, extracted from our documents, written down many years after Jesus' death and above all edited and compiled more than a hundred and fifty years later as the manual of belief of an already constituted Christian community, preoccupied by its cult and not by its worldly history.

The contradictions in the Gospel accounts of the discovery of Jesus' empty tomb, and the extreme barrenness of the one statement they make in common—that the tomb Jesus was placed in on the evening of his death was found empty the third day after that—indicates that the earliest tradition knew of no witnesses to the physical resurrection of Jesus from the tomb. Not only that, but it is evident that for the first few centuries after Jesus' death the whereabouts of Jesus' tomb remained unknown; it was only "located" by Saint Helena, mother of Emperor Constantine, in 326 C.E. as the result of "divine inspiration."

The earliest tradition relies on the appearance of Jesus to some of his disciples in a vision, initially to Simon the Rock, then to others. It was not, that is to say, the tradition of the discovery of the empty tomb that launched the faith in Jesus' resurrection. In fact, the mere discovery of an empty tomb would have remained inexplicable without elaborate proof that it actually meant what it was supposed to mean. In any case that meaning would have been apparent only if someone saw Jesus afterward.

In the very logic of the situation it is evident that it was the conviction of Jesus' reappearance that started the stories about Jesus' being laid to rest in a tomb later found empty. This logic is simply confirmed by the fact that the details concerning the tomb story fail to hang together.

We have no actual record of the resurrection in the sense of any eye-witness accounts, trustworthy or not. The Gospel records do not pretend to describe the earliest visions as seen by Jesus' followers; on the contrary, we have nothing but a ritually stylized account of how the earliest Church, some fifty years and more after the events, expressed its view of the resurrection of the Christ.

The oldest record we have of Jesus' appearances after death is that of Saul of Tarsus, which was at least twenty-five years after Jesus' death and could not very well be put more vaguely.

> I . . . received that Christ died for our sins in accordance with the scriptures, that he was buried, that he was raised on the third day in accordance with the scriptures, and that he appeared to Cephas [Simon the Rock], then to the twelve. Then he appeared to more than five hundred brethren at one time, most of whom are still alive, though some have fallen asleep. Then he appeared to Jacob, then to all the apostles. Last of all, as to one untimely born, he appeared to me. (1 Cor.15:4–8)

In this passage Saul gives us the basic outline of the earliest belief. It has practically no details of any kind, such as appear so much later in the Gospels themselves; Saul evidently had no knowledge of such details. The words "he appeared" are too simple to sustain any elaboration, and the fact that he uses the same phrase to apply to himself, while indicating elsewhere that he never actually saw Jesus in the flesh, is itself highly significant. It is the same word as that used to refer to the vision that "appeared" first to Simon the Rock, and it pinpoints it as exactly that—a vision.

Indeed, the starkly simple quality of these visions is attested by the very bareness of the word. The notion of "he appeared to," or "was seen by," which is the meaning of the Greek word used *(ophthé)* implies a complete independence of any of the legendary scenes recorded in the secondary or tertiary layers of the Gospels, which represent a later attempt to buttress Jesus' reappearance by circumstantial details, such as his having dinner with his disciples, etc., as in Luke and John. As indicated above Saul used this same word in describing his own vision of Jesus; consequently, since in Saul's case there is no question of his having actually seen Jesus in person, we must conclude that Simon the Rock and the rest of Jesus' followers simply had an overpowering awareness of the presence of their leader—actually an excellent way of singling out the most characteristic single feature of a hallucination, or in any case of the emotional interpretation given to a visual phenomenon of a certain vagueness.

An ampler, far more stylized account of the visions of Jesus that underlay the early tradition is given in Matthew:

> Now the eleven disciples went to Galilee, to the mountain to which Jesus had directed them. And when they saw him they worshipped him; but some doubted. And Jesus came and said to them. "All authority in heaven and on earth has been given to me. Go therefore and make disciples of all nations, baptizing them in the name of the Father and of the Son and of the Holy Spirit, teaching them to observe all the I have commanded you; and lo , I am with you always, to the World's End." (Mt.28:16–20)

Here the final sentence gives us the purpose of the entire account. It leads up to this reaffirmation of the Christian faith as it took shape generations after the death of Jesus. The details in it are interesting, however, because of the admission, presumably ineluctable, that some of the disciples had doubts.

Historically this leads to the presumption that the faith in Jesus' resurrection, guaranteed by the visions, spread only gradually, doubtless beginning with Simon the Rock and, according to Saul's catalogue of these visions, affecting first the twelve disciples, then the remaining circle of Jesus' followers. These doubts of Jesus' resurrection must have been very solidly established in the earliest tradition; they are attested by a celebrated passage in the Fourth Gospel:

> Now Thomas, one of the twelve, called the Twin, was not with them when Jesus came. So the other disciples told him, "We have seen the Lord." But he said to them, "Unless I see in his hands the print of the nails, and place my finger in the mark of the nails, and place my hand in his side, I will not believe. Eight days later, his disciples were again in the house, and Thomas was with them. The doors were shut, but Jesus came and stood among them and said, "Peace be with you." Then he said to Thomas, "Put your finger here, and see my hands; and put out your hand, and place it in my side; do not be faithless, but believing." Thomas

answered him, "My Lord and my God!" Jesus said to him, "Have you believed because you have seen me? Blessed are those who have not seen and yet believe." (Jn 20:24–29)

There is no need to emphasize the profound significance of the last sentence for the Church. It has, of course, been its cornerstone ever since. Its very indispensability for the creed indicates its remoteness from any conceivable historical scene, even if the phrase attributed to Thomas, "My Lord and *my God!*" were not wholly inconceivable in the mouth of any Jew of Jesus' own milieu.

An incident that may give us a key to the mechanism, so to speak, of the launching of the faith in the resurrection is the curious passage at the end of the Fourth Gospel:

After this Jesus revealed himself again to the disciples by the Sea of Tiberias; and he revealed himself in this way. Simon the Rock, Thomas called the Twin, Nathanael of Cana in Galilee, the sons of Zebedee, and two others of his disciples were together. Simon the Rock said to them, "I am going fishing." They said to him, "We will go with you." They went out and got into the boat; but that night they caught nothing. Just as day was breaking, Jesus stood on the beach; yet the disciples did not know it was Jesus. Jesus said to them, "Children, have you any fish?" They answered him "No." He said to them, "Cast the net on the right side of the board, and you will find some." So they cast it, and now they were not able to haul it in, for the quantity of fish. That disciple whom Jesus loved said to Simon "It is the Lord!" When Simon the Rock heard that it was the Lord, he put on his clothes, for he was stripped for work, and sprang into the sea, but the other disciples came in the boat, dragging the net full of fish, for they were not far from the land, but about a hundred yards off. When they got out on land, they saw a charcoal fire there, with fish lying on it, and bread. Jesus said to them, "Bring some of the fish that you have just caught." So Simon the Rock went aboard and hauled the net ashore, full of large fish, a hundred and fifty-three of them, and although there were so many, the net was not torn. Jesus said to them, "Come and have breakfast." Now none of the disciples dared ask him, "Who are you?" They knew it was the Lord. Jesus came and took the bread and gave it to them and so with the fish. This was now the third time that Jesus was revealed to the disciples after he was raised from the dead. (Jn 21:1–14)

This entirely contradicts the preceding chapter, which is unmistakably the natural ending of the fourth Gospel and refers to the appearances of the resuscitated Jesus in Jerusalem. The final chapter in our present fourth Gospel abruptly transfers the locale of Jesus' appearances back to Galilee, and by doing so changes the perspective as well. It is no longer a question of the glorious apostles consecrated by the spirit of Christ as his vicars on earth, but of poor fishermen, discouraged by the frustration of their campaign against Jerusalem, who have gone home to take up their former occupations.

This switch in perspective is abrupt, and so out of harmony with the glorifying tendency in the Gospels I have referred to that in accordance with our criterion of authenticity it is at bottom bound to carry conviction, regardless of how it too has been stylized to conform with the general tendency.

The localization in Jerusalem of Jesus' reappearance after death is attested by two passages in Luke (24:13–53), chapter 20 in the fourth Gospel (the excerpt given above and the conclusion to the extant version of Mark). On study, however, they may be seen to be secondary, both in the framework of the text and for logical considerations, to the earlier tradition that situates them in Galilee, where Jesus' followers no doubt fled after the Jerusalem fiasco.

There is also some confusion with respect to the number of times Jesus was supposed to have "appeared" to his followers, and in what order these appearances took place; it seems most likely on the whole that the very first appearance was to Simon the Rock, and then doubtless to the other disciples ("the twelve").

The vacillation in the very earliest tradition about these basic details may be seen in comparing the above-mentioned passages from Saul's First Letter to the Corinthians with the record of appearances given in the Gospels: on the one hand Saul's list is too long, since he includes 500 disciples, then Jesus' brother Jacob, then all the apostles, who are not mentioned in the Gospels, and on the other hand too short, since he omits the incident given in Luke of the disciples on the road to Emmaus. In addition Saul seems quite ignorant of the secondary legends concerning Jesus' tomb, both about his body's being placed in it and about its disappearance.

The manner in which everything else is arranged in the Gospels gives one the unmistakable impression that the kernel of the entire tradition, which is the fact of the belief of Simon the Rock, and doubtless of the other immediate companions, in the resuscitation of Jesus because of their having seen him in a vision, has been densely overlaid, in accordance with the very nature of the Gospels and the New Testament as a whole, by subsequent details of an edifying nature, designed to base the authority of the primitive Church on the "apostolic tradition," and thus to justify the very existence of the Church, which, as we have seen, was the last thing Jesus could have been thinking of.

The exception to this is of course the above mentioned record of doubts among the very first followers of Jesus. The account of their doubts, especially the curious episode of Doubting Thomas, by preserving a scrap of knowledge in the informational vacuum of the first generation after Jesus, vouches for the gradualness of the growing faith in the resurrection itself.

The appearances of Jesus do not require an explanation, that is, an explanation of something considered to be supernatural. For our purposes it is quite enough to establish the formation of the belief that they had taken place. Historically speaking, there may be a difference in whether Simon the Rock actually saw a vision or merely thought he saw one; but since we can only perceive this history through documents that record the beliefs of historical individuals it does not matter for us whether Simon the Rock was right or wrong. A vision is simply that—something thought to be seen.

As for the "objective" basis of this subjective impression, there is nothing, of course, in the Gospels or the New Testament as a whole that would enable such a discussion even to be started, especially since there was no line of demarcation at that time between such things. There was not, that is to say, any body of opinion that would have been able to deny *a priori* the possibility of resuscitation, and *a fortiori* the possibility of seeing someone resuscitated. The belief in miracles, still widespread today, was even more so then.

The resuscitation of Jesus was not, of course, considered to be a mere renewal of life in a terrestrial body; it was not, that is, a duplication of Jesus' own miracles in raising Lazarus and Jairus's daughter from the dead. In their cases the presumption was that they had in effect died prematurely and in due time would die normally. Jesus' resurrection, on the other hand, was a miracle of an altogether different order; it made him invulnerable to death for all eternity. It was understood, that is, as the equivalent of his glorification at the right hand of God; it is this that gives the miracles of his "appearing" to his disciples and others its essential meaning, and also demonstrates its nonphysical nature. It is also a reminder of the somewhat curious fact that although the divinity of Jesus was well-established by the time the Gospels were composed and edited, long after

Jesus' death, the impression they give of him is entirely human; his divinity is referred to only once or twice as it were artificially, by mention in the title of a Gospel or by having an outsider (like the Roman centurion) mention his being the Son of God.

In any case, the disciples clearly were not prepared for Jesus' resurrection; as we have seen, when Jesus explained to them how it was all going to take place, as recorded in Mark (8:31, 9:10 and 32) they were completely obtuse. The only assumption we can make is that Jesus never said anything of the sort, but that after the faith had been established it must have been repugnant to the earliest chroniclers that their Lord had not foreseen everything, so the appropriate rectifications were retrojected as the faith evolved. For that matter the whole insistence, in the Gospels as well as on the part of Saul, that everything had been accomplished in fulfillment of the Scriptures seems puzzling. No such belief in the death and resurrection of the Messiah is recorded among the Jews at all, and certainly not in the Hebrew Scriptures.

Now, the oldest portions of the Gospels indicate that the disciples made their way back to Galilee at first; this is perhaps demonstrated most succinctly by a phrase put in Jesus' mouth in Mark: "But after I am raised up I will go before you to Galilee" (Mk 14:28). Accordingly, we find Simon the Rock and a group of other disciples, shattered by the collapse of their movement and by their leader's dreadful death on the cross, going back to Galilee heartbroken. Jesus' above-mentioned pseudoprediction, in Mark: "You will all fall away; for it is written, 'I will strike the shepherd, and the sheep will be scattered' " (Mk 14:27) actually sums up what must have happened; as a fictional device to humiliate the presumed inspirers of the apostolic tradition it seems pointless.

Consequently we must imagine that after leaving the scene of disaster full of grief, doubtless in the mood retained by the above-mentioned passage in Luke—"But we had hoped that he was the one to redeem Israel" (Lk 24:21)—they nevertheless could not believe that things had come to an end. Despite the clear record of their incomprehension and flight, which, substantially soft-pedaled as it no doubt is, conveys by that very fact the completeness of their rout, they could not resign themselves to acquiescing in the apparent verdict of the events.

Simon the Rock seems to have been the first to have seen Jesus resuscitated, or rather, as we have seen, had a vision of him resuscitated in glory. Simon's primacy is based on the authority of Saul, on the story of the miraculous catch of fish in the fourth Gospel (Chapter 21) reproduced above, as well as on a phrase in Luke (24:34) and another in the fourth Gospel (20:6). (The various women who figure in the stories of the empty tomb are clearly there for the purpose of rounding out the legendary account of the tomb, which as we have seen is altogether secondary to the primordial recollection in the tradition of Simon's vision.) Once the fact of Simon's having had a vision of Jesus is accepted, the mechanism may already be thought to have been triggered; the mere multiplication of visions afterwards is even easier to imagine, in view of the well-known contagiousness of collective visions and hallucinations. Let us glance at the conditions that kindled the outburst of the new faith.

Jesus' followers, shattered by defeat, go back to Galilee; but they do not abandon their hopes. They, or at any rate some of them (in view of the doubters), cannot accept his permanent absence—his death. All that we must imagine to explain to ourselves the very first impulse that was to develop with such complexity, is a state of emotional tension that as we see led to a vision coming first to Simon the Rock, doubtless the closest to Jesus of all his followers, and then to some of the others, gradually followed by the rest of the group. For our purposes this is sufficient. In any case there is nothing more to be hoped for from the complete void in our information for this period. Not only are we at a loss to explain how the group of Jesus' followers that had first gone to Galilee retraced their steps and established themselves in Jerusalem, where the "Mother Church" was to come into being, but we are almost equally in the dark for the actual inception of the missionary movement that spread the new faith elsewhere.

A word of caution repeated: The basic source of confusion in the study of this extraordinary development—why Jesus' followers are not Jews—is that the later Church took as its starting point a belief that in fact failed. This belief was part of the movement started by Jesus and held by him and his first followers. With the failure of the Kingdom to appear, and with the crushing of the movement by Rome, there was no occasion for a new faith. The very glorification of Jesus that served as the starting point of the new religion was inherently alien to everything Jesus himself had been interested in. The early Church, springing up over his crucified body and taking the resurrection and glorification of the Savior as the central theme of the new cult, abandoned Jesus' actual life and his own aims.

Jesus' Gospel, as we have seen, was the proclamation of the imminence of the Kingdom of God, accessible to those who had repented; this was transformed by the Church into the Gospel of Christ, the doctrine of salvation through his death and resurrection. The oldest Church message made individual salvations dependent on the person of the Christ, while the oldest message we can disentangle from the complexities of the Gospels, contained in Matthew 10 (Jesus' instructions to the disciples), is silent about Jesus himself. In these instructions Jesus says nothing at all about the necessity of a period of trials and tribulations before the coming of the Kingdom, nor is there any suggestion that his own death would be in any sense at all a prerequisite for its advent.

In short, the cross itself marks the line of demarcation between Christianity as a religion and its origins in Jesus' life and activity, between the prehistory of the religion and the religion itself. Without the death of Jesus, there would have been no Christianity at all. In the epigram of the French scholar, Alfred Loisy, "What Jesus proclaimed was the Kingdom of God, what happened was the Church." Or, as Saul put it: "If Christ be not raised, then our preaching is in vain, and your faith is in vain" (1 Cor 15:14).

The cross was the central symbol of the entire mechanism of salvation; it was the very repulsiveness of the cross that led Saul to say, "Jews demand signs and Greeks seek wisdom, but we preach Christ crucified, a stumbling-block to Jews and folly to Gentiles" (1 Cor 1:22–23), and it was the dynamism inherent in this contradiction that led him to transform the catastrophe into the arch-symbol of hope.

But for the Jews proper the Cross remained a bafflement, since not only was the very notion of a failed Messiah a logical contradiction for them, but crucifixion was considered to be a punishment of someone accursed by God, according to Deuteronomy 21:23 as recalled by Saul: "For it is written, 'cursed be every one who hangs on a tree' " (Gal 3:13). Consequently, among Jesus' Jewish followers in Palestine the crucifixion remained what it was to remain for Jews generally, a scandal that in essence could only be apologized for and played down, and at best had to be compensated, or overcompensated for by the resurrection, which both canceled the disgrace of Jesus' death and explained it away.

Because of this basic and above all unavowed transformation of perspective the transition between Jesus' activity and the belief in the Christ—the belief in individual salvation through the Savior's crucifixion and glorification—is quite obscure, especially since the most striking thing about the earliest origins of the nascent sect is, as mentioned before, its thoroughgoing identity with Judaism. Whatever the impulses that led the initial band of disciples to come to Jerusalem, we have only the Acts of the Apostles and Saul's Letters as a source of information; as we shall see, there are profound disagreements between them.

Let us stress a vital chronological detail; the Gospels, though written a generation later than Saul's Letters, describe events that took place substantially before Saul's Letters were written; Acts, also written much later (at least forty years) than Saul's Letters, partially overlap them as a description of events. In a still larger sense, since Saul's version of the evolving religion was ultimately successful, everything in both the Gospels and Acts probably came under the influence of his ideas in one form or another.

We have already referred to the fact that Jesus' followers, headed by his brother Jacob, were assiduous worshippers at the Temple in Jerusalem. This, oddly enough, is the keynote on which Luke comes to an end, when after reporting the risen Jesus' final words to his followers, the chronicler goes on: "And they returned to Jerusalem with great joy, and were continually in the Temple blessing God" (Lk 24:53). This simple sentence is surely the leitmotif of the description of the little community that seems to have formed in Jerusalem around a common devotion to Jesus. It is repeated often:

> Many wonders and signs were done through the apostles. And all who believed were together and had all things in common; and they sold their possessions and goods and distributed them to all as had need. And day by day, attending the Temple together and breaking bread in their homes, they partook of food with glad and generous hearts, praising God and having favor with all the people. (Acts 2:43–47)

> And they were all together in Solomon's Portico. The people held them in high honor. (Acts 5:12,13)

> And every day in the Temple and at home they did not cease teaching and preaching Jesus as the Christ. (Acts 5:42)

Nor was it a mere question of attendance; the point is both emphasized and unintentionally allowed to slip in that they were even punctilious with respect to the laws of ritual purity.

> But Simon said, "No Lord; for I have never eaten anything that is common or unclean." (Acts 10:14)

> So when Simon went up to Jerusalem, the circumcision party criticized him, saying, "Why did you go to uncircumcised men and eat with them?" (Acts 11:2,3)

> But some men came down from Judea and were teaching the brethren, "Unless you are circumcised according to the custom of Moses, you cannot be saved." (Acts 15:1)

The unequivocal statement is also made that not only were many Pharisees members of the little group:

> But some believers who belonged to the party of the Pharisees rose up, and said, "It is necessary to circumcise them, and to charge them to keep the law of Moses." (Acts 15:5)

but that even priests had joined them:

> And the word of God increased; and the number of disciples multiplied greatly in Jerusalem, and a great many of the priests were obedient to the faith. (Acts 6:7)

And taken as a whole the group congratulates itself on being "zealous for the Torah."

> And when they heard it, they glorified God. And they said to him, "You see, brother, how many thousands there are among the Jews of those who have believed; they are all zealous for the Torah." (Acts 21:20)

These passages indicate that for a whole generation after Jesus' death his followers were pious Jews and proud of it. They attracted into their fold members of the professional religious classes, and did not deviate even from the burdensome ceremonial laws.

Nor was that all. Not only did they attend the Temple, they actually preached that *Jesus was the Messiah* (Christ). We have already seen that the mere belief in the Messiahship of a human being was not blasphemous in terms of the Torah, nor was it blasphemous to say as much about oneself. It might be considered a quirk, blunder, mania, obsession, or delusion, but it involved no question of piety. Hence there was no reason why a Jew should not have followed Jesus' obedience to the Torah, while cherishing a belief about the character of one human being. Since in this Jewish milieu there could be no question of *worshipping* Jesus such a belief was essentially a private matter.

It is true that the corollary of this belief in the minds of the very first Jerusalem community was that Jesus, selected by God as his Messiah, was going to come again. This was the first displacement, so to speak, or the first transformation of the original hope of Jesus and his followers; they were now awaiting the return of the Messiah in glory instead of the Kingdom of God. It was this glorious return that was to herald the installation of the Kingdom. Thus, while for all practical purposes they were still concentrating on the same thing, a profound difference had taken place. From the point of view of potentialities, Jesus' followers now understood the divine economy through the prism of their attitude toward Jesus *personally*; and this fact alone laid the foundations for the future magnification of Jesus, to his progressive elevation from the Jewish Messiah, to the Vice-God, ruler of the cosmos, and to God himself, at least in one of his aspects.

Let us glance for a moment at the situation of the small group of Jesus' followers, no doubt the core of the much larger following he must have had to warrant the attention of the Roman authorities.

Though Simon the Rock's vision had, emotionally speaking, wiped out the humiliation of Jesus' death on the cross, there was still a complete vacuum of ideas; Jesus had not, after all, established anything, neither a new belief nor a new rite. Hence his followers had nothing left but Judaism. It was Simon the Rock's vision that was to give rise to a new chain of events. At precisely this point there was a fusion between a plain, straightforward fact—a vision that was believed in—and the interpretation of that fact. I have already quoted Saul of Tarsus's interpretation: "Unless Christ was resurrected, our faith is in vain" (1 Cor 15:17), which gave this fusion of fact and interpretation a lapidary formulation.

Now the transformation of the grief of Jesus' mourners has brought about a new situation. Whatever had been believed by Jesus and his followers beforehand about the Kingdom of God has been replaced by a belief about Jesus himself. This was, as we shall see, the first of three stages in the magnification of Jesus, from Jewish messianist to lord of the universe, to deity.

A special interpretation of Jesus' execution was fundamental; the ignominy of the crucifixion had to be explained away. In and for itself the resurrection was a dramatic explanation; anyone raised from the dead and glorified at the right hand of God must have been marked for some grand purpose; it was now clear that he had been singled out by God as part of a cosmic plan.

Jesus' immediate followers still believed, as far as Judaism in general was concerned, what Jesus himself had believed; that Yahweh was about to intervene in history, smash the pagan powers, restore the fortunes of the Jews and rectify this world. They now merely added to this the subsidiary belief that the singling out of Jesus by his resurrection meant that the Kingdom would be accompanied by his glorious return. All this was well within the confines of the basic simplicity of Judaism.

The stages of this early transposition are easily traced: "Lord, wilt thou restore sovereignty to Israel?" (Acts 1:6). This is plainly a mere reaffirmation of the ancient belief, shared by all Kingdom of God activists, that the Kingdom of God would restore the fortunes of the Jews. A little later: "Jesus of Nazareth, a man singled out by God and made known to you through miracles, portents and signs, which God worked among you through him" (Acts 2:22). This repeats a theme of the same writer: "[Jesus is described by the Emmaus pilgrims as] 'a man who was a prophet, powerful in words and deeds before God and all the people. . . . We had been hoping he was the man to redeem Israel' " (Lk 24:13,14). This was no more than the traditional Jewish idea of a prophet, enhanced by the conviction that he would be the one to "redeem Israel." This old view had to be confirmed by Simon the Rock's Vision. It had to be turned into the concept that Jesus, who had begun as a prophet, had been *made* special by God: "God has made this Jesus . . . both Lord and Messiah" (Acts 2:36).

Thus at first things were not very different; one element had been transposed. The Kingdom of God was still believed in—now, however, linked to the person of Jesus, for whom a great future had been signaled by the divine decision to elevate Jesus to the right hand of God and thus guarantee the validity of his role as Messiah. In practical terms this meant, in the beginning, that the original conviction that the Kingdom of God was about to be installed was now linked to the person of Jesus; the Kingdom would be installed *after* Jesus had come back again.

Thus for the time being the Kingdom of God was not abandoned; it was merely linked to another experience. The early believers in Simon the Rock's vision knew, unlike predecessors, say, who had merely been convinced of an interpretation of scriptural passages that suited them, that the Kingdom of God *had* to come now that it was associated with the overwhelming, palpable fact of Jesus' having been singled out, in full view, so to speak, of the believers in the vision, as the manifest herald of the Kingdom. In this way the proclamation of Jesus' death, intertwined with his resurrection, instantly presented itself to those who believed in it as the demonstration of God's ultimate and indeed imminent triumph.

This conviction was held by a handful of people near the scene of the vision in Galilee—perhaps a dozen or so at the most. They did not stay in Galilee long; they left for Jerusalem. No doubt it seemed obvious to them that if the Kingdom of God was about to break forth that could happen initially only in Jerusalem—the same reasoning, of course, that had impelled Jesus himself to go there.

They must have had acquaintances, perhaps from previous pilgrimages: they took their meals in a modest house. They would have no difficulty in forming a synagogue of their own without attracting attention; only ten Jews were needed for a quorum.

The group is very small: there is Simon the Rock, whose vision had been accepted by others (his very sobriquet "the Rock" might have been due to this founding vision). There is also Jacob (Major) and John ben-Zavdai, and Jesus' brother Jacob (Minor), known as Upright Jacob, who must have derived some influence from his kinship with Jesus even though at the outset of Jesus' career he had apparently been against it (as in Mark and Matthew): he had had a vision of his own, very early on (I Cor 15:5,7).

They have the appearance of ordinary Jews: they are "assiduous" in attending services in the Temple, where Upright Jacob was soon to be celebrated for his piety. In principle nothing distinguishes them: Their characteristic belief—that Jesus, executed for sedition by the Romans, had been resurrected—was in no sense a belief that lay outside Judaism. It was merely an eccentric, as it were personal quirk, though it was also, to be sure, an aspect of politics, as we shall see.

The believers in Simon the Rock's vision—from now on I shall call them "Jesists"—still believe in "the One," Yahweh, the God of Israel; their only writings are the Hebrew Scriptures; they share the general Pharisee belief in the resurrection of the dead, the Last Judgment, and, of course, the imminent Kingdom of God. They know themselves to be, like everyone else, sinful; they need God's mercy. They have in their minds a view of the heavenly world, of hosts of angels, of the underworld populated by Satan and the evil spirits: For them the earth is the playground of the "powers." They believe, like all normative Jews, in beings intermediate

between God and the world. God's attributes are more or less personified—
"Wisdom," "Word" (*Hokhma, Memra*). For them Jesus was the Messiah,
who had been the Son of David—i.e., the Jewish Messiah, descended
from the great King David, now expected to come back and rule a regenerated world as the Son of Man. For them this Messiah was to come down
from heaven and judge the righteous and the wicked. (Mt 25:31–32).

The Torah—the core of Judaism—is fundamental. It was only later, of
course, that the question of the primacy of the Torah was to occasion the
splitting away of a new faith. For the first coterie of Jesists this did not even
arise: The Torah was taken for granted.

This Jesist coterie not only shares the same idea of the World's End as
all the Kingdom of God activists, they have the identical stance of dynamic
expectation. Both the Jesists and the other Kingdom of God activists
believe in the absolute sovereignty of Yahweh, and also in his active help
in restoring dominion to Israel; both loathe the Romans as pagans who
worship men as gods; both cherish the Torah and the Temple as absolute
values; and both are violently opposed to paying the Roman taxes. Jesus
had been executed, after all, just like countless Zealots. Both groups detest
the priestly aristocracy; both, finally, are followed by the "people of the
land" against the rich and powerful. For both, in short, three categories of
people are enemies—pagans in the Holy Land, the "publicans" who collected taxes for the Romans, and sinners against the Torah.

For the Jesists in Jerusalem the only problem about Jesus' messiahship
was that it seemed to contradict the traditional role of the Messiah. Still, if
a scriptural basis could be added to the impact of Simon the Rock's vision,
this problem might be gotten around, and a harmonious explanation might
be presented both of Jesus' messiahship and its apparent failure.

The Jesists quickly found a cogent explanation of the contradiction.
Jesus, who had come as Messiah to destroy the Romans and save his people, had died as a martyr for Israel and also for Israel's sins—i.e., his people had failed to respond. He had been turned over to the Roman procurator: all would be set right when he came again, this time, as guaranteed by
the vision of Simon the Rock, at the right hand of God.

There was plainly no place for pagans in this tight design. The very
vindication of Israel implied not only the destruction of Rome, but the punishment of the pagans in general: "When the Son of Man comes in all his
glory and all the angels with him, he will sit in state on his throne, with all
the nations [pagans] gathered before him" (Mt 25:31). Jesus, as Messiah-

judge, accordingly, was simply meant to judge all mankind, from the point of view of a resurgent Israel.

At the same time the Jerusalem Jesists had moved a little away from the original view of Jesus as a mere man delegated, like the classical prophets, to carry out the will of Yahweh. For the prophets of old such a man might have been a mere human being.

But the very fact of the vision, of seeing in Jesus no longer a human being they had all known, but a being resurrected by the favor of God and glorified at his right hand, was a step in the direction of transcendentalizing Jesus. The initial, rather simple view that Jesus, by being resurrected, had passed instantaneously from the earthbound to the heavenly condition already made Jesus no longer a mere man. Still, this might have been easily assimilated because of the proliferation in contemporary Jewry, alongside the old-fashioned notion of a purely human messiah, of visionary, apocalyptic Messiahs playing superhuman roles. Thus the figure of Jesus, though remembered by living people as a real human being, was susceptible of the sort of magnification possible for people caught up in the tension of waiting for transcendent events. Jesus began ascending, even in Jerusalem. But this was not yet apparent; its "implications," in any case, were not to be drawn within a purely Jewish milieu. The Jerusalem Jesists remained wholly integrated with the Temple milieu throughout their existence.

Initially the Jerusalem Jesists must have been impressed by the rapid percolation of the news of the vision to so many different parts of the Jewish Diaspora. The news of the vision was no doubt accompanied by its explanation that Jesus had been *meant* to die in order to rise again, i.e., the view that Saul had "received' upon joining the Jesists shortly after the crucifixion. When the views of the Jerusalem coterie lapped over into the numerous congregations of pagan converts and semiconverts to Judaism—the "God-fearers" and others—that too would have seemed to be promoted by God's grace. It took a few years before the Jerusalem Jesists felt called upon to react to the success of the "Hellenizing" ideas being mingled with their own in the Diaspora.

It is obvious, indeed, that the Jerusalem Jesists had no intention of evangelizing the pagans: that would have seemed incomprehensible to pious Jews whose ideas still revolved around the destinies of Israel, the Kingdom of God, and a Jewish Messiah. The proselytization that did finally begin was associated with the expulsion of some Greek-speaking

Jews after the execution of their leader, Stephen. It was these followers of Stephen who first began "preaching the Lord Jesus" to the pagans in Antioch after first having been active with the Diaspora Jews there (Acts 11:19–21).

The harmonizing chronicler of Acts (see critical appendix) inserts a special incident to bridge over what must have been the original antipathy of the Jerusalem coterie to the very idea of taking their views to the pagans. Acts, mentioning the conversion of Cornelius, the Roman centurion, introduces this by indicating that God had had to prepare Simon the Rock for this by a special revelation (Acts 10:1, 11:18).

If they did, after all, accept the fact that their special view of Jesus might profitably be communicated to pagans, they must have insisted that at least those pagans be converted to Judaism, via circumcision, a primary requirement: (Acts 11:22), the "door of faith" opened by God "to the pagans" (Acts 14:27).

This concession—not a real one, in any case, since conversion simply made a pagan a full Jew—implied no change of views on the part of the Jerusalem Jesists, who remained unwavering in their fundamental view that Israel remained the chosen people as before. The vital necessity of this notion is indicated by Saul himself, even at the very moment of evolving ideas designed for absorption by pagans, as he shows in the powerful metaphor comparing the pagans to a "wild olive . . . grafted" on Jewry, and exhorting them to remember that it is not they who sustain the "root," but the root that sustains them (Rom 11:17,18).

The metaphor itself, indeed, may be a seductive way of pointing out to his superiors in Jerusalem the profitability and justifiability of carrying their ideas to the pagans—another door of faith.

For the rest, what distinguished the Jerusalem Jesists from their surroundings a little was their feeling that they were somehow the elect, since they alone perceived the true role of Jesus in bringing the Kingdom expected by countless Jews. It was they alone, they no doubt thought, for whom the great day of Yahweh forecast by the classical prophets and being fought for by Zealots, Daggermen, and activists of all kinds, would bring happiness. In the turbulent Israel of those days this idea was not uncommon.

Initially there was no organization at all, nor could there have been, since at first there was no reason to think the original group would last— the very idea of enduring was obviously the antithesis of the hope and longing that had brought them to Jerusalem in the first place. This small, familylike group could not have lasted long; in this stage it consisted of "brothers," "believers," "all with one heart, one soul" (Acts 4:32). Perhaps their conduct was guided, like that of other Jews, by a few ethical precepts. The Sermon on the Mount, a cluster of rules for ordinary conduct, without speculation, no doubt came from this early period. It might have suited their self-esteem:

> You are the salt of the earth . . . the light of the world. . . . If your justice does not transcend that of the . . . Pharisees you will not enter into the Kingdom of God." (Mt 5:13)

At first there was no interest in the real-life Jesus they had all known. Waiting for the World's End, there was no reason to write down anything about a flesh-and-blood Jesus, about his person or his career, or his relations with friends and enemies, or even the World's End miracles that had been attributed to him.

Within the small coterie the only divisions noticeable even a decade or more after Jesus' death were into "apostles, prophets and teachers" (1 Cor 12:28); there was still no bureaucracy and no allocation of offices to monitor or control the ideas of the coterie. There were no sacred persons and no hierarchy. The group's program was simply to wait for Jesus the risen Messiah to come down from heaven, smash the pagan power, and install the Kingdom; there was no need for organization.

Still, as the group kept growing, and as the Second Coming kept being postponed, some need for administration was felt. The earliest record (very late) mentions only two aspects of organization: holding all things in common and making a general distribution of goods according to individual need (Acts 2:43, 4:32). It was this, no doubt, that planted the seeds of the Church as an institution: The Church arose, in germ, out of the community chest.

The "primitive communism" traditionally attributed to this phase of evolution was, to be sure, a later idealization (Barnabas's gift of his possessions to the community is reported as an exception [Acts 4:36–7]). The community chest itself was to give rise to the tradition of the inherent meritoriousness of poverty and of good works, which meant doing things for the common good and for the poor.

Since the glorious return of the Risen One was expected from one moment to the next no propaganda was carried on by the first Jesists, though of course they communicated their beliefs. They could not have remained incognito in the Temple milieu, especially since they would have been known to be associated with the abortive enterprise of Jesus, notorious vis-à-vis the authorities, even though there is no indication of any further activity that might have made them suspect once they were living a quiet life in Jerusalem.

In the absence of organization what was important was personal qualities—charisma, the grace bestowed on certain "saints" by the "Spirit," linked almost at once, no doubt, to the risen Jesus, who unlike the old-fashioned prophet, whose authority came from God, possessed the Spirit directly through his glorification. It was the Spirit that created incentives for action, not bureaucracy, hierarchy, or organization. It will be a long time before those inspired by the Spirit will be replaced by an actual organization and even longer before the initially elected functionaries organize the group as its masters.

Thus at the outset, before there is any question of such organization, the administration and authority of the first coterie are conceived of as being entirely under the auspices of the Spirit (1 Cor 12:28). Basically, the "Spirit" was a way of talking about spontaneous or at least pseudospontaneous psychic activity. It was not, in its nature, limited by anything; that is, it could not be bureaucratized. It marked that stage of group life that preceded any form of organization. In and for itself it validated, as the symbol of free-floating decisions, whatever was going on in the life of the early coterie.

The Spirit could show itself in more than one form, mainly ecstasy and prophecy, in the sense of edifying the listeners by "explaining" the Scriptures or, perhaps, the recollection of what Jesus had said or was thought to have said, and phenomena like glossolalia—i.e., babbling in public—explained as repeating powerful, mysterious ideas from some "unknown language." (To outsiders, of course, this might look like plain drunkenness [Acts 2:13]). The rule of the Spirit, no doubt, itself marks both the beginning of propaganda—that is, the articulation and promotion of a self-consciously different point of view—and the rudiments of organization entailed by the postponement of the Second Coming. To maintain themselves as a group in the midst of an environment they were part of, though with a characteristic difference, the earliest coterie had to organize itself simply to persist.

The first pivot that was to bring about the germination of a faith unsuspected by either Jesus or the first Jesists appeared within the Jerusalem coterie. In a Jewish milieu the mere messiahship of Jesus, however fitted out with transcendental elements, could not, perhaps, have prospered for very long; it would seem to have required realization in a practical sense. Thus the ascension of Jesus was held back by the milieu in which it had begun. Even though his ascension overshadowed his humanity (such as his biological descent from King David), it was itself limited to concepts valid only in Judaism.

The Jerusalem Temple was the goal of pilgrimage for Jews throughout the world, and it was natural for the Jerusalem Jesists to communicate their excitement to countless numbers of other Jews who were constantly arriving. Thus the primitive, more or less tightly-knit group of Jesists was soon diluted by Greek-speaking Jews from the Diaspora, whose familiarity with pagan culture, no doubt, made it easy for them to believe in personal resurrection. It was they who were to take the initial ascension of Jesus and amplify it, as we shall see, endlessly.

It was from the moment that such Diaspora Jews, influenced by the Jesists, stayed on in Jerusalem, no doubt in a special synagogue with regional associations, that the gradual formation of a new type of community must be assumed. For it would seem clear that once the contagion of the vision had affected them the reason they stayed on in Jerusalem was again a simple one—they were waiting for the risen Jesus to appear for the second time, this time bringing with him, of a certainty, the Kingdom of God.

The views of the Jerusalem Jesists did not detach them from the movement for the Kingdom of God that was beginning to churn up the country and that was to culminate in the 66–70 insurrection. Just as they could pray "assiduously" in the Jewish Temple, so their view of the Kingdom of God, a mere variant of the general belief, did not preclude the identification of the Jesists with their fellow activists in the swelling tide of insurrection.

It was the Diaspora Jesists (the "Hellenists" of Acts) who, while accepting the primordial lesson drawn by the original believers in the vision—that God had singled Jesus out as the Messiah-soon-to-return—expanded the idea far beyond its original scope. A ferment began that, by leading to the magnification of the person of Jesus, by stressing what was originally a minor difference between the immediate entourage of the lost leader Jesus and the ordinary mass of Jews living within the framework of traditional Jewish ideas—the Sadducees, Pharisees and so on—escalated that minor difference to a higher level of significance. At first the original core of Jesists must have influenced only small numbers of Diaspora Jews;

then, gradually, as that number increased, and as the Diaspora Jews became more numerous relative to the original core, the initial harmony in the fervent expectation of the Second Coming began to be eroded by the survival of the original group, by the need to cope with real life while waiting for that second coming of Christ.

And because the Greek-speaking Jews, who had a wider range of ideas, philosophical background, and interests through their Greek-language background, inevitably began not only to expand the simplicity of the original notion of Jesus' role but to project it beyond the boundaries of Jewish tradition, the break between them and their fellow believers widened into a split. The initial difference, curiously enough, is recorded on a most mundane plane. There were disagreements about the allocation of food at the tables that in the very beginning were communal, i.e., the community must have been small enough to warrant such tables (Acts 6:1–7).

The Jerusalem Jesists were to become symbolized in the early tradition as "the twelve," counterposed to "the seven," referring to the Greek-speaking Diaspora Jews. "the Twelve" were later considered to have been the "apostolic" element, representing the "Word of God," while "the seven" represented material services, i.e., the future deaconate. Nevertheless, though tradition (i.e., Acts) presents the Greek-speaking seven in this anodyne way, what exacerbated the falling-out was the predilection of the Greek-speaking Jews for propaganda. The group is epitomized in the figure of Stephen, who was "argued with" by members of some regional synagogues (Acts 6:9, 10), and accused of denouncing both the Temple and the Torah.

Stephen was arraigned before the Jewish authorities (the Sanhedrin). He not only defended his views but expressed them, as it seems, in a particularly violent form, culminating in a savage denunciation of Jews as such for having failed to accept Jesus the Messiah. He was sentenced to death by stoning for apostasy.[1] Thus, within little more than a decade after Jesus' execution the idea had already sprouted in the Jesist milieu that the Torah and the cult—the essence of Judaism—had been superseded, in principle, by the resurrection of Jesus and its consequences.

The Jesist community was split: The Greek-speaking Jews—Stephen's partisans—were deported from Jerusalem. They scattered, some of them going at first nearby, to the provinces of Judea and Samaria, and a little later further north, to Antioch in Syria and to Cyprus. It was in Antioch—

a great capital—that some unknown Diaspora Jews took the first step outside the Jewish enclosure. It was there, for the first time, that while some of the Greek-speaking Jews (natives of Cyprus and Cyrene) "spoke only to the Jews, some of them, coming to Antioch, spoke to the Greeks, announcing to them Lord Jesus" (Acts11: 19–21). It was in Antioch, too, that the word "Christians" was coined. At that time, to be sure, it meant no more than "Jesist," someone who believed in Jesus as Messiah ("Christ" was the Greek translation of the Hebrew-Aramaic word "Messiah").

The Greek-speaking Jews who had left Jerusalem must have been a mere handful; they were only going home or to places they would feel at home in. Nor could the "Greeks" referred to above have been ordinary Greeks. Normal pagans could not have understood either the Kingdom of God, the concept of "repenting," the point of the resurrection of a Jewish Messiah, or for that matter the concept of one almighty God.

The pagans harangued by the exiles from Jerusalem must have been the numerous "God-fearers" clustered around countless synagogues throughout the Mediterranean. Wherever Jews had settled, the orderly rites and their immemorial antiquity had attracted huge numbers of pagans, who though fascinated by Judaism, were loath to take on the burden of circumcision and the dietary laws. It was accordingly such "God-fearers" who were the first to hear, in their own language, the "good news" brought to them by the Greek-speaking Jews.

The new, enhanced view of Jesus, the failed nationalist leader and would-be messiah who had been "hanged on wood" by the Romans, spread very rapidly, from Palestine to Syria, to Rome itself, and to Egypt. Wherever there were Jewish communities—they were scattered all over the eastern Mediterranean area and beyond—it would have been natural for Jews returning from Jerusalem pilgrimages to bring with them the exciting news that a Kingdom of God activist had actually been raised from the dead and been *seen* glorified. The use of the word "Christians" as a species of Jew must have spread equally rapidly. In any case, little groups and assemblies, generally associated in the first generation or two with Jewish synagogues, must have been accessible to the abundant speculation fostered by the idea that Jesus' resurrection was an integral part of a divine plan.

The very existence of such coteries in a society that went on living a normal life entailed the emergence of a cult of some kind. Mere feeling cannot remain very long in the form of feeling alone: It must be given some sort of public, that is, social expression. The awareness of being distinguished from other Jews, if only by the quirk of a special belief, in and for itself stimulated the coagulation of both ideas and rites. In turn the practice of such a cult reinforced the bond already felt by those sharing the same belief: the cult became the manifestation of togetherness.

This meant, quite simply, that the person of Jesus the Messiah, the *raison d'être* of the coterie to begin with, soon became the focus for the crystallization of the cult. As a group, the believers, the "Saints," would, in the early period, concentrate on Jesus and the longings they associated with his power. What they longed for now was not only the Kingdom of God, like other Jews whose imaginations were inflamed by the tension of the epoch, but for *him* to return with the Kingdom.

This was soon to abbreviate itself, as it were, to the simple fact of his coming, longed for with ardor. And to bring that about it was equally natural to invoke his name, which in the beginning meant that in praying to God the Jesists designated, with feeling, Jesus as the guarantee that their prayers would be answered.

Thus when the small coteries found a recruit, he or she had to signalize allegiance to the coterie by demonstrating faith in the name of the risen Jesus. Invoking that name became, accordingly, the emblem of the new association. This was what became the core of whatever the early ceremonial was. It provided a potent mechanism for assuming the status of a member of the new elect.

Everyone in that era took it for granted that some form of power was inherent in the very essence of a name. In the recollections of the Jerusalem Jesists, moreover, Jesus had demonstrated through his World's End miracles that some aspect of the divine power was inherent in his very person. The potency inherent in names as such is illustrated often:

In my name they will expel demons. (Mk 16:17)

Was it not in your name that we expelled demons? (Mt 7:22)

In the name of Jesus Christ . . . walk! (Acts 3:6)

The name of Jesus . . . has strengthened this man. (Acts 3:16)

The antiquity of this turn of mind is attested by what have been a most ancient formula: "Lord, come!" (or: "Let the Lord come!"—*Maran atha !* in Aramaic).

Thus the very name of Jesus the Nazarene justified and enhanced its use for cultic purposes. The figure of Jesus became not merely the aim of communion, but its very instrument. This took place, of course, against a background of conventional synagogue practices. All the first coteries were, after all, pious Jews naturally grouped around synagogues. Thus the earliest Jesists, too, read the Scriptures, sang psalms, and prayed together.

They tended to select, to be sure, passages from the Scriptures that had a point for *them,* i.e., that highlighted prophecies and so on that Jesus was thought to have realized. Very soon they had begun exercising their minds ferreting out passages from the Hebrew Scriptures and putting them together as a body of "testimonies" to the truth of their belief. No doubt they favored psalms full of hope, those that exalted the promise, since this was their primary concern. Their prayers, too, must have concentrated accordingly on the supplication for the glorious return of their Messiah— the meaning of "Lord, come!"

Thus, even though the framework of their prayers and supplications remained Jewish, and even though they thought themselves, in the first few generations, to be Jews, such coteries had already launched a dynamic, as we can see, that in its nature tended to create a split between them and Judaism. The mere fact that the background of their hopes at this time was constituted by Jewish tradition had little to do with the true emotional intent of their behavior; that intent, linked as it was to a dynamic innovation expected to take place in the universe, was inherently likely to break with normative Judaism—unless, of course, it actually took place.

At the same time, whatever their belief in Jesus' special role was, the Jesists in Jerusalem went on sharing the general Kingdom of God perspective that had become commonplace among the Pharisees and lower strata of the priesthood, in contrast with the pro-Roman quietist attitude of the Jewish aristocracy and upper priesthood. That perspective, of the World's End accompanied by the restoration of Jewish dominion throughout the world, naturally entailed comprehensive opposition to the Roman Empire, the chief obstacle to the realization of the divine plan.

Since all activist Jews believed this, there was no distinction between the Jerusalem Jesists and the other activists, such as the Zealots, Daggermen and so on, vis-à-vis the Romans. The crucifixion of Jesus was not embarrassing to the Kingdom of God activists from a political point of view; he had after all died a national hero—a victim of pagan oppression.

There was at first no natural transmission to the pagans of the early, national view of the risen Jesus; the basic framework of the national idea was wholly Jewish. Hence, even though the focal position of the Temple created a network of relations between Palestinian and Diaspora Jewry, there was not as yet a bridge to the pagans, which was formed only with the expulsion of the Greek-speaking Jews from Jerusalem.

There were, accordingly, three stages in the magnification of Jesus. The first involved a small transposition of traditional values, from Jesus as messianic pretender and herald of the Kingdom of God to Jesus as Messiah-soon-to-come-again and as bringer of the Kingdom of God. The first magnification was still well within the human scale; the second created an angle of elevation, as it were, that was later on to bring in its train still another type of magnification. The third stage in the magnification of Jesus, arising, in a way, out of his magnification in the second stage, revolved around Jesus as in and for himself a divinity whose significance transcended by far all history, including, of course, Jewish history.

For the evolution of this third phase we have a record in the letters of Saul of Tarsus, later to be known as St. Paul, Apostle to the Gentiles.

Saul's Letters were to constitute the core of what was, much later, to become the New Testament; they can be considered, accordingly, the main-spring of the religion whose formation was catalyzed by his ideas. We shall see how Saul, against the background of the Kingdom of God agitation among the Jews, mediated through his own experiences the essential elements of what was to become Christianity.

Saul worked out all his ideas—inherited, perhaps, from some unknown predecessors—between some time shortly after the crucifixion of Jesus and some time long before the outbreak of the Jewish insurrection against Rome in 66. However, they were not to acquire importance until after the destruction of the Temple in Jerusalem in 70. As we shall see, that event cleared the way for the conquest of his ideas.

Saul, too, had a fervent belief in the imminent advent of the Kingdom of God, but he made two changes in the general faith that were to survive the failure of the Kingdom to materialize. He linked the formula for entering the Kingdom initially to the figure of Jesus as Son of God, and he abandoned the Jewish national/religious rejection of Rome. These two elements combined were to replace the Jewish people with the whole human race as the target of the propaganda arising out of the new faith.

Saul's Letters make him the only identifiable individual in the New Testament, though not much is known about him. Still, his Letters, in their passionate intensity, were to have a permanent effect on the Jesist fellowships gradually taking shape in the vast reaches of the Roman Empire. In his own lifetime it was still possible to think of the Kingdom of God as merely having been postponed, and it was this postponement, by presenting Saul with a tormenting enigma, that was to bring about the germination of the Christian faith and its embodiment in a universal Church.

Saul's role in the shaping of all the institutions of Christianity—quite unforeseeably for him, since he thought the world was about to end—was primordial. This makes his indifference to Jesus the man all the more striking. The lush creativity deployed in the conceptual universe he constructed in the portrait of Christ Jesus, Son of God, Light of the World, Savior of the Universe, contrasts starkly with what he says about Jesus the man. This is all we learn of Jesus from Saul's Letters:[2]

Jesus was a Jew born of a woman under the Torah. (Gal. 3:16, 4:4)

He was descended from David. (Rom. 1:3)

He preached only to Israel, according to the promises (made by God to the Jews). (Rom. 15:8)

He obeyed God to the point of accepting death on the Cross. (Phil. 2:8)

He chose Apostles. (Gal. 1:17,19)

He was reviled and crucified. (Rom. 15:3, I Cor. 15:3, Gal. 2:20, 3:13, etc.)

He instituted the Eucharist on the night of his betrayal. (I Cor 11:23)

The mention of the Eucharist is, of course, priceless for the history of this fundamental sacrament.

Saul also makes a few remarks about Jesus after his death:

He rose on the third day. (I Cor 15:4)

He showed himself to Simon the Rock, the Apostles, and others (in visions), including Saul himself. (I Cor 15:5–8)

He is now sitting on the right hand of God, awaiting the great day when he will come again. (Rom 8:34)

It will be seen that apart from its skimpiness Saul's summary of what he considers the salient elements in the life of Jesus omits, very remarkably, the nature of Jesus' death, "accepted" as part of his "obedience to God." All real-life tension has been removed; the whole struggle carried on by the Kingdom of God activists is reduced to Jesus' being "reviled and crucified."

It is instructive to observe how the realistic Kingdom of God, meant to replace the natural world and restore the fortunes of the Jews—the belief of countless at the time Jews, including Jesus—was etherealized and denationalized by Saul, who (at the same time) retained the trigger idea of God's decision, which would accomplish the process in the twinkling of an eye whenever God saw fit.

Now, how did Saul's ideas evolve into Christianity?

7

Saul's Problem

How exciting it would be to have a clear view of Saul! If only we could see the man behind his passionate, obsessive, logical Letters! The Letters are so lively, despite their remoteness in time, that we often feel very close indeed; even in the most modern readers they may strike a potent chord. Yet of course a rapprochement is out of the question; the Letters cannot flesh out the personality of their author. They are indispensable for a view of Saul's times and for that matter of his temperament, but they are not parts of an autobiography, they are real Letters.

It would be presumptuous to "analyze" Saul. Without unconscious material, without dreams, without free associations, without the various underpinnings of data that only a living subject can provide, analysis is plainly impossible.

Saul's scanty indications about his person are hardly any help. He often refers to something he calls a "thorn in his flesh," and to himself as "untimely born"; he mentions bearing on his body the marks of Jesus Christ (Gal 6:17) and indicates that he was very short, with a terrible voice, but none of this makes a portrait. Nor is it eked out by the perhaps authentic tradition that he was "quite bald, bow-legged, with eyebrows meeting above a long nose and a red, florid face."[1] Nor can we make much of the suggestion that he had to have himself declared "clean" of leprosy (by the Temple priests in Jerusalem [Acts 21: 20–27]).

Of course his feelings about women, too, would be a gold mine—if we knew what they were. As it is, there is practically nothing to build on, in spite of the widespread tendency to turn Saul into some sort of woman-hater, based mainly on his most celebrated remark, that "it is better to marry than to burn."

The only women Saul mentions specifically, to be sure, are those of a "canonic" age—women too old to be either wives or mothers. Widows are real widows, so to speak, only if they are over 60 years old and have had only one husband (I Tim 5:3,9). Otherwise they "should keep silence in the synagogues . . . If there is anything they want to know, let them ask their husbands at home. For it is shameful for a woman to speak in the syna-gogue" (I Cor 14:35). None of this tells us much.

An account of his "conversion" might be helpful; his own is so meager—a mere mention of it—that however interesting, in a negative way, it tells us nothing. To be sure, the triple description given in Acts may help; it is per-sonal, circumstantial, and plausible, derived, perhaps, from Saul himself.

The first mention in Acts says that "a light from heaven flashed about him, and he fell to the ground and heard a voice (of Jesus) saying to him. 'Saul, Saul, why do you persecute me?' 'Tell me, Lord,' he said, 'who you are.' The voice answered, 'I am Jesus, whom you are persecuting.' . . . The men traveling with him heard the voice but saw no one. . . . Saul arose, and when his eyes were opened could see nothing . . . for three days he was sightless, and neither ate nor drank" (Acts 9:3–9).

The second mention is no more explicit. Here the people with Saul see the light but cannot hear the voice; Saul "couldn't see because of the brightness of the light" (Acts 22:3–16). The third mention, much skimpier, doesn't contradict the first two. The absence of his companions' reaction to what Saul experienced doubtless implies that the event was "private"—no mention is made of a general manifestation that the chronicler would no doubt have taken pleasure in setting down (witness the anonymous record-ing of the "five hundred" eyewitnesses to Jesus' resurrection).

The meager description may sound, of course, like an epileptic fit; many have thought so. Yet it seems impossible to assert this with any assurance, though the loss of hearing, falling down, and the prolonged fast-ing may imply as much. Nevertheless the explosive nature of the episode and the great pain it was doubtless accompanied by seem to point to a lengthy period of psychological travail beforehand. We are surely entitled to assume that Saul's seizure was a way out of some torment. But what could that have been?

Now, a problem seldom discussed is Saul's life before his "conversion" on the road to Damascus. None of his letters have survived from the first fourteen or fifteen years afterwards. What had he been doing all this time? What had been his feelings about the life-and-death struggle of the Jews against Rome?

The present accounts of Saul's early activities are, to put it baldly, nonsense. The notion that Saul could have persecuted the Jesists is preposterous, if only because on the one hand the leader of the Jerusalem Jesists, Upright Jacob, was a bona-fide priest of the Temple in which all the Jesists together with numerous Pharisees and priests kept praying "assiduously," and on the other hand because it is impossible to see how Saul, with no official standing of any kind, could have "persecuted" anyone.

We are told:

> Saul ravaged the community, entering house after house and dragging off both men and women to prison. (Acts 8:1–3)

> "I had them punished repeatedly in all the synagogues and compelled them to revile Jesus. Being mad with them beyond measure I even hunted them to towns across the border." (Acts 26:10–11)

We seem confronted by simple-minded hagiography, far removed from the events and with no interest in factuality.

For that matter, when Saul reports similar persecution on his part (Gal 1:13) we are bound to regard it as a sort of literary embellishment, a means of heightening the contrast before and after his conversion. It gives us a glimpse, indeed, of the peculiarly chaotic fragments of documentation that were stitched together, long after the events, in order to give the nascent community a foothold in some tradition, however tendentiously focused.

Now, Acts records a strange coincidence. During Saul's final visit to Jerusalem (between 53–58), a Roman centurion mistakes him for Theudas, an Alexandrian Jew who had stirred up a revolt and led some "four thousand Daggermen" out into the wilderness (21:38). Theudas had surely claimed messianic status.

In any case, Saul seems to have been a friend (or disciple) of Theudas's,[2] whose appearance seems to have coincided with the absorption of Judea into the empire, when the question of direct tribute to Rome came up again. (It had been suspended in 41 when the Jewish King Agrippa I was allocated Judea among some other territories at the death of Emperor Gaius; Agrippa I died in 44.) Acts (5:34–37) links Theudas, perhaps anachronistically, to Judah of Galilee, founder of the Zealot movement. "Leading out into the wilderness," as noted above, was a militant messianist anti-Roman operation—It was one way of disrupting society. Theudas was, no doubt, a variety of Zealot or Daggerman, though for the Romans, to be sure, all insurrectionists were the same as Daggermen.

In view of the Jesists' reputation as insurrectionists, i.e., as carriers on of Jesus' own secular activities, it is even more significant that Saul was also called "a plague-carrier, a fomenter of revolt among all the Jews of the empire and a ring leader of the [Jesists]" (Acts 24:5). "These subverters of the empire have reached here now. . . . All of them are violators of Caesar's decrees, and declare there is a rival king, Jesus" (Acts 17:7). Accordingly, Saul's association with Theudas would be vital as an indication of his activities before he took on his far better known role.

Saul's withdrawal after his conversion for two years into "Arabia," as so many translations have it, was not into present-day Arabia, but into the Arabah in the lower Jordan valley, a hide-out for insurrectionists fairly close to the Dead Sea. Now, in the Arabah he could hardly have been devoting himself to mere speculation, or communing with his soul, or brooding about personal salvation, or for that matter constructing schemes of salvation for mankind in the abstract. If that was all he was doing, why would he have aroused the hostility of the pagan king of Nabatea centered in Petra? Or in Damascus, where, inexplicably enough, only the Jews are his enemies? (2 Cor 11:32). Thus Saul, as well as others like him (Silas), is occasionally presented as a Zealot.

Saul himself mentions having been taken for a Zealot by various Diaspora communities. And it may be tempting to take another look at his remark that he was extremely zealous for the traditions of his fathers (Gal 1:14): if he is, in fact, using the word "zealous" here in the sense reserved for the Zealots, themselves originally known as "Zealots for the Torah" (Macc 2:27), this may be an indication, obscured by centuries of misunderstanding and mistranslation, of an original connection.

Saul's personal background fits into this view of his early interests. He was born into a prosperous family; his father, originally from Gush-Halav (Gischala) in Palestine, a hotbed of Zealot intransigence, bought and bequeathed to Saul citizenship in Tarsus[3] in Cilicia (now in the northwest corner of modern Syria), a bustling town through which the streams of traffic originating all over Asia Minor would descend into Syria and then fan out through the Fertile Crescent, including Palestine.

Now, if Saul had often been taken as a Zealot by the Jews of the Diaspora, might he not have *been* at one time a Zealot? Might not these peeps into a different situation, these fragments, which have slipped past the apologetic tendency of the chronicler and become embedded unnoticed in our present texts, constitute a recollection of Saul's previous career? A career as a Zealot, which was transformed only with the fiasco of the Jesus enterprise, when Saul internalized his revolt against the powers of this world—Rome—by generalizing and transcendentalizing the messianic hope? Or if he had persecuted the Jesists in the sense of opposing them, might he have been a militant in a rival "tendency"—that of John the Baptist? Or of Theudas, whom the Roman centurion mistook him for?

Or might he have turned aside from physical resistance altogether? Might he not, in the wake of the Jesus fiasco, have abandoned the flesh-and-blood, active, this-worldly resistance of the militant messianists in favor of what could easily be felt to have been a still more far-reaching upheaval—the immediate installation of the Kingdom of God, only this time through the agency of Jesus' resurrection, experienced by him explosively as a dazzling way out of the heart-breaking disappointment over the fiasco itself?

We are reduced to Saul's character, after all, and must look at his Letters to see whether we can extract some history from them—if only in the form of psychology!

At first sight the story of Saul's career seems coherent: A devout Jew, he persecutes the "mother Church." Suddenly, on the road to Damascus, he is smitten by a vision of the risen Jesus addressing him from on high. Converted, he becomes a missionary to the pagans on behalf of the new faith, contending with the violent opposition of the Jews; he is arrested in Jerusalem during a riot in the Jewish Temple and sent to Rome where he dies; he lives on through his writings.

Very tidy. Yet even a cursory glance at the traditional account is troubling: the more we look into Saul's background the odder everything seems. The crux of the matter, plainly, is Saul's feeling about Jesus, or rather, since he seems not to have known Jesus personally, his relationship to Jesus' career. Thus the transformation of hatred into love calls for a brief glance at Jesus' death and its meaning for Saul.

Though no deep psychological "material" can be found in Saul's Letters, the general impression they make is unmistakable. He was obsessed by two things above all—a fear of death, and an obsessive compulsiveness about the observance of minutiae. The two preoccupations are intertwined; they must have been the matrix for the solution he found for his problem.

For Saul the overriding issue was simple. How could death be defeated? This was what he thought constituted the radical failure of the Torah: It could not guarantee immortality. Yet there was one element that held out hope. If death was the wages of sin, and one could somehow avoid sin through perfect obedience to God's will, then there might be a chance for a sinless man to avoid death. This was, of course, the case of Jesus, and Jesus' resurrection was the proof that God had in fact banished mortality for him and, by extension, for all those who believed in him and could somehow be made one with him.

Saul, morbidly afraid of death, must have had an access of flaming hope at the first news of Simon the Rock's vision on the Sea of Galilee. Then his common sense reasserted itself. How could such a thing be? But perhaps after all!?

If Saul is not merely exaggerating his previous hostility to the Jesists as a rhetorical device to heighten the significance of his seizure, its explosiveness can doubtless be attributed to the tension created by the attractiveness of the new belief the moment he heard it. He must have felt, from what is evident about his morbid fear of death and his longing for immortality, that the possibility of resurrection was really brought near at hand by the reported experience of Jesus, a fellow messianist. In that case his initial reaction must have been one of horrified, but fascinated disbelief: he then did manifest hostility and in fact fought against it precisely because of its fascination.

Saul's morbid fear of death was intertwined with his equally morbid and hence inevitably frustrated punctiliousness.

Though Jews in general thought the observance of the Torah in and for itself a comfort as well as a guide, for Saul it was inherently unsatisfactory. It was simply not possible for him to live up to its requirements. For Saul, as for all Jews, death, the result of sin, had been brought into the world by Adam through a single act of disobedience (Rom 5:12–21); hence, since disobedience to God is the cardinal sin in Judaism, a failure to keep even one single commandment, however trivial in appearance, brought about a similar condemnation: "For all who rely on the works of the Torah are under a curse, for it is written, 'Cursed be every one who does not abide by all things written in . . . the Torah' " (Gal 3:10). Saul even went so far as to blame the Torah itself for the very fact of sinning: "If it had not been for the Torah I should not have known sin. I should not have known what it is to covet if the Torah had not said, 'You shall not covet' " (Rom 7:7).

After his conversion, Saul made much of his remarkable but hopeless zeal for the Torah beforehand: "I was blameless," he says, "as far as the Torah can make you blameless" (Phil 3:6). "You must have heard . . . how enthusiastic I was for the tradition of my ancestors" (Gal 1:13,14).

Thus, even though Saul became more and more scrupulous—typically!—it was to no avail; he could not measure up to God's demands (Gal 1:14., Phil 13:6). Nothing was more natural for him, accordingly, than to blame the Torah, the solace of Israel and all its sinners, for sin itself!

In other words, man could not in his nature be right through the mere observance of the Torah; he could be saved *only* by an independent decision of Yahweh's. Yahweh graciously *chooses* to save the sinner. The corollary of the sinfulness of the Torah itself is, of course, that as long as one is caged by the Torah one is bound to be, like Saul, "a prisoner of the law of sin that lives in his body" (Rom 7:23). His obsessiveness about religious observance was tied up with just this morbid fear of death. For Saul it was Jesus' unique distinction to have been so perfectly obedient to God that he had been resurrected by God's direct action and made, moreover, Lord over all things.

The explosiveness of Saul's "conversion" generated his blinding vision, on the road to Damascus, that Jesus had been not only resurrected—as in Simon the Rock's Vision—but deified. As we shall see, all the ideas he developed after his conversion derived their power, both religiously and magically, from this stupendous, simple idea, the Incarnation—the indwelling of God in the body of Jesus, a human being.

It is illuminating to discern the process whereby Saul transformed his innovations into an intellectual complex that was to become, unforeseeably, a new religion. Specifically, the mechanism that exhilarated Saul after his seizure on the road to Damascus was his sudden, blinding insight that through the modality of Jesus' own resurrection, God had done for Saul something that he, a "prisoner of the Law of sin," could never have achieved for himself: perfect obedience. The belief engendered by his seizure had thus cut through the vicious circle of the compulsive obsessive's need to conform with *all* requirements and his simultaneous inability to do so. Put this way, of course, it all sounds like the paradigm for a neurotic syndrome.

Thus the specific effect achieved by Saul's new-found faith, first of all in the fact of Jesus' resurrection and then in the significance of that fact, was the conquest of his morbid terror. Jesus, a Jew, no doubt an ecstatically messianic Jew like Saul himself, had been saved from death—so Saul, too, could be.

Saul puts it movingly: "What a wretched man I am! Who will rescue me from this body doomed to death? Thanks be to God through Jesus Christ our Lord!" (Rom 7:24).

Similarly, he was able to "cease trying by my own efforts for the perfection that comes from the Torah"; he wanted "only the perfection that comes through faith, and from God" (Phil 3:9).

Saul's fervor, as shown by his seizure, as well as by the urgency with which he hammers his feelings into the heads of his audience, indicates that he had undergone a psychic upheaval that left him trembling with expectation. In being so abruptly overwhelmed by the factuality of Jesus' resurrection, more particularly by its meaning for himself, and enthralled as he was by a messianic fervor, by the utter conviction that the universe was on the brink of an explosion, Saul must have expected to be snatched up at once into eternal life in the Kingdom of God. In the first flush of his seizure he was convinced that the world to come was quite literally at hand then and there, so that he and everyone then alive would witness it personally: "We shall not all sleep, but we shall be changed, in a moment, in the twinkling of an eye, at the last trumpet" (1 Cor 15:51–2). Hence everyone living at that moment would not have to die at all, but could simply don his or her glorified body: "For this perishable nature must put on the imperishable" (1 Cor 15:53).

Yet his first glow died down somewhat. His ardor had to be restrained by his awareness that the World's End had not, in fact, come about, even though his conviction never wavered that it was on the very threshold of appearing, together with the redemption it was supposed to implement. The imminence of the World's End was not remotely a metaphor; like everything in Saul's thought, it was solid, palpable, *factual*. The point, remarkably obvious, requires only a few quotations for establishment.

Saul's generation was to "outlive the World's End" (1 Cor 10:11); in the time to come they were to pronounce judgment upon the angels (1 Cor 6:3). "The fashion of this world is passing away" (1 Cor 7:31); "as long as we have time, let us do good" (Gal 6:10). Redemption is nearer "now" than when Saul and the Jesists in Rome had been the first believers (Rom 13:11); the looked-for day is already "at hand" (Rom 13:12); God is "shortly" going to tread Satan underfoot (Rom 16:20). Philippians, too, is infused by the same World's End feverishness.

Saul never describes the messianic kingdom, the preamble to the eternal Kingdom of God, and of course the relations of the two concepts varied greatly in the minds of different thinkers. But there was no question in Saul's mind of its imminence; this is indicated by the very nuances in his timing. When he says, for instance, that redemption was nearer "now" than when he and the Roman Jesists had been the first believers, he seems to take as his starting point the date of his visit to Rome twenty-five years before; hence, when he adds, in the next line, that the "night is far gone, the day is at hand," he seems to be reckoning with a span of forty years.

That is, since Saul reckons the messianic kingdom as having been triggered by Jesus' resurrection, the lapse of twenty-five years since then may imply a remainder of fifteen years before the messianic kingdom comes to an end and the eternal Kingdom of God is installed. That is, Saul assumed a maximum duration of forty years for the messianic kingdom. Here, too, he was accepting a conventional estimate.[4] But it constituted a maximum estimate—the outside limit.

There is, of course, great elasticity in the notion of "at hand." Even the maximum interval of forty years, most of which had elapsed, was brief. Saul thought that death itself was on the very verge of destruction (1 Cor 15:26); hence he regarded the deaths of the elect, those firm in their allegiance to Jesus, as special exceptions; Saul thought Jesus' glorious return was on the very threshold of arrival, within a few years at most—i.e., another fifteen from the time of writing his First Letter to the Corinthians twenty-five years after the crucifixion, and really, as far as his emotions were concerned, weeks or even days. He was enthralled, quite simply, by the conviction that his generation was the final generation of mankind, to be infallibly succeeded by the World's End.

Curiously enough, it was just this temporary hitch, this slight delay that by demanding an explanation was to bring in its train a seminal complex of ideas encased within Saul's fundamental argument. An argument in its nature is anchored in a structure; hence, premises and conclusions had to be interlocked in order to buttress Saul's purpose—to explain the hiatus between Jesus' resurrection and the Kingdom of God. Saul's explanation, psychologically inevitable though it was, could be evolved in its turn only out of the ideas he was familiar with. His psychic problem, provisionally solved, as it were, by his blinding identification with Jesus, had to be articulated intellectually through the views that he shared with countless Jews but that in his special situation had to be aligned along a different axis.

Saul had to explain a strange, really quite incomprehensible time lag. What could it have meant for God to have plunged once again into history to resurrect and immortalize a human being? If that had been God's way of launching the whole process of installing his Kingdom, why had he not finished it? Why the postponement?

If the messianic kingdom had been initiated by Jesus' resurrection, why had it not yet been consummated? How, indeed, could it have been initiated *without* being consummated? How could there be an intermission? And what could it mean? Above all, if Jesus' resurrection was meant to usher in the Kingdom of God, *how could those who believed in that go on dying?* It was Saul's explanation of natural death, in the teeth of the hopes arising out of Jesus' resurrection, that forced on him an intellectual breakthrough that was to make him, long after his death, a world-shaker.

8

Saul's Breakthrough:
The Postponement of the Kingdom

Saul explained, or rather explained away the postponement of the Kingdom by a complicated theory of cosmic contention between God-forces and Devil-forces, which included the angels.

This aspect of Saul's thought was inevitably short-lived. Since the Kingdom never came, the very concept of its coming lost its urgency a generation after Saul's death. The idea itself simply expired. No longer evoking any emotion, it received lip service for some time, then faded away. Saul's theory of cosmic contention became wholly archaic. In the modern era, indeed, it is almost incomprehensible; for all practical purposes it is unfamiliar even to many scholars.

For Saul, the author of world history was Adam; the author of recent meaningful history—i.e., the sacred-secular history of the chosen people—was Abraham. Both together engendered all lines of all human history, lines that all converged in the figure of the Messiah as herald of the World's End. Saul's blinding flash on the road to Damascus merely told him that the point of culmination had been reached in Jesus.

If Saul's fundamental expectation had been realized, if the natural world had, indeed, ended with the glorious return of the Messiah and the subsequent installation of the Kingdom of God, there would, of course, have been no necessity for argument, proof, deduction—in fact for anything at all. But the world remained obdurately *there*. What was the explanation?

Jewish fantasies about the World's End, which with the book of Daniel, generations before Jesus, and with countless other apocalyptic schemes had begun to proliferate as a reaction to Hellenism, could scarcely be called hard-and-fast; the notion of exactly what forms were to be taken by the Kingdom of God naturally baffled analysis. Roughly, however, the relationship between the Messiah and the Kingdom of God was a simple one. Originally, in the simple scheme prevalent during the lifetime of Jesus (which he too might well have believed in), the Messiah, drawn from Daniel, was, quite simply, to usher in the Kingdom of God, bringing about a state of bliss upon the conclusion of the one final judgment for all survivors of the final generation and for all the rest of the resurrected from all mankind. Thus there was one state of bliss, ushered in by the Jewish Messiah, one final judgment, and one Kingdom of God.

All previous theories of the World's End had one resurrection of mankind, placed either before the messianic kingdom[1] preceding the Kingdom of God or afterwards.[2] Before the problem acquired special urgency with the career of Jesus, Jewish thinkers had taken it for granted that those participating in the Kingdom of God would have died normally, to be granted eternal life along with the rest of the dead through the general resurrection. This "normal," as it were commonsensical, fantasy could withstand the assault of logic simply because such a historical conjuncture had never come about. All lay in the indecipherable future.

But Jesus' miraculous resurrection had changed all that—after all, that was the whole point of it. Nor could the resurrection, however miraculous, be considered an isolated event; it had to mean something stupendous, i.e., the World's End. Hence Saul regarded himself and his generation as being suspended in a process that was ineluctably working itself out. Jesus' death and resurrection merely constituted the first stage; the final stage, coming at any moment , was the Kingdom of God. Thus the hiatus between Jesus' resurrection and the installation of the messianic kingdom was a fundamental problem for Saul. The postponement was wholly incomprehensible in the framework of all received ideas, since hitherto the Messiah's appearance was itself to have been the signal for the transformation of the cosmos. How could the Messiah come unless the Kingdom of God followed him at once?

In the teeth of the evidence—normal-seeming death as well as a normal-seeming world—Saul had to *prove* that redemption was no longer merely *at hand*—as both Jesus and John the Baptist had proclaimed—but in fact was *already* there because of Jesus' resurrection. He had to take the stupendous novelty of Jesus' resurrection and, functioning within his Jewish milieu, show that it had superseded the Torah.

Saul's philosophical problem was really imposed on him by his polemical problem. He was obliged to argue with various believers in Jesus and, at a time when there was no such thing as agreed-upon doctrine, he was subjected to various kinds of partial disbelief that obliged him to contrive *ad hoc* answers. Many Corinthians, for instance, while not denying the resurrection of Jesus himself—what could they have believed in if they had?—denied the *general* resurrection altogether (1 Cor 15:12–18, 29–33) and thus denied any resurrection for themselves. (We have no idea what they believed in general; we have to deduce that from Saul's polemics.) These Corinthians believed that only those who were alive at Jesus' glorious return could possibly share in the messianic kingdom. Saul was reduced to taking the point they had in common—Jesus' resurrection—and then, on the basis of the shared belief, proving its true implications to the skeptical Corinthians. This was what led to Saul's earliest conundrum about the ongoing deaths of those who believed that Jesus' resurrection and glorification led to the messianic kingdom.

The partial disbelief of the Corinthians, which obliged Saul to create *ad hoc* solutions, had to be generalized the moment the first believer died before the Kingdom came. And since, as death went on, the early believers in Jesus' special role had to cling to their hopes in the teeth of the evidence, Saul found himself obliged to maintain that those who had died, as long as they believed in Jesus' redemptive function, would infallibly be resurrected at the glorious return. Thus, at first he was forced to lay it down that any deceased members of the Corinthian congregation had died only because they had celebrated the Lord's Supper in an unworthy manner (1 Cor 11:29–32)—i.e., they had not died normally.

It was Saul's desperation over the brute fact of people's continuous dying because of Jesus' apparent failure to install the messianic kingdom, as he had been supposed to by all tradition, that forced Saul to resort to such subtle extravagances to explain away the facts of life and death—i.e., the ordinary world. He had to work out a special, indeed, altogether peculiar theory of the general redemption involved in the World's End.

Saul agreed with some other Jews in distinguishing between two states of bliss: the bliss of the kingdom installed by the Messiah and the bliss of the eternal Kingdom of God itself. The survivors—the elect—of the final generation (his own) naturally shared in both. For them the messianic kingdom and the Kingdom of God were to have the identical impact. But those who had died before the messianic kingdom could not benefit from the messianic kingdom itself; they had to be kept in reserve, sleeping, so to speak, until the Kingdom of God itself was installed.

Saul, following others,[3] regarded the messianic kingdom as transient, but thought that both the resurrection of the dead and the judgment of the resurrected from all mankind throughout history could not take place until after the termination of the messianic kingdom, which had to give way to the eternal Kingdom of God. At the same time Saul regarded the entry into the messianic kingdom as the privilege of the elect of the final generation.

It was against this background that his originality came into play. A remarkable invention was well nigh forced on him, so to speak, by the necessity of explaining why believers were still dying after Jesus' resurrection. He was obliged to invent two resurrections.

He had to claim that the first participants in the messianic kingdom were already in the resurrection "way of life." Yet he also said that the elect of the final generation, even those who had died before the advent of the messianic kingdom, were going to be able to share in it by means of Jesus' resurrection. How was that possible? If the messianic kingdom was transient, how could its participants be immortal?

It is instructive to see how Saul used the intellectual tools at his disposal to contrive a new idea. Believers in Jesus had already demonstrated their loyalty; they had a right to share in the Kingdom of God—what would their faith have been worth otherwise?

Because of the unforeseen hitch in the date of the glorious return, the death of believers in the interim was, one might have thought, just like the death of any other human being beforehand, i.e., they too would have to wait for the general resurrection of the dead at the end of the transient messianic kingdom and the beginning of the eternal Kingdom of God. Now, for such believers to share the prerogative of the final generation, and so share the Messianic Glory despite their premature deaths, some device had to be found. Saul solved the puzzle by fiat. He simply laid it down that those who had died firm in their faith before the advent of the messianic kingdom did *not* have to wait for the resurrection at the end of the messianic kingdom, but could be granted—by his own brainwork!—a special privilege. They would be awarded an earlier, *special* resurrection for themselves alone; that would enable them to share the glory of the messianic kingdom on precisely the same footing as the elect of the final generation.

For Saul it is not the dead in general who are resurrected by the messianic kingdom, but only those who have died full of faith in Jesus Christ. Thus Saul, though he maintains the notion of the messianic kingdom as the prerogative of the final generation, and links it to the conception of the resurrection of the dead in general, imposes a special condition on the general idea. The resurrection of the prematurely dead elect would be followed by the resurrection of other people later on, at a second resurrection, in which all the people who had ever lived would turn up for final judgment at the end of the messianic kingdom and appear before the throne of God, to be dealt eternal life or eternal torment.

With our own perspective we can see what a complicated problem this must have been during the genesis of the new religion; it seemed to interpose a purely artificial, arbitrary, fundamentally unreasonable barrier between common sense and the ardor of expectation. From a superficial, merely logical point of view, since the messianic kingdom was transient, those in it could hardly be expected to have eternal life; they would normally be thought of as sharing the type of existence of the world they lived in. Yet Saul, in the teeth of logic, forced by the exigencies of polemics, by his own need for reassurance, declares that anyone still alive when the messianic kingdom arrives will have been transformed. Despite all appearances they will have been invested with eternal life as part of the resurrection of the dead in general. He assures the Corinthians, for instance, that it had no consequence one way or the other whether they were alive or not when the messianic kingdom was installed—they would then change their mortality for immortality (1 Cor 15:5–53).

His polemical isolation, in short, obliged Saul to tamper with a tradition that he otherwise accepted; he had to distort it to accommodate a fact—the death and resurrection of Jesus. Saul's remark that "if we believe that Jesus Christ has died and risen again, God will also bring with him through Jesus those who have fallen asleep" (1 Thes 4:14) is meant to extrapolate from the resurrection of Jesus the resurrection of those who have died believing in the redemptiveness of his role.

Saul, obliged to accommodate historical facts, had to manipulate them theoretically to extract, somehow, the desired propagandistic objective. The mere fact that Jesus the Messiah had himself died and been resurrected *before* the kingdom as a whole had materialized forced Saul to abandon an otherwise matter-of-course traditional view of the World's End and prove to the Corinthian deniers of the general resurrection that believers were already granted eternal life even in the transient messianic kingdom.

The problem of believers dying before the glorious return was really insoluble. Saul was bound to assume that the resurrection was to come before the Kingdom of God, since otherwise he would be obliged to face the indigestible contradiction that natural people and resurrected people would be living side by side in the messianic kingdom. He avoids this by assuming that those living in the messianic kingdom have taken on the resurrection medium of existence just like the Messiah himself. He drives this point home by a curiously simple-minded argument. He equates Jesus' resurrection with that of ordinary people in the Corinthian congregation: "For if there is no resurrection of the dead, then Christ is not risen" (1 Cor 15:13).

Thus Saul had created a new idea—tenuous, to be sure, and outside his historical situation ultimately, no doubt, preposterous, but indispensable in solving his current problem. Yet it left him in a logical mess; he is obliged to concede that death is still in existence, i.e., remains a power until the messianic kingdom is terminated. How, then, can dying believers elude death's clutches *before* death is destroyed, before death is defeated at the time of the general resurrection into the eternal Kingdom when death, *because of that,* is forced to release them?

For that matter, how can people slip into the resurrection medium of existence in general, without passing through the gates of death and resurrection, in that order?

It was, after all, far from self-evident that before the messianic kingdom believers in Jesus were already resurrected, while survivors were transformed; hence Saul had to carry on a long, passionate, sustained, and intricate argument to prove it. Just because it was wholly unexpected, indeed, stunningly against all reason, his novel argument had to be anchored in a comprehensive theory.

Building on his new theory, he contrived a still more ingenious idea, which was to have the most far-reaching consequences. The necessity of explaining an incomprehensible phenomenon—how mortals could live side by side with the eternal resurrected in a transient messianic kingdom—forced Saul to construct a grandiose institution, an institution contrived precisely to implement his new idea. He generalized the existence of the believers in Jesus—the new sect of Jesists—and created an outsize, symbolic dimension for them as a collectivity. He contrived a new condition of the universe, the being-in-Christ, and created a metaphysical institution to implement it, the mystic body of Christ.

This bridge-concept enabled Saul to assure all believers that even though they had died before the glorious return they would not be plain dead, like all other human beings who had died, but would be raised up at the glorious return in a sort of preliminary resurrection. Even if they had "fallen asleep," as long as they had done so "in Christ," all would be well (1 Thes 4:16, 1 Cor 15:18,23). Those still alive would, of course, be transformed without further ado from the ordinary mode of being directly into the eternal.

It is impossible to exaggerate the literalness of Saul's conception of the "corporeal solidarity" between the elect and the glorified immortal body of the risen Christ; they partake of a common bodily identity.

> Having been crucified with Christ, it is no longer I who live, but Christ who lives in me. (Gal 2:19,20)

> You know surely that your bodies are members making up the body of Christ. (2 Cor 6:15)

> Just as a human body, though made up of many parts, is a single unit because all those parts, though many, make one body, so it is with Christ. (I Cor 12:12)

> Now you together are Christ's body, but each of you is a different part of it. (I Cor 12:27)

These turns of phrase are not mere metaphors, figures of speech or the like; they depict for Saul a state of absolute reality. Any attempt to lessen the full-bodied, concrete, palpable meaning of Saul's phraseology leads to a complete misunderstanding of his theory of the divine time-table and of his own activity. The crudity of his language reflects the materialism of his thought. Believers were thought and felt themselves to be "in Christ" *bodily.* Saul's emphasis on the focality of the body pointed up what was for him of paramount importance, both personally and philosophically.

Saul's conception is profound, indeed revolutionary, though it borders, to be sure, on the demented. *He had created a special race of people.* The believers who shared mysteriously in the death and resurrection of the Savior were extricated from the ordinary category of existence. Their belief is not mere belief; it *ipso facto* makes them mystical participants in another condition of nature, the death and resurrection of a divine being. Despite all appearances, accordingly, these believers are not natural people like others, but people who have *already* passed through death and resurrection along with Jesus: thus, when the messianic kingdom opens up, they will be intrinsically capable of sharing in the resurrectional medium of existence, while everyone else will simply die a normal death.

In the same way, those who have already died prior to the glorious return, while seemingly dead like everyone else who had died, are not really dead like that at all, but are capable of rising again before the others—i.e., before the general resurrection at the end of the messianic kingdom—because of their death and resurrection along with Jesus, provided, of course, that they too have died "in Christ."

Saul's certainty that the Body of Christ was not a metaphor but a plain unvarnished fact of life underlies his key remark: "There are no more distinctions between Jew and Greek, slave and free, male and female, but you are one in Christ Jesus." (Gal 3:28)

For Saul men are, in the current epoch, *not equal*; they fall into various classifications. This is, indeed, the very reason Saul's doctrine of predestination is important. It establishes the schedule of approach to God. It is not a man as such who is enabled to enter into a relationship of some kind with God, but the human being who is *elected*; it is the act of mystic choice that opens to human beings the way to a state of blessedness through being ultimately united with God.

This is also made clear by the hierarchy Saul establishes not only between Jews and Gentiles, but between men and women. It is obvious to Saul that since woman (according to Genesis) was formed from the substance of man, she is inherently second-class (1 Cor 11:7–11). Saul in fact has a hierarchical tableau as the starting point of his mysticism. Disregarding the distinctions between Jews and Gentiles, he arranges the table of degrees as follows: God-Christ-man-woman; he puts it succinctly: "Every man's head is Christ, the head of the woman is the man and the Head of Christ is God" (1 Cor 11:3).

It is the aim of the being-in-Christ to wipe out precisely this hierarchy—for it is, according to Saul, only "in Christ" that the elect segment of the human race attains a blissful sameness. It is the basis of his insistence that the being-in-Christ will in fact terminate once and for all the whole present division of mankind. Only in Christ will all divisions vanish. There will be no Jews, no Greeks, no men, no women; i.e., *the world will be another world.*

Some scholars have discerned the influence of Stoicism on Saul, yet the essentially passive, unhistorical nature of Stoic mysticism—at bottom really a theory of timeless, unchanging nature pervaded by an essence thought of as divine—is in sharp contrast with the history-obsessed Jewish view that a transcendent God had created nature and was in some sense behind it. Saul's view is Jewish; it is essentially that of a drama. The historic process, supernaturalized, consists of the emanation of the world from the mind of God, its alienation from God, then the ultimate return to God. This means that it is mere common sense, or logic, to say that everything comes from God, or through God, and may go back to God, but can never—in the current epoch—be *in* God. This is precisely the significance of the World's End. People and the world—every Greek, Jew, man, woman—will be in God (Rom 11:36) only at the *end* of the drama.

Pantheism in any form is incomprehensible to Saul. He takes it for granted, once again expressing a commonplace Jewish idea, that God and nature are totally distinct. On that basis he assumes that men are separated from God by a further insurmountable barrier, the dominion of angels. It is the angelic powers that make a direct relationship between God and man impossible. The principal advantage of being one of the elect in Christ is that this sad state of angelic dominion is ended—the end of Romans 8 is a hymn of joy—when the love of God is no longer blocked from finding its way to the elect by the autonomous power of the angels (Rom 8:38–39).

Christ must overcome these powers as the messianic age progresses, and when death, the last enemy, is destroyed, then the power bestowed on Christ will no longer be needed; at that time God will be all in all (1 Cor 25:26–28); i.e., there will be a being-in-God when the present world passes away once and for all. In short, Saul's relationship to the mystical notion of a union with God is determined by historical factors—the unfolding of the great drama. This requires a transition in time—the era in which a union with Christ is possible precedes the era of the union with God.

This is simply another way of pointing up Saul's Jewish World's End theory; history must proceed, then stop. The Jewish view of God in history thus contains the seeds of its termination—God is infinite, history is not.

Saul's creation of an eccentric state of nature, a special and as it were quasi-biological category of mankind consisting of the rising of all dead believers at the inception of the messianic kingdom, together with those still alive, and the simultaneous transformation of both groups into deathless beings, has, of course, staggering implications. And it was Saul's luminous, hysterical key concept of the being-in-Christ that implemented this remarkable idea and found a modality for it by integrating it into a general system of ideas.

Saul's curious, perhaps unique notion revolutionized, moreover, our sense of time; he reanalyzed the timing of the successive ages of the cosmos. Before Saul the normal view of time was sequential: a *then* follows a *now.* According to this banal view the death and resurrection of Jesus had taken place in the recent past and, by virtue of having taken place, had made it possible for Jesus to return in glory in the near future, bringing with him the messianic kingdom immediately preceding the Kingdom of God.

Now, after Saul, it was possible to think of successive ages as being in some way simultaneous. His conception of the true significance of Jesus' death and resurrection enables him to proclaim that his generation was already encompassed by the messianic kingdom. Since Jesus' death and resurrection could not have preceded the messianic kingdom, but constituted a messianic event *per se,* the meaning of the event was obvious—quite simply, the messianic age had already dawned!

As part of this, equally obviously, Jesus' resurrection could not have been the only event of its kind. It had to be the initial event of a whole series of events whose totality would constitute a new world. This was why Jesus was "the first fruits of those that have fallen asleep" (1 Cor 15:20).

Hence Saul's generation was, to his mind, already in the period of the messianic resurrection, even though the resurrection of others still lay in the future. Saul drew this logical inference from the cardinal fact of contemporary history, that Jesus had not merely been snatched up to heaven (that would have meant little), but had undergone death and resurrection.

How, then, did Saul explain why the world still looked the same? People were going about leading workaday lives; the Jews were still subject to the Romans, whose power kept spreading everywhere; the little bands of those who believed that Jesus had somehow played a special role were still cogitating on the meaning of it all, since he had seemingly, after all, come to the same disastrous end as countless other Jewish activists.

Saul managed to extract an entirely different conclusion from this seemingly normal world. He could see forces working away that were entirely different from those conceived of by others. For him Jesus' resurrection demonstrated one thing beyond all argument. The powers of the supernatural world, the powers of resurrection, were burrowing away beneath the seemingly natural world. Though people blinded by appearances remained unaware of it, the resurrection of Jesus had *already* triggered the installation of the supernatural world.

This blinding insight, perhaps the ecstatic frenzy underlying the remarkable blurring of the distinction between successive periods of time, enabled Saul to intermingle two worlds hitherto entirely distinct, the transient and the eternal worlds, just as he had intertwined the concepts of then and now. For him faith, no longer a trusting reliance on something expected to take place, was equipped to digest *current* certainties of the psyche.

This has nothing to do with the notion, fashionable nowadays, of spiritualizing grossly material concepts—quite the contrary. The conception, like all Saul's ideas, was severely materialistic. It was dependent on an objective condition of the universe, whose objectivity was, indeed, still further intensified by Saul's conception of faith. This alone gave it a peculiar magnetism, not so much for his own generation, perhaps, as for generations far in the future.

Saul's intermingling of the ephemeral and the eternal laid the foundations of a special attitude of mind that gave rise to a special brand of mysticism. Like everything else in Saul's conceptualization of his experience, his mysticism, too, is wholly objective—it has nothing to do with mere projections of emotion, mere acts of thought, mere expressions of the psyche, etc. People gifted with insight simply have to see what is happening *in fact*. In doing this they become aware of a condition of the universe, a fact of life, a state of history, that they are at one and the same time in the ephemeral world of today and in the world of eternity. What they have to grasp is the functioning of real, cosmic forces, the forces of supernatural existence, comprehensively undermining the outward appearances of the workaday world. Since the resurrection of Jesus, in short, reality is normal only in appearance; true reality is exploding!

Functionally speaking, the task of the elect—the believers in the salvational role of Jesus—was to constitute the arena in which the supernatural forces had advanced the farthest. At the glorious return the irresistible impact of these supernatural forces was going to be manifested precisely via the instantaneous transformation of the elect into the resurrection medium of existence.

Saul had upset all previous theories of the World's End. He had pulverized the conventional view of time as mere sequence, and had created a special dialectic of progression: simultaneity amidst sequence. At the same time, of course, that very conception was linked to a fact of history. It was this conception of history that was to have far-reaching consequences. Still weightier with historical consequences than this grandiose notion of the being-in-Christ, however, was the institution it was ultimately to give rise to: the universal Church. As an idea, the being-in-Christ was bound to remain disembodied. It had to be, and like all Saul's ideas it was concretized. Saul had to show how it was that the elect could benefit practically from the fact of their faith; how the community of themselves and the Savior, a community established by that faith, could come into existence.

To make sense of his basic concept—the sharing of the elect in the resurrection medium of existence prior to the general resurrection of the dead from the entire past—he had to give the concept a more general groundwork. For this he contrived the broader idea that the divine powers already at work within the person of the Messiah could somehow permeate all those linked to him by spiritual fellowship. Saul had to make the notion of this permeation intelligible as a structural element in his theory of the World's End.

The material concept of the body-of-Christ is, in fact, the indispensable, material underpinning of the condition of the universe constituted by the being-in-Christ. It is not at all the mere totalization of the multitude of congregations believing in Jesus; it is a vital modality for implementing the concept of being-in-Christ. Saul's phrase that we "are all baptized into one body" (I Cor 12:13) is, for him, no more than a statement of fact. Thus Saul, by finding a palpable parallel, an organic, or institutional supplement to the merely ideational configuration of the being-in-Christ, made a socio-religious innovation, the preordained "community of saints," physically embodying the communion established by the intermingling of divine powers between the Savior and those who believed in him.

In and for itself this idea was rooted in the old Jewish notion of the elimination of sinners from the elect, i.e., from the *real* people. It rested on the notion that the elect nation, the Jews, contaminated by evil-doers of one kind or another, had to be purged, leaving only the elect remnant on hand to assume the role of the elect to the messianic kingdom; i.e., the nation had to be sifted, a concept organically bound up with that of election.

For Saul the true believers were "called" to sainthood (1 Cor 1:2; Rom 1:7); he identified this preexistent community of the saints with the inhabitants of the preexistent heavenly Jerusalem.[4] This was linked to his use of the Greek word *ekklesia* (congregation) not merely for a specific congregation, but for the spiritual, yet tangible collectivity, the mystic body of the Church.[5]

His notion of the mystic communion of the believers in Christ, contrived to fit his view of the cosmic condition in the wake of the stupendous fact of Jesus' resurrection, had to answer fundamental and, from the point of view of vulgar common sense, logical questions. How was it possible for the elect, walking about on earth looking like natural people, to share a fellowship with Jesus, the Messiah who was already in a supernatural category of existence? How was it possible for them to realize their fellowship with the supernatural Messiah before their own resurrections?

The commonsense point of view—the conventional Jewish view of the time—was a simple one, anchored in the equally conventional view of time as sequence. From that point of view it might have seemed natural for the elect to share the fellowship with Jesus only in the sense of a belief in his special role, on the one hand, and then, in the further consequence of that belief, in their looking forward to a future realization of their solidarity with him at some time in the hopeful future, after the messianic glory had obliterated the workaday world.

For Saul this was no good at all. In the interregnum between the resurrection of Jesus and his glorious return Saul claimed something special, that even now, with people walking about looking ordinary, the solidarity of the elect was *already* working itself out. In the teeth of everything that looked like evidence, that was a present fact; for that matter it was *only* through such solidarity that the communion with Jesus in the messianic kingdom would ever be possible.

That was the entire burden of Saul's argument. It is the privilege of the elect to share resurrection with Jesus before the rest of the dead are resurrected. The significance of the predestination of those called to the messianic kingdom is this: They are predestined to acquire the resurrection medium of existence *in advance* of the messianic kingdom. This is entirely in line with Saul's thoroughgoing, material, quite nonspiritual attitude toward history and anthropology. The predestined solidarity of the elect, both with the Messiah Jesus and with each other, has a character that for Saul is practically physical.

Thus the stupendously novel fact of Jesus' resurrection and glorification has had this effect. It has created a special mode of existence in the universe. It has given rise to a community of human beings unlike all others, bound to each other and to Jesus in a unique manner. Because of Jesus' resurrection the entire corporeity of the elect to the messianic kingdom has been permeated through and through by resurrection. In Albert Schweitzer's phrase, they are like a "mass of piled up fuel, which the fire kindled there immediately spreads through."[6]

It is because of this quasi-bodily identity that the elect, despite their looking just like anyone else, are now integrated *literally* with Jesus; it is this that enables them to slip directly into the resurrection medium of existence whether they are living or dead. This very simple, though of course quite revolutionary and, perhaps, disturbing idea, was meant by Saul literally and expressed succinctly: "He has died for us in order that we, whether we wake or sleep, may be alive with him" (1 Thes 5:9,10).

This was very reassuring for believers: even though they might have died before the glorious return, they haven't missed anything. They enter the messianic kingdom via a special, preliminary resurrection, which gives them, as it seems, an enormous advantage over ordinary nonbelievers, who will have to wait for the general resurrection following the end of the messianic kingdom.

As for the believers still alive at the glorious return, coming at any moment, they will not have to die at all to move into the resurrection medium of existence. They have *already* died and risen again with Christ, after all, through their faith; hence they enter in on the resurrection way of life by a mere transformation. They simply drop the outer garment, so to speak, of their seemingly natural existence, and there they are, resurrected.

This train of thought entailed still another fateful consequence. The resurrection of Jesus has triggered the resurrection of the dead in general and the launching of the supernatural realm following the World's End. This is a prime fact, even though the replacement of mortality by immortality is operative, at the outset, only in the corporeity of those elected to the messianic kingdom, and even though there, too, it is not yet in gross physical evidence.

This is entirely consistent with Saul's logical construction. It fits in precisely because of the essential unity of this whole stupendous phenomenon—the temporal identity, far beyond vulgar sequentiality, of Jesus' manifestation as Messiah, his resurrection, and the inception of the messianic kingdom, including the resurrection and transformation of the elect of the final generation. All these are merely phases or aspects of the one event, not merely causally, but temporally.

Saul's train of thought is logical; it arises harmoniously from a set of assumptions. Because of this the logic requires in its nature the substantiation of the fact that warrants the train of thought in the first place. It required the messianic kingdom to make its appearance when Saul thought it would—at any moment, and in any case within a maximum duration of forty years from the date of Jesus' resurrection. That was the only condition that enabled Saul to insist that the whole phenomenon was happening *there and then.*

Knowing, with utter inner certainty, that an outer phenomenon was already in the very process of happening, that the immortal world, properly envisaged, had already risen in successive eruptions from the stuff of the ephemeral flux, Saul could see the total logical insignificance of the merely apparent delay between Jesus' resurrection and his glorious return. It was a mere gap, handily bridged by Saul's contrivance of the being-in-Christ, though a bridge, to be sure, cannot be extended indefinitely.

If it is true that Jesus, whose career was also set in motion, after all, by a theory of the World's End, expected his own death to play a role in the materialization of the end, Saul's view can easily be shown to fit in with that—only, with the resurrection of Jesus, the divine timetable had moved into another phase.

Saul's idea is simple, all-encompassing. It makes it possible to postulate a situation in which the believer's entire being, down to his most ordinary thoughts, feelings, and actions, can be brought into a highly charged atmosphere, an atmosphere, indeed, of personal mysticism, accessible to everyone, that by virtue of its immediacy, of precisely its "objectivity," can achieve a scope, durability, and strength that would seem to elevate it beyond most other varieties of mysticism.

It is because of its "objectivity," its historicity, its dramatic potentialities that Saul's being-in-Christ constituted an experience different in potency from, though identical in structure with the Hellenistic mysteries, in which daily life simply went on independently of the mystical experience of the believer. Saul's mysticism could take in everything, all aspects of life and of the individual's total experiences. It could insulate everyone within a warm cocoon.

Now, all of this was part of a general argument contrived to answer the fundamental riddle that had called forth Saul's innovations. Why, after all, had Jesus failed to return in glory immediately? What was he—or God—waiting for? What was the point of it all?

This redoubtable puzzle called for a redoubtable solution; Saul devised a rather "Jewish" one,—using intellectual arguments to buttress extremist remedies. In saying that "God has consigned all men to disobedience that he may have mercy upon all," (Rom 11:32) Saul is plainly not referring to "all" the elect, nor to the eternal bliss, which he takes for granted as being distinct from messianic bliss.

Saul and the Jerusalem Jesists were in accord on this point, that Jesus as the Messiah had not died for *all* mankind—an idea incomprehensible at that time—but for a definite group of people, i.e., the elect to the Kingdom of God. The Jesists might have believed that there had been a change of perspective between the time when Jesus had expected the Messiah (Son of Man) to appear, before his disciples had "gone over to the cities of Israel" (Mt. 10:23)—i.e., a matter of days or weeks—and the point when he thought that he had to die alone, but in any case that his death would free the elect from the premessianic tribulation. That is, at the end Jesus might have thought that the Kingdom of God could not come until the premessianic tribulation was over, but that if he died in a way that God could accept as the equivalent of that tribulation, i.e., as a ransom, the Kingdom could be ushered in at once.

Now Saul, too, accepted this in principle. He, too, was thinking only of the final generation and its share in the messianic kingdom; from that vantage point he was thinking only of convincing the entire elect, since that was a necessary phase before Jesus—in Saul's rectified timetable—could return in glory at all. This was, in fact, the miracle required to explain the glorious return expected by Saul in his own lifetime; he was saying that Jesus would infallibly reappear the moment all mankind, or at any rate, the elect of the entire human race—i.e., all pagans as well as all Jews—was converted.

What an extravagance! Manifestly a desperate makeshift, forced on him by the utter insolubility of the delay in the glorious return, it nevertheless leads us to the core of his concern—the destiny of Israel. This was not only because of his audience—Jews and Judaized pagans—but because in the depths of his being Saul himself remained, somehow, a devout Jew. What he had to cope with, above all, was the Torah.

9

Wrestling with the Torah

If we glance at the finished product of Saul's upheaval without, for a moment, looking into the genesis of his ideas, we are bound to be impressed by its structure. A divine, preexistent Being condescends to become embodied in a normal man whose crucifixion, willed by God, reconciles the universe and God by extinguishing sin together with the mortal body housing the Divine Being; this opens the road to personal salvation for all human beings. In Saul's words:

> [Jesus Christ] though he was in the form of God, did not count equality with God a thing to be grasped, but emptied himself, taking the form of a servant, being born in the likeness of men. And being found in human form, he humbled himself and became obedient unto death, even death on a cross. (Phil 2:6,7)

This atoning sacrifice of a divine figure is part of the cosmic struggle between the God-forces and the devil-forces.

Every element in this dynamic conception, the very notion of *struggle* between the multiplicity of powers governing the universe, is evidently alien to monotheism, whose essence, after all, lies in the elimination of all mythological structures, all autonomous magic, all deflections from the all-encompassing will of a unique creator. The structure of "Paulinism" is identical with that of a pagan mystery religion, of the sort that drenched the eastern Mediterranean during this whole era. Various as the pagan mysteries were in cult and ritual, there was one constantly recurrent, fundamental theme—a sacramental participation in the death of a deity via some form of assimilation. In the worship of Isis, for instance, the adept dons a divine garment making him immortal; in the Osiris cult the adept is dissolved into his god via baptism.

Except for the name of the deity, Saul's baptism is similar to the Isis, Osiris, and Attis cults. Nor can it, in and for itself, be derived from any form of contemporary Judaism, even though, as I shall show in a moment, the actual content of his magical procedures has been extrapolated from Jewish ideas. Indeed, Saul's dependence, for content on Judaism, and for structure and procedures on the various mystery religions of the Hellenistic east, is an illuminating instance of the syncretism that characterized his milieu.

If magic is defined as a procedure whereby a willed action, of a natural kind, is such as to set in motion supernatural forces, and if the notion underlying a sacrament is anchored in the presupposition that supernatural forces may be linked to earthly, natural objects, then it is plain that Saul's two fundamental sacraments, baptism and the Eucharist, performed a magical function. For Saul these sacraments were the media of salvation; they effectuated the essence of redemption as arising, in a novel manner, from the dying and rising again with the Christ.

This was a long jump away from the symbolism in lavish use among the Jews; Saul's sacraments were *not* symbols; as channels implementing the action of the Holy Spirit, they constituted miracle-working procedures.

It cannot be overemphasized that for Saul what counted was the intense physicality of the entire cultic process he helped adapt. Though his own "mystery," as he himself calls it, was structurally identical with various mystery religions of his time, it had an entirely different axis of inclination. It is this that explains Saul's career in a milieu of messianic monotheists, steeped though his thought was in mythology and magic, its framework and its starting point were anchored so firmly in Judaic presuppositions that it took time before the full import of his innovations could be grasped.

All these innovations came about, in fact, because the concept of the World's End, a mere axiom for Saul as for countless messianists of the epoch, was inevitably intertwined with argumentation the moment the hiatus between the stupendous concept and its delay had to be explained. Saul was obliged to devise an argument to span the gap between his dream and what seemed to be the reality. Indeed, the fact of his having to argue at all stemmed from this primordial dilemma, the need to explain away the unthinkable—the delay in the glorious return.

If things had worked out as Saul must have felt outside Damascus, the world would have ended then and there—all would have been well. But as he saw the natural order simply going on as before, he had to cast about for an explanation of the bizarre inactivity of the universe. Hence he had to build an argument. He did this in the manner imposed by the nature of argumentation. He extracted cogent conclusions from accepted premises. Judaism was his starting point, but he gave it a special interpretation.

To establish the concept of the being-in-Christ, he was obliged to fill in the hiatus between the Messiah's resurrection and his glorious return with an intricate mythological structure. The hiatus itself, a mere vacuum, had itself to be structured somehow to dominate the minds as well as the emotions of his audience. Starting out from Jewish premises, with Jewish ideas, and addressing himself to audiences permeated by Judaism, Saul inevitably found a Jewish groundwork for his mythology.

Whether or not Saul was really trained "at the feet of Gamaliel," as he said (perhaps as a way of establishing his credentials), his insistence on his Jewishness can scarcely be exaggerated.

Even from a technical point of view, Saul's approach to Jewish tradition, the only tradition in which his basic concepts—Messiah, redemption, the elect—had any sense, was anchored in rabbinics, in which his polemical requirements demanded only that he concentrate like other Pharisees (not the aristocratic, conservative Sadducees) on the "oral" Torah rather than the "written" Torah. His contrasting the letter and the spirit of the Torah (2 Cor 3:6) meant no more than that.

Even after his seizure outside Damascus he retained a Jewish framework for all his ideas. Indeed, it was only within the Jewish tradition that he could make his own psychic upheaval meaningful. Yet his mind was so infused by mythology that even in his destruction of the Torah by means of the Torah he falls back, doubtless unwittingly, on the mythological underpinnings of his psyche.

The great "stumbling-block" in his presentation to audiences familiar with Judaism was the malediction in the Torah (Deut 21:23): "Anyone who hangs on a tree [cross] is accursed." Saul uses this very malediction to demonstrate (Gal 3:13) that it was precisely the crucifixion of Jesus, a horror from all points of view, that cancelled the Torah.

Saul believed that Jesus had already been exalted above all beings, including angels, through his death and resurrection. This authority, while incontestably vouchsafed him by God, could not, however, be entered into until the start of the messianic kingdom, at which time, with his inherent authority now fully deployed, he would deliver his partisans from the coming wrath (1 Thes 1:10).

Saul's fundamental idea, without which his life remains unintelligible, is that the messianic age, having been launched by the resurrection, will shortly be consummated. The modality of this is part of the contest between the divine powers and the angel powers. Since Jesus' death has enfeebled the angel powers, redemption is already *partially* attained.

This is shown, among other things, by the superfluousness of the "angels of the presence"—those angels who defend the elect before God against the accusing angels. These angels are superfluous, as Saul explains the intricacies of this myth, because it is God himself and Jesus who declare that the elect who have been accused are, in fact, innocent (Rom 8:31–39). Because of this it is of no consequence whatever that the elect, now absolutely assured of God's love and consequently of their justification, may or may not be tormented until the angel powers, doomed by Jesus' death, are finally done away with once and for all.

This whole process, initiated by the wedging of Jesus' death and resurrection into the world order, is to be consummated by the total destruction of the angels' rule via the glorious return. As with the Kingdom of God proclaimed by John the Baptist and by Jesus, the glorious return of Jesus will not be announced by any harbingers whatever (1 Thes 5:1–4). It will, quite simply, be *there*—an instantaneous transformation just like the advent of the Kingdom of God, which it conceptually, spiritually, and historically duplicates.

Saul invests his new idea with motifs taken from various apocalyptical and rabbinical writings; he mirrors his vision of the glorious return in purely Jewish phraseology. He merely transfers it from the traditional target, Yahweh, and ascribes it all to the action of Jesus the Lord.

Saul takes the events of the World's End for granted. He disregards, for instance, the distinctions made in the Apocalypse of John, where the Last Judgment decides who gets eternal bliss and who gets eternal death (represented as the second death in Rev 20:6,15 and depicted as eternal torment in the lake of fire). Saul also takes for granted as well-known the general resurrection and, immediately following, the Last Judgment on all men and on the defeated angels (1 Cor 15:23–28). For him all this is simply part of the end (1 Cor 15:24).

The details with which he invests his stark and simple idea merely enhance the wonder of it all. The Lord is to descend from the skies escorted by mighty angels flaming with fire; so panoplied, he judges the world (1 Thes 4:16, 2 Thes 1:7–10). Elsewhere this is reserved for God alone.[1] There are a few other features also drawn from Jewish fantasy: the cry of command upon the glorious return, the archangel's voice, the heavenly clarion trumpeting forth (1 Cor 15:52). The coincidence of the general resurrection with this stunning event is also Jewish.

Those believers who have already "fallen asleep"—evidently not *really* dead—will wake up; believers still alive will be transformed into a special condition of existence attendant on the resurrection of Jesus. All believers, the awakened and the transformed, will then be snatched up into heaven to meet the Lord in the air. From then on they will all abide with him forever (1 Thes 4:16–17).

Saul even uses the same phrase attributed to Jesus about the unknowable date of the whole transformation—"like a thief in the night" (1 Thes 5:2). The whole concept sounds entirely rabbinical.[2]

Saul expands the function of inherited material. The same trumpet mentioned by Isaiah as meant to call together the scattered children of Israel (Isaiah 27:13) is extrapolated by Saul as a modality for calling on *all* the dead elect to enter the messianic kingdom: "For the trumpet shall sound, and the dead shall arise incorruptible, and we shall be changed" (1 Cor 15:52).

All nature, too, passes over from mortality to immortality (Rom 8:19–22). In this sense the redemption of the believer is not in the least a transaction between him, God, and Jesus, but part of an overwhelming event, i.e., the World's End, in which he has the privilege of participating.

Saul's whole being was filled by the conviction that the world was ending there and then, and that his generation was to be the last generation of mankind. The old era (*aeon*), though still strong, was already declining (". . . the rulers of this world, who are doomed to pass away" (1.Cor 2:6); "the World's End has come" (1 Cor 10:11) upon *this* (his own) generation. "The form of this world is passing away" (1 Cor 7:31), that is, the natural world is finished, the celestial is underway: "The old has passed away, behold, the new has come" (2 Cor 5:17).

But in spite of all his efforts to prop himself on the Scriptures, Saul succumbs to the temptations of mythology. He is obliged to fill the vacuum of the hiatus between the present day and the return of Christ.

Saul portrays the messianic kingdom, the preamble to the true Bliss, when God "will be All in All," as a situation of violent strife, the arena of the struggle with the angel powers. This echo of pagan mythology is still alive and potent for him; he is so steeped in the mythological thought underlying the mysteries that he makes so fundamental a matter as the transition to the Kingdom of God revolve around an actual contest. For a pious Jew, after all, the angels had no *real* authority; they were merely delegates, like all else in the universe, of God's absolute power.

In any case, these angel powers will eventually be overcome—Saul doesn't say when—by Christ and his people; finally Death, who seems to be not only lord of the dead, but an angel power himself (cf. the "sting of Death" in I Cor 15:55), will be robbed of his power (1 Cor 15:23–28).

Saul's ideas have been presented for so long as elaborations of timeless "theology" that an effort must be made to discern their real framework. Rooted in his emotional distress, his ideas were contrived to solve a problem that for him was purely historical, while at the same time, of course, transcendentally significant.

Saul regarded himself, quite simply, as a devout Jew—but a Jew *in a new era.* From the Jewish point of view, to be sure, the new era was meant to take in the whole world, since it was an action instituted by the Creator of the universe. On the other hand, only the Jews were involved in understanding the expected transformation; it was the divine timetable as framed by the Hebrew Scriptures. It was the Jewish achievement to pierce the veil of the divine intention that was now to be manifested through the final cataclysm involved in the implementation of that intention. A pagan untouched by Jewish ideas could not have grasped the notion of a divine plan to begin with.

For Saul the role of Jesus as Messiah merely demonstrated the validity of the whole plan, though in and for itself the general Jewish belief was not restricted to a belief in any specific Messiah. The Jewishness not only of Saul's point of departure, but of his audience, can hardly be exaggerated. The congregations he wrote his Letters to, whether or not made up of "ethnic" Jews, were plainly steeped in Jewish ideas. They must have had a fairly extensive Jewish training.

A short list of the references he makes to the Hebrew Scriptures, with no clarification, is illuminating.

Saul takes for granted a knowledge of the Torah and of the importance of circumcision, although outsiders would surely have required a lot of explanation, especially of circumcision (in its nature altogether bizarre to pagans, indeed grotesque). Saul expects his correspondents to be aware that Jesus had died and risen again in accordance with these same Scriptures; he even assumes they will get the point of his references to Abraham, Isaac, Hagar, and Sarah, which he uses to build up his arguments. Moreover, he seems to assume that even such abstruse notions, altogether idiosyncratic from an outsider's point of view, as the spiritual rock, Moses' tablets of stone, the covenant, the sin of Adam, and the stone of offense were quite familiar to his audiences.

A single passage shows Saul's unquestioning assumption that his listeners have a completely Jewish education:

> For whatever was written in former days was written for our instruction, that by steadfastness and by the encouragement of the Scriptures we might have hope. (Rom 15:4)

There can be no doubt that all those addressed by Saul had arrived at the point of being his audience via the Hebrew Scriptures. He was not an "apostle to the Gentiles" at all; he was an "apostle," whatever may be the value of the word, to Jews and to converts to Judaism. Saul was operating, in short, in an entirely Jewish milieu, under the authority, as we shall see, of a priest in the Jerusalem Temple. His differences with other agitators within the same milieu revolved around the mere interpretation of a remarkable event treated within the matrix of traditional Jewish authority.

This is surely one of the explanations for a characteristic often regarded as a foible. Despite Saul's "universal" theme, and despite the pains he had taken to create an intellectual structure encompassing his views of cosmic upheaval, he nevertheless kept harping on the credentials of the Jews. He plainly assumed that Jewish descent is primary, despite his own theories.

In a context in which Judaism was taken for granted as the springboard for all serious thought, the very fact of his insistence shows that he was putting a brake on his own "universal" exposition. He was holding his audience back from "going too far," from going overboard along the lines of his own innovations, by reminding them that, in spite of everything, Jews "came first" both in time and in importance. His own behavior remained entirely that of a devout Jew:

Do we then overthrow the Torah by this faith? By no means; on the contrary, we uphold the Torah. (Rom 3:31)

So the Torah is holy, and the commandment is holy and just and good. (Rom 7:12)

After this Saul . . . cut his hair, for he had a vow. (Acts 18:18)

For Saul . . . was hastening to be at Jerusalem, if possible, on the day of the Pentecost. (Acts 20:16)

Then Saul purified himself . . . and went into the Temple, to give notice when the days of purification would be fulfilled and the offering presented. (Acts 21:26)

Saul's handiwork, accordingly, is the compromise between his received ideas, his emotional disposition, and the specific historical crisis he was involved in by the fusion of the two.

His starting point—the conviction that death was due to Adam's primordial sin of disobedience, as well as to the various sins committed by each individual in his own lifetime (grounded in Gen 4:17–19)—was derived from the core of the Hebrew Scriptures, in which the will of Yahweh is bedrock. At the same time, his obsessiveness made him disregard the notion of the covenant between Yahweh and the Jews, a covenant that in its nature expressed a reciprocity of relationship. Saul talked about the Torah as though it were a mere summary of injunctions, impossible, moreover, to live up to, and then played off the fact of sin, looming so large in his tormented psyche, against these unfulfillable demands.

For Jews the power of sin could never destroy faith in the essential "fulfillability" of the Torah; it was there, after all, to enable people to remain in harmony with their Creator. Saul disregarded not only this concept of the fear of God, but the equally indispensable Jewish concept of repentance (*teshuvah*), which for all Jews could, in and for itself, break the mastery of sin. Strangely, a rather kindred Greek notion (summed up in the word *metanoia*) also had no effect on Saul, whose view of the relationship between Yahweh and man disregarded not only the Hebrew prophets, but also the "summons to repentance" preached by John the Baptist and, as it seems, by Jesus, too. Saul had no interest in man's ability to return again to God, still less in man's freedom of decision. It is plain that his compulsive obsessiveness imposed on him a sort of rigidity that could be broken only by extremist, explosive formulations.

The basic notion of reciprocity inherent in the idea of covenant was blurred in the Greek translation of the Hebrew Scriptures current in Saul's day (the Septuagint) by the use of a Greek word (*diatheke*) that seems to have expressed a somewhat ambiguous notion, hovering between the meaning of covenant and something rather more like the word "arrangement." Saul, in disregarding the reciprocity of a covenant, eliminated this ambiguity altogether. The covenant between the Jews and Yahweh became a unilateral declaration of God's will, an "arrangement" instituted and authorized by God alone. Disregarding the fundamental concept of partnership involving mutual obligations, Saul refused to accept the Torah as essentially an instrument for the realization of the covenant.

This arbitrary, rather wilful splitting up of the essential unity between the Torah and the Covenant enabled Saul to clear the way for a basic requirement of his polemic on behalf of a new view of what Judaism meant in the new era, the establishment of a rationale for presenting Jesus Christ as the "end" or "purpose" of the Torah and hence of its abrogation.

Yet it was vital for him to attack the Torah by means of the Torah. Addressing Jews or pagans already somewhat shaped by Judaism, Saul used the Hebrew Scriptures as a source of his own argumentation on behalf of a suspension or elimination of those same Scriptures. Starting from a characteristically Jewish notion, Saul presented the death of Jesus the Messiah as an atonement. In its turn this led to the doctrine of righteousness through faith.

His use of the argument drawn from Scripture has generally been called "rabbinical"; perhaps casuistic is not too strong a word for it.

The root of Saul's notion of faith was his need to find some technique for bypassing the Torah. Since he had to take the Torah as his starting point, he had to find in it a prop to enable him to extend a quotation from the Torah along lines that suited both his rabbinical posture and his propagandistic aims. The fact that Abraham could be said to have believed God, and that this was "reckoned to him for righteousness" (Gen 15:6), was for him an effective argument for the supersession of the Torah. If Abraham was righteous *before* the revelation of the Torah on Sinai, what was the enduring value of the Torah? Hence righteousness could be, and in Abraham's case *was* achieved without the Torah at all, but exclusively through faith. Accordingly, the same notion could apply to all those who believed in the salvation instituted by Yahweh through the atoning death of Jesus Christ, the new Savior.

Another argument was drawn from Habakkuk (2:4); Saul repeats it very precisely:

> For in it the righteousness of God is revealed through faith for faith; as it is written, he who through faith is righteous shall live. (Rom 1:17)

> Now it is evident that no man is justified before God by the Torah, for "He who through faith is righteous shall live." (Gal 3:11)

For Saul these two quotations obliterate all else in the Hebrew Scriptures.

The reason he requires them is self-evident. They lead directly to the stupendous fact that the messianic hope is independent of the Torah altogether, since the early prophets who had first formulated the messianic hope had not yet known the Torah as law. By demonstrating that Abraham was given God's promise long before the covenant was made with Israel, Saul utilizes the groundwork of the Torah as a tool to destroy its validity.

This standpoint is polemically so effective that it enables Saul to lean over backward, seemingly, to praise the Torah for its marvelous attributes—he calls it "good," "holy," "spiritual," "divine," and so on (Romans).

Saul's argument is directed not at the mere qualities of the Torah, but at its origins. He really means that the Torah is *too* good for the Jews and indeed for people in general; it is so very good it cannot be lived up to at all. It was exactly this that was intended by the angel powers intent on subjugating men—to give them a Torah that was altogether beyond them, since the "good," the "holy," and the "divine" are evidently beyond human capacities.

Thus Saul could sound superdevout vis-à-vis the Torah; at the same time his basic argument loomed up bigger and bigger in the polemical context of his career and emerged with crushing force after his audience had been prepared for the abandonment of the Torah by his apparent praise of it.

He draws, further, still more specific advantage from his argument about Abraham. First recalling that the Promise was made to Abraham's "seed," he then points out that the word "seed" is in the singular; hence Abraham's "seed" ultimately can be no more and no less than Jesus himself. He then goes on to expand this notion; he makes Abraham the father of the pagans as well as of the Jews. Hence, the true seed of Abraham are all those sharing the being-in-Christ, i.e., all believing Jews and pagans alike (Rom 4:11–25).

Saul's conceptualization of sin also reflects his reimportation of mythology into his own brand of Judaism, imposed on him by the necessity of structuring the hiatus between the resurrection of the Messiah and his glorious return.

Generally speaking it was a rabbinical commonplace that each man was capable of bringing about desirable behavior through free will. Most Jewish teachers (together with Rabbi Aqiba, a few generations after Saul), expounded the absolute freedom or the human will, with the banal corollary that generally speaking the observance of the Torah enabled man to free himself from sin. This was just another way of saying what was obvious. The Torah, by virtue of its existence, counterbalanced the evil impulse, since it was, after all, given to man to harmonize the whole of his nature, including his will power.

But some Jews were more pessimistic; Rabbi Eliezer ben Hyrcanus, for instance, who lived shortly after Saul, gives a more or less parallel account of human sinfulness. Some rabbis even hypostasized the evil impulse, not merely as an impulse, but very nearly as an autonomous alien god dwelling in man's body.

Thus Saul's own view of sin was distinguished only by its extremism. He gives a more or less personal explanation of sin (in Rom 7) exemplifying various rabbinic views. He fortifies the rabbinic doctrine of the struggle between the evil impulse and the good impulse (*yeser ra'* and *yeser tobh*) by describing them as arrayed against each other in what sounds like a mythological hangover of the era before the birth of monotheism. Thus, in conceptualizing his rejection of the validity of the Torah, much too feeble an instrument to withstand the powerful upsurge from his unconscious, Saul falls back into the mythological world preceding monotheism and revives the notion of autonomously contending forces.

Saul conceived of forces dualistically arrayed against each other—spirit against flesh, will versus ability, the law of God and the law of sin. All were engaged in a mortal struggle within the human heart. The struggle was not equal. On the contrary, the law of God—the Torah—could set in motion no more than man's will power, whereas man's actual behavior was determined by the very nature of his flesh, which is sinful (Rom 7:14–23).

Intellectually commonplace, Saul's doctrine of sin was given its remarkable dynamism by his temperamental extravagance, his psychoneurosis. He was a pessimist extremist.

It is in fact his intense suffering that makes him amplify his conception of the World's End, the only thing big enough to save him. He is over-ridingly preoccupied by articulating, without much detail, his demonstration of how history will be terminated, a preoccupation forced on him by the simple fact that history had not ended. He gives details only to show how the Messiah, after vanquishing the angel powers, hands back his authority to God, who *then* becomes "all in all." It is there that world history stops. Everyone who by virtue of coming forth from God and then returning to him has proved his obedience to him, belongs to God entirely and forever. Everyone else is allotted eternal damnation.

In accordance with the thoroughgoing materiality of his thought, Saul conceives of eternal bliss not at all as spiritual, but as an aspect of the world-condition entailed by the bodily resurrection and by the being-with-God all-in-all.

If Jesus thought, as some believe, that the Torah came to an end with the inception of the messianic kingdom, Saul, obliged to take into account the intervening fact of the death and resurrection of Jesus (which places Saul in a later phase of the divine timetable), incorporates this notion of the end of the Torah by putting it into the second phase—the Torah has already been partially invalidated at least by the very fact of the resurrection of Jesus.

Saul has already taken a step far beyond Judaism.

Judaism, anchored in a transcendent God beyond nature, always had the problem of mediating between such a God and nature. While here and there in the earliest parts of the Torah God simply appears, or at least is heard, later on the angels came to be thought of as indispensable intermediaries between the transcendent God and the people.

Yet obviously the Torah was given by God, on Mt. Sinai. The scene, entirely unambiguous, might ordinarily have been thought to be decisive. For Saul's scheme, however, it was essential to have a Torah not given by God at all, but by the angels, who wanted to enslave men to themselves. Thus Jesus' resurrection from the dead was efficacious in the sense that it shook up the angel powers, and thus extracted all authority from the Torah.

This strange idea is peculiar to Saul. He needs it to insert a mythological element—of contingency, contention, and struggle—enabling his thought to cope with the transcendence of God, who otherwise would have been conceptually hard to cope with. If *God* had given the Torah, how could it be invalidated?

Saul's starting point in his polemic against his fellow Jews, which was, all unknown to him, to take him far beyond Judaism, was thus his quite arbitrary insistence that the Torah entailed the dominion of the angel powers. This in its turn formed part of an intricate explanation of the modality by which the death of Jesus had set in motion the divine timetable, i.e., by assuming that the natural world was under the dominion of the angel powers, Saul inserted another quirk of mythological contention into what had hitherto been, within Judaism, the simplicity of Yahweh's relationship to mankind.

Saul's mythological complication had, to be sure, a certain simplicity of its own. He said that the angel powers had simply been hoodwinked by the death of Jesus; they had allowed it by misunderstanding his perfect obedience to God, hence his not being subject to death. By allowing Jesus to be killed they had been deceived into exceeding their competence, and hence had contributed to the destruction of their own power. Throughout this process the Sanhedrin and the scribes had been no more than tools of the angels (1 Cor 2:6–8).

Having thus been outwitted, the angels suffered two losses. Not only was their dominion undermined, ultimately to be overthrown completely, but they had also lost the actual power they had through the Torah itself. This last was especially useful to Saul since it enabled him to bypass very handily the traditional "stumbling-block," the malediction* in the Torah on "whoso hangs on a tree." Since it was obvious that Jesus the Messiah could not be accursed even though he had been hanged from a cross, this was a fundamental exception to the validity of the Torah, and since the Torah is a unity, if there is one case where it is invalid it is invalid *in toto*.

This was what showed that the angels had been hoodwinked. If they had known what was really going on they would have done their utmost to *save* Jesus, since without Jesus' death the Messiah would not have appeared immediately. He had appeared, after all, because of the very fact of that death; hence the Torah would have conserved its validity.

A remarkable piece of casuistry!

This destruction, or perhaps evasion, of the concept of the Torah's validity, was, to be sure, merely a structural element in the solution of Saul's cardinal problem, i.e., the being-in-Christ of the community of

---

*It is far from clear that this *is* a malediction. How could the countless kingdom of God activists crucified by the Romans have been cursed by God? But Saul required this concert for his polemics.

saints, or the mystic body of Christ. This concept was what really solved the cardinal problem—the deaths of the elect after the resurrection and before the glorious return. Since Jesus' death and resurrection had *ipso facto* ushered in the messianic kingdom, all believers were at least partially redeemed—in any case far more than they had realized.

This was the chief reason for Saul's frantic travels—he had to persuade his audiences of facts already in their possession that they had underestimated.

Thus, at the outset, the matrix of Saul's ideas had been conventionally historical. His vision of the messianic age had been essentially the Jewish drama of world history in successive stages. His exposition of his own personal Christ-mysticism was distinguished, in fact, not so much by its magical procedures, indubitable though these are, as by its objective realism, like all his ideas.

Despite his malaise within Judaism, despite his frictions with Jewish leaders, despite the "problem" of the Torah, for Saul, grappling with Yahweh's plans, the Jews remained the cardinal, indeed, the only *real* people. For Saul it was essential that Israel be converted to a belief in the salvational role of Jesus the Messiah:

> I want you to understand this mystery, brethren: a hardening has come upon part of Israel, until the full number of the pagans come in and so all Israel will be saved. . . . As regards the gospel they are enemies of God, for your sake, but as regards election they are beloved for the sake of their forefathers. (Rom 11:25–28)

It was because Saul was waiting for the pagan elect to be converted in their capacity as authentic pagans, not as judaized pagans, and because he was gripped by the conviction that time was running out very quickly, that he felt obliged to scurry about the known world; he had to make sure that no one had any excuse not to join the elect merely because he had not yet heard the word (Rom 10:18). There was, in fact, a profound difference, for Saul, between pagans pure and simple and pagan converts to Judaism. This is, ultimately, the reason he cannot consent to obliging pagan converts to accept what all previous Judaism had required as a minimal requirement for admission to Israel—namely, the acceptance of the Torah (circumcision, food laws, etc.).

It would have been quite easy for Saul to bypass the whole question.

The miracle worked on converts by baptism was supposed to be wholly objective, i.e., a magical change, hence it by no means required the convert to "understand" it. The believer is supposed to be inducted, through baptism, into an objective world order in which through the resurrection of Jesus the supernatural resurrection powers are already sapping the natural world order; because of this the baptism is effective on the believer regardless of his consciousness, which is quite superfluous. Once the belief in Jesus is present, the objective effect of baptism brings about the union with Christ automatically.

For Saul, accordingly, it is a fatal error to treat the Torah as though it had any validity whatever after Jesus' death and resurrection. If the convert is supposed to submit to the Torah, it means that he is claiming his share in the messianic kingdom on premises that belong, in fact, only to Jews. The error lies precisely in the shockingly gross oversight that by doing this the pagan convert is fundamentally abandoning Jesus altogether. He has missed the whole point of the redemptive resurrection. Instead of Saul's profound concept of the being-in-Christ, the pagan convert has the utterly outmoded, quite misleading concept of the being-within-the-Torah, a completely foolish idea. By that fact alone the pagan convert gives up his being-in-Christ; he excludes himself from the mystic body of Christ and lapses back into a state in which he will no longer have any chance for redemption at all.

Saul's arguing around this point often sounds cranky. It is because he is looking at the Torah, a cardinal problem, from different points of view at different times, and for different categories of people—Jews, pagans, converts to Jesus, converts to Judaism. It must not be forgotten that throughout Saul's lifetime the Jesists were merely a current of opinion within the Jewish community, and that the central group of Jerusalem Jesists led by Upright Jacob were observant Jews. In Saul's time the ferment that later was to result in a split between Judaism and its offshoot was only beginning. The small congregations scattered around the eastern Mediterranean, where different people with different views on all basic questions struggled to formulate those views against the background of a general expectation of the World's End, were in a state of chaos.

Saul's handling of the Torah is perfectly logical, indeed extremely simple, though it sounds somewhat contradictory. It is, perhaps, no more than a "pilpul," as Jewish exegetes of the Torah might say, a piece of casuistry imposed on him by the apparent failure of the universe to respond correctly to the resurrection of Jesus.

Saul seems to say that the Torah is simply invalid. On the other hand he acknowledges its authority without reservation for those who accept it. This hangs together with his saying that Jews—born Jews and full converts—should follow the Torah, as Saul himself did all his life. Believers in Jesus from among the pagans, however, must not acknowledge the Torah; if *they* do they are denying the role of Jesus.

Thus the real question is, just how *is* the Torah valid? And hence, what is the correct attitude of the believer in Jesus toward the Torah? Saul, obsessed by the conviction that the natural world is dominated by angels, gives a simple answer to the question. The Torah is part of the natural world, dominated by the angel powers; hence the degree of validity of the Torah is equal to the degree of validity retained by the natural world now in the throes of upheaval. The death and resurrection of Jesus, the initial, paramount fact that has initiated the transition from the natural to the supernatural world, has dealt a death blow to the angel powers, but it has not yet eliminated them altogether. Though launched, the messianic kingdom in its entirety has not yet arrived.

Hence the Torah is valid wherever the messianic kingdom is not yet in full control. Where the supernatural world is already realized, both the dominion of the angel powers and the authority of the Torah have retreated or lost their validity. Wherever the natural world, on the other hand, is still real, the dominion of the angel powers and of the Torah is still absolutely all right.

Now, within the mystic body of Christ constituted by the being-in-Christ—the community of believers in Jesus Christ—the supernatural world is, despite all appearances, already in force. It is a sphere already bursting with the forces that had brought about Jesus' resurrection. But everything outside the sphere of the mystic body of Christ is still part of the natural world and will remain so until the advent of the messianic kingdom, heralded, initiated, but not yet accomplished by the death and resurrection of Jesus.

Once one grasps the simple fact that Saul is absorbed by the notion of a situation of dynamic but lopsided transition it is easy to see the consistency of his analysis, however extravagant its starting point. He merely affirms the coexistence of two different, but equally valid attitudes toward the Torah from these two different points of view. The Torah is either valid or invalid according to whether it coincides with one world order or another—the being-in-Christ or the being in the natural order still under the dominion of the angel powers. In a word, the Torah stops where the messianic kingdom begins.

Which really takes us back to the starting point. It was a Jewish view, too, after all, that the Torah was valid only insofar as the Kingdom of God had not yet come; afterwards it would be superfluous and would cease. Thus it is the same old question. Was Jesus the Messiah or not? Or, put a little differently: Was his resurrection proof of his messiahship?

The reasoning behind this notion is also simple. It is obvious that the World's End must terminate the Torah; in the nature of things the end of history, involving as it does a total confrontation with and absorption by the direct presence of God, creates an ethic that transcends time-bound institutions. The Torah, created by God for this world, is out of place in the messianic kingdom.

The traditional Jewish view had some ambiguities in it. The prophets of the period before the Babylonian Exile, who invented the notion of the World's End, were really preoccupied with an absolute ethic independent, essentially, of the Torah. In a way they might be said to have created morality by insisting that since the one God gave rise to everything in the universe, the terrible condition of the Jews was their own fault, somehow, and in articulating that somehow they created absolute standards of morality. Yet the prophets of the Babylonian Exile later conceived of the Torah as itself leading to the messianic kingdom, and of its observance as naturally guaranteeing the observant Jew a "portion in the world to come."

This was plainly illogical. What could be the meaning in a supernatural world of a Torah designed to accommodate a natural world? Yet the Torah was so overwhelmingly important for Judaism that it was impossible simply to disregard it; hence the late Jewish apocalypses avoid explicitly denying the validity of the Torah in the messianic kingdom; they simply pass it by in silence.[3]

It is true that the Jews thought the Torah eternal—preexistent in the mind of God even before it was revealed to Moses and the Jews on Mount Sinai. Yet for that very reason it could lapse into abeyance once again, i.e., as before Sinai, once the messianic kingdom was installed. If evil is done away with, why the Torah?

No doubt it would have been simple, practically speaking, if Saul had assumed an indifferent attitude toward the Torah. It would surely have kept him out of trouble, since it was to be just this subtle, nuanced, fluctuating "dialectical" notion of his about the Torah's shifting degrees of validity that was to get him into hot water in Jerusalem. But he was too inflamed, too systematic, too exigent, too "logical." His mystical doctrine of the being-in-Christ, if it meant anything at all, had to be applied with consistency; his logic forced him to enunciate propositions that were out of tune with Jewish preconceptions.

Saul was so consumed by eagerness for the glorious return, so utterly convinced of its imminence, that it governed his practical, day-to-day outlook too. The imminence of the glorious return was really his criterion for assessing day-to-day behavior. He really thought that, since the glorious return was for all practical purposes *here,* no changes had to be made in ordinary life. Thus he laid it down that no matter what condition of life the convert to Jesus found himself in he should simply stay there, since the redemption via the messianic kingdom was already at hand. This meant, practically, something quite simple: Jews stayed Jews, pagans stayed pagans; i.e., no one budged till kingdom come.

It was this that no doubt explains his indifference to slavery (today, of course, entirely unfashionable!). Why bother at all about release from slavery for the few moments still to be spent in the natural world before its final extinction? Similarly for his quietist attitude toward the authorities, his theory that the government—any government—is in and for itself authoritative as an expression of God's will.

Saul's sole exception to his general ruling is marriage. He thought a Jesist should marry rather than be unchaste. To his mind the justification of this exception was that marriage was a change of petty consequence as compared with the far greater evil of unchastity that was to be avoided at all costs (1 Cor 7:9, 28, 36–40). For Saul unchastity was one of the three sins that bring death (the others being circumcision *after* baptism and participation in heathen sacrificial feasts). All three sins were heinous because they obliterated the paramount fact—the mystic body of Christ.

Consistently enough, Saul lived as a seemingly observant Jew all his life. It can scarcely be doubted that he always thought of himself as entirely faithful to his ancestral traditions:

> I would willingly be . . . cut off from the Messiah if I could help my brothers of Israel, my own flesh and blood. (Rom 9:3)

He conformed with his punishment of thirty-nine stripes by Jewish officials five times (2 Cor 11:24); he said he was "a Jew to the Jews, to gain the Jews" (1 Cor 9:20), and he "lived as though under the Torah, to gain those who are." To be sure, in his case this corresponded to an inner indifference to the Torah that had always proved so helpless in the face of his psychological torment. However, on the threshold of the World's End, since the Torah had lived itself out, why not seem to observe it? When Saul said "circumcision counts for nothing, uncircumcision counts for nothing" (1 Cor 7:19), he merely gave this indifference an epigrammatical form.

Yet his feelings remained profoundly Jewish, so much so that he was profoundly perplexed, perhaps embittered by the obduracy of his fellow Jews in not seeing what he thought he saw with such blinding clarity, that the God of Israel and of the universe had finally launched his ultimate project of redeeming mankind, both Jews and pagans, through the death of Jesus and his resurrection.

Nor was he in any sense cut off by his ideas from the mainstream of contemporary Judaism, since we know from the collective turnout in the war against the Romans in 66–70 that the bulk of Jewry agreed with him in essence that the World's End was beginning to bubble everywhere and that God was going to settle things in his own favor once and for all.

It would not be too much to say that two generations of Jews were consumed by the feverishness of the messianic fantasy—feverish just because it was thought to be about to be realized. In this respect Saul was typical of his milieu. His Letters were plainly written against a background of a contagion that extended throughout a huge area; whatever his relations with the Jerusalem Jesists in detail they were grounded in a common belief in the World's End. It would have been preposterous, at that time, even to ask Saul whether he was a "Christian"; it would have meant, very precisely, nothing whatever. The question of abandoning his people could never even have occurred to him; Judaism was the core of his life. Otherwise, indeed, what could the very word "Messiah" have meant to him?

In short, what separated Saul and his fellow messianists from other devout Jews, at that particular crossroads—crossroads to us, not to them— was merely a difference of opinion about what would have seemed to all contemporary Jews a question of fact. Had the Messiah come or not? Or rather, if Jesus had been made Messiah by his resurrection, did that mean that the World's End was on them or not?

It was, accordingly, precisely Saul's Jewish piety that led to his death— or rather, it was his outward acceptance of the Torah that, intertwined with his own reservations, was to bring it about. His remark about being "all things to all men, to the Jews a Jew, to the Greeks a Greek" was a mere aspect of what may be called his public relations presentation; in reality he remained ardently pious all his life. Only his modifications proved fateful!

Still, his general theory, however logical and symmetrical, could not bridge over many practical problems that Jews were bound to face in their intercourse with pagans, more particularly those pagans who had come into Judaism via their faith in the resurrection of Jesus. Devout Jews, for instance, could not eat with pagans at all; it was indeed this practical problem of behavior that gave rise to the first violent conflict within the new, still amorphous congregations. If the Lord's Supper was to be properly celebrated, for instance, how could Jewish exclusivism at the table be circumvented?

Circumcision, too, presented a tangle. Saul was ready, for instance, to sanction, in the teeth of his own convictions, the circumcision of Titus, a Greek, and Timothy, a half-Greek whose mother was Jewish. It is quite possible, to be sure, that Saul gradually changed his mind over a period of time, and saw the full implications of his own theory about the being-in-Christ only later; it may also have been because in personal encounters he was, as it seems, ineffectual (2 Cor 10:10, Gal 1:10).

But in spite of the above exceptions Saul was entirely consistent in forbidding circumcision to any pagans at all. The pagan, in consciously allowing himself to be circumcised, signalized his enduring, hence illegitimate submission to the flesh. This annihilated the very concept of the being-in-Christ; it was a form of kowtowing to the angel powers sustaining the Torah.

It was Saul's logic that was ultimately to make his life unbearable and indeed bring it to an end. All his difficulties, polemical and practical, as roving recruiter for the new idea, stemmed from his insistence on a rigorous application of his theory of the status quo to the cardinal question of the Torah.

Looking back, we can see it was hopeless from the outset. No one could have accomplished Saul's self-imposed task—unless, of course, the great upheaval took place!

Saul was obliged to persuade devout Jews, who naturally thought the Torah enabled them to attain true righteousness, that it was in fact of no consequence whatever, while at the same time it still retained its binding power on them as Jews even after they had become believers in Jesus' salutary role.

It sounded like a mere logical contradiction. Also a practical one, since the theory of the Torah's efficacy was not, after all, a mere theory, but was anchored in practices accepted for untold generations.

Saul's insistence that devout Jews dine with pagans, which catapulted him into a bitter controversy with Simon the Rock (Gal 2:11–16), merely heightened the peculiar trickiness of his position. He was really requiring Jewish believers, still devout in the ancient faith, to shed their piety and embark on a new idea, buttressed only by Saul's fanatical insistence on his own understanding of Jesus' resurrection as the prelude to the World's End.

It may be conceivable that if the agreement with Simon the Rock (adumbrated, a little sketchily, in Gal 2:7–9) had been lived up to—*per impossibile*—there would then, somehow, have been two types of congregation in existence—one for devout Jews, the other for pagans who had "come to Jesus" without bothering about Judaism. But in Saul's lifetime the Temple was still a supreme fact in the lives of all Jews, both in the Jewish communities scattered throughout the Diaspora, and in the assured community in Palestine, famous for its antiquity and, even though under the heel of an imperial power, solidly rooted on its own soil. Saul, while representative of the messianic mainstream of Jewish national life, was still going against the current in his emphasis on the singularity of the Jewish messiah as he conceived him.

It was out of the question for Saul to create at that time another type of Jewish community, nor, since the World's End was at hand, could there have been any reason to. The early congregations were made up of both devout Jews and more or less judaized pagans; it had been the very magnetism of Judaism that had, after all, attracted the pagans in the first place. It would seem impossible to have had any real ideological unity without suppressing one approach or the other.

More important, the original apostles were all very much alive; associates, intimates, and relatives of Jesus, they wore the mantle of authority vested in them by his still-living history. They were a repository, so to speak, of the succession of leadership; it was only natural for them to maintain that their authority covered all believers in Jesus.

Thus there was an inevitable conflict between Saul, a turbulent, somewhat twisted person whose authority really came only from his own frenzy, and those who could claim to have inherited their authority somehow from Jesus himself, and who no doubt cited many remembered sayings of Jesus, all of them distinguished, as we can see from echoes in the Gospels, by a narrowly parochial cast.

In such circumstances it was no doubt equally natural for Saul to develop a sort of megalomania to transcend his sense of his own short-comings. He was bound to consider himself uniquely capable of perceiving the inner working-out of the mechanism of the body-in-Christ. His rivals were, he thought, "blinded by Satan"; that was why they were incapable of grasping the fundamental futility of the Torah at that historical conjuncture. He also thought them merely cowardly. They were afraid of the persecutions lying in wait for them if they fought for the "cross of Christ" in the only logical way it could be fought for (Gal 6:12).

Saul's specific timing of the World's End was linked to a form of arithmetic he had devised and ascribed, perhaps a little mysteriously in its turn, to God. When the number of those who, through their belief in Jesus' salvational role, implement their election to the messianic kingdom, then the World's End will be at hand. The elect must actualize their election by merging in the being-in-Christ.

That was the reason for Saul's desire to push on to Spain. His motives were exclusively theological, or perhaps theological-cum-mathematical. He says this unmistakably:

> Making it my ambition to preach the Gospel not where Christ has already been named, lest I build on another man's foundation, but as it is written: "They shall see who have never been told of him, and they shall understand who have never heard of him." This is the reason I have so often been hindered from coming to you. But now, since I no longer have any room for work in these regions, and since I have longed for many years to come to you, I hope to see you in passing as I go to Spain. (Rom 15:20–24)

Since Saul was appointed by God himself as part of the divine plan, he was the only one who could grasp this. Thus he was uniquely equipped for a unique role that at the same time was indispensable for the functioning of the divine timetable.

Yet his constant disclaimers, very humble-sounding, of the value of his own person—he seems to harp on his fundamental worthlessness—sound like aspects of genuine megalomania.

It is this note of megalomania, stridently clear, that may give us a final insight into Saul's temperament. It is hard to withstand the impression that like many others of the same "type," Saul took special pride in his sufferings.

If I must boast, I shall boast of the things that show my weakness. (2 Cor 11:30)

I will all the more gladly boast of my weaknesses that the power of Christ may rest upon me. For the sake of Christ, then, I am content with weaknesses, insults, hardships, persecutions and calamities, for when I am weak, then I am strong. (2 Cor 12:9,10)

We rejoice in our sufferings, knowing that suffering produces endurance.(Rom 5:3)

Even if I am to be poured as a libation upon the sacrificial offering of your faith, I am glad. (Phil 2:17)

The same thought, with its suggestion that it was *because* of Saul's weakness that he found strength in his faith, is reflected in the following:

For Christ was crucified in weakness, but lives by the power of God. For we are weak in him but . . . we shall live with him by the power of God (2 Cor 13:4)

This was also, to be sure, a reflection of the millennial Jewish tradition of finding in present misery a harbinger of future joy. Indeed, it may be that the Jewish invention of the entire conception of the World's End may itself be a sort of model for Saul's masochism—the happy illusion that the misery of the moment will eventually be set right in the ecstasy of the guaranteed future.

For that matter Saul's achievement in converting a symbol of absolute degradation—the punishment of the cross, a favorite Roman device just because of its humiliating cruelty—into a triumphant symbol of glory was in its very nature a piece of Jewish prestidigitation.

Saul epitomized par excellence the apocalyptic strain in Jewish thought. For the classical prophets—Amos, Hosea, Isaiah—there was only one world, in which the grandiose events of its own end took place, events that, even though they included the restoration of the House of David and the future glory of Israel in a world without images that had returned to the one God, were themselves encased within the same world.

The apocalypticists, however, split the world dynamically into two antithetical and successive ages—this World and the Coming World—in which darkness was counterposed to light and the antithesis between Israel and the pagans was expanded into a cosmic antithesis of contending forces—light vs. dark, purity vs. sin, life vs. death, God vs. anti-Divine powers.

This was the background against which the ideas of the resurrection of the dead and the rewards and punishments of the Last Judgment, paradise and hell, and the mingling together of the promises and threats to the Jewish people were paralleled by features of individual retribution at the World's End. Specific apocalypses, though unaccountably reserved for the initiates, were nevertheless pegged onto the old analyses of the classical prophets.

Countless Jews, exacerbated by Roman oppression, had turned to apocalyptic, which in its dramatic dialectic always encompasses elements of both horror and consolation intertwined. History, instead of being consummated, is turned inside out. It is destroyed at the very moment that it is transformed into an antithesis through a light that, as Gershom Scholem says, "shines on it from somewhere altogether different."

What was perhaps most striking about Saul's place in the turbulent messianic movement of his time was that, while exemplifying the Jewish elan of the epoch, he was governed by the same universalizing passions as the Pharisee missionaries themselves, equally enthralled by the World's End hysteria. His seizure on the road to Damascus merely gave his passions another target, a little further along the line of the World's End projections. Now that Yahweh had launched the final, triggering miracle of Jesus' resurrection, the assurances of the World's End found in the classical prophets, embellished by the messianic fervor of the epoch, could be thought to be on the very brink of fulfillment.

Saul's exaltation had propelled him far beyond the mere historicism of Judaism; whether or not he had been personally attracted by paganism in the forms he had been familiar with before his seizure, he was to find such pagan ideas, perhaps because they reflected the vast unmovingness of nature and the tranquil cyclicism of the universe, more meaningful than dynamic historicism.

Saul was really seeking a meaning that was deeper—more deeply embedded in his own unconscious, in his own neuroses, whatever they were—than the superficial, purely political activities of his fellow Jews and of his own activity beforehand, if he had indeed ever taken part in the this-worldly Zealot enterprise of smashing the Roman state with the help of God. Saul could no longer be satisfied by the obvious, open, clear, matter-of-fact point of Jesus' execution—i.e., a Roman act of war against an enemy of Rome—and sought in the mode of execution, enhanced by his acceptance of the vision of the risen Jesus, a deep, mysterious, otherworldly meaning.

His ardent imagination had sought and found a total solution; it was not only Israel that needed redemption from pagan oppression, but all mankind. The entire universe was a battlefield between the demonic power holding the world in thrall and the installation of the Kingdom of God now attested by the unique destiny of his fellow messianist, Jesus.

Saul transformed the modest enterprise of national redemption via the armed action of masses of people aided by God into a cosmic enterprise involving the nature of the universe. The small-scale liberation of the Jews from bondage to a big power, an entirely feasible project of national independence realized many times over in history, was dwarfed by Saul's titanic new conception, smelted in the crucible of his personal misery—the salvation of all men from a universal condition. Of course this whole switch of perspective was bound to get him into trouble with his fellow Jews, but since he was fervently convinced that the period of waiting was extremely short, really nothing, that could not matter.

Absorbed in elaborating this grandiose piece of imaginative extravagance out of the depths of his psyche, why bother with the flesh-and-blood disciples at all? Indeed, why should they be called the "real" disciples at all?

In the short run, of course—though even that short run was amazingly long: twenty-five years!—Saul was soon to find himself a little embarrassed, though, as we shall see, he managed to hold out for some time.

Saul's mysticism had solved a peculiarly Jewish problem. Jews had always been incapable of an identification with God; the absolute split in Judaism between the transcendently divine and the mundanely human was too deeply rooted to be overcome. But, as a mystic, Saul could manage to identify himself with a fellow Jew and fellow messianist, perhaps even a fellow Zealot.

He identified himself with a fellow Jew to whom *something stupendous had happened,* something so stupendous that by identifying himself with him, by calling him Son of God, and by securing in this way a guarantee of eternal life, he had really found a mechanism for identifying himself with God anyhow.

A mere identification with the transcendent God of the universe, if conceivable for a devout Jew, would really have been a symptom of radical derangement, entirely pathological; Saul in that case would have been totally ineffectual, a mere psychotic. But a subsidiary, roundabout identification, so to speak, with another human being who is then identified with God, procured Saul a double benefit.

On the one hand, his identification with God in spite of the roundabout approach was reinforced by the guarantee of immortality, and on the other hand his effectiveness in the real world could be grounded in genuine, productive, and no doubt deeply satisfying personal activity. In Saul's solution of his basic problem—the hiatus between Jesus' career on earth and his glorious return as usher of the messianic kingdom—there was ample room for a healthy, active life: exhorting, preparing, educating, explaining, arguing.

Thus Saul's identification with Jesus could give him a fruitful career, so to speak, in ordinary society. It kept him sane, and in any case gave his energies a framework of social purposefulness and a certain influence, however restricted, in his own lifetime. The baffling contrast between the Messiah's arrival and the seeming continuity of the world, which it was the purpose of Saul's life to make comprehensible, created a fruitful tension between the two states of mind—the exhilarating assurance that the messianic age had started, and the awareness that the world was manifestly still unredeemed. The tension kept Saul planted on the ground—gazing at the heavens in ecstasy.

Thus Saul thought himself the only human being in the whole world who had penetrated the meaning of Jesus' resurrection and the timetable of the World's End. This, combined with his polemical need to shift the Torah into the background of the World's End altogether, made him counterpose himself, quite naturally, even to Moses. His designation of the Torah as the "dispensation of death," i.e., an adjunct of the current workaday and now superseded natural world, hence irrelevant to the Kingdom of God, where death would be vanquished, was balanced by the conception of himself as the bringer of the "dispensation of the Spirit," in contradiction to, or rather, perhaps, as a potentialization of the old dispensation. Since the "splendor" of the new dispensation was necessarily greater than the old—"what is permanent must have much more splendor"—his train of thought inevitably magnified his own role (2 Cor 3:7–14).

Saul's megalomania was not, for him, megalomania at all. Like all else in his mind, it was merely factual. Though his statement that he had been "set apart" before birth (Gal 1:15) sounds, to be sure, like megalomania pure and simple, it seems to have no necessary connection with his vocation. His view of himself arises in an entirely natural way from the manner in which he conceives his pivotal role in the divine timetable.

If the glorious return could not come about until the pagans had had an opportunity to hear the good news, and that was to bring about the convincing of the Jews, and Saul was the only one who could see this, it was entirely sensible for him to consider himself indispensable for the consummation of the action initiated by the contemporary irruption of God into human affairs. Because of this Saul considered himself the linchpin of the cosmic transformation, and as such the natural target for the enmity of the angel powers. He was the only one who had grasped the mechanism of their destruction, which was why he thought they wanted to undo him as they had Jesus.

For Saul, Isaac and Jacob represented the new congregations of that branch of messianism anchored in the faith in Jesus; Ishmael and Esau symbolized the obsolete, stubbornly astigmatic Jewish synagogues that had not understood this. The body-of-Christ became the chosen brother; the synagogue became the rejected brother (Rom 9:6–13). It was in this way that election was transmitted from Abraham's "in the flesh" to his merely spiritual descendants, while those Jews who because of their "hardness of heart" still refused to be convinced were turned into the rejected offspring.

Ultimately, of course, things would turn out well anyhow. Even though the "old Israel"—i.e., ordinary Jews—had been turned into an enemy, it was still in God's plan to allow them to be redeemed through the instrumentality of Jesus Christ, and very shortly, to boot. Thus harmony was ultimately inevitable, with everything neatly dovetailing.

For Saul, accordingly, remaining a devout Jew in the oldfashioned sense at a time when something entirely novel had just taken place was to oppose oneself to God's will, to be *really* an apostate!

10

Saul's System

It was, of course, Saul's magnification of Jesus that catalyzed his ideas into what may be called a system. Saul magnified the Jewish Messiah—an entirely human figure—in such a way as to lend the impulsive mixture of his borrowings from various traditions a peculiar dynamic that long after his death was to jell into the theology of a universal Church. The incarnation—the indwelling of God in the body of Jesus—was its linchpin.

In taking the story of God commanding Abraham to sacrifice his son Isaac—very nearly a conventional episode in the lessons drawn by Jews from their meditation on God in history—and applying the motif to God himself, Saul recast the meaning of the phrase "Son of God." He did this in a way that produced a close approximation, indeed a copy of the pagan mythologies a thousand years before.

The sonship of God is spoken of quite easily in the Hebrew Scriptures as well as in various apocalyptic writings. Such ideas, like the hypostatization of the Torah, are plainly metaphors, symbols, allegories at most. They do not purport to convey descriptions of a state of nature. But when Saul took the phrase "Son of God," traditionally not much more than an honorific epithet, and focused it on Jesus, he was making a statement about the essence of reality. It was essentially incomprehensible to monotheists.

The Jewish conviction of the utter contrast between the Divine and the human, between God and the world, was absolute. There was no margin for compromise. Nor can Saul's extremism be ascribed to his Diaspora milieu;

the Judaism of the Diaspora was fundamentally identical with Palestinian Judaism, though neither one, to be sure, was the monolith of unyielding rigidity often made much of.

When Saul, apparently unconsciously, took phrases hitherto reserved for Yahweh, whose name was "above every name," to which "every knee should bow," and used these phrases about the name of Jesus, he could have done so only through being overwhelmed by his emotions, since for him this transfer of attributes should have constituted a real problem.

He seems to have appropriated these phrases because they were embedded in the Scriptures; thus it was his use of Scripture to validate his "points" that sufficed to recreate, oddly enough, the mythological framework discarded by Judaism long before the Scriptures came into being.

It may well have been the enhancing of the sacrament of baptism, which had swiftly become the hallmark of membership in the evolving sect, that provided a ritual peg, so to speak, to prop up the explosive feeling underlying Saul's original vision, as transformed for social use.

In a milieu dominated by a constant effervescence that combined Jewish messianic fever and the longing of uprooted pagans for personal salvation, baptism itself gave a tremendous impetus to the ascension of Jesus.

Jesus himself came to be worshipped, not as himself—a Jewish Messiah who had ignominiously failed—but by means of an inflated conception fictitiously linked to the historic Jesus as a point of contact with the world. In reality this stripped the entire meaning of his actual career from any connection with Judaism or messianism in favor of an infinitely more grandiose idea—that of the Lord. Saul has a characteristic statement: "You and my spirit being gathered together in the name of the Lord Jesus, with the power of our Lord Jesus" (1 Cor 5:4).

This transposes us to the state of mind of the early members of this eccentric coterie. Even without analysis such a sentence indicates that to anyone who found it meaningful the name of the Lord, indeed, the very word "Lord" in and for itself, already constituted a potent factor in the genesis of a cult. Pagan worshippers must have felt stirred to their depths by the assurance of the "real presence" given by such a proposition of the authentic action initiated by the powerful name of Christ Jesus. It seems most likely that this word "Lord" became the fundamental name for the new deity as the personality of the historic Jesus, stripped of all historical attributes through the automatic working out of the forces implied in his deification, was necessarily fitted out with details.

The word "Lord" (in Greek *Kyrios*) had generally been used by Greek slaves for their master; never used for the classical deities of the Olympic pantheon, it was current for the petty gods of salvation in Asia Minor, Egypt, and Syria whenever these were referred to in Greek. Saul uses it for the relations between Christ and his slaves, (I Cor 7:22); in the notable passage in Philippians (2:9–10), too, after calling Jesus "Lord," Saul applies to him the phrase reserved for Yahweh ("at whose name every knee shall bow" etc.). It is, of course, Saul's unconsciousness of this switch in the targets of this honorific phrase that indicates the depth of the psychological-socio-cultic process underlying the shift in perspective.

Thus the axis of differentiation between the Jerusalem Jesists and the semipagan fellowships forming on Greek-speaking terrain in the Diaspora was this contrast between the Jewish concept of the messianic Son of Man and the pregnant notion of the Lord launched by some unknown predecessors of Saul and endlessly amplified by him.

This differentiation was cardinal; the Son of Man, the concept of a superhuman but still not divine personage figuring in the pageant of the World's End fantasied by the Jews and quite meaningless to a non-Jew, was a mere factor of the World's End. He was a dimension, so to speak, only within the framework of the messianic kingdom. Beforehand he had no existence for any one on earth. Simply kept in reserve in the wings of the celestial playhouse until his cue was spoken, he would then step onstage to play out his portentous role.

This, the starting point of the new faith, was soon amplified. For the semipagans recruited to the new belief, the dimension of the "Lord" was not at all a part of the World's End, it was a mystic exaltation experienced *there and then.* It was a current condition of nature. For the feverish initiates it meant the real presence of the Lord Christ Jesus at the very moment of the realization of the communion of his worshippers. It was a device that served as the mechanism of identification between the new mystery launched in Antioch and the current mysteries of the Hellenistic world. For it was this element that made them all identical. The adepts of the pagan Mysteries also felt the mystic presence of their Savior at the very moment of their psycho-physical identification with him.

In calling Jesus, the Jewish Messiah, "Lord Jesus," Saul had changed the original concept, still the summation of the Jerusalem Jesists' faith, to something fused with the style of thought, and above all of emotion, associated with the Mysteries. By transforming the Jewish Messiah—a man charged with the power of Yahweh to redeem the chosen people and hum-ble their oppressors—into the messenger and incarnation of God, charged with giving salvation to *all* men and guaranteeing them a future life of bliss that would enable the soul of each and every individual to fulfill its true destiny, Saul had unconsciously amplified, generalized, and dislocated the axis of belief.

Whether or not contemporaries were aware of the potentialities of the contrast between these two notions—the Son of Man and the pagan Lord—they were inherently irreconcilable. The concept of the Son of Man com-ing on the clouds of heaven to install the messianic kingdom could never have expanded beyond the confines of Judaism (unless, of course, the Son of Man *had* come).

Thus Saul's two-pronged concept—on the one hand faith in the risen Jesus, lord of the universe, and on the other hand the ritualized worship of Lord Jesus, assimilated by Saul from his pagan milieu—ultimately became the launching platform of a new faith. Faith was shifted from the "Nazarene"—the focus of expectation for the Jerusalem Jesists—to the "Crucified One," i.e., a celestial personality prior to the creation, the incar-nation of the Spirit of God now come down to earth to generate a new mankind for which he would be the new Adam.

This cosmic myth was anchored in the key concept of the Son of God, a concept alien to all Jewish thought, since how, after all, could the unat-tainable, transcendental God of the universe engender a child in a human body?

Jews famously called anyone inspired by God, even a righteous prince, a "servant of God." In the Septuagint this is a simple Greek phrase (*pais tou theou*), in which the Greek word *pais* means both servant and child. Thus the transition between *pais,* servant, and *hyios,* son, was very smooth; it is a commonplace of Saul's writing.

Yet while this trivial pun may have facilitated Saul's approach to this grandiose concept, it could scarcely have caused it. In his assertion that "God spared not his own Son but delivered him up for us all" (Rom 8:32), Saul plainly soars beyond verbalism to a profound mythological concep-tion of human destiny. The ramifications of this mythology reverse the monotheistic process of extirpating mythological remnants and lapse into a long extinct stage of thought.

Saul's Jewish piety made it unthinkable merely to *deny* Yahweh; hence he makes a careful distinction between him and the Lord Jesus. For Saul the Lord remains, somehow, dependent on God (1 Cor 3:23) and obeys him "even unto death" (Phil 2:8); he is subject to him in all things (1 Cor 15:28). Saul sums this up in a global statement:

> To us there is one God, the Father, of whom are all things, and we unto him; and one Lord Jesus Christ, through whom are all things, and we through him. (1 Cor 8:6)

The confusion inherent in this statement is as sweeping as the statement. It had not even crossed Saul's acute, energetic mind to cope with a profound problem—the relationship between Jesus and Yahweh. It was not to be settled, indeed, for hundreds of years, until the concept of the Trinity was contrived to cope with the problem theologically if not to solve it intellectually. In Saul's time it was utterly insoluble, since the conflict between the rapidly ascending Christ Jesus, Lord of the universe, and Yahweh, the Creator of the universe—to both of whom the phrase "unto whom every knee shall bow" was applied in Saul's milieu with apparently equal force—is plainly absolute. Saul's indifference to what should have been a first-class conundrum for him illustrates the degree to which he was not, in fact, a theologian at all, but a feverish historian.

The reason Saul could disregard the whole point is evident. It did not matter. He had total trust in the impending resolution of all problems through the divine cataclysm mankind was on the brink of, and since the total transformation heralded by Jesus' resurrection was about to erupt, mere logical analysis could be shrugged aside.

Incapable of or indifferent to the elaboration of a genuine theory of the relation between God and Jesus, Saul was satisfied to describe Jesus in a shabby, somewhat threadbare metaphor; for Saul the Lord was, quite simply, "the Spirit" (2 Cor 3:17). He was content with a sort of rough-and-ready analogy that somehow brought Jesus into line with the concept of the one God and that was pointed up by the notion that Jesus was, at the same time, the Son of God.

The unconscious erosion of Saul's monotheism by pagan mythology had advanced far enough for him to regard the Lord as more or less a category of creation all by himself, the category "nearest" God, perhaps, and hence to be qualified as "divine." This was a substantial concession that was more striking in its way than even his use of the sacraments—which I shall discuss in a moment—since it represents the notion of grades of divinity, also outmoded by monotheism a millennium before. But just as Saul considered the clash of cosmic forces—angel powers and demon powers—a true source of cosmic divine action, while nevertheless looking on God as the total source of authority, so he conserved the notion of a special category of creation epitomized by Jesus the Lord. His passionate mind ignored logical flaws in one as in the other.

Saul's magnification of Jesus on this vast scale through the use of phrases hitherto reserved for Yahweh, and more particularly the transformation of Jesus into an object of cultic *worship,* meant quite simply the apotheosis of Jesus. In the short run, while ecstasy, the immediacy of expectation, and the feverishness of the milieu could anchor the nascent faith in the emotions of its believers, Saul's indifference to clarification was not disturbing. Yet clarification was bound to be insisted on sooner or later. The original theory could not withstand indefinitely the gradual simmering down of hope and the reconquest of the coming generation by the workaday world. As Jesus ascended, he inevitably coalesced in thought as well as in feeling with Yahweh. The Lord became God.

It was in this way that the twin notions of Jesus' execution being on the one hand a "stumbling-block for the Jews"—how could a Messiah be hanged?—and on the other a folly for the pagans—how could a Jewish national goal interest them?—were bypassed in favor of a "higher," more general and far more grandiose scheme. Without Saul's being aware of it, in short, his handiwork already constituted, in and for itself, a form of syncretism, even a form of Gnosis that a couple of generations later was to be expanded into complex systems.[1]

The incarnation itself, of course, did not solve the problem of the hiatus between the resurrection of the divine Jesus and its consummation in the messianic Kingdom of God leading to the Eternal Kingdom.

Saul soared above this inexplicable hiatus by using baptism, the Eucharist, and two pregnant concepts, the being-in-Christ and the mystic body of Christ.

In Saul's day no communal religion was even conceivable without a body of rites. In the pagan Mysteries the most emotion-charged rites revolved around various sacrifices designed to appease the wrath of the divinity, to secure his favor, and, most potent, to establish a fellowship between believers, uniting them with the divinity and demonstrating tangibly that they constituted a genuine "mystic" body.

The Jews had long since extracted from all such rites their magical component, and had converted them into mere symbolical acts signalizing various events, either historical or psychological. But Saul, through baptism, carried the work of ritualization and magicalization still further. He took the bread-breaking that in the Jerusalem Jesist community meant no more than the symbol of a non-"mystic" fellowship and expanded its significance.

The Jesists had made no link between the "bread-breaking" of the Last Supper and the execution of Jesus. For them it had no special value, nor was it a reflection of any expressed desire of Jesus'. But Saul forged an unbreakable link between the bread-breaking at the Last Supper and the redemptive drama of the passion. In soil already tilled and fertilized, he sowed the seeds of a sacramental sacrifice of atonement and mystical fellowship; in this way he created the key mechanism of the stupendous Mystery: not merely a commemorative, but a living symbol of the great work effected by the cross and perpetually to be re-created with every repetition.

The very epitome of a pagan idea, sometimes minified in scholarship to the phrase "a morcel of paganism," is found full-hewn in Saul:

> The Lord Jesus, the night he was betrayed, took bread, and when he had given thanks he broke it, and said: "This is my body, which is for you. Do this in remembrance of me." In the same way, also, the cup, after supper, saying, "This cup is the new covenant in my blood. Do this, as often as you drink it in remembrance of me. For as often as you eat this bread and drink the cup, you proclaim the Lord's death until he comes." (1 Cor 11:23–26)

The profundification of baptism effected by Saul was equally efficacious, equally pagan, equally magical. "For as many of you as were baptized unto Christ did put on Christ" (Gal 3:27). In structure this was precisely identical with the taurobolium and similar pagan rites, even though unlike the manner in which, in the pagan Mystery, the initiate became "an" Osiris, etc., the believer in Christ Jesus was not made "a" Christ. Yet in imagination, and above all in feeling, it was on the identical plane; a human being was linked to a divinity by a *procedure*.

Just as the adept in the Mysteries identifies the concept of "putting on" Christ with a holy garment of salvation, so in Saul's Mystery the adept's baptism is equated with a descent into death. He surges out of death after three plunges, in accordance with the rising of Christ from the tomb on the third day, and consequently from then on is guaranteed glorification on the model of the Lord's glorification.

Thus, despite the structural similarity, so to speak, between the Eucharist and various commonplace forms of sacramental participation in the death of a deity in the Mystery Religions, there is an essential difference of scale. The omnipotence of the one God, Creator of the universe, magnifies the effect of the rituals linked to him. Thus the Eucharist, by identifying the believer with the crucified and glorified Son of God, brings about a permanent alteration of reality—the immortality of the believer. In this way Saul, without changing the pagan procedure itself, heightened the symbolism to embody a quite different and infinitely more dynamic idea. Instead of becoming "a" Christ—quite inconceivable—the believer can regard the procedure as a guarantee of salvation.

For Saul the nub of the matter was the modality of guaranteeing each believer a personal share in the glory entailed by the World's End. Believers required, very naturally, some assurance of salvation at the very moment that the expected glory was in process of becoming a fact. How else could they be sure of acquiring the glory on judgment day?

At the outset the sacraments of the first Jesist fellowships were thought of as guaranteeing the messianic glory itself. It was taken for granted that believers were bound to survive to the advent of the messianic kingdom, which in those days was felt to be "at hand"—on the very point of exploding. In the very beginning, indeed, in the wake of Jesus' execution, or, rather, in the contagion that swiftly radiated outward from Simon the Rock's vision on the Sea of Galilee, it was assumed that whoever was baptized and attended the Lord's Supper was guaranteed survival in his or her natural body before the advent of the messianic kingdom; anyone who died before then was thought to have shown unworthiness of messianic bliss.

Even without Saul this primitive belief would have had to be modified. A link would have had to be welded between the resurrectional power of the sacraments and the glorious return. The link was indispensable if only because the number of those dying naturally kept increasing as the messianic kingdom kept failing to appear (see chapter 8). If the new faith was to survive, this expanding chasm between theory and fact had to be plastered over. Hence as a more comprehensive system of beliefs was tailored to fit a growing community, it was vital to create a link between the resurrectional power of the sacraments and those who had already died. This was peculiarly difficult. How indeed could a conception be devised that would create such a miracle, a procedure *now* that would have an effect on the past?

This was the function of Saul's invention. The being-in-Christ was consummated by the mystic body of Christ. It was this twin notion that was the vehicle for the implementation of this unusual idea. It established a natural link between the corpses of those who had been baptized before their death into the body-of-Christ and the resurrection medium of existence in the messianic kingdom.

It must be repeated that the forgiveness of sins through baptism was entirely *objective*; it had nothing to do with perfecting the individual's ethical nature, but merely guaranteed him deliverance on judgment day. Baptism was supposed to annul all sins committed beforehand. Saul did no more than carry on this view of the sacrament; it was no doubt current in the Jesist coteries he was familiar with. Saul's view of the efficacy of baptism—of its objective, or magical value—comes out in the question he asks in his argument with the Corinthian fellowship: "If the dead do not rise at all, why do men have themselves baptized for the dead?" (1 Cor 15:29).

The wording of this simple question shows that Saul's belief in resurrection was accompanied by a belief in the potency of a procedure that could bring it about. Since this magical device was linked to a general idea, in its nature capable of indefinite expansion, the fusion of the two was capacious enough to encompass well-nigh endless potentialities.

Saul, intent with his whole being on the immediacy of the messianic upheaval, feeling with a throbbing certainty, one senses from his Letters, that this condition of the universe was a fact warranting special urgency, had rounded off the whole complex of ideas current in his day in a unitary whole. He had created a mystical and intellectual basis for that unity by integrating the whole complex with the magical power of the sacraments.

A few simple ideas from the milieu of Palestinian Jewry were transposed to the Greek-speaking Jewish Diaspora. The escalation in the potency of these ideas in the very process of transition, an escalation in which Saul's ideas, long after his death, were to play a primordial role, was the direct consequence of a historical see-saw; the importance of Hellenism was to grow enormously after the obliteration of the Temple milieu in Palestine in 70.

There seems to have been no discord at first between the Jews in Antioch and the semi-Judaized pagans; they even ate together (Gal 2). This situation was apparently to be disturbed later on, to be sure, because the

Jesist leaders in Jerusalem were to object. But at the outset, before the "ideological" process had advanced, there was no occasion for friction. Yet at the same time the Jesist coterie, both Jews and semi-Jews, must have felt itself to be a fellowship distinct from an ordinary synagogue. Thus it was natural to utilize a conventional Jewish rite, baptism, which had originally symbolized purification from sin, and by extension a modality of initiation into a group similarly purified, as the hallmark of allegiance to the new group.

John the Baptist's baptism, an entirely Jewish phenomenon, seems to have had the same origin as the outpouring of the Spirit linked to its appearance in the Hebrew prophets. Grounded in the notion of the World's End, it guaranteed that the baptized one would be saved on judgment day.

Jesus himself, to be sure, never baptized; also, the way in which the early Jesist coteries took over John the Baptist's method of baptism is untraceable.The Jewish communities of this feverish period must have had many differences of opinion about the details, timing, sequence, rationale of personal voluntarism, and so on. Still, there are some revealing traces in the documents.

Because of the way in which the Baptist is carefully, diplomatically but insistently relegated to second place after Jesus while at the same time being accorded full honors in that status, it is obvious that very early on the Baptist's entourage merged with the Jesists. Hence baptism, as linked to John, was simply taken over as part of the merger. That may explain the curious lapse recorded in the editorial handling of the chronicle absorbed into the Gospel of John, where the statement that Jesus "baptized more than John" is followed at once by a flat denial, namely, "Jesus himself did not baptize" (Jn 4:1,2).

The chronicler, writing two generations or more after the events, at a time when the Baptists and the Jesists were one, must be implying that the Jesists had increased more than the Baptists, had become numerically strong enough to absorb them; but then he reminds his readers that Jesus personally had never baptized at all. The institution was so strong by then that any disclaimer of its connection with the putative founder of the sect must have had indisputable factual evidence against it.

The author of Acts, for instance, preoccupied with harmonizing the past with his current outlook, had to make Saul's ideas the outcome, indeed the culmination of his predecessors' views. To do so he had to overcome difficulties. For him, it is clear, those baptized by John the Baptist were quite inadequately baptized (19:1–7), and John's baptism had to be supplemented, at the very least, by the "laying on of hands" as transmitted by Saul. At the same time the chronicler feels obliged to show that Saul was just like all the other "apostles." He makes a false analogy between those baptized "into John's baptism," plainly a false identification with the much later baptism "into Jesus Christ"; then he equates Saul with the other apostles on the theory that his "laying on of hands" had the same special efficacy—equally false—as that of the Apostles. He has retrojected a much later state of affairs to an already forgotten, though recent past.

Regardless of how the two groups fused, the modality of transforming the messianist John the Baptist's rite into the baptism of the early Jesist fellowships seems to have taken place in two different ways.

The ardent hope of the World's End was immensely concentrated during its transformation into a belief in Jesus' personal role. The moment the small coterie of Jesists was inflamed by the conviction that Jesus had become the Messiah, their expectation of the World's End had a far more definite content. The descriptions of the ecstasies of the newly converted around this time make it plain that the baptism of the Spirit was felt to be a reality, that is, baptism with water was at once equated with baptism with the Spirit.

The initial transition between the personally authoritative baptism by John and the institutionally authoritative baptism of the early Jesist coteries thus came about through the succession of historical facts. As soon as John's baptism was absorbed by the early fellowships and equated with baptism by the Spirit, mere water baptism was necessarily felt to be outmoded. There was no need, in the midst of an evolving mythology, to recall the superficial historical link. The potency of symbols requires no fortification by reminiscence.

It became a matter of course, for those coming into the new coterie from the amorphous pagan population, to emphasize baptism as a rite of passage from the state of unbelief to the state of belief. Baptism came to mean, doubtless very early on, that one baptized in the new congregation was not only purified from his sins on entering the fellowship, but was actually sanctified into a consecrated group, and that his sanctification had marked him out for the Kingdom of God, moreover, by means of the name of Jesus Christ, which was almost immediately transposed so as to constitute a sort of potent divine name—"Christ Jesus." In this way baptism became the rite par excellence of the new fellowship, the fundamental criterion of communion outmoding all other standards and nullifying the former legal ideas of impurity arising out of physical contacts.

In a word, baptism itself soon became the bond of brotherhood. By realizing the communion of the faithful "in Christ" it already constituted an emotion-charged induction into a Mystery.

Saul's ardor, though cerebralized in a complicated way, was essentially matter-of-fact, down-to-earth, in a word, physical. His identification with Jesus was not remotely metaphorical, any more than it was a mere passive participation in the spiritual being of Christ. It was a genuine, matter-of-fact, personal experience of Jesus' death and resurrection.

This is illuminated by Saul's idiom. It might have seemed natural for him simply to borrow the vocabulary of the Mysteries, and to use the word "rebirth" to describe the status of the initiate, as was the case in the taurobolium, for instance, where the candidate for initiation has the blood of an ox poured over him and is then considered to have been "reborn." (In Johannine literature, indeed, the word "rebirth" seems to be used as a matter of course, unself-consciously.)

Yet Saul insisted on the rather complex, violent notion of *participating* in an already experienced resurrection; in fact he never mentions the word "rebirth" in the sense made familiar by the Mysteries. (In Galatians 4:19, for instance, he means only that he has fathered the faith of his recruits, not that they are actually born again.)

The real reason Saul couldn't use the word "rebirth" was that to his mind the dying and resurrection with Christ was a statement of fact. It described a real situation in the world.

This is of a piece with Saul's inability to regard the pagan experience of deification, i.e., identification with an actual god, as similar to the experience of a believer who has died with Christ and been resurrected with him. Whereas in the Mysteries, such as the taurobolium, the adept *becomes* the divinity through the mystical identification with the divinity via the actual blood, in the being-in-Christ the dying and rising again cannot, after all, turn the initiate into Christ; it can only induct him into a fellowship with Christ through sharing or repeating Christ's own experience.

To some extent this was because of the general Jewish inability to consider even the possibility of a human being's becoming one with God. Saul regarded the spirit of Christ as in some sense the same as the spirit of God, a basic fuzziness in his thinking, as indicated above, that was cleared up only centuries later by the concept of the Trinity.

The way Saul dealt with the sacraments will illustrate the basic differences between his mysticism, rooted in the fellowship with a Divine Being, and the mysticism of the Hellenistic Mysteries, in which the initiate became, for a limited time, a sort of god.

In the Mysteries the symbolic procedure is heightened to the point of realization; it has magical power. For Saul, on the other hand, the symbolism merely records a historic fact, the dying and resurrection of Christ, as having been realized, once again, in the believer, and realized, moreover, continuously from the moment of baptism on.

In the Mysteries, the magical procedure must be repeated, as though the reservoir of power engendered by the magic of the initiation had been gradually consumed, and to be restored had to be gone through all over again. In Saul's thought the experience itself is constantly duplicated. It is another aspect of Saul's singular realism, a realism, I hasten to repeat, that is attendant on Saul's cataclysmic view of history. This extraordinary dynamic, derived from Saul's intense experience of the mystical identification entailed by the being-in-Christ, through its formulation as a here-and-now mystical experience, endlessly repeated, of the believer in the death and resurrection of the Christ, gave Saul's views a lasting impact.

Scholars have wrangled about this matter. Many who regarded Saul's Mystery as simply one more Hellenistic Mystery were embarrassed by its patent objective realism, of a kind quite different from the mere psychological realism of the Mysteries, On the other hand, those who, intent on emphasizing Saul's originality, were concerned to deny any Hellenistic influence, were disturbed by just this grossness of Saul's thought, its matter-of-fact, concrete historicity.

It is plain, in any case, that while Saul's mystical conception of the union with divinity was different in content from the Mysteries, it was identical in structure and, most important, in magical efficacy.

It is evident that Saul regards baptism and the Eucharist as acts of power leading to redemption. They are magical procedures (though we shall see in a moment that they are, because of the general framework of Saul's ideas, no more, perhaps, than "semi"-magical). He says flatly that baptism triggers the being-in-Christ and the consequent dying and resurrection along with him. Anyone baptized "unto Christ" is united in body with him and with the other elect who are "in Christ" (Gal 3:27–8), and because of this undergoes the dying and resurrection of the Christ himself (Rom 6:3–4).

If proof were needed that this is not a mere metaphor, but a statement of an "objective" fact, i.e., a belief in the magical efficacy of the rite, it can easily be seen in Saul's argument that those people who baptized themselves *on behalf of* the dead, so that the dead could themselves benefit from the whole procedure, not only were not superstitious, but were showing that the resurrection was a fact pure and simple.

For Saul baptism was effective as burial and resurrection because it took place in the name of Christ, himself buried and resurrected; thus baptism brought about the effect of the redemption inherent in the mysticism of the being-in-Christ.

This was not original on Saul's part; he was merely carrying on the tradition he had found ready-made amongst the Jesists, that baptism guaranteed the forgiveness of sins through allegiance to the Messiah and the consequent prospect of ultimately sharing the glory that was to shine forth at his return. Saul was merely contriving another modus operandi for this simple idea through his own original contribution, the being-in-Christ concept and the mysticism involved by it. Similarly, while equating baptism with the passage of the Israelites through the Red Sea, he equated the Lord's Supper with the eating of manna in the desert and the drinking of water from the rock (1 Cor 10:1–6).

For Jews the eating of manna in the desert, the drinking of water from the rock, and the passage through the Red Sea were realistically presented episodes in the attainment of the Promised Land by the Israelites, episodes undergone by the entire Jewish people; they were simply part of Jewish history. They were never thought to be sacramental; they had simply happened, meriting no more than commemorative symbolism.

But since they had happened as exemplifications of God's will in planting the Jews in the Promised Land, they were, for Saul, divine interventions. Thus it was easy for him to enhance the historico-divine episodes on the way to the Promised Land by ritualizing them; their divine component was enough to give them a magical effect. For Saul a ceremonial act carried out in accordance with God's will contributed to salvation; in this way it became a sacrament.

Similarly, the belief in the World's End, via baptism and the Eucharist, became an integral part of the glory inherent in the messianic kingdom; thus the two sacraments paralleled the Israelites' experiences en route to the Promised Land. Since the Promised Land was the salvation of the Israelites, their experience with water (in the Red Sea and drinking it from the rock) simply highlighted the mysterious modality of water in their redemption.

Hence baptism and the Eucharist merely recapitulated the drama of redemption in the different, current era. Recapitulating the redemptive acts of God in the desert, they signalized the consecration of the elect to the messianic kingdom, i.e., to salvation in the messianic age.

Thus Saul assimilated two basic Jewish ideas, the atoning efficacy of the travail of the righteous and the suffering of the Messiah. He added a further prop by drawing an obvious parallel between Jesus dying through a divine command and God's command to Abraham, without warning or explanation, to sacrifice his son Isaac (Gen 22:9). (Saul called Jesists the children of the promise, like Isaac [Gal 4:28, Rom 9:7 ff]).

Saul extracted these three ideas from the arsenal of Jewish tradition, mixed them together and pointed them in a direction that was to prove to be sensationally anti-Jewish. He had constructed a novel procedure for salvation; the fusion of these three concepts created a dynamic idea that was entirely novel.

It was the transformation of the sacraments that created a bridge between Saul's palpably materialistic, history-shaped ideas and the ahistoric, timeless ideas that, much later, were to give the Church its foundation.

In the earliest Christian faith—that of the Jesists, the Palestinian entourage of Jesus—the idea of redemption had been linked to Jesus only insofar as he was lord of the messianic kingdom; his death was the necessary modality for the forgiveness of sins that in its turn was a necessary condition for entering the messianic kingdom. In this sense the validity of this conception of Jesus as lord of the kingdom was anchored in the validity of the whole World's End theory; hence it might have been thought that this whole complex of ideas might well have expired together with the expectation of the World's End.

But Saul's fiery temperament had enabled him to develop a feeling for a mystical union with Jesus that was entirely different in texture, so to speak, from a mere belief in Jesus. Or rather, what in a cooler, more balanced nature might have been satisfied with a mere belief in a certain chain of events—in that era not, really, very extraordinary—was escalated by ardor into an exalted feeling of psychic union. This brought redemption much closer to the actual person of Jesus and heightened his importance limitlessly.

Now, Saul magnified the magical element in this transformation still further. For him redemption no longer meant the mere assurance of participation in the messianic kingdom, but a *resurrection* to that participation. Just as his whole being had been swept into a new phase by his explosive identification with the risen Jesus, so his emotionality remained the source of a hyper-magnification both of Jesus and of the virtues inherent in the union with Jesus. This was to survive the collapse of his historical ideas—his Jewish starting point—and serve as the vehicle for an entirely new train of mystical thought.

The magic that was merely potential in the original Jesist belief in the Messiah's role was actually realized by Saul. Had Saul been in a situation in which there would have been some point in reflecting on all this, he would not, to be sure, have cared particularly, since after all he believed everything was about to end there and then. Thus the original belief in a redemption brought about in the natural world by the Messiah as usher of the new age gradually took a form inherently alien to monotheism—personal resurrection *through* Jesus Christ.

The whole range of this remarkable intellectual turning inside-out is encapsulated in a single phrase, Saul's assertion that those who have died "in Christ" will instantly rise upon his return (1 Thes 4:16).

This simple phrase, which for Saul had meant something self-evident—a mere aspect of the installation of the messianic kingdom as part of the World's End fantasied by Jews—was to serve as the springboard for an entirely novel view summed up in the notion of immortality, pure and simple, to be acquired through Christ. (It was this phrase that acted as midwife to what has generally been called the Hellenization of early Christianity.)

This was the macrocosmic aspect of what in microcosm has been said about the heightening of the magical role in the sacraments. Saul established a causal link between the sacraments and union with the risen Jesus; hence the sacraments, quasi-magical to begin with, played a causal role in the acquisition of immortality through resurrection. It was this fortification of the magical role in the sacraments that ultimately led to the idea of the Lord's Supper as a food that *in itself* conferred immortality.

It would have been out of the question to Hellenize Jesus the risen Jew of Nazareth, who was at most the usher of the Jewish messianic kingdom, but Saul tucked his original, brilliantly pregnant scheme of the resurrection via the being-In-Christ into the amplification, in the wake of Simon the

Rock's vision, of Jesus the Messiah. And it was this derivative belief of resurrection through the being-in-Christ, in Jesus as bringer of the resurrection—no longer of the Kingdom!—heightened by the magicalization of the sacraments as guaranteeing the being-in-Christ and hence the resurrection itself, that was to play a primordial role in a universal Church.

Thus the sacraments conceived of by Saul as mediating the resurrection to a messianic glory reserved for that particular generation came to bestow immortality absolutely, through a vehicle conceived of as valid for all future generations.

In short, in this sphere, too, Saul had devised a piece of functional magic originally conceived of as effective only in influencing a specific historical situation, but as history frustrated his thought and went rolling on as before, his *ad hoc* devices were ossified into integral components of a reality whose perception was institutionalized on an altogether different basis. Saul's ideas became integral parts of a world-stuff to which access could be achieved independently of God.

Pagan mysticism is rooted in nature; it is timeless. Intertwined with the fabric of the universe, it can exercise an effect on the world by means of magic. The power of its symbolism is derived from the enhancement of the symbols reflecting a fundamental world condition in the present. A person consciously repeating a symbol imports the myth into his own immediate present; he reexperiences the timelessness inherent in nature. Thus symbols reenact shifts in the natural condition.

Now, for Saul and other Jews, what was happening was not at all a timeless condition of nature, but a historical event. In Saul's mind, forces stemming from the Maker of the universe had been set in motion; they had, in fact, already transformed the world. Those forces had manifested themselves through the dying and rising again of Jesus Christ; since then their potency had been demonstrated via a specific category of people—the elect of the final generation. The potency of those forces was merely triggered by baptism.

In the pagan Mysteries what happens is, at bottom, a personal decision that affects one's destiny—one chooses to recreate or duplicate the events of the timeless world order through the ardent application of a symbol. But in Saul's mysticism, one is merely swung along into the wake of the transformation of the world order in a given historical era. The transformation itself, as part of the installation of the Kingdom of God, has nothing whatever to do with one's own decision; that decision merely enables one to participate in the transformation. The believer slips into the tide of the divine intention.

When Saul's historical analysis was nullified by the historical facts, his failure became institutionalized in the Church. Through the efficacy of the magical procedures applied by the Church the individual once again personally determines his own schedule of salvation; he chooses to demonstrate his personal involvement through the application of magic. And though the Church embodies the beliefs of a huge collectivity, the world itself is not transformed; the individual's decision functions with respect to himself because it sets in motion the symbols made potent through the system of the Church. This is peculiarly obvious in the transformation of the sacraments.

Since mankind as a whole had had its fate settled through predestination, the sacraments—initially meant, as I have indicated, for the messianic kingdom, not for the ensuing eternal bliss—had a role to play only for the elect of the final generation. To Saul's mind, oddly enough, Jesus had no role to play for mankind *at all*; for Saul, believers took part in Jesus' actual experience, in dying and rising, via the magic inhering in the sacraments; to his mind baptism was an indispensable preamble to the Lord's Supper; without baptism believers could derive no benefit from it.

Now, in the evolution of the early fellowships into a Church, the original meaning of baptism was to vanish together with the shriveling of the whole concept of the World's End. Since Saul's baptism was supposed to be effective only for the final generation, where it depended on the quasi-physical concept of bodily identity with the mystic body of Christ, the idea necessarily became meaningless when the World's End was no longer expected.

The sacraments, which had begun by guaranteeing a share in the messianic glory, were now generalized to overspread the entire orbit of the evolving Church. When the World's End theory vanished, immortality pure and simple was to become the foundation of the Church.

The distinction, for Saul fundamental, between messianic bliss and eternal bliss was simply wiped out. The whole conception of the privileged final generation of the World's End, a conception that must have given intense ecstasy to those under its sway, was outmoded. The Final Generation, not being, after all, final, became an obsolete idea. And as it receded into history itself, as people kept dying, there was no longer any distinction whatever between messianic and eternal bliss; they coalesced. The messianic kingdom expected by Saul with such urgency came to be equated with the Kingdom of God, and that too was postponed beyond the scope of ordinary emotionality.

Saul did not, perhaps, invent anything; he merely made an amalgam, a mixture of ideas of different origins, with different purposes, contrived to soothe his wretchedness. To do so he plunged far back into history.

Monotheism had, of course, repressed many unconscious elements and sublimated others, in creating a structure that could express an elevated spirituality and at the same time channelize emotions, too—up to a point. But it could not do so for Saul. His anguish made him recoil from the radical simplification inherent in monotheism. Paganism, with its reliance on the emotionalization of magic, its surrender to mysterious forces grounded incomprehensibly in the world, provided him with a gratification linked to a structure of ideas that as a Jew he could not consciously, perhaps, accept, but that, when justified, as he saw it, by the stupendous fact of Jesus' resurrection, he could digest as part of the divine plan, and digest with genuine enthusiasm, to boot, perhaps just because it had, for unconscious reasons, always attracted him.

In Saul's emotions everything repressed in premessianic Judaism surfaced. Jews had replaced, for instance, the ancient human sacrifices—traces are embedded in the Hebrew Scriptures—with a system of animal sacrifices, and later on with merely symbolic sacrifices. This meant the replacement of magical by commemorative acts.

Saul revived this ancient procedure, shifted it back to its real-life setting by having it take place via the consumption of a human being designated as a god, and at the same time enhanced the potency of that by creating a different system of symbols around an act that was, at bottom, both crassly materialistic and wholly magical. The Eucharist plainly represents the antique sacrificial notion of a divine-human sacrifice; a "morcel of paganism," it has retrogressed to a stage long before monotheism.

The Eucharist, representing the most primitive method of identification with a loved object, a symbolic way of achieving total ingestion, could be taken as an effective, well-nigh literal way of acting out the harmonization of man's relationship with the Father.

The ritual is peculiarly potent for those who can accept it because it represents the fusion of two opposite notions: the proclamation of hope fulfilled and the commonsense awareness of hope deferred. The early believers in Saul's Eucharist—profoundly different in content, though of course in form reminiscent of the mere communalism of the Passover meal—could become "one body" with the deathless glory of the Savior Lord, a symbol whose potency is heightened by its sensuality. Thus they could anticipate an integral participation at the World's End, while simultaneously, within the framework of the here and now, thrilling to the rich emotionality of a life-rhythm established by this and other sacraments.

This was not, in all probability, Saul's own initiative. The pagan type of fellowship meal was taken over by him; it consisted of transforming a communal meal into a memorial feast revolving around Jesus' death *profoundly understood*. Once this had come into existence, it was bound to heighten its significance by the ingestion of a symbol of Jesus' body. This symbolical ingestion became the sacrament; the whole meal was transformed from one commemorating the Passover meal in which Jesus had merely taken part, into one in which he was eaten. The Lord became both the feeder and the food.

The ingestion of the Lord's body has the further advantage, from the point of view of psychic economy, of providing a victim that is not harmed by the ingestion. It enables feelings of aggression to be both satisfied and sublimated, since the victim, without being annihilated in the very process of consumption, provides the sole nourishment that is effective.

Saul thought believers consumed the Lord's body *literally*; but for him the real body was the spiritual body, which was not at all immaterial, but constituted the very substance of "resurrection corporeality." Because of this the Lord's Supper united the believer with the body of Christ, which, in cosmic terms, was the only real body. Hence, since Christ the Lord had vanquished death once and for all, it was only the Lord whose existence was real, in the sense that God had intended existence to be real before Adam's sin had laid a curse on all mankind whose elect was only now, in Saul's lifetime, being ransomed through Jesus' atonement.

One is bound to admire the range and potency of Saul's mythology—he retailored the universe to his hysteria.

This idea of the Eucharist seems to be light-years removed from the simplicity of Jewish commemorative communal dinners. It could hardly be retrojected to Jesus' own lifetime. What could it have meant to contemporary Jews at an actual Passover meal, before the ritual was reinterpreted in the light of the resurrection, to be told by Jesus the "true" significance of the normal bread-breaking and wine-drinking?

Saul's Eucharist is thus very conservative, in the sense of reverting to ancient, suppressed, semi-instinctual modes of feeling, while at the same time it is, in a sense, progressive; it opens up to countless individuals the possibility of joining a new type of universal community.

The irony here is, no doubt, vast. For Saul a natural, real-life event—the dying and the resurrection of Jesus, which had happened in his own lifetime—was the matrix of both his Christ-mysticism and the sacraments that helped initiates share in the coming transformation of the universe.

This event, cosmically historical, was translated into the lives of ordinary people as a personal experience they all could share; they too could die and rise again *in real life.* This notion created a dramatic tension embodied in the Church, a tension that Saul himself, convinced the World's End was at hand, never could have foreseen. It was because of the imminence of the World's End that the sacraments, as well as the being-in-Christ mysticism, were merely ephemeral, transient, *ad hoc* accommodations soon to be nullified by the messianic kingdom.

Saul's sacraments were created on behalf of the elect of the final generation. They were thus only semimagical, so to speak, by being severely restricted in time. They had their inception in Jesus' death, i.e., in the immediate present, and remained efficacious until the glorious return—the immediate future. Fundamentally, what modified the resemblance, indeed the identity between Saul's magical procedures—the sacraments—and the magic of the Mysteries was their intellectual framework.

In the Mysteries the magic was absolute, though circumscribed; their magical mainspring tapped the energies of the mysterious realm of the world in areas where it was not subject to some particular divine power; for all pagan religions this meant the vastness of the realm beyond divinity. This meant that in the Mysteries magic within its limitations could be efficacious for all men at all times. The magic is, accordingly, pure, timeless; it functions only because it is no more than a condition of nature.

For Saul, on the other hand, all was taking place then and there on the plane of human history; all his procedures were geared to a specific act of historical transformation, everything that for him as for countless other Jews of his time was entailed by the World's End. This was the monotheistic limitation, so to speak, on the efficacy of Saul's magic. For him the magic was bound to be restricted to the performance of what may be called a historical function. The sacraments did not, in and of themselves, bestow the gift of salvation; they merely facilitated a participation in a new phase of an evolving world order, in this case the final phase.

For Saul the sacraments, despite their magical ingredient, were essentially historical, i.e., ephemeral. They started off in the immediate present—the death and resurrection of Christ—and remained valid until the immediate future—the glorious return. They had no further validity; indeed, in the nature of this train of thought they automatically became superfluous with the consummation of the cosmic transformation. Beforehand they had no function, they were simply inconceivable. Afterwards, they were inevitably bound to annul themselves. They were, in fact, contrived for precisely that particular generation, the elect of those "upon whom the World's End is come" (1 Cor 10:11).

Thus, while Saul's mythology has the structure of a Hellenistic Mystery, its momentum, rooted in the Jewish drama of history, gives it an inner consistency that radically distinguished it not only from the Mysteries but for that matter from all other forms of mysticism—its direct interconnection with the World's End. Saul's frenzied emotions, by fixing on what seemed to him to be the fact that both worlds, the ephemeral and the eternal, were already coexisting, already *there,* gave a natural background to his mysticism, which apprehended a simple reality, not created by thought, and gave his passions a solid underpinning.

This sheer physicality, linked to the World's End, also characterizes Saul's view of faith. For him faith had nothing whatever to do with the spiritualization of an old-fashioned Yahwism that has so often been ascribed to him. Faith, like all Saul's basic ideas, revolved around the conditions of the new age.

The notion that righteousness comes from faith, i.e., from a merely subjective attitude, is a gross misunderstanding of his thought. In reality the righteousness of the individual is itself a mere by-product of the fundamental world-change; it is the first effect of the being-in-Christ. It would be absurd to think that righteousness is derived from faith; that is out of the question. Faith itself acquires meaning only as an aspect of the being-in-Christ, i.e., as a consequence of the baptism that triggers the whole relationship. It is thus really an aspect of the messianic age; it is an actual condition of the universe, like the resurrection a medium of existence itself.

Like his view of the sacraments, Saul's view of ethics revolved around a palpably physical concept—the installation of the messianic kingdom. In this respect, as we can see from our own vantage point, he had taken a step backward from the general view of ethics apparently held by Jesus and John the Baptist.

For Jesus, for the Baptist, no doubt for the early coteries of Jesists, all ethics was summed up in the simple notion of repentance, a transformation of the heart consisting of penitent feeling for the past and a determination to live henceforward, liberated from earthly lusts, in the expectation of the messianic kingdom. The ethicalized conduct following baptism was supposed to be in itself the fruit of repentance. Broadly speaking, it may be said that commonsense Jewish ethics was supposed to be lived up to in full as a preliminary condition of the hoped-for Kingdom of God.

Saul took over this view, but made it fit into his general scheme. For him repentance was no more than the ethical act required to lead up to baptism, which because of its magical nature was far more than repentance, since it represented the materialization of the primordial act of having died and risen again with Jesus and hence, through participating in the body of Christ, of being able to walk about in a condition that, despite appearances, was no longer earthly. The freedom from earthliness, sinfulness, lusts, iniquities of various kinds, and so on was not a mere ethical state; people were not merely better, they were inducted into an other-worldly state of being altogether.

Like the sacraments, ethics constitutes an element in the sphere of the mystical dying and rising again with Jesus. In this respect it is the totality of being, and not at all merely the fruit of repentance, as it had been for Jesus, John, and the Hebrew prophets. It is the fruit of the Spirit, a manifestation of the being-in-Christ (Gal 5:22).

Of the two doctrines of righteousness enunciated by Saul, ethics is associated somehow not at all with righteousness by faith, but with the being-in-Christ. To deny all value to works of the Torah, Saul emphasizes—perhaps, in his polemics, overemphasizes—the inherently preposterous idea that faith requires no works *at all.* His categorical rejection of any inherent value in ethical behavior, his exclusive emphasis on the link between faith and its true anchorage in the body-of-Christ, makes any spiritual interpretation of "Paulinism" systematically wrong-headed.

For Saul, ethics is a natural function of the redeemed state; it is a mere aspect of an other-worldly, already realized identification with the risen Jesus, and with the elect constituting the body-of-Christ. Because of this it engenders the right behavior independently of any personal volition; in no case is the individual responsible for his own behavior.

Beforehand, sinners are incapable of good works, since they have not been baptized; afterwards, redeemed by baptism, sinners must produce good works as it were *automatically,* since it is not they but the effect of the risen Jesus on them that produces good works.

Properly speaking Saul has no ethics at all. If ethics is understood as a goal of free will, or in any case of a personal desire for good behavior, it is plain that Saul is talking about something entirely different. For him it is only the fruit of the mysticism inherent in the being-in-Christ that is merely *looked at* from the point of view of will. It is wholly supernatural, and thus of no concern to the workaday world or the people living in it.

The essence of Saul's thought is strikingly simple. Since Jesus is about to return in glory at any moment, all contrary appearances are deceptive. If the supernatural forces already working out the fact of resurrection and its incalculable consequences for the universe, revolving around the key concept of the World's End, are accomplishing their work without showing any external signs of it—except for Saul himself and his audience!— it is possible to live, externally, as though one were an ordinary mortal.

Saul's practical recommendations authorized a renunciation of the world that was not at all dramatic, violent, or conspicuous. It could be utterly quietist in appearance; indeed, it had the unnoticeable style of inner liberation. This was in sharp contrast with the style of other world negations, most obviously, of course, with the violent world-rejecting style of other Jewish messianists. If Saul had ever been a practicing activist "forcing the end" in the Zealot manner, his later ideas were the opposite; one could appear to be doing *nothing.*

> Brethren, the appointed time has grown very short; from now on, let those who have wives live as though they had none, and those who mourn as though they were not mourning, and those who rejoice as though they were not rejoicing, and those who buy as though they had no goods, and those who deal with the world as though they had no dealings with it. For the form of this world is passing away. (1 Cor 7:29–31)

This would evidently mean, in practice, that life would go on looking as it did before—but what would that matter? The true liberation of those who had entered the body of Christ via the being-in-Christ was necessarily internal; its potential would be realized only in the imminent messianic kingdom.

Since Saul's ethics are rooted in another condition of the world, he does not disregard ethics in the ordinary sense at all. He never expresses the idea, common enough in later Gnosticism and indeed in all elite conceptions, that those who have become superior beings, redeemed through their personal insight into the condition of the universe being brought into effect by the resurrection of Jesus, are thereby raised above ordinary people and the normal notion of good and evil in the workaday world. He does not deny ordinary ethics; on the contrary, insofar as the ordinary world continues he takes it for granted that normal views should prevail.

Furthermore, although Saul naturally holds the view that salvation through the risen Jesus is the cardinal category, when this is not directly involved he makes a point of indulging those who have not yet seen the Light. Though the freedom he has achieved through the being-in-Christ is fundamental, raising him above the mundane, small-minded concerns of finicky individuals who are excessively worried, for instance, about accidentally eating meat from pagan sacrifices (1 Cor 8:1–13, 10:23–33), and as a free man "in Christ" he can sneer at debates over distinctions between holy and unholy days, clean and unclean meats (Rom 14:19, 15:2), he does not push his notion of freedom so far as to offend those with different views if there is no need to. It is true that he maintains the primary conception of freedom from the Torah (as in 2 Cor 3:17, "Where the Spirit of the Lord is, there is liberty") as a matter of principle (Gal 2:4–5, 5:1, 5:13), but when the Torah is not playing a role of specific principle he enjoins free men not to make a point of their freedom when others are hostile or offended, but to make concessions to those who have not yet got the point.

For Saul it is not the action in and for itself but the underlying state of mind that settles the question of good or evil. It comes under the heading of expediency: "All things are lawful, but not all things are expedient" (1 Cor 6:12).

Saul is indignant at the very notion of brethren suing each other in secular courts (1 Cor 6:2–3) in a world on the very brink of extinction; they should perceive the utter futility of seeking earthly justice for those already belonging to the messianic kingdom.

He is determined, in fact, not to make trouble except for fundamental principles. Though it might have seemed a matter of course for him to soar above all dietary distinctions in the Torah, he does not; he requires his followers to submit to all sorts of limitations on what they eat to avoid embarrassing those "weaker" than themselves.

Everything is indeed clean, but it is wrong for any one to make others fall by what he eats; it is right not to eat meat or drink wine or do anything that makes your brother stumble. The faith that you have, keep between yourselves and God; we who are strong ought to bear with the failings of the weak. (Rom 14:20–15:1)

Saul does not go to the trouble of making a systematic exposition of this simple idea; it actually boils down to mere good manners, and is doubtless to be interpreted as a way of not attracting attention to trivialities in relations with a group in which he was trying to promote his ideas on important matters. It is of a piece with his acceptance of authority and other aspects of a status quo that precisely because it was ephemeral need not be disturbed more than was necessary to achieve salvation.

This gave his views on ordinary practical matters a curious commonsensicality that when divorced from his burning conviction about the messianic kingdom could and did simply fit into the workaday world and prepared the way, ultimately, for the Protestant work ethic (see chapter 13).

Despite his frenzy about the World's End, for instance, he is against indolence and sloppiness as spiritually dangerous. Thus he commends work, a little unreasonably from the point of view of the collapsing world, because he thinks it promotes spirituality in social life. In an evident hangover from old-fashioned Jewish ideas of practical life, thrift, self-respect and so on, he also commends work as an autonomous value, since it brings about independence; for him that is indispensable for an ethical person.

Aspire to live quietly, to mind your own affairs, and to work with your hands . . . so that you may command the respect of outsiders and be dependent on nobody. (1 Thes 4:11–12)

This sounds, of course, like respectable, rather banal advice, but the point is that since the world is ending anyhow we should go on living ethically in an *ordinary* sense until the great change. At the same time, to be sure, it seems clear that he has a natural, though perhaps grudging respect for "old-fashioned" virtues.

God loves a cheerful giver (Proverbs 22:8), and God is able to provide you with every blessing in abundance, so that you may always have enough of everything and may provide in abundance for every good work. (2 Cor 9:7–8)

The very thing that may be thought of as having kept him sane, despite his obsession with an idea that proved to be a delusion, after all, was his conviction that even though the great events in the offing were to be brought about objectively—by God's will—they nevertheless did not allow believers to remain indolent.

Just as he was against sloppiness and sloth, indiscipline and disorder, so he was for action; his conception of the messianic kingdom called for involvement and activity. There was, in his mythological view of cosmic clashing forces, a bitter contest going on between the forces opposing God and those championing him. Those God-championing forces consisted of the elect in loose conjunction with the Messiah. The contest made the messianic kingdom by no means a place for repose, but an area of incessant activity, even though the victory of the God forces was, of course, inevitable.

Hence discipline, order, respect for authority, and peaceable disposition were all vital. Even on neutral public occasions, such as public worship, for instance, Saul was preoccupied with "decency" and "order":

All things should be done decently and in order. (1 Cor 14:40)

God is not a God of disorder, but of order, not of confusion but of peace. (1 Cor 14:33)

For while there is jealousy and strife amongst you are you not of the flesh, and behaving like ordinary men? The works of the flesh are plain: immorality, impurity, licentiousness, idolatry, sorcery, enmity, strife, jealousy, anger, selfishness, dissension, party spirit, envy, drunkenness, carousing and the like. I warn you . . . that those who do such things shall not inherit the Kingdom of God. (Gal 5:19–21)

Practically speaking, in fact, Saul is wholeheartedly for good works!

It may be his blanket endorsement of authority *as such* that was to have the most portentous consequences.

Let every person be subject to the governing authorities. For there is no authority except from God, and those that exist have been instituted by God. Therefore he who resists the authorities resists what God has appointed, and those who resist will incur judgement. For rulers are not a terror to good conduct, but to bad. Would you have no fear of him who is in authority? Then do what is good, and you will receive his approval,

> for he is God's servant for your good. . . . For the same reason you also pay taxes, for the authorities are ministers of God. . . . Pay all of them their dues, taxes to whom taxes are due, revenue to whom revenue is due, respect to whom respect is due, honor to whom honor is due. (Rom 13:1–7)

It is obvious, to be sure, that Saul's commendation of authority, whatever it might have been responsible for, is simply the result of his general conviction that the world is passing away, hence that believers should behave with decorum to spend the short time beforehand in as orderly a way as possible. Since the believer is already free of this world he can behave as though things were different from what they are.

Superficially Saul's endorsement of authority sounds as though it might have been rooted in a concept like "noblesse oblige," an attitude expounded by Stoics long after his death but no doubt present in his lifetime too. The power of the late Stoic emperors, for instance, was supported in theory by a notion of the state that implied its obligation to do good.

But Saul had no interest in such general considerations. His theory was derived entirely from the conjunction of two Jewish ideas. One was the general notion, developed among the Diaspora Jews as a consequence of their status as guests of a variety of host societies, that it was mere common sense, reflecting *force majeure,* to accept the dominion of foreigners as long as Judaism could be practiced. For quietist religion in general, government had to be accepted; what could be done about it?

It was this theory that was expressed in the authorization of sacrifices to Caesar in the Temple in Jerusalem and on his behalf in synagogues throughout the Diaspora. If it required a more general exposition it could be found in a Talmudic compilation: "Pray for the prosperity of the government, since but for the fear of it men would tear each other apart."[2]

Still more philosophically, even those convinced that the World's End was upon them might think that secular powers were also derived from God: in monotheism *everything* is derived from God.

On the other hand, it was of course obvious that with the World's End looming up there was no need to believe in the actual validity of such secular powers; pernicious institutions bound to vanish at any moment. Saul combined this idea with the parallel one, of *apparent* quietism, and produced an intelligent, practical compromise.

For Saul, the temporal powers were bound to succumb at the World's

End and vanish together with the whole of the current world order, and were only for the time being actually ruling. Hence, since it did not matter one way or the other, the elect should pay no attention to them, avoid standing out as mischief-makers, and go about their daily business quietly. It is a pious fiction. Just as Saul advises the elect to behave as though there where no such thing as private property, and so does not call for it to be abandoned, so he advises the elect to act as though the authorities, in any case about to be wiped out, were absolutely all right.

Had believers fallen out with the authorities there would, of course, have been riots—in fact, exactly what kept happening in Palestine for generations before and after Jesus. This was just the situation that Saul was no doubt preoccupied with avoiding. Whatever might have been his mundane views before his seizure on the road to Damascus, whether or not he had himself ever been a militant messianist, later on, after the fiasco of Jesus' enterprise, he held diametrically opposed views. What he had abandoned was only the gross, external, activist form of agitation against the temporal powers of this world, in favor of submission to an other-worldly upheaval arranged by God directly. He was agitating for a spiritual, inward release from the bondage of this world, buttressing his novel theory by a denial of the entire temporal order in such a sweeping form that nothing so trivial as armed action was remotely relevant.

Jesus had appeared as herald of the Kingdom of God; then, changing his mind in midcareer, as it seems (in reaction against a Roman outrage), had flung himself against the normal world to "force the end." Saul, perhaps realizing that in the current situation moving against the Roman State was inherently hopeless, saw in consequence something more important; there was really no need to. God himself, by resurrecting Jesus, had brought about an entirely unprecedented state of affairs, dwarfing, from the Jewish point of view, the whole problem of the Roman State.

In sustaining this fiction, based on the principle that temporal regimes were to be treated as though they were carrying out God's commission, Saul could simply soar above any facts to the contrary—that countless governments were behaving *unjustly,* in ways that God could not conceivably approve. On behalf of this theory of "as though" Saul even disregards the many times he himself was wrongfully treated by authorities, which in other contexts he freely complains about (2 Cor 11:23, 25).

Thus he found himself constrained by two Jewish attitudes, or rather by the articulation of those attitudes in his own interpretation of current affairs, to praise authority absolutely with an extravagance no one had ever used before. His endorsement is indeed so intemperate, so far-fetched even in its style, that one is bound to assume that Saul's urgency arose out of the need for dissociating the Jews from any suspicion of trouble-making (Palestine was certainly getting nearer the boil) in favor of his paramount objective, promoting the salvation entailed by his theory of the World's End.

In his feverishness, Saul could actually hypostatize an ordinary historical event, taken as an example of God's intervention—passage through the Red Sea—isolate an element, magicalize it, and insert the resulting potent, independent element into another intellectual structure. His lapse into deep archaism, starting out from historic levels of Jewish consciousness, thus found itself buttressed both by history and by ancient magic.

Since Saul, like Jesus himself, and for that matter all the countless other apocalypticists, hotheads, zealots, malcontents, enthusiasts, fantasts, and dreamers Palestine was teeming with, considered the universe to be on the threshold of an imminent transformation, he naturally viewed himself and his generation as the focus of the vortex of God's plainly manifested intentions—the World's End.

Saul had reserved a special place for himself in this general scheme. For himself personally death was not to be the beginning of a perhaps somewhat pathetic intermediate state of existence; *he* was to join Jesus instantly (Phil 1:21–24). Essentially, he wanted to stay alive for the sake of the body of Christ, the new congregation of believers, and to see the fruits of his labors. He regarded himself as entirely superior to the other apostles, since it was up to him to preach to the entire world his own version of Jesus' role.

In Saul's mind, nevertheless, the fate of the Jews remained of paramount consequence. The Jews also had to be able to join the elect, and since the hardening of their hearts to what seemed to him a luminously obvious idea—though restricted to himself—was a mysterious element in God's whole enterprise, Saul was obliged to preach his Gospel to the whole world so that the Jews, *out of sheer envy,* would be converted after learning of the general conversion of the pagans (Rom 1:13–14, 17–24). This was absolutely vital to his scheme, since the glorious return could not take place until then. Thus it was only to save Israel that Saul looked to the Gentiles!

And the Jews could, after all, be saved, since according to Saul their disobedience, while mysterious, was still no more than ephemeral. Their election was not changed by it in the least; God had, as it were, discounted the whole thing in advance.

In a moment we shall see the consequences of Saul's initially logical, though passionate and capricious conviction of the World's End: how his ideas, which in their living substance were entirely historical, i.e., "practical" and contingent, were dislocated, transformed and calcified in a direction undreamed of. They were to become—theology.

In his lifetime he had to contend with something quite different—politics, or perhaps more accurately, intrigues.

11

Saul's Rivals

Despite later apologies, including Saul's, the plain fact is that Jesus' crucifixion was regarded by all Jews as a humiliating form of torture. Hence, though Jesus might have been looked up to, even revered as a martyred hero of the Jewish resistance to the detested Romans, his influence, initially, would have been entirely secular. Jewish Messiahs were expected to be victorious. Why else would they have been Messiahs?

Only the factor of emotional exaltation leading to faith could forestall the disintegration of Jesus' secular movement. The magnification engendered by faith created the belief that Jesus was to return in glory, that his death was a mere interruption in a scheme guaranteed by Yahweh.

It was Simon the Rock's vision on the Sea of Galilee that inflamed Jesus' entourage and generated a new scenario as the true explanation of Jesus' career. It created a plausible explanation of why his death—only a *seeming* death, witness the vision!—was a mere interruption, and why his glorious return, in the crisis of the age, would finally attain his objective, the objective of countless devout Jews. Thus the apparently hopeless situation involved in Jesus' crucifixion became the starting point of something quite different—a new hope grounded in a new theory.

Though Saul seems never to have seen Jesus in the flesh, his own vision of the risen Jesus involved him at once with the Jesists in Jerusalem, and thus with the fortunes of the Jewish community in Palestine, itself the center of the vast Jewish Diaspora, the countless communities of Jews scattered far and wide throughout the eastern Roman Empire and beyond, from Egypt and Asia Minor as far as Persia.

Immediately after Jesus' execution, or rather after Simon the Rock's vision, a small community of those affected by the vision established itself in Jerusalem. The news of the vision spread from this community to the Greek-speaking milieu of the Jews from the Diaspora who had set up various synagogues in Jerusalem, and from these little groups of Greek-speaking Jews had circulated into the Diaspora itself.

Saul joined the Jesists around 34, a few years after the crucifixion; he met Upright Jacob a few years later, in Jerusalem, where he went to consult Simon the Rock. He merely saw Jacob at the time without trying to consult him. But on his next visit to Jerusalem, some fifteen years later—around 51—he records Jacob's primacy among the Jesists, designating him as the first of the "three pillars"—an impression confirmed by the reference in Galatians (2:1,9), where Simon is said to have docilely yielded to Jacob's envoys in Antioch.

The Jewishness of the Jerusalem Jesists can scarcely be exaggerated. Whatever their differences with Saul later on, and whatever Saul's own attitude toward the fundamental question of the status of Judaism, it is plain (from Acts) that the Jesists were no more than devout Jews entirely integrated with the Temple milieu, its customs and rituals. The evidence for this was so solidly embedded in the earliest documents that it survived the apologetically motivated disdain for the Jews as a whole that is generally obvious in the Gospels and Acts.

The Jerusalem Jesists were, quite simply, an integral part of Israel until their extinction together with the Jewish state. Their sole perspective was the "restoration of the Kingdom of Israel" via the glorious return of their Messiah; meanwhile they were led by Jesus' brother, Upright Jacob.

The early group of Jesists seems to have been run on dynastic lines. It was no doubt natural, after Jesus' death, and after his brothers had somehow, despite the hostility recorded in the Gospels, become partisans of his views, for a brother to claim the leadership of his followers.

Since we cannot discern the nuances of what the belief in Jesus consisted of, and since our documents were undoubtedly shaped by the official view of later generations, we can only surmise the original line of differentiation in the opinions that proliferated in the wake of Simon's vision.

Jesus' resurrection did not imply that he was *there* any longer. Whatever the reality of the resurrection as felt by the earliest visionaries, it had nothing to do with Jesus' physical presence—he had conquered death *once and for all,* and was now in heaven (Acts 1:11). Accordingly, the first Jesists had a dual problem. What was the meaning of what had happened? Also, why had it happened that way?

It is plain (from Acts, *despite* the chronicler's intention) that at the outset the Jerusalem group had no ambitions for propagandizing the pagans. Why should they? They were operating within a narrow framework of expectation; their expectation was couched in Jewish terms, indeed was meaningful only in such terms. What could the "restoration of the Kingdom to Israel" have meant to pagans?

It is the manifest irrelevance of all such ideas to any pagan that gives us the key to Saul's title "apostle to the pagans."

For Saul's Letters plainly indicate that he was in no sense addressing plain, ordinary pagans. On the contrary, both he and his audience are entirely at home in the universe of the Hebrew Scriptures; they both take for granted basic ideas that have sense only for those already imbued with Judaism.

But though the Jesists had no intention of proselytizing among the pagans, the news of the resurrection as evidenced by Simon's vision and others was so stupendous that the Jesists could hardly keep it to themselves—they *had* to preach.

Within the Jewish milieu an explanation was devised instantly. All had been foretold! An explanation drawn from the Hebrew Scriptures was found at once. (The anecdote of the two disciples on the road to Emmaus [Lk 24:13–21] breathes the simple piety of a provincial milieu.) Since the belief in the risen Messiah had never been known before, it must have been extracted from its scriptural matrix, so to speak, by the tug of the vision. The Scriptures could be brought in to confirm the vision only after the vision itself was believed in (Lk 24:25–7; Acts 3:18). Thus, to a sympathetic listener, it was easy to explain the riddle of Jesus' crucifixion. But the major problem was still there—the Kingdom of God. Where was *that*?

That too could be explained to a receptive audience without too much difficulty. The Kingdom of God was there, too! It was just a bit delayed. The longed-for upheaval was now linked to the glorious return of Jesus, the risen Messiah decked out with supernatural powers, on the clouds of heaven.

For the Jesists who settled in Jerusalem immediately after the crucifixion, doubtless to wait for the installation of the Kingdom of God in the only place it could really begin, the initial credo was remarkably simple: "Christ died for our sins in accordance with the Scriptures"(1 Cor 15:3).

This was soon amplified to mean that Jesus, who had come to redeem Israel, was frustrated by the hatred of the Romans, and no doubt—if a remark put in Simon's mouth (Acts 3:14–18) is not an anachronism—by the blindness of the Jews (i.e., they had not followed him in sufficient numbers). Nevertheless, almighty Yahweh would infallibly vindicate his Messiah by sending him back to earth, this time with power and glory, to "restore the Kingdom" to a repentant Israel. The Jesists were simply to prepare for that repentance.

For the Jesists, accordingly, both Jesus' career and his crucifixion concerned only Israel, in the clutches of the Roman idolaters. The pagans had nothing whatever to do with this conception; it was a purely internal Jewish matter. The chosen people were being harassed by the powers of this world. Indeed, the pagans *in general* had to be punished as part of the overthrow of the Roman Empire (the Last Judgment, for instance, begins with the pagans lined up before the Messiah of Israel waiting to hear their fate [Mt 25:31]).

During the very earliest period following the vision of the risen Jesus the World's End hysteria was maintained, as it seems, by the ecstatic experiences of the faithful; these must have been fairly commonplace. For a limited time, the World's End hysteria was capable of overcoming the disappointment over the failure of the glorious return. With unusual rapidity, it seems, ideas began fermenting everywhere; only a few years after the execution of Jesus different theories were vying with each other in the numerous congregations of the eastern Mediterranean.

The ripening crisis in Palestine had naturally affected the Jewish world as a whole—the far-flung Diaspora congregations, all owing allegiance to the Jerusalem Temple, that made up Saul's horizons. Aside from their ties to the Temple, the congregations scattered throughout the Diaspora were, to be sure, variegated. Countless synagogues had attracted varying numbers of pagan "God-fearers" and outright converts.

The intellectual atmosphere of the scattered Jewish congregations, deeply involved in the agonizing situation in Palestine, must have been so chaotic that Saul could rove about for decades explaining things in ways that only much later were to make him fall foul of the Jesists in Jerusalem. There was no bureaucracy, and the authority of the Jerusalem Jesists could have been expressed only through the voluntary submission of the believers in Jesus' singular distinction; hence the situation was shapeless enough for Saul to work out his own ideas more or less unhindered. There was, indeed, nothing at that time, really, even to wish to control. The basic schema that arose in the immediate wake of Jesus' execution was so simple that it was bound to be expanded in one direction or another, especially since the time before the glorious return had to be filled in somehow or other with explanations of the delay. These inevitably led to some embroidery on the central themes of the Messiah and his function.

Clearly, Saul was working out his private miseries on the periphery of a situation that from an intellectual point of view remained chaotic for decades. Since the fight against the Romans must have been the dominant factor in Jewish life in Palestine for many years, Saul's own contributions to what was later, very slowly, to become doctrine, could go unnoticed in the Diaspora. It was in fact only after he had been preaching for some time that he seems to have come to the attention of Upright Jacob, leader of the Jerusalem Jesists.

Saul's personal point of view could scarcely have been alien to the little coteries of enthusiasts in the earliest period after the crucifixion of Jesus. The presuppositions of his views were present, in one form or another, in the Greek-speaking Jewish milieu he was addressing himself to; he felt he was merely reminding his audience of the implications of something whose essence they had already accepted.

Saul had surely found a body of received ideas waiting for him. He was no innovator. This is obvious from his own writings, and from the fact that the coteries of Antioch, Rome, and elsewhere were already in existence, no doubt with views of their own, before he set up as a wandering recruiter. All believed in a single elementary teaching: that the advent of the messianic kingdom was assured through the death and resurrection of Jesus. Thus it was upon a foundation of ideas inherited from his immediate milieu that Saul began speaking of what he was now constantly to refer to as "his" gospel.

Since despite his eventual confrontation, as it seems, with Upright Jacob, Saul kept writing to people for many years—twenty or twenty-five—without vexing the Jerusalem Jesists, his views, singular or not, must have been at bottom acceptable, or at least indiscernible. His praise of the Torah, his constant emphasis on the primacy of the Jews, his seeming devotion to Jesus the Jewish Messiah, were all unchallengeable.

The very style of Saul's Letters indicates the chaotic, contentious atmosphere of the time among the coteries of Jews and judaized pagans infected by the excitement linked to Jesus. The anxiety pervading his Letters makes it obvious that Saul felt himself to be at a disadvantage—he was, in fact, struggling against rivals. He refers specifically to a "different Jesus" and "another gospel" (Gal 1:6–9; 2 Cor 11:4). There is a feeling of something akin to helplessness that arises from even a casual reading. Saul's influence is circumscribed; he seems to be in an inferior position vis-à-vis superiors wielding unchallengeable authority over the Jesists, both Jews and pagans. It is obvious from the Letters that there is some sort of control being exercised over the new grouping made up of Jews and semi-Jews, and that the control emanates from the Jerusalem Jesists.

Moreover, only three men in the Jesist community of Jerusalem have a decisive voice—the ones Saul refers to, sometimes ironically, apparently, as the "pillars," e.g., Upright Jacob, Simon the Rock, and John the son of Zavdai (Zebedee). Of these three, Upright Jacob is acknowledged to be the head (Gal 2:9; 2:12); confirmation of this is to be found in the much later account of Acts (12:17; 15:13, 19; 21:18). In the Gospels, to be sure, the impression is conveyed that the apostles—whatever might have been their real function—were led by Simon the Rock, while Upright Jacob's name occurs only in a hostile context (as one of the family all of whom thought Jesus crazy [Mk 3:21, 31–35; 6:3; Mt 12:46–50; Lk 8:19–21]).

The pillars were evidently the supreme authorities for the small Jesist congregations. This is clear from Acts (15:13–21) in which Jacob's proposals are simply accepted with no debate of any kind, and it is reported without explanation (21:18) that on Saul's last visit to Jerusalem he went in "to Jacob and all the elders were present." In Saul's own Letters, too, written at a time when Jacob was still alive, Saul accepts, without the smallest objection, an obligation laid on him by the pillars to collect money for the Jesists in Jerusalem, and undertakes to do so with zeal (Gal 2:10; I Cor 16:1–6; 2 Cor 9:1–15; Rom 5:25–27).

Jerusalem is plainly the executive center of the new views. A special commission is reported as handling the propagandizing of the Samaritans (8:14ff); the problem of the pagans' conversion in Caesarea is debated by it (11:1–18); another commission is sent out by the Jerusalem group to investigate the Antioch congregations because of the propagandizing of the pagans there (11:22, 23); and a formal council settles the terms of admission for pagans into the community of the Jesists (15:6–29).

Saul is in close touch with the Jerusalem community (9:27–30; 11:25, 26, 30; 15:2ff; 18:22). Giving them a personal report is the reason for his final visit to Jerusalem (21:18, 19), which ended, as it seems, with his death, though nothing is said of what must have been the responsibility of the Jerusalem Jesists for it.

More particularly, there is evidence that Jacob had authority outside Palestine, and over a notable body of pagan recruits. In Antioch Simon, the "pillar," submits without protest to a rebuke delivered by Jacob's envoys because Simon had sat down at table with pagans (Gal 2:9, 11, 12). In short, Upright Jacob, the "Lord's brother," is preeminent (Gal 1:19).

The formula is recorded by Saul:

> Christ died for our sins in accordance with the Scriptures, he was buried, and he was raised on the third day in accordance with the Scriptures, and appeared to Simon the Rock, then to the Twelve. Then he appeared to more than five hundred brethren at one time, most of whom are alive though some have fallen asleep. Then he appeared to Jacob, then to all the apostles. Last of all, as to one untimely born, he appeared also to me. (1 Cor 15:3–8)

This formula seems to have achieved an actual liturgical shape very early. It indicates the hierarchical status in the earliest congregations of the resurrection witnesses, the only ones actually mentioned by name besides, of course, Saul himself. Saul's personal status has to be buttressed in a variety of ways because of his tardiness in rallying to the new tendency and because of his reputation as an opponent, apparently, before he was overwhelmed by his emotions on the road to Damascus.

A conundrum is looming: What could Saul have been teaching, while under the authority of Upright Jacob, that allowed him to go on as long as he did before falling foul of him? And what were his true relations with the Jerusalem Jesists?

It is difficult to grasp the differences between the Jesists and Saul before his seizure outside Damascus deflected and intensified his ardor. It is impossible, in particular, to grasp the reasons for his "persecution" of the Jesists, even if we dismiss the fury made so much of in Acts (7:58; 8:1–3; 9:1–2). That is surely part of the design intended to bring out the sensational contrast before and after his conversion; his own remarks about his aversion to the Jesists before his seizure (Gal 1:13 and 1 Cor 15:9), if genuine, are enigmatic.

If an emotional antagonism alone is looked for it might seem most likely that if Saul too had been a Zealot, as seems probable, he might have had some factional differences with other Zealots, and that his ardent polemical temperament later exaggerated those in retrospect, and then, precisely at a point when he had gone overboard for an extravagant solution of the dilemma of Jewish messianism—how to conquer the world on behalf of a God who was doing nothing to help—made him heighten his opposition to the Jesists to the point of explosiveness, thereupon resolved by his seizure.

If, that is to say, he had been a fanatical Zealot before his crisis, he might well have been so bitterly disappointed by the failure of the messianic agitation, specifically by the humiliating fiasco of Jesus' own movement, that he switched over to a point of view that soared far beyond the parochial encumbrance of the destinies of Israel, whose problems he had now undertaken to solve through his own far more grandiose projections. None of all this can be seen with certainty.

Saul's personal crisis in its own way projected him beyond the circle of the Jesists, though in that feverish atmosphere this too was not apparent for some time. Nothing survives from Saul's initial fifteen-year period of activity after his seizure, hence there is no way of knowing what he was thinking, how much he had absorbed of what views from the congregations he was familiar with, and in general what his own distinguishing notions were.

What is certain is that his own evolution, insofar as it involved the formulation of a set of beliefs—themselves a mere addendum to the feverish expectation that must have gripped every messianist household—did not take as its starting point the simple-minded hope of the Jerusalem Jesists. Saul did not start out from the contemplation of the concept of Jesus and proceed along the bridge of whatever beliefs about him were held in the Jesist community; he must have developed his characteristic attitudes via a Jewish congregation in the Hellenistic world.

Not only did Saul not know Jesus, but he had nothing to do with the formation of the early Jesist groups, which aside from Antioch and Rome had sprung up in Phoenicia and Cyprus (Acts 11:19).

There was, no doubt, something inherently sterile in the beliefs of the Jerusalem Jesists; after all, since they had no thought of abandoning traditional Judaism, they were really limited to a cluster of attitudes that could lead nowhere unless their basic hope came true—unless Jesus did, in fact, return in glory on the clouds of heaven. The Jesists had a simple problem, solved in a simple way.

If Jesus had been resurrected, and it had been not a mere resurrection, like that of Lazarus, for instance, but his glorification at the right hand of Yahweh, that could have meant only one thing; Yahweh had intended to distinguish Jesus uniquely—he was the Messiah!

This was convincing to those whose ardor had led them to accept Simon the Rock's vision; it was easy to tuck this magnified conception of Jesus into contemporary messianic speculation. Jesus was instantly identified with the "Son of Man" outlined in the book of Daniel, a model for feverish fantasying about the World's End.

But Saul doesn't even mention this; even if he knew about it, which may be likely, he had no interest in it. Thus, even in this simple matter of the chief attribute of the failed Messiah, he was already at odds with the Jerusalem Jesists, though the meaning of this was not yet clear.

For the Jesists, Jesus' death did not demand any idea of atonement as an explanation; for Saul, the formula he found ready in the Hellenized Jewish congregations was peremptory: "Christ died *for our sins.*"

Saul himself utilized another formula, also taken over from the pagan milieu; this formula, fundamental not only in all his Letters but also in all the New Testament writings emanating from the pagan milieu, was centered in the word and the concept of the "Lord."

Similarly, though the Messiah could never have been conceived of as himself a sufferer, it proved possible later to find an appropriate phrase in the classical prophets: "Despised and rejected of men, a man of sorrows and acquainted with grief . . . he was despised and we esteemed him not" (Isaiah 52:3ff).

This was surely out of the question as a reference to any Jewish Messiah, if only because the idea of a sacrificial death, or the expiatory sufferings of a Messiah, could never have meant anything to a Jewish audience as long as they believed in the Torah. For the devout of Israel, after all, the messianic hope did not constitute an obstacle to the Torah, but its natural sequel.

Thus neither Saul's doctrine of the Messiah nor the early Jesist conception was a mere extension of any strand of Jewish traditional messianism, but the natural consequence of a novel historical fact—the execution of Jesus. It was the fruit of the speculation that became rife after Simon's vision.

Chronologically, Saul was merely an organizer of the second phase; he says as much in a celebrated passage in which he says quite clearly that he had "received" a tradition from others before "delivering" it to the Corinthians (1 Cor 11:23). The true architects of the nascent faith, as it seems, were the founders of the Antioch congregation, whoever they were. It was there that the word "Christian" was coined and the "Lord Jesus" was first preached, not merely to the Diaspora Jews, but to the "pagans" (Acts 11:19–21), no doubt to the pagan "God-fearers" clustered around the synagogues, inspired by the followers of Stephen, the first martyr in Christian tradition. (Even as late as the composition of Acts, pious chroniclers thought it so bizarre for a Gentile to believe in Jesus that a special revelation for Simon the Rock himself was felt to be necessary [Acts10]).

What Saul did, essentially, was to establish the orbit, both intellectual and emotional, by means of which what had once been a divine project for the benefit of the Jewish people was transformed into a religion of salvation closely modeled on the prevalent Mysteries. But all this was happening on a terrain that was spiritually far removed from the activities of the Jesists in Jerusalem, nor do we quite see, beyond a few dim echoes in Saul's Letters and the wholly tendentious, i.e., piously falsifying chronicles of Acts, exactly how they reacted to it.

It is scarcely conceivable that the founders of the Antioch congregation and Saul himself could have been acting *consciously* outside the confines of Judaism, a massive institution supported by a powerful government, with an internationally famous, rich and solidly established shrine. Nor was it possible, as we shall see, for Saul or doubtless anyone else still within the framework of official Judaism merely to disregard the wishes of the central community of Temple-worshipping Jesists led by Jesus' brother, Upright Jacob.

Now, if we realize that the Jerusalem Jesists simply went on believing that the Kingdom of God in its nature entailed the destruction of the entire secular order—the Roman power plus its props in the local aristocracies— there must have been a schism within the Temple hierarchy itself, between the quietists—with some notable exceptions, as we shall see—supporting the Roman status quo, and the seditionists, including the lower orders of the Temple hierarchy.

The Jewish orthodoxy of all groups is manifest. The Jesists were all narrowly encased in an unquestioning allegiance to the Torah; more significant, as we shall see, they were embroiled in the national resistance to Rome.

It is evident that many priests and Pharisees were members of the little community of Jerusalem Jesists (Acts 6:7; 15:5). Many Jesists took the Nazirite vow, as did Saul (Acts 31:23–24; 18:18). Jacob mentions many Jesists as "zealous for the Torah" (Acts 21:20); even if this does not mean that they were in fact Zealots, it testifies at least to their militant orthodoxy. Nor is this in the least surprising, in view of the substantive identity between the various groups of national activists. This is demonstrated by the absence of any indication that when priests joined the Jerusalem Jesist community there was any change at all in their professional status.

The seditionists represented an integral part of the intractable segment of Palestine Jewry. There were enough of them, after all, to bring about, only a few years after Saul's death, the fatal revolt of 66–70, which brought matters to a head in the Temple itself.

This really meant that sedition vis-à-vis Rome was in the very air of the Jesist community, and that Upright Jacob was or had become a faithful follower of his brother with respect to the cardinal aspect of his brother's hopes—the installation of the Kingdom.

Saul's assumption of the mystic unity of the Church—the mystic body of Christ in the vision of an ideal community of God encompassing the flesh-and-blood congregations of fellow believers in Jesus' salvational role—automatically entailed the acceptance of the authority of the Jesists in Jerusalem, the unquestioned center of the nascent faith (Rom 15:19; Gal 1:17ff; 1 Cor 16:3).

This may have been because all the crucial events in the dramatic career of Jesus took place there (except Simon's vision) but also, no doubt, because Jerusalem was bound to remain, quite simply, the religious center for all Jewry.

The indications of Saul's subordination to Upright Jacob are legion. Throughout Galatians, at the very moment he is struggling to flaunt his independence, he shows himself to be dependent on the Jesists in Jerusalem; he accepts their temporal priority, calling them "apostles before me" (Gal 1:17). Most important, he accepts the burden of collecting alms for the Jerusalem group not only without protest, but with zeal (Gal 1:10).

He shows his dependence on the real-life Jesus at the very moment he is obliged to establish his own position. Though he tries to equate his experience with that of the apostles, he puts himself a long way down the list, after the five hundred anonymous people who saw the risen Jesus; only then does he thrust himself in, calling himself "untimely born," to boot.

At the same time, of course, he prides himself on his uniqueness; he implies that his mandate comes straight from God, hence has nothing whatever to do with the apostles, whose status is no more than an echo of mundane reminiscences (1 Cor 15:1 ff). He says that God "revealed his son to me, that I might preach him among the Gentiles" (Gal 1:15,16).

The conflict embedded in all Saul's Letters revolves around two things, the indispensability of circumcision for would-be members of the nascent sect, i.e., the most extreme example of the burden of the Torah, and Saul's own authority.

Even a casual reading of the Letters indicates that Saul's defense takes three forms, each of which is no doubt aimed at an attack coming from one of three directions.

First of all, he lays great stress on his own independence of the Jesists in Jerusalem (he says with heat that his own conversion had been brought about by direct action on the part of the Savior himself).

Then, in a very awkward-sounding passage, he claims to have gone to Jerusalem much later as a result of a "revelation" there, but at the same time he is obliged to report to the Jerusalem leaders about his agitation among the Greek-speaking congregations in the Diaspora synagogues, "lest I had run in vain" (Gal 2:1–10), i.e., lest the Jesist leaders simply nullify his efforts.

Then, after reporting an incident to do with the circumcision of his pagan recruit Titus, he is obliged to admit, in a very roundabout way, that in spite of his disclaiming any special concern for the Jerusalem Jesists, his work had, in fact, been recognized by the three pillars (i.e., Upright Jacob, Simon the Rock, and John, son of Zavdai).

The nature of this "recognition," to be sure, remains vague. Saul claims there are two gospels, one for the "circumcised"—i.e., the observant Jews—the other for the "uncircumcised"; he assigns the former to Simon, the latter to himself. Nevertheless, at the same time, he makes his celebrated remark on being all things to all men: "To the Jews I became as a Jew, that I might gain Jews" and explicitly contradicts his allocation of territory to Simon and to himself, as between circumcised and uncircumcised.

Saul tells all this to the Galatians because, presumably, some rivals had been giving a different explanation of this particular trip of his to Jerusalem, questioning his attitude toward circumcision and forcing him to invent a somewhat conciliationist explanation of the peculiar dichotomy in the agitation promoting the messianic elevation of Jesus.

The episode of the table-fellowship in Antioch is surely illuminating. Simon at first sits down at table with some pagans, i.e., no doubt pagan "God-fearers," but when some envoys arrive from Upright Jacob he retreats. This shows that he was subject to the authority of Jacob; it must have led to a falling-out of some kind, since, if they could have been reconciled on this point, Saul would surely not have missed a chance to tuck it into his general ingratiating attitude toward the Jesists. The Antioch episode makes it clear that whether or not Saul had been given some support by the Jesists beforehand, it was nullified by what happened at Antioch.

It must have led to a crisis. Let us assume that Saul had received some sort of general mandate from the Jesists, tried to apply it in detail in Antioch, and Simon fell in with it at the time. But the moment the general mandate was applied in a specific case—of crucial importance for a whole body of legislation in the Torah revolving around the food laws—it was countermanded by Upright Jacob; Simon, seeing the point, knuckles under.

Thus the attack on Saul's competence is implicit throughout Galatians, which does not, to be sure, record the outcome of the conflict. In 1 Corinthians, however, Saul actually enumerates *four* conflicting views: his own (by implication), Simon's, Apollo's, and, strangely, that of the party of "Christ" (which, since in the original it could have meant no more than "messianist," might have been some other group magnifying Jesus on a merely human scale [1Cor 1:12; 3:22]).

Acts very obviously distorts what must have been the real situation by describing Simon's attitude to circumcision as being the same as Saul's at a time when it was precisely this conflict on a fundamental issue that was getting Saul into hot water with the Jerusalem leaders. For that matter Jacob, too, is seen making only a few simple moral and dietary demands on the pagan converts (Acts 15:19–21).

It may well be that the very success of the contagion among the pagan "God-fearers" confronted the Jerusalem group with a fait accompli, to which they responded, at least initially, by insisting that the pagan adherents of the new belief, i.e., in the special role of Jesus as Jewish Messiah, become full-fledged Jews, i.e., accept circumcision as well as the other obligations of the Torah. It was precisely this situation, in fact, that created the axis for the first conflict we can discern between the entourage of Jesus and the growing number of pagans outside Palestine who had come under the influence first of Judaism in general and then of the specific variety of Judaism bound up with the messianic hope represented by Jesus.

The Gospels and Acts, though composed long after Jesus' death, contain a kernel of historicity whenever they display antipagan attitudes; these are likely to be factual since they run counter to the apologetic tendency as a whole (our cardinal criterion).

Hence we see that these antipagan attitudes, to be thought acceptable, must have survived in the first community of Jesists, and have characterized that community until long after the crucifixion, indeed, for generations. Unhistorical in their own attitudes, the chroniclers unwittingly reflect a situation that must have prevailed during the period prior to Jesus' death, when the countless ecstatic or activist messianists were enthralled by the Kingdom of God.

The significance of circumcision, from the Jesists' point of view, was obvious; it had, indeed, a political overtone. It warranted the authenticity of the conversion to Judaism. Thus Saul's categorical dismissal of circumcision as not having the smallest significance in and for itself—"neither circumcision counts for anything nor uncircumcision"—was clearly something that was bound to destroy him and ultimately did. It was all part of the accusation made by Jacob that Saul had been "teaching all the Jews who are amongst the pagans to forsake Moses, telling them not to circumcise their children nor to observe the customs" (Acts 21:21).

We can perceive, accordingly, even through the veil created by the bias of Acts, an original differentiation within the small subsection of the Jewish community, a differentiation whose consequences were to become apparent only after the cataclysm of 66–70 and the obliteration of Jewry as a normal community rooted in its own land. The differentiation could scarcely have been apparent to the participants—a characteristic of history!—since whatever the friction over details or even principles might have amounted to, it was completely overshadowed by the expectation of an imminent upheaval that was in essence the same for all activist, ecstatic groupings, i.e., the reentry of God into history.

For the small group of Jesists in Jerusalem, the center, however inchoate, of the scattered enthusiasts throughout the Diaspora, that reentry was a simple repetition of what they had, no doubt, expected with the appearance of Jesus himself—the Kingdom of God, installed this time through the glorious return of Jesus. This ardent belief in the imminent upheaval was shared by the Greek-speaking Jews in the Diaspora; the difference, which was to become overwhelmingly important, was only that for them, during the brief period of waiting, it was natural, under the pressure of a pagan environment, to begin transforming the fact of Jesus into the concept of Jesus, and then to embroider on that. A singularly fruitful activity!

The reason Saul's eccentricities went unnoticed as long as they did was their relative insignificance vis-à-vis the expectation that gripped the entire community. Ultimately, to be sure, they got him into trouble with Jacob and the other pillars in Jerusalem, but for years, as Saul traveled back and forth among the tiny congregations of the northeastern Mediterranean, embroidering his fantasies onto the received figure of Jesus the Jewish Messiah and trying to extract a meaning from the concept to justify his own embroidery, it must have seemed that he was, in a way, doing no more than explaining something to unimportant audiences of judaized pagans who would in any case soon be swallowed up by the great transformation and thus pass into the Kingdom like all the other elect.

It was no doubt only with the passage of time, as the great change failed to materialize and Saul's ideas became fixed by dint of repetition buttressed by further projections of his psyche, that the pillars expressed their disquiet and, still without falling out with Saul, asked for some reassurance.

Consequently, since Saul must have been familiar with the insurrectionist mood of the Jerusalem Jesists, who were, after all, merely carrying on Jesus' own activist line, he obviously must have felt at home in the milieu. He was, in fact, solving the same religious problem that was being solved by the Jerusalem Jesists. How to obliterate the world order. While providing the somewhat one-sided, unelaborated, simplistic approach of the Jerusalem Jesists with a more spacious intellectual framework, he was wiping out, in his own mind, the foundations of the workaday world by explaining a state of affairs that was already in some sense present, and that needed clarification only because so many Jews refused to grasp it. Thus he had to interpret the state of affairs arising out of the resurrection of Jesus and to circumvent the baffling incomprehension of so many of his fellow Jews.

In this period before the destruction of the Temple, when Upright Jacob was a priest officiating normally in the Temple, there was nothing in the original Jesist faith that could have seemed offensive to other Jews. Believers in Jesus were living normal lives, as far as the Temple was concerned, merely being wrapped up, like countless Jews at the time, in fantasies about an imminent final catastrophe. There was no occasion for the control of thought; all was still under the canopy of the Temple.

Indeed, the only reason for any control at all was in connection with money. If the early Jesists were merely waiting for the glorious return, the Jerusalem group must at first have made demands on its sympathizers for money and nothing else. That may explain why envoys were sent out to find support. In any case that in itself signalized the subordination of the foreign congregations to the authority of Jerusalem.

Yet eventually, as we know, Saul's differences with the Jesists, though overlaid by the common frenzy about the World's End, eventually surfaced—or rather, they surfaced before the destruction of the Temple in 70. Afterwards, as we shall see, they triumphed.

Acts is our sole source for the spread of the nascent faith as viewed from the perspective of the Roman defeat of the Jews. Yet from a historical point of view, oddly enough, Acts is simultaneously priceless and worthless. Its overriding apologetic intent is manifest; the author has set out, it is plain, to demonstrate that by God's grace the faith of the tiny community in Jerusalem, numbering some 120, bloomed mightily, and at the end of the chronicle had come to the great capital of the world, Rome, there to be preached "openly and unhindered" (28:31).

Acts harmonizes everything. There were no real clashes, divergences of opinion were peaceably compromised; though the "mother Church" had priority, there was no disagreement with anyone. Saul, who had died at least forty years before the composition of Acts, had been a great apostle, authoritative, etc.

There are two quite different versions extant of how the new belief was carried abroad. Both Acts and Saul's Letters concur with respect to the territory that was Saul's principal arena, i.e., the vast area northwest of Palestine, taking in Crete as well as the cities of Greece and going on to Rome (a congregation was in existence there well before Saul, as he indicates). But they disagree completely about how the new ideas were disseminated.

Neither Acts nor Saul pays any attention to the spread of the new belief south of Palestine, notably in Alexandria, Egypt, where there was an enormous community of Jews that like other Jews must have been agitated by the sedition simmering in Judea. Neither Acts nor Saul mentions any Jesist activity there, though Acts refers (19:1–7) to some sort of intellectual fermentation in Alexandria revolving around Apollo, the enigmatic figure Saul also mentions as a competitor.

Now, since John's ritual of baptism must originally have been entirely independent of Jesus' activity, it is evident, from the pains taken in the

Gospels and in all references to the Baptist to accord his career with that of Jesus, that the Baptist, however exemplary, was nevertheless subordinate—from the subsequently triumphant point of view of the Church—to the Messiah, Jesus.

The Baptist's followers, whatever the details of their beliefs, must have been close enough in tendency to the Jesists for both coteries to have coalesced early on; groups representing these various points of view were dwelling amicably together in the same congregations, as in Corinth. Hence, before Saul's ideas emerged as "Pauline" in a fixed form long after his death, it was not at all strange for Jesists to accept people who believed only in John's baptism. They were still unaware of the later development that was to turn the Baptist into a mere forerunner of Jesus.

Now, whatever John's baptism meant in the messianic ferment of the time, it could surely have had nothing to do with the notion that Jesus was the Savior of mankind. Accordingly, whatever made Apollo a luminary in Alexandrian Jewry, he represented a belief that, though independent of Saul's own complex, subtle and logical interpretation of the meaning of Jesus' career, could circulate freely in congregations where Saul, too, had a foothold.

The nascent faith must have spread very rapidly. Simon the Rock, for instance, seems to have been known to the recruits in Corinth; Saul mentions him as the inspirer of one of the four groups there. Furthermore, Saul, though he expresses himself circumspectly, makes much of combating people with a "different gospel." He does not invoke his own authority, but merely calls on those he had inducted into the Jesist group to cling to his own interpretation instead of straying after others (Gal 1:6ff; 2 Cor 11:1ff).

Though Acts is remarkably taciturn about all frictions in the earliest community of Jesists, its reticence is far from perfect. The apologetic bent of the chronicler, while pervasive, lets a few revealing discrepancies slip through. It is intriguing to see how fragments of earlier, doubtless historical situations have been conserved. The entire last half of the book, for instance, is preoccupied with grounding Saul's authoritativeness, though a contrary reminiscence has nevertheless been preserved. While Saul was "trying to convince" some Jews about Jesus on the basis of the Torah and the Hebrew Scriptures, "some were convinced by what he said, while others disbelieved" (28:23,24). Surely an echo of a fact!

It is against this apologetic background in Acts that the mention of Apollo (18:24) must be judged; it seems to puncture the chronicler's camouflage. Apollo, Saul indicates, must have been important in Corinth (1 Cor 1:12; 3:4, 21–23, 4:6); his following is put on the same level as that of Saul himself, of Simon the Rock, and of the group referred to as "of Christ." He must be the same Apollo mentioned in Acts as a notable leader in the "apostolic generation"; if so, it is a big puzzle.

Apollo looks quite odd. Though he is said to have "carefully taught the things concerning Jesus," and was, indeed, "mighty in the Scriptures," as well as "fervent in spirit and instructed in the way of the Lord," yet he quite incomprehensibly knew "only the baptism of John." Apollo does not seem even to realize that Jesus had played a special role at all.

Not only did Apollo not share Saul's views about circumcision, to say nothing about Saul's grandiose conceptions of the body of Christ, the dying and rising again with Christ, and so on, he did not even know that John had predicted the advent of Jesus. In fact, Acts says, in its usual sugary style, two of Saul's friends had to "expound to Apollo the way of God more carefully." Apollo, totally unaware of any of the later "ideology," sounds as though he must have been a mere baptist messianist, no more, no less.

Historically, this may tell us a lot. There must have been a record of this Apollo as having been active in Alexandria, a place otherwise entirely disregarded by both Acts and Saul, with a different view of the messianic turmoil agitating the Jewish communities. Apollo must have been carrying on a line of agitation in Alexandria altogether at variance with Saul's; by the time Saul's Letters came to be revered the mention of Apollo could not be edited out. Documents mentioning Apollo could not simply be swept under the rug; they were assimilated in a well-meaning, piously fraudulent style, so that the general impression of harmony in the idealized earliest community need not be disturbed while the references were being stitched into the conciliationist fabric. The chronicler of Acts, unaware of our own, history-minded criteria, simply handled with earnest obtuseness documents reflecting an entirely "schismatic," i.e., as yet unharmonized situation in Alexandria.

In their present context the references to Apollo are bound to remain unintelligible. John's baptism, looked at from the much later, entirely unhistorical view of the early hagiographers, was nothing but a dim prototype of the baptism in the Holy Spirit and fire that had been assigned to Jesus, whom the Baptist was supposed to have merely pointed to as the coming one mightier than himself (Lk 3:15–17).

Thus in Corinth we have a cluster of mutually exclusive points of view in an amorphous milieu being worked on by different individuals in different ways. The account of Stephen's martyrdom is rewarding.

Stephen, in his trial before the Sanhedrin (Acts 7:1–53), not only denounces the Jews for their obduracy, but also attacks the Temple, at least partially. Since the Gospels never attacked the Temple as such, and indeed conserved many remarks made by Jesus confirming the validity of Temple worship, the speech put in Stephen's mouth before the Sanhedrin contradicts the harmonizing tendency of the chronicler. If Stephen did in fact act against the practices of the Jewish Temple, his stoning must demonstrate a contrast between himself, whatever he represented, and the other Jerusalem Jesists led by Upright Jacob, who remained on unharmed after Stephen's execution.

The distinction between Stephen and the "twelve apostles" is unmistakably indicated (Acts 8:1), though the chronicler, to be sure, doesn't bother to explain why the "apostles," the leaders of the Jerusalem Jesists, were exempt from the harassment of Stephen and his group. In fact, the "seven deacons," supposed to be merely menial administrators of the Jesist community, seem to go in for just the same kind of agitation as the "twelve."

This curious discrepancy may simply stem from the general purpose of the chronicler of Acts—who is also the author of Luke—to trace back the history of the Jesists to Jerusalem. Hence the much later split in the community, a split that emerged only after the destruction of Jerusalem in the war against the Romans, would also be traced back to Luke's ideas of its origins, and a thoroughly anachronistic speech, full of hatred for the Jews, could be ascribed to Stephen.

Though Acts might plausibly have made much of Stephen, whose career seems to have been so promising from the point of view of propagandizing the pagans, it unaccountably drops him completely and switches over to a build-up of Simon the Rock's missionary exploits, an episode that culminates, again quite unaccountably, with his acceptance of Cornelius, the Roman, and some friends of his into the messianist community. Simon has to defend himself, it seems, against the orthodox Jesists in Jerusalem led by Upright Jacob.

This amounts to saying that Simon and Saul had identical attitudes— another instance of harmonization. It can hardly be anything but a fabrication along the lines laid down by the very nature of the apologia; it is a jagged, spasmodic effort to reconcile Simon the Rock and Saul, who on all recorded points must have diverged.

The rest of Acts is devoted to Saul; it makes him the exclusive promoter of Christianity, though for the time in hand this would seem to have been utterly anachronistic. Alexandria, where Jewish messianism must have had a strong foothold, in view of the size of the Jewish community and the turbulent episodes recorded of relations between Jews and pagans, is not even mentioned, nor is any indication given that the Jesists in Rome had been there before Saul.

Acts gives a brief account of the Jesists' attitude to some innovations in admitting pagans to the early congregations. Saul and Barnabas—little else is known about him—are described as having had great success amongst the Antioch pagans. Some of the Jesists in Jerusalem seem to insist—perhaps via envoys—that the acceptance of the Torah is indispensable for the admission of new believers. A delegation from Antioch led by Saul and Barnabas goes to Jerusalem; they have a collision with some of the Pharisees among the Jerusalem Jesists (Acts 15:1,2,4,5). The whole question is settled in a "general council" of the "apostles and elders," presided over by Upright Jacob. The council hands down a judgment that is entirely along the agitational line ascribed to Saul. Upright Jacob, speaking for the general council, declares all pagans totally exempt from all requirements of the Torah; all they have to do is observe a few elementary moral principles—doubtless an echo of the "Noachide" laws thought by Jews to apply to all mankind—and some dietary restrictions. Moreover, the Jews who had complained about the abrogation of the Torah in Antioch are specifically condemned; Saul and Barnabas, steadfast, are lauded.

But in Saul's lifetime his characteristic views were *not* approved by the Jerusalem leaders. His Letter to the Galatians, written in the heat of the fray two generations at least before the harmonizing efforts of Acts, violently attacks the whole idea of forcing circumcision on pagans before letting them into the Jewish messianist movement.

Saul completely omits any reference to the so-called general council mentioned in Acts as having established harmony between these two conflicting views in favor of the departure from the Torah that *in fact* had become the hallmark of the nascent faith. Saul never mentions any settlement of this dispute in his favor; in view of his obvious concern with placating or mollifying the Jerusalem Jesists, whether they were his opponents or merely his rival fellow believers, we can see that in Saul's lifetime his views were unacceptable.

Saul's fund-raising on behalf of the "saints in Jerusalem" was vital to him. It was to represent the fruitfulness of his efforts among the congregations of Greece and Asia Minor. Romans 15, written before he left Corinth for Jerusalem, says that the money was for the "poor among the saints"; i.e., the alms were to enable the Jerusalem Jesists to go on waiting for the imminently expected glorious return.

The purpose of the collection was to show that the pagans had indeed found salvation in the Jewish Messiah, i.e., that Saul's amplification of Jesus' role had in fact borne fruit. The collection represented several years' activity on Saul's part; it had to be handed over in Jerusalem in a dramatic way, i.e., to show, by the presence of at least eight companions representing pagan congregations (Acts 20:4ff), the sensational effect of such a public demonstration. The world at large would become aware of the potency of Jesus' role in the salvation of the human race by the mass conversion of the pagans—i.e., mankind. Saul conceived of this—as indicated elsewhere—as the penultimate stage of the cosmic drama whose climax was to be the glorious return. The prophets Isaiah and Micah would be vindicated; with the pagans converted, the Jews could be too, whereupon the divine scheme would be consummated.

Saul might, perhaps, have considered that the dramatic presentation of the collection would put him in a good light in general, and make up for the disquieting reports that had no doubt been filtering into the Jerusalem milieu. In this way a general reconciliation might be brought about between himself and his previous mentors, if that was how he still thought of them. In any case, as we shall see, his aims were frustrated. All his hopes, whatever they might have been, foundered on the conflict he ran into in the Temple. He met his death as a direct result of a riot in the Temple, though the circumstances must be extracted from the pious camouflage of Acts and its subsequent editors.

Saul was to emerge after his death from the obscurity and, perhaps, the obloquy of his later career. From the point of view of the generation that followed he was the chief thinker of the nascent sect, as indeed he was to remain during the efflorescence of Christianity. But throughout the ending of Acts, throughout the apologetic vagueness and willful inconsequentiality of the whole account, a sinister thread of portending disaster can be discerned. Broken off and camouflaged by the requirements of the apologia, this thread remains visible as a testimony to Saul's end.

The trip that Saul, unaccountably at first, seems to be obliged to make to Jerusalem is mentioned several times. First we are simply told that he must "go to Jerusalem" before "seeing Rome" (Acts 19:21). A little later Saul explains the trip by the need to give alms to his nation (27:17); then we are told he is prevented from sailing from Greece to Syria by a Jewish plot, even though he is simply bringing alms to the Jerusalem community and members of the Temple hierarchy (20:3). Then, bypassing Ephesus in his haste to get to Jerusalem by Pentecost, he summons the elders of the Ephesian congregation to Miletus for the express purpose of hearing him. Saul is very apologetic; he stresses that he is "innocent of the blood" of all those present; he is going to Jerusalem entirely pure, but does not "know what will befall" him there. He sums up:

> I know that after my departure fierce wolves will come in among you, not sparing the flock; and from among your own selves will arise men speaking perverse things, to draw away the disciples after them. (20:17–38)

The passage is full of unexplained foreboding. He seems to be going to Jerusalem despite the warning of the Holy Spirit; suffering, perhaps death, may be lying in wait for him. He tells his sympathizers that he will never see them again; he gloomily foretells the troubles that will come about when he is gone. Before his arrival in Jerusalem he is warned by a prophet speaking through the Holy Spirit that he will, in fact, be arrested by the Jews and handed over to the pagans (21:10–12).

Despite all these premonitions, recorded with no explanation, Saul persists; the reader must believe the trip was unavoidable. The chronicler seems to be telling the reader the minimum allowed by his apologetic intention.

The crucial episode is, of course, Saul's conduct in Jerusalem. After he reports on his work to Upright Jacob in the presence of the elders (21:18,19), the whole group "glorifies God." Then Jacob points out what has already been made clear about Saul's opposition to pagan circumcision and to the Torah (21:20–22).

Now, though the chronicler draws no inferences from all this, they are obvious. The Jerusalem Jesists are committed to the Torah; all are hostile to Saul for his behavior in the Diaspora. From their own point of view, as we know from Saul's Letters, they were entirely justified.

This is what leads to the test imposed on Saul's public orthodoxy (21:23,24). Here, too, the background is convincingly matter-of-fact—

that is, put in by the chronicler unwittingly. The central authority is never questioned. This must reflect the historical reality; Saul was bound to accept the decisions of the Jesist core anchored in the Temple. It was to them that he made his report, and they who indicted his misconduct.

The handling of Saul's death in Acts points up the crucial issue of the entire account—the very issue, indeed, that constitutes the reason for the chronicler's apologia. Logically, Saul's reinterpretation of the Torah—or rather of the interaction between the Torah and redemption after the resurrection of Jesus—led to a negation of the unique position of Israel (Gal 1:10; 1 Cor 16:1–6; 2 Cor 9:1–15; Rom 15:25–7).

This made it easy for Upright Jacob to put Saul in a dilemma. Saul had to show that he had been living up to the Torah, that there was "no truth" in what they had been told about him (Acts 21:24). He was to pay the charges for four Nazirites to shave their heads; he was also to purify himself with them.

The Nazirite vow was an ancient and expensive custom, considered a persuasive symbol of piety.[1] Upright Jacob himself was a Nazirite; his head had been shorn, he did not drink wine or strong drink and ate no meat.[2] (This was why, indeed, he was called "Upright.")

Since Saul was accompanied by some representatives of his pagan following, the test was, no doubt, staged primarily for them, as well as for the Jews (Acts 20:4, 21–29).

It is the most decisive demonstration of Saul's subordination to Upright Jacob. Had Saul refused the test he might have been killed on the spot as an apostate; by submitting, he compromised himself in the eyes of his recruits.

In the confused narrative of Acts all these events lead, somehow, to a riot; despite Saul's demonstration of orthodoxy he is recognized by some Jews from Asia Minor as an enticer away from Judaism. He is also accused of having brought into the Temple an uncircumcised pagan (an offense subject to the death penalty). In the riot Saul is arrested, as it seems, for his own safety; he is jailed and ultimately sent to Rome.

Thus he was arrested *not* as a Christian, an incomprehensible idea at the time, but as having violated a Temple taboo by starting a riot on the sacred premises. The arrest took place under the authority of a section of the priestly hierarchy represented by Upright Jacob and the other Pharisees, priests and elders who made up the Jesist coterie. Saul's arrest, accordingly, was independent of whether he was thought to be an apostate or not.

The account of Saul's arrest in Jerusalem and his remarkably long, tortuous trip to Rome is stiff with improbabilities of all kinds. He is even supposed to have dealt directly with the Roman Jews while in Roman custody on a capital charge! But it is the silence of Acts about his death that stands out in the whole muzzy chronicle.

Saul's appeal to the Romans, which he was entitled to make as a potential citizen of Tarsus, must have been futile. Otherwise Acts would surely have made a point of it. It would obviously have been to the chronicler's interest to record Saul's release, which one might expect from his free-and-easy treatment by the Romans. If Saul had been acquitted there would have been every reason to mention, indeed flaunt it; that would have fitted in very well with the chronicler's apologia. Or, since Acts takes great pains to reconcile Saul and the Jerusalem Jesists it piously refers to as the "mother Church," we might expect some indication that they had helped him.

But not a word is said about whether the Jerusalem Jesists did anything to help Saul during the five years—at least—before his trial came up in Rome. Ending up on its characteristic note of harmony, Acts merely makes an anodyne comment on Saul's arrival and sojourn in Rome, "preaching the Kingdom of God and teaching about the Lord Jesus Christ quite openly and unhindered." At the same time, very curiously, Saul goes on living there more or less on his own terms (at his own expense, of all things!).

Saul now disappears; his death may be put around 55 C.E., a few years before Upright Jacob's. But though he drops out of history, he was to have an effect after his death; his posthumous success—very strange, as we shall see—can be understood only against the background of the events leading up to and culminating in the catastrophe that befell the Jews in 70 C.E.

12

The Roman-Jewish War: The Destruction of the Temple

Whether or not Jesus' enterprise had the secular importance that seems indicated by the existence of a police writ against Davidides that lasted till the end of the first century, there is no doubt that from Pontius Pilate's term of office on (ca.26–36) until the Jewish revolt of 66–70, the country was seething with armed uprisings, intrigues, and conspiracies. Crucifixions were countless.

The various forces of the country—religious rebels, priestly aristocrats, Roman officials, the Jewish royal family, and the Jewish peasantry and artisans—interacted in plunging the country into a bloodbath.

After Pontius Pilate the tension steadily mounted between the Roman administration and the Jewish population of Judea, Samaria, and Galilee. The rapacity of the procurators was on a collision course with the turbulence that came increasingly under the focus of the Kingdom of God activists. Pilate himself, whose apparent ineptitude led to one misjudgment after another, was finally undone by a blunder that involved the growing Kingdom of God fervor.

Some Samaritans (a sect that accepted only the Pentateuch of the Hebrew Scriptures), after having been roused by one of the many messianic agitators "stirring up the people," had gathered to ascend their holy mountain (Mt. Gerizim) to gaze at the sacred utensils buried in their Temple. This was obviously the prelude to some messianic sally.

Pilate loosed on them a heavily armed force; a great many Samaritans were killed, others jailed, the rest dispersed. Pilate executed the most eminent prisoners.[1]

He had gone too far. The Samaritans complained to the legate of Syria (Vitellius), who sent Pilate back to Rome to answer charges of malfeasance. Pilate's end is unknown.

The Romans considered the control of the high priesthood vital. Ever since the riots against Herod the Great's successor, Archelaus, in 4 B.C.E., when the mob demanded the immediate liberation of political prisoners and the removal of a detested High Priest[2] and coupled this with a demand for the election of a high priest of "greater piety and purer morals,"[3] the insistence on their own elected high priest had remained the rallying cry of militant Jews. In 67 C.E., some five years after Upright Jacob's death, it was implemented by the followers of John of Gush-Halav in Jerusalem, then under Roman siege. It was because of the inherently insurrectionist nature of the demand for an elected high priest that the Romans, from the banishment of Archelaus in 6 to Pontius Pilate's recall (i.e., from 6–36), had kept the high priest's mantle in their custody, to prevent its appropriation by an "impostor." The centrality of the high priesthood thus played a key role in Jewish affairs.

The Jerusalem aristocrats were, generally speaking, quietist. It was natural for them to tailor their activities to the Roman presence. But the lower strata of the priesthood were simmering with the politico-religious mutinousness that was churning up the Jewish community as a whole. It was this state of virtual civil war that led to Upright Jacob's death.

The simmering that had been going on for decades under the leadership of Judah the Galilean's family and partisans began to step up its intensity in 52–60 (under the procuratorship of Antonius Felix), when according to Josephus the country was teeming with "brigands" and "impostors" who kept "deceiving" the people. Josephus associates these "brigands," moreover, with "wonder-workers," i.e., those claiming to bring about "wonders" like those attendant on God's intervention on behalf of his people in the past, as in the conquest of the promised land and during the Exodus from Egypt. During this decade, Josephus wrote, a new type of "bandit" made its appearance—the "Daggermen" (*Sicarii*) who specialized in the assassination of renegades (Jewish quietists and collaborators). The Daggermen mingled with crowds assembling during religious festivals; they would snatch out their daggers from under their robes and stab their victims. His account makes it clear that Daggermen and Zealots were equivalent.

The activity of the Zealots was not limited to Palestine, during the fifties, for instance—fifteen to twenty years after Jesus' execution— Zealots and other militants kept visiting all the Jewish communities in the Diaspora in an attempt to rally support to a messianic revolt against the Romans. At one point the Jews were expelled from Rome by Emperor Claudius for messianic sedition. In Alexandria the Jews were warned against itinerant Zealots, a "pest that threatens the whole world."[4] It was the notoriously incendiary character of the Jesists that made it plausible for Nero to accuse them of having set fire to Rome.

In Palestine there was a dense intermingling of economic and political factors in the strife between the high priests and the lower priesthood. The lower priests, because of the combination of national loyalty and their material interests, were at one with the Zealots against the High Priests. The Jerusalem mob must, in fact, have been Zealots; the Daggermen had already shown their hostility to the priestly aristocracy by killing Jonathan, the high priest. Titus, son of Caesar Vespasian, is supposed to have told a war council that the Jewish Temple had to be destroyed in order to extinguish the Jesists' belief that Jesus was going to reappear as Messiah.[5]

Around 59, some decades after the execution of Jesus, the high priests of the Temple, chosen from among the priestly aristocracy, who ever since the reign of Agrippa I had been appointed by the Herodian princes, were still further estranged from the lower priesthood. Josephus, without explaining the widespread hatred of the high priests, merely says they were at odds with the lower priests and the leaders of the Jerusalem mob. The two factions kept clashing violently. Each side used thugs against the other (the Romans, unaccountably, held off). The high priests' chief maneuver was to withhold the tithes from the lower priesthood (practically their only source of revenue).[6]

In 60 Festus, the Roman procurator, began an energetic repression of Zealots, Daggermen, and other diehards, including the followers of an "impostor" who had been leading people off into the desert in a form of militant civil disobedience.[7] Around the same time Nero triggered what was to become the Jewish War by settling a local quarrel between the Syrian and Jewish inhabitants of Caesarea, in Palestine, in favor of the Syrians. It was this decision of Nero's that had made Festus suppress the Jewish militants.[8]

Two years later Festus died; between his death and the arrival of his successor (Lucceius Albinus), Ananus, son of a high priest, was appointed High Priest himself by King Agrippa II. Though the high priests had to be confirmed by the procurator, Ananus took advantage of the hiatus to convoke the Sanhedrin to put Upright Jacob on trial together with some others.

The emergence of Upright Jacob is obscure. Not only was he not an apostle, he was not even a candidate to make up, after the death of Judas, what must have already been considered the symbolic number of twelve (Acts 1:15–26).

The question of Upright Jacob's role is fundamental. Was he, as Acts would indicate, no more than a pious Jew praying "assiduously" in the Temple with his pious associates? Was he a priest? Was he a *high* priest? Was he really the leader of the Jerusalem Jesists? If so, what did the Jesists want? Why were they organized in the first place?

Though he is mentioned as a member of the Jerusalem community (Acts 1:14), generally speaking Acts systematically soft-pedals his role in contrast with its treatment of Simon the Rock. The effect is strange; it gives us a glimpse into a complex situation in the earliest community without enabling us to grasp anything more than the fact itself.

Upright Jacob must have rocketed up in the Jerusalem Jesist community. He is mentioned together with Simon the Rock, as a special witness of the resurrection, in an otherwise anonymous list that was very early, since Saul mentions it to the Corinthians (i.e., about the tradition he had received from the Jerusalem group [1 Cor 15:5,7]). Consequently, if Simon the Rock had been a Jesist leader, he must have been dislodged by Jacob soon after the crucifixion. Since, according to Acts, Simon led the Jesists until he was imprisoned (by King Agrippa I around 43–44 C.E.) the question would remain, what had Jacob been doing for a decade?

Acts' reticence on Upright Jacob's ascension is only bizarre, to be sure, from a mundane point of view. By the time Acts was composed and edited the Jesists had become irrelevant to the events that had, historically, molded the chronicler's viewpoint. He had to digest, somehow, the Jerusalem period in the immediate wake of the crucifixion of Jesus while remaining perforce quite indifferent to the real life of the Jesists.

Now, Upright Jacob, like his brother Jesus, might well have been a descendant of King David; there would have been thousands of such descendants around this time. There seems no reason to doubt this genealogical background—whatever its significance—if only because of Saul's matter-of-fact reference to Jesus as a "son of David" (Rom 1:3); it would seem unthinkable that Saul would have said such a thing only two or three decades after Jesus' execution if it hadn't been believed.[9]

There was a tradition[10] that Upright Jacob was not only a brother of Jesus', but a twin brother. This notion could hardly have been invented after Jesus had become well known, since it would have provided adversaries with a handy explanation of Jesus' resurrection. There was, furthermore, a tradition that Judah Thomas—i.e., Judah "Twin"—was also a twin of Jesus' (Jacob was considered a suitable name for the second of twins [Gen 25:26]).

Upright Jacob's trial is tantalizingly mysterious. Josephus, calling him the brother of the "so-called Christ" (implying the omission, no doubt by a zealous Christian generations later, of a preceding passage mentioning Jesus unflatteringly), does not explain just why Jacob and his associates were accused of breaking the Torah and were in fact stoned to death.[11]

Josephus whitewashes them all. He says the "most fairminded" of the citizens, those most observant of the Torah, protested secretly to King Agrippa II, asking him to restrain Ananus in the future. Agrippa was in fact pressured into removing Ananus as high priest, and the new procurator, Albinus, rebuked him severely.[12]

The citizens were annoyed for two different reasons. One was Ananus's action as such, the other his illegal convocation of the Sanhedrin. It has been suggested that a new procurator's authorization was needed to convoke the Sanhedrin to renew Roman authority over its functioning (this is the only instance of a procurator's authorization being needed to convoke the Sanhedrin).

Josephus leaves the execution of Jacob himself completely in the dark; nor does he clarify the religious offense involved, though its nature is clearly implied by the charge and by the punishment (stoning). At the same time it seems to contradict the indignation of the "very observant" citizens; Jacob could hardly have been known as a transgressor of the Torah.

Upright Jacob was renowned for his cultic zeal; aside from the two important vows he had taken (Rechabite and Nazirite), he was supposed to have been constantly in the Temple.[13] He was also known to have worn linen, never wool; Josephus tells us that the Levites, under Florus (Albinus's successor as procurator) were given permission to don the linen tunic of the priesthood. Furthermore, some later sources[14] indicate that Jacob was at one time high priest, a few years after Saul was sent to Rome to his death; they maintain that Jacob "wore the priestly diadem on his head," and had the right to enter the Holy of Holies "because he was a Nasorean and connected with the priesthood."

Upright Jacob . . . was of David's race, being the son of Joseph, and was a Nasorean, as Joseph's first-born and therefore dedicated (to the Lord), and moreover . . . he officiated after the manner of the ancient priesthood. Wherefore also he was permitted once a year to enter the Holy of Holies, as the Torah commanded the high priests.[15]

Now, it seems likely that John the Baptist made his appearance long before Jesus, i.e., around the time of Archelaus (4 B.C.E.–6 C.E.), which is, indeed, the only thing that might explain the otherwise incomprehensible passage in the Gospels where Jesus, talking about the "storming of the Kingdom of God," says that "from the days of the Baptist until now it has been forcibly seized by men of violence" (Mt 11:12; Lk 16:16). "Until now" would be odd if Jesus, who was supposed to be only a few months younger than the Baptist, was thinking of a very short passage of time.

John the Baptist was no doubt the first Zealot elected high priest (the Zealots were, of course, against all high priests appointed annually by the Herodians and later by the Romans). After the Baptist's death the office seems to have passed to Yohanan ben Zavdai (John son of Zebedee),[16] one of the two "sons of thunder" (Boanerges), who was executed under Agrippa in 44 C.E., perhaps because of his claim to the high priesthood. There is even some evidence (not in Acts) that his brother Jacob (James) was also executed at the same time.[17]

Thus, if Jacob had been elected high priest during the turbulence constantly simmering in Jerusalem, which began to reach a pitch of high tension under Festus, it was an act of the deepest political significance, all the more so since an account of this murky episode written a century after Josephus seems to retain an element of an older tradition, namely, that Jacob was killed *just* before the Roman siege of Jerusalem.[18]

Now, if Jacob had assumed the function of a high priest, but, because of the civil war atmosphere, in the eyes of the regular Sadducean hierarchy was a bogus, unauthorized high priest, it was natural for Ananus, whom Josephus, despite his own quietist tendencies, treats with disdain, to get rid of Jacob through guile, since the Romans would have been outraged by the arbitrary assumption of authority on the part of the Sanhedrin and its lynching of a popular leader, as we know Jacob to have been because of the strong protests.

Accordingly, Jacob's opponents in the Temple hierarchy invited him—now an old man—to address the crowds assembling in the Temple for the Passover celebration. Doubtless he proclaimed his brother to be about to return to glory and undo the pagans, whereupon he was shoved over the wall, as it were inadvertently, and hit on the head with a wooden club by an officer of the high priest who was standing around in plain clothes to make it look like an accident. In this way the regular priests could explain to the Romans that Upright Jacob had fallen off the roof by accident, perhaps, because of his age, from dizziness. The Jesists themselves thought the killer was no more than a fuller who did Jacob in out of sheer personal fanaticism.[19] Thus the Sadducean ruse was entirely successful.

The Talmud seems to have conserved an echo of this. A Tannaite tradition of the third or fourth century has it that someone condemned by the Sanhedrin to stoning at a time when the Sanhedrin lacked the power to execute its own sentences would somehow "fall from the roof," i.e., God would intervene to carry out the Sanhedrin's sentence.[20] This phrase, "falling from the roof"—an anodyne wording, which does not sound at all like stoning—may conserve a reminiscence of Jacob's actual fate, since the idea of a fuller walking about the Temple during the Passover feast with the tools of his trade seems absurd.

Thus an explanation of Jacob's assassination emerges. Since we know from Acts that the lower orders of the Temple represented the militant wing of the Pharisees—Zealots proper as well as Pharisees—and since we know that the Sadducees and the Jerusalem aristocracy were generally pro-Roman (i.e., quietist) we can perceive that Upright Jacob was, quite simply, a political opponent of the Sadducees like his brother. Moreover, he was so influential that the Sadducees, girding themselves against the renewal of messianic agitation, the paramount factor of this whole era in Palestine, were alarmed at the likelihood that the agitation might now be focused on the person of the recently failed Messiah, Jacob's brother Jesus. But when they tried to interrogate him in public, to trap him into stopping the agitation about Jesus' imminent glorious return, Jacob infuriated them, perhaps to their surprise, by making a public proclamation of his belief. The Jerusalem mob got very enthusiastic, greeted his proclamation with the outcry of "Hosannah to the Son of David," i.e., an affirmation of solidarity with the anti-Roman messianists, Zealots, Daggermen, and others. Upon Jacob's death the Roman siege of Jerusalem started forthwith.

On the basic question, accordingly—the identification of Jacob with the Zealots—our main sources are in accord despite discrepancies in detail. The rapprochement of Jacob's disguised murder and the inception of the Roman siege[21] gives a plausible rationale for the whole incident, reinforced by the mention in Josephus of the degree of pacification that Albinus had to undertake the moment he arrived in Palestine and found himself confronted by the ravages of the Daggermen.[22]

The outline is clear regardless of specific dates. Upright Jacob, leader of the Jesists in Jerusalem, a facet of the militant movement, was inevitably embroiled in the messianic crisis of 62 C.E., during the hiatus between the two procurators (Festus and Albinus). Thus it seems likely that Jacob's death in 62—or, if it took place a few years later, on the eve of the Roman siege of Jerusalem—was merely one incident in the civil war atmosphere that pervaded the Temple.

After Jacob's death in 62 C.E. the leadership of the group seems to have been transmitted to Simeon ben Cleophas,[23] a first cousin of Jesus' (son of his paternal uncle). Under Domitian, i.e. between 90 and 110 (when Matthew, Luke, and Acts were compiled), Simeon, a centenarian,[24] together with Jesus' grand-nephews, i.e., sons of his brother Judah, were all arrested, but the nephews were released as harmless[25] while Simeon was tortured and killed.

There is a similarity in dynastic principle between the organization of the Jesist group and that of the Zealot movement launched by Judah of Galilee; it may imply that before Jesus was magnified, as it were ideologically, after his crucifixion, there had been a normal dynastic authority in the militant movement he had led. Hence Upright Jacob would have a position of natural leadership through blood relationship, which only much later, as the nascent faith coagulated within the evolving mythology after the destruction of Jerusalem, was interpreted as an element in a hierarchy conceived of as having been articulated by ideology.

In his guarded account of this complex background Josephus sheds some light on the backstage situation after Albinus's arrival in 62; he indicates that Albinus's personal corruption had made him take bribes from "powerful" people to turn a blind eye on their seditious activities;[26] i.e., the people Josephus calls the "revolutionary party"—the Zealots—were powerful enough to suborn a procurator. This was all the easier, of course, because one of the chief inducements in becoming a Roman satrap was the pickings. Thus the procurator's accessibility to the Zealots illustrates their massive influence for years before the actual outbreak of the insurrection of 66.

Josephus's aim in slanting his account is clear. On the one hand he is intent on blaming the excesses of the various procurators for the catastrophic Roman war—Albinus's successor is presented as a monster of the foulest description—and contrasts their enormities with the exemplary patience shown by the Jews; when he mentions the Zealots he minifies their activities. Even during the two years in office of the depraved, corrupt and avaricious Florus, Josephus says nothing at all about the Zealots.

In many ways the Romans had great respect for the Jews and for Jewish institutions; still, a strong Jewish society in Palestine was *ipso facto* ominous, if only because, in addition to being a bastion against Parthia in the east, it was coupled with widespread Jewish proselytization throughout the Roman Empire. The proselytizing movement, though unfocused, had had a profound effect, through social osmosis, on the pagan masses. It was considered a menace not only because of the Roman ideal of a state religion accepted by society at large, but also because of its effect on the highest strata of the realm. Hence, while Judaism was constitutional for born Jews, the movement of conversion seemed to imperil the Empire itself, one more serious danger added to the many shredding its social fabric.

Judaism had attracted many converts among the Aramaic-speaking peoples conquered by Rome; indeed, the remarkable dispersion of Jewish communities throughout the known world, commented on even a century before Jesus,[27] must doubtless be explained by conversion, especially among women, for whom circumcision naturally was no deterrent. It was so attractive around this time, indeed, that it had even penetrated the court at Rome; the Empress Poppea Sabina was a semiconvert.[28] In Damascus and Antioch, apparently all the women practiced Jewish rites.[29]

Around 46 the whole of the royal house of Adiabene became Jewish, apparently through the royal harem;[30] some of the Adiabene princes were even to become Zealots. During the Roman war[31] a potent factor in the sharpening of the crisis with Rome was the widespread poverty, especially painful in the countryside. Even in the cities, the true focus of Greco-Roman culture, "the splendor . . . was created by and existed for a rather small minority. . . . The large masses of the city population had either a very moderate income or lived in extreme poverty."[32]

The situation on the land was undoubtedly far worse, especially in Palestine, which was far from being the richest part of the empire. There any crisis at all would tend to ruin a great many peasants, turning them into victims of money-lenders and forcing the loss of their property. Economically and socially deracinated people would of course be particularly susceptible to the economic propaganda that had always accompanied the

Kingdom of God agitators. One of the first acts of the rebels in Jerusalem in 66 was the setting on fire of the public archives, the repository of the money-lenders' bonds, "in order to win over a host of grateful debtors and bring about a rising of the poor against the rich"; they were naturally loathed by the moderates.[33]

The slaves, too, of whom there were a great many—generally converts to Judaism—were also inflamed by the socioeconomic objectives of the insurrectionary party; in the war one of the Zealot leaders, Simon bar Giora, proclaimed the emancipation of all slaves.[34]

The harshness of the taxation seemed to go beyond the actual capacity of the country. Part of the general Roman system of taxation included land tax, a poll tax, a water tax, a city tax, meat taxes on staples (meat and salt), a road tax, a house tax, etc.[35] Taxes were ubiquitous. Though this was characteristic of the empire as a whole, its effects were most marked in impoverished Palestine, where the economic situation was exacerbated by precisely the political instability that had been coming to a head for decades before the war.

Tax collectors, generally Jews, had the worst possible reputation, preserved for us in the Gospels, in which the word "publican," in the perspective of the Kingdom of God agitation, meant no more than "sinner."[36]

Corruption of this kind also extended to the Jewish aristocracy, which waxed fat on what amounted to extortions from the masses. The high priestly families, all very rich, were also venal; bribery could secure appointment to many lucrative jobs. The secular aristocracy, headed by Agrippa II, was also notorious for violence and oppression.[37]

Bribery extended throughout the regime; bribery of the procurators themselves was of course routine; it was, as I have indicated, one of the reasons the post was attractive. Saul, for instance, was expected to bribe Felix to be let out of jail (Acts 24:26). The last and worst of the procurators, Florus, "became a partner" of the Kingdom of God activists, whom he avoided molesting.[38] Tacitus himself, though as a rule hostile toward Jews, singles him out as a prime cause of the war that broke out in 66: "the Jews' patience lasted until Gessius Florus became procurator."[39] Albinus, too, could be bribed to release Daggermen.[40]

These instances demonstrate the power of the Kingdom of God activists. It was so pervasive that for a limited time that it could even attenuate the political conflict.

It would surely be an exaggeration to say the procurators were headstrong and acting against imperial interests as interpreted in Rome. On the contrary, since they could easily be deposed it must be assumed that in broad outline they were considered to be reliably interpreting the decisions of the center.

The procurators, to be sure, had no agreed-on policy on how to handle the explosive situation in Palestine; there were personal rivalries between some of them (e.g., Cumanus and Felix). Florus, who seems simply to have detested Jews as such, had no program for dealing with the insurrection his own policies had helped provoke. Even though he was supposed to have intentionally instigated the insurrection to cover up his own rapacity and corruption,[41] he had no plan to put in operation once the insurgents managed to launch the uprising.

An enormous element of social protest can, in fact, hardly be overestimated in considering the insurrection of 66–70. The population as a whole was divided into the pro-Roman elements of the upper classes, a vacillating body of people in the middle, and a majority of plebeians, who eventually, under the leadership of the Kingdom of God activists, carried the day. The element of social protest explains the entry of plebeians in general into the insurrectionary movement. The burning of the money-lenders' bonds was bound to seem attractive to the poor.

Social protest united even those otherwise differing widely. The two Zealot leaders in 66–70, Simon bar Giora and John of Gush Halav (Gischala), even though of different social background, both loathed the pro-Roman Jewish aristocracy. (John was a prosperous businessman). John's men went in for "ransacking the houses of the rich";[42] later both launched a general attack on the upper classes indiscriminately.[43]

The Samaritans, too, though long-time enemies of the Jews and in the recent period under the special protection of the Romans for just that reason, backed the insurrection,[44] evidently because of socioeconomic motives that made the uprising transcend its own Jewish setting, especially since the Samaritans too had a Kingdom of God perspective.

There was even a possibility that the economic upheaval presaged by the social protest inherent in the insurrection might have spread to other countries, creating another problem for the Roman administration.[45]

In addition, there was a great influx of young Jews, including upper-class young men, into the Kingdom of God movement; youth in and for itself, in fact, was a significant cause of the insurrection.[46] One of the leaders of the Daggermen, Ben Batiah, was the nephew of Yohanan ben

Zakkai, the mentor of the peace party;[47] Eliezer, captain of the Temple (an office just below that of high priest), who precipitated the revolt, was the son of the high priest Hananiah (Ananias).[48]

On the other hand it was the quality of the Kingdom of God agitation in its most acute form—the essential religious motif of the uprising as a whole—that made it difficult for non-Jews to take part in it. The Shammaites—a tendency believing in a specially strict interpretation of the Scriptures—generally middle-class and upper-middle-class, were also strong Zealots. This gave a heavy religio-national tincture to the insurrection that isolated the Jews and made it impossible to take full advantage of the element of social protest and extend it to those suffering the same afflictions outside Palestine.

At the outset, in fact, the uprising was entirely national in character; it was only later, as the war became more and more bitter, through the perception, no doubt, of its hopelessness as God failed to intervene, that the element of social protest surfaced dynamically and led to a civil war between the various insurgent groups—Daggermen, Zealots, the groups associated with John of Gush Halav, Simon bar Giora, etc.—that both reflected and heightened the social upheaval.

The leaders of the uprising had formed no strategy in case of victory; their feeling must have arisen exclusively out of a burning religious conviction that all problems of strategy would be solved quite simply by the intervention of God. Moreover, the elements that united for the purpose of the insurrection were far from uniform or harmonious in any sense. If not for the loathing inflamed by the Roman administration, especially by the last procurator, Florus, the radical differences between them would no doubt have come out even earlier.

Both the Jesists and the Zealots, as well as the other Kingdom of God activists, were immersed in the same movement of armed revolt against the Romans. Since there was a variety of currents flowing along the same anti-Roman course, nothing would have distinguished the Jesists in this respect from the others. They differed only through their conviction that the Kingdom of God would be installed after the glorious return of Jesus. This no doubt explains why so many members of the Jesist coterie in Jerusalem could be Zealots. Since being a Zealot also implied a feeling, or a mood, the broad milieu that was seething with anti-Roman agitation could have contained many sympathizers not necessarily engaged in a specific organizational activity.

For a long time after Judah the Galilean, the activity of the Zealots took place mainly in the countryside outside Jerusalem; it was not until around 63, some thirty years after the execution of Jesus, that Daggermen began stirring in Jerusalem. It is more than likely that the Zealots in the countryside would have been living more or less normally in villages and on farms, participating in specific operations as they arose and then fading quietly back home. But as the war atmosphere came to fever pitch toward 66, all currents converged on Jerusalem.

The events leading up to the catastrophe of 66–70 are plain. In the wake of the serious clash between Jews and pagans in Caesarea, Florus's excesses exacerbated the Jews. Florus raided the Temple treasury, to boot, which led to a collision between the Jews and the Roman military. Jewish losses were heavy, but Florus had to leave Jerusalem to report to the Legate of Syria (Cestius Gallus) that a revolt had broken out; the Jews may have been, in addition, remiss in collecting or transmitting the tribute due Rome.

The priestly authorities, quietist vis-à-vis Rome both for reasons of common sense and because that common sense itself insulated them against the messianic fever, with its expectations of instantaneous divine intervention, found themselves allied with Rome against the diehards from among their own people.

Josephus puts a persuasive, lofty, and indeed moving speech into the mouth of King Agrippa, who makes a common-sense plea, based on futility, against challenging the Roman Empire. Agrippa gives his plea a religious justification by pointing out that the Romans' success must have had divine sanction, after all, which meant that the submission of the Jews to Rome was enjoined by God, and that the Zealot ideal of a theocracy (i.e., "Kingdom of God") was entirely out of place. In short, the Jews had to hand over the tribute to Rome, face realities, and calm down.

But the torrent of militancy proved to be too strong. The rebellion broke out shortly after, in the autumn of 66, and pervaded the Temple again when Eliezer, commander of the Temple, persuaded the lower priests to disregard the higher priests altogether and stop the sacrifices offered on behalf of Caesar and the Roman people—a declaration of war—while various Roman garrisons in Palestine were massacred out of hand.

Unaccountably, the Romans reacted sluggishly. It was three months before the governor of Syria (Cestius Gallus), the chief military support of the procurator in Palestine, dispatched an army; during this time a wave of violence flooded the country. The Jews of Caesarea were totally massacred;

in reprisal a dozen pagan cities, including some Syrian villages, were devastated and countless pagans killed. There were anti-Jewish riots and massacres in Tyre, Alexandria, and many other cities.[49]

The war was prolonged by a strange event. The Roman army, a strong force of legionary and auxiliary units, entered Palestine and advanced on Jerusalem without much opposition in Galilee or Samaria, and was about to engage in an attack on the very walls of the Temple, when for some unknown reason Gallus ordered it to fall back and retreat northward out of the city. The retreating forces were mercilessly harried and killed.[50]

The morale of the rebels shot up deliriously. The retreat of the Roman army forces was so unexpected, so unlikely, so inexplicable, that it could be grasped only as the finger of God once again intervening on behalf of the fighters for Yahweh. It was surely one of the greatest defeats ever inflicted on the Roman legions, and was exacerbated, moreover, by having been inflicted by amateurs in a key area of the empire, between the Egyptian granary and the lush farmlands of Syria, and on the route to Parthia, Rome's chief contemporary enemy.

The peace party's hopes vanished. The euphoria induced by the victory had the fatal effect of sweeping the Jews, as a collectivity, into the war.

In the spring of 67 Vespasian, a veteran commander whose appointment by Nero indicates the importance of the Jewish uprising, moved into Palestine with three legions and a strong force of auxiliaries.[51] He had to lay siege to a whole string of fortified towns barring the way to Jerusalem. This complicated his campaign, since though the Jews were amateurish as fighters in the field their ardor and energy were very effective elsewhere.

Vespasian, perhaps with an eye on the contest for the imperial succession that broke out after the death of Nero in 68, moved very slowly and cautiously through the countryside north of Jerusalem, gradually isolating it. The sluggish pace of the campaign further buttressed the rebels' hopes.

In 66, at the very beginning of the revolt, Menahem, Judah the Galilean's grandson, who had slaughtered the Roman garrison of Masada, giving him an armory as well as a fortress that was practically impregnable, went to Jerusalem to have himself crowned king. This was, no doubt, a synonym for Messiah; Menahem, too, expressed the religious impulse that had kindled the national uprising.

Menahem headed his own group of Daggermen; claiming both charismatic and dynastic authority in the holy war, he had presented himself as "king,"[52] only to be assassinated by rival Zealots. From then on there was a civil war among the insurgents.

The sluggishness of the Roman campaign in 68–69, following the inexplicable retreat of Gallus's army at the outset of the war, had strengthened the insurgents' mood of exaltation. The great festivals were celebrated at the Temple to general attendance.[53]

The final and decisive battle was the siege of Jerusalem, initiated at last by Titus, Vespasian's eldest son, in the spring of 70, a little before Passover. The Roman army now consisted of four legions and a great force of auxiliaries. Vespasian, now emperor, with a need for prestige, urgently required a victory in Palestine, where the Roman legions had been held up for four years.

The Jews, hitherto divided in bloody strife between the two chief factions led by John of Gush Halav and Simon bar Giora respectively, now united in ferocious resistance. Jerusalem was divided by great walls. There were three major strong points: the Temple itself, the Antonia fortress, and the Herodian palace, which had massive towers. Hence a besieging army could not merely breach the outer walls, but had to attack the city section by section. This meant fighting in tight quarters, which untrained combatants could excel in, and hence an intensification and prolongation of the siege.

It was no doubt one of the most frightful in history. The city was wholly hemmed in by a massive Roman walling-up of the entire area; famine and sickness helped the Romans. All offers of terms were rejected by the Kingdom of God enthusiasts, who until the very last moment seem to have expected God to intervene. Indeed, if, as some think, Revelation 11:1–3 is a fragment of a Zealot document, it reflects an early aspect of the siege, in which the outer court of the Temple was "trodden by pagans" but the sanctuary was still untouched, and the rebels still thought God would intervene to prevent the desecration of the actual sanctuary.

Despite the ferocious resistance, the Romans stormed the inner sanctuary; tens of thousands of Jews were massacred or burned to death in the fire that razed the entire Temple, while the victorious Romans sacrificed to their standards and saluted Titus as Imperator.

The seizure of the inner Temple paralyzed all Jewish resistance; they were now merely slaughtered by the legionaries. By the time the bloodbath was over Jerusalem was a vast heap of smoking ruins covered with corpses.[54] The debacle meant the virtual end of the revolt (other strongholds, including Masada, were captured a little later).

The Jewish state had been annihilated; pagan soldiers were now encamped on the ancient shrine of the Jews.[55] Though there was another insurrection under Bar Kochba in 132–35, the national existence of the Jews was suspended until the twentieth century.

Titus brought his booty back to Rome, including the seven-star Menorah salvaged from the burning Temple. Simon bar Giora was taken to Rome to be executed in Titus's triumph at the foot of the Capitol; John of Gush Halav was imprisoned for life.

The war had inflicted titanic losses on the Jews, estimated by Josephus at well over 1,300,000 casualties. The results were summed up, very simply, in the third Gospel: "And they shall fall by the mouth of the sword, And be led captive into all the nations; and Jerusalem shall be trodden down by the Gentiles." (Lk 21–23)

13

"Paulinism"—A New World

Saul's ideas were to prevail because of the destruction of the Temple milieu in Jerusalem and, more broadly, because the Jewish debacle of 70 wiped out what had been a center for the far-flung Jewish Diaspora, even though enough Jews, despite the vast bloodletting, were left in Palestine to undertake still another insurrectionary enterprise, equally abortive, two generations later under Bar Kochba.

Yet another event encased Saul's ideas within an entirely different framework and transformed them so profoundly that the transformation took place unnoticed.

That event was, so to speak, a non-event: *the world did not end.* And since the World's End never took place, all World's End theories began to shrivel very soon after the Jewish debacle of 70. Saul's ideas, unconsciously restructured, were absorbed by later generations of recruits to the nascent faith and molded to the needs of a living society.

Had the Temple not been destroyed, had the solid, ramified powerful Jewry of Palestine not been pulverized by the Romans in 70, it is hard to see what future Saul's ideas could have had.

How could the nascent faith that was to be anchored in his passionate Letters have evolved if it had remained encapsulated within the ancient Jewish religion, grounded in its Torah and sustained by the ardor of a people rooted in its land?

The version of Jesus' career believed in by the Jerusalem Jesists could scarcely have been able to survive for very long the failure of all World's End theories. Though the magnification of the person of Jesus was doubtless an inevitable consequence of the initial vision of the risen Jesus glorified, the containment of that magnification within the confines of Jewish monotheism precluded the transcendental turn it proved to be capable of among pagans. It is hard to imagine that it could have been capable of ideological ramification; the lush growth of the complex, subtle pagan notions grafted onto it would have been impossible in a world of thought in which the parameters of the divine and the human were laid down with the unyielding starkness of monotheism.

Thus it was the military-political defeat of the Jews in 70 that changed the social setting of Saul's ideas and hence the fate of the ideas themselves. The extermination of the Jerusalem Jesist community along with the nationalist movement it was part of gave the Diaspora paramount importance for the nascent faith. With the disappearance of Jewish centers of authority—as distinct from the spiritual influence exercised by rabbis over the far-flung Jewish communities—the coteries of Jesists scattered throughout the Hellenistic world could evolve as fortune befell them.

The destruction of the Temple, in fact, settled the "problem" of the Torah that had been so painful for Saul. The whole conflict around the entry of pagans into Judaism was obliterated by that stupendous event, which shifted the development of the slowly forming doctrine onto an entirely different plane, that of "Christology" in the jargon of the new coteries of pagan Jesists. It was only after the destruction of the Temple that a point of view entirely independent of Judaism could assert itself.

Later on, to be sure, an attempt was made to create a link between the original community of believers and the subsequent Church in the form of a legend that they had escaped, somehow, to a little place (Pella) on the other side of the Jordan, but the legend remains a flimsy, transparent piece of propaganda.[1]

No doubt the first step in dislocating all accounts of Jesus from the plane of history to that of theology was the apologia in the Gospel of Mark. The nature of Mark's milieu, probably Rome, obliged him to effect a transposition in which the theological viewpoint, now necessary because of the shift from the concept of the Jewish Messiah to that of the lord of the universe, utterly overshadowed, distorted, and well-nigh obliterated mundane factuality.

By the time Saul's ideas were canonized, long after his death, by the earliest Church fathers, they had already become incomprehensible. The Church fathers were gripped by them because of their universality, since by now, with the recession of the Jews as targets for recruiting, Saul's ideas could encompass all mankind. It was only natural, in the absence of anything else, for Saul's outpourings, through the passion that informed their logic, to soar beyond their time-bound premises and become the groundwork of a new canon, itself conceptualized as an eternal institution.

Even though the second generation that followed the destruction of Jerusalem was already incapable, because of its own time orientation, to grasp the inwardness of Saul's hysteria about the World's End, the way had been cleared for the simplification of Saul's outsize conceptions. The mysticism that had enthralled Saul himself, the mysticism rooted in the ardent expectation of the World's End, had been utterly forgotten by the next generation, which, its enthusiasm spent, was obliged to accept life in the workaday world, while Saul's ideas, transposed, proved powerful enough to become the vessel for a new faith adapted to its pagan milieu.

For generations the activities of Jewish missionaries had been very successful: "God-fearers"—pagans who accepted the God of Israel without submitting to circumcision or the dietary laws—were numerous. No doubt they formed the core of the congregations that much later were to become Christian. (Acts indicates that Saul's own recruiting campaigns were most successful among the "God-fearers.")

Classical Hebrew prophecy had created a very natural bridge between any human being and the Torah; Saul made much of Isaiah's reference to Israel as "the light of the nations." It was precisely in Saul's milieu, the Greek-speaking population of the eastern Mediterranean, that the movement for the conversion of the pagans had become urgent; in his day it must have reached its peak.

Antioch was a natural place for the new faith to begin coagulating; it was there that something new was told to the "Greeks"—i.e., to the pagan hangers-on of Judaism "as well as to the Jews" (Acts 11:20). The word "Christian," coined there, meant no more, at the time, than a follower of the Christ ("Messiah" in Greek). Yet the simple translation was to prove capacious enough to sustain a staggering amplification of meaning.

The third largest city in the Roman Empire, Antioch, like so many other Hellenistic crossroads, was cosmopolitan, bringing together beliefs prevalent throughout the Hellenized east as well as in the empire as a whole. The Jewish colony was very big, and surrounded, as it seems, by converts, both full converts and God-fearers.

Though not so many ordinary Jews took up the new hope linked to Jesus, there must have been many recruits to it among the converts and God-fearers. At this stage, of course, ordinary pagans could not have been attracted, since the basic terminology of the whole approach was so densely interlaced with the key concepts of Judaism that it would have been, quite simply, unintelligible to any outsider. In any case the new admixture of recruits soon gave the semi-Judaized pagans a preponderance in the Antioch Jewish colony.

Between 100 and 200 C.E., when Christianity struck root in the Hellenistic world, educated people were all the more accessible to eastern religions because the official religion of the Greco-Romans was already a syncretism, a blend established after the Roman conquest of the already Hellenized east and made up of the deities of both conquerors and conquered. No doubt the elite did not believe, exactly, in this syncretized state religion, but in public they respected it, if only on the general theory that the masses had to be curbed by *something*.

Augustus's attempt to restore the old Roman religion had succeeded only with respect to some temples and temple rites; it had done no more than enhance the civic potency of the official ceremonial. It was really an aspect of mere patriotism, since the official religion had only a few rites, with no theology, no dogma, and above all no emotion. The masses for their part remained, as it seems, devoted to petty local deities and sorcerers.

Now, there was nothing in the elite of that age to withstand the lush emotionality of eastern religiosity. In the absence of any science, with primitive, shapeless, and meager empiricism the only foothold in reality, the way was left open to arbitrary philosophical speculation of all kinds. It was a terrain on which ideas of all kinds could be endlessly combined.

But what was doubtless decisive in the genesis of Christianity was the pulverization of society as a whole. Social disintegration, upheavals, uprootings, transfers of populations, warfare with enslavements, went on for a century and more. Solace was at a premium.

Stoicism protected only the elite against affliction. For that matter even the skepticism of the enlightened was flooded by the deeply felt ceremonies of the eastern cults. Stoicism, definitely on the decline by the end of the second century, left the pagan world ready for the sweeping combinations, arrestingly simple, of the ideas superimposed on Saul's originally time-bound formulas.

In 190 C.E., with the advent of Septimus Severus and his clan, the

Roman Empire was finally taken over by African and Syrian princes; women were imbued with the mystic ardor of the East. Fervor of all kinds was epidemic.

The element common to all forms of this religious contagion converged on a single target, the salvation of the individual.

And with the pagan world longing for such salvation, which implied the release of the soul from the bondage of matter and individual immortality through union with God—the common objective of the Mysteries, of Gnosticism, of Neo-Platonism—it proved to be easy for nascent Christianity to play a panoramic role. Structurally identical with the Mysteries, the incarnation, the redemptive crucifixion, and the resurrection contained an infinitely greater content derived from the magnification of the deity that was, no doubt, the cardinal element taken over from Judaism.

Later on, to be sure, Saul's syncretism was to give rise to more complex systems, while the Church, gradually consolidated on the groundwork of Saul's own syncretism, was to insulate itself against contending extravagances of thought and define its own doctrines in an exclusive way. This was accompanied by endless bloodshed, since the central concepts of the Mystery from then on embodied in the Church were so subtle, so rarefied, so alien to all reason, that the evolving orthodoxy could be enforced only by violence.

Only a little more than a generation after his death Saul was warped almost beyond recognition; by 100 C.E. he had already been integrated with the category of "theological literature"—brittle, artificial, lifeless, utterly unlike his anguished, living Letters, throbbing with urgency. What the Church really took over from Saul was his peripheral, basically ornamental notions—his shallow, moralizing maxims, his aversion to sex, his primness.

To sum up this striking shift in perspective, it may be said that everything he had to say about the Torah, his whole intricate, yet simple and logical extrapolation from received ideas, was pulverized. With the evolution of dogma in the early Church, especially in the period immediately following him, the genetic core, so to speak, of his views was smashed to smithereens.

It was possible for schismatics (like Marcion) to pick up one strand of Saul's thought—his seeming hostility to the Torah—and by disregarding its organic connection with the glorious return create an antinomian structure whose plausibility depended on its omissions. For Tertullian and Irenaeus, the essence of religion itself became nothing more than a banal recommendation of etiquette. Since law could scarcely be disregarded in the living society that survived the theories of the World's End, the early Church Fathers merely replaced the Torah with a new law, summed up by a rootless legalism that was considered enough to make a believer meritorious.

It is illuminating to see, more specifically, how Saul's constellation of ideas and emotions was elaborated and transformed by two Church Fathers, Ignatius and Polycarp.

Ignatius, writing after the turn of the second century, was authoritative for various congregations in Asia Minor. Both he and Polycarp seem to have been steeped in Saul's writings; they both make much of his formula "in Christ"; they harp on themes for which Saul's vocabulary is indispensable.

Yet despite their immersion in Saul's ideas there is a vast omission. They have really dropped Saul's basic idea altogether as well as the source of his logic—the key concept that after dying with Jesus believers have *already* been resurrected together with him. They have taken over the general formulation of Saul's mysticism, but neither its actual content nor its logical structure.

This is specially instructive since it indicates the modality by which a living idea of Saul's, rooted in a specific conviction about a specific historical era, was emptied of its content in a different era. Saul's formula was filled up with notions that from then on were to preoccupy the Church.

Just at the point where individual believers lost their capacity for feeling that they, personally, formed part of the final generation "on whom the World's End has come" and were the only ones to benefit by a participation in the messianic kingdom already partially installed, the heightening of mere expectation into a productive emotional state that could create mystical communion ceased to be possible. Saul's writings could still be quoted mechanically, but if an active mind was to cope with the new situation arising out of the failure of the World's End theory, it had to rework the theory along lines that gave it coherence in some other framework of thought, freed from the World's End fever.

That framework was found waiting in Hellenistic stereotypes that the extinction of the Jerusalem Jesist community cleared the way for. Whatever might have been the consequences had the Jerusalem Jesists somehow survived—quite incalculable, of course—when the Jesists disappeared Hellenistic ideas could work themselves out without hindrance. The elimination of the Jerusalem Jesists removed what may be called the Jewish brake on the paganizing process; it allowed the ideas current in the complex Hellenistic world to play on the simple idea and on the still simpler emotion expressed by Saul.

It was not apparent—it remained indeed, a puzzle for centuries—that this was happening; Ignatius could hardly be expected to be aware of a historical process. *We* see it now; *he* experienced it then.

Ignatius applied Saul's formula "in Christ" in an entirely general way, quite independently of the structure of ideas that for Saul constituted its real content. He filled it with a quite different doctrine, that of the fusion of flesh and spirit that is supposed to take place within the Church through the fellowship with Christ. That fusion of flesh and spirit now became the guarantee of immortality through resurrection.

Saul's view had also rested on the assumption that resurrection was the handiwork of the divine spirit; it was just this similarity that enabled Ignatius to disregard the true thrust of Saul's thought. It sounds, in fact, like a mere streamlining of Saul's idea. It retains the concept of dying and rising again and merely drops Jesus.

Nevertheless Ignatius, quite unconsciously, had completely replaced one idea with another. The dynamic of Saul's complex notion was simply forgotten.

The difference between the two similar-sounding notions of the spirit is fundamental; Saul's history-minded, physical view of the world transformation was replaced by a theory of timeless magic. There is an utter contrast, conceptual as well as historical, between the two views of spirit and flesh.

The contrast between the two notions and the mechanism that effected the shift are easily seen. For Saul there could be no question of any union between spirit and flesh; for him the flesh is simply eliminated through the dying and rising again with Jesus; the spirit, fused with the psyche as part of the integral corporeity, transforms it into the glorious body after the glorious return.

The death and resurrection of Jesus brought about redemption simply because Jesus was the future Messiah, and it was *as* the Messiah that he died in playing out the great drama of the World's End; it was because of this that Jesus' death could be conceived of as an atoning sacrifice for the elect. Simultaneously, since he was both a preexistent being and the future Messiah—the once and future king—his seeming death entailed his inevitable resurrection and therewith the triggering of the resurrection era.

But Saul's views were alien to Ignatius and his successors, themselves living at a time when the World's End theory, even where it survived as an article of faith, had been drained of life.

Ignatius believed in the resurrection of the actual *body* of the believer (a notion also taken over from the World's End fantasies of contemporary Judaism). In this scheme of ideas the actual flesh of the body was made capable of immortality through the inward action of the spirit. Ignatius did not think flesh inherently perishable, hence unfit for the working out of the resurrection, but regarded the fusion of the spirit and the flesh as a natural process that had merely been exemplified for the first time in the case of Jesus. It was an unexplained, unmotivated miracle; beforehand the flesh was not capable of immortalization, afterwards it was.

In the pagan thought of the time, the redemptive activity of Jesus consisted merely of his coming into the world as a union of the flesh and the spirit, and *because of that* making possible the cognate union of flesh and spirit that led to the resurrection of the elect. In Ignatius's mind the death and resurrection of Jesus merely make manifest the category of resurrection derived from the mode of Jesus' own resurrection; it is a process embedded in nature.

One mechanism had been replaced by another. To Saul's mind the mechanism that brought about the transmission of the spirit in the imminent messianic kingdom was the believers' dying and rising again with Jesus; without that specific mechanism, itself dependent on the complete physicality, the historical actuality of the world-change, the idea, in and for itself, would have been incomprehensible. As the World's End theory withered away, the mere phrase "in Christ"—Saul's shorthand for the complex, but clear and logical concept of being-in-Christ—was used as though it were a merely abstract idea. He would surely have found it unrecognizable.

What sounds like a technicality, perhaps a matter of mere semantics, was heavy with potentialities, for it explained the function of the Church, which was to mediate the transmission of the spirit to *natural men*. This was light-years removed from Saul's historically minded, this-world-changing conception.

Saul assumed that the spirit fused with the spiritual part of man's nature; Ignatius, embarked on a different course altogether, though the vocabulary remained the same, took it for granted that it was the inherently miraculous working of the spirit that united it with the fleshly body. In Saul's idea the resurrection has already begun through the union with

Christ in the being-in-Christ, in Ignatius the Spirit merely prepares the believer for the resurrection through the abstract union with Christ, mediated by the church. Thus the concept of the spirit—bursting with unperceived ambiguities—became an unavowed bridge between two radically different ideas.

For Ignatius the cardinal feature of Saul's thought had been transformed, again, of course, unconsciously. Whereas for Saul baptism had been an indispensable preamble to the Lord's Supper (Eucharist), for Ignatius the cardinal element had become the Eucharist, which baptism merely led up to. In the bread and wine the fusion of matter and spirit was brought about in exactly the same way as the fusion of spirit and flesh brought about by the bodily identity with Jesus; the Eucharist merely manifested a modality of the redemption. Both the bodily identity with Jesus and the fusion of matter and spirit duplicated the existence of the Savior in a form lending itself to transmission.

What had been for Saul the body and blood of Jesus to be partaken of at the Lord's Supper was turned into a fundamentally different, though structurally similar concept. The Logos Christology turned the body and blood into the *flesh* and blood of Jesus, and in that way interpreted the wine and bread consumed at the Lord's Supper.

Thus, though the root of this remained the initial step taken by Saul— the magnification of Jesus' person as part of his deification—this itself, steeped in a Greek idea about a human being's potentiality for divinization, was then systematically extended.

There is a similar parallel—and a similar contrast—in the way the solidarity between the elect and between the elect and Jesus was handled by Saul and by Ignatius. For both of them the being-in-Christ arose out of a mystical conception that in its turn was ultimately rooted in a mystical view of history—the preexistent community of the saints.

For Saul, the death and resurrection undergone by the elect collectively, and by the elect together with Christ, was no more than the working out of the predestined solidarity of all of them together plus Jesus.

For Ignatius, however, this mystical notion, soaring beyond history, was replaced by a magical notion of a current participation in a fusion of flesh and spirit that had been accomplished, mysteriously, in the very person of Christ. It was simply part of the substance of the new deity.

The same may be said about Saul's idea of freedom from the Torah. This had made sense only in connection with his theory of the World's End.

As an absolute, mere freedom in general could have no place in a real society. Hence it proved necessary to build up legal norms once again as the Church solidified on improvised foundations. In the very first generation after Saul this basic idea of freedom from the Torah as an aspect of the dichotomy he established between the Torah and Jesus—radical and simple—went far beyond the orbit of the thinkers who were gropingly, as it seems, promoting new ideas in their scattered fellowships. The author of Acts, for instance, having failed in his own time-bound milieu to grasp Saul's fundamental doctrine of freedom from the Torah, disregards it altogether. He has simplemindedly reduced Saul's doctrine of justification by faith—a logical extrapolation from the incipient messianic kingdom—to the mere forgiveness of sins.

In short, all the details, all the modalities of operation, that in Saul's mind were indispensable for the implementation of *transitions*—into the elect, into the being-in-Christ, into the messianic kingdom—were radically misconstrued and dropped from the Church's horizons. This was all part and parcel of the Church's abandonment of Saul's reasons for suspending the Torah vis-à-vis pagan converts, as well as his solution of a problem that in his own lifetime simply had to be solved, i.e., the problem of the status quo; should people undertake anything new before the glorious return? Saul's answer had, of course, been simple: "Everyone should remain in the state in which he was called" (1 Cor 7:20). But by the time the glorious return had fizzled out, this orbit of ideas had become irrelevant. The Church was already coping not with Saul's fantasies, but with the workaday world.

The intellectual configuration, so to speak, that made Hellenization possible was independent of a mere event; it did not have to wait, for instance, until the theory of the World's End was undone by the world going-on. The Hellenization of Saul's constellation of ideas had begun only a generation or so after him, at the end of the first and the beginning of the second century, while the inflammation expressed in the World's End theory was still raging.

Essentially, the process was autonomous. The pagan milieu was bound to assimilate parochial Jewish notions of history in its own way. Even before the Jewish husk, so to speak, of the old ideas, shriveled rapidly with the shattering disappointment on the one hand of the World's End not happening, and on the other, more concretely, with the extinction of the Jerusalem Jesist community after 70, the autonomous functioning of a Hellenistic style of thought had already established itself.

Hellenization had not begun as a mere reaction to the disappointment that no doubt grew progressively over the failure of the messianic kingdom to appear. It began as a process inherent in the assimilation of an alien idea; thus it was bound to begin long before the mere slackening of enthusiasm for World's End fantasies.

The idea of a resurrection guaranteed by union with the risen Jesus was a seedbed for countless pregnant ideas drawn from philosophy, logic, and so on; indeed, the *assurance* of that resurrection, since it seemed to fly in the teeth of all evidence, had to be elaborated through brainwork.

It was only Saul who had believed, after all, in the link between the resurrection of Jesus and the World's End; only he could take seriously the notion that the resurrection into the messianic kingdom was guaranteed by the fact that Jesus' resurrection had *already* triggered the transition to the messianic kingdom, that believers had *already* died and risen again with Jesus and were thus guaranteed participation in the resurrection style of existence at the glorious return.

Saul's successors could no longer make do with this primitive ardor, so plainly at odds with mundane facts. The ardor was bound to dim below the point where it could summon up genuine enthusiasm. Ardor like Saul's could exist only when the resurrection of Jesus was felt with such intensity that it could suffice to launch a new universe; in its turn that had to be experienced with such overwhelming certainty that the believer could link the cosmic upheaval to his own person.

The misunderstanding of Saul's basic thought was remarkably rapid. He had already been Hellenized completely by the second generation after his death; a couple of generations later his World's End delusion—the anchorage of all his ideas—was to be utterly indigestible. The entire mechanism he had devised to explain the working out of Jesus' death and resurrection was simply dropped.

It took no more than a generation for the ardent conviction infusing Saul's system to expire. Even though the hopes bound up with the World's End survived, as it seems, into the second century, and the theory clung to life as part of the nascent faith (as we can see by the writings of some Church Fathers),[2] the true ardor of expectation had nevertheless been relegated by the second generation or so after Saul to a nebulous, amorphous future; it had been edged back to the end of the World's End.

Saul's views had arisen organically out of his milieu because both he and his milieu still believed in the imminent installation of the messianic kingdom; hence Saul's ideas could be dramatically effective, in their novelty, without at the same time seeming preposterous. But with the extinction of the expectation of the World's End, the only positive element of Saul's opinions was their generality, as a vehicle for proselytization. In this way Saul's improvisations, essentially *ad hoc* contrivances to encompass the world change he thought had already begun, were calcified; they were then codified on an entirely different intellectual and emotional basis.

Just as Saul had misconceived Judaism because of his frantic conviction of the World's End, so the Church, insisting that it was the only heir of true Judaism, necessarily misconstrued Saul by dropping the immediate expectation of the World's End, without, curiously enough, even noticing the omission.

Christian theology may be said to have begun with the lobotomizing of Saul's ideas; it then made fruitful use of this conception of the union of flesh and spirit by extending it to explain, first of all, the fusion of the divine and human in the person of Jesus—a source of endless difficulties!—then the function of Jesus in the bringing of salvation, then, further, the mediation of redemption by the magicalized sacraments.

If theology arises in the first place to fill the vacuum of religious disappointment, the process is illuminated by the fate of Saul's ideas. The World's End, which never came, very soon generated a *doctrine* of the World's End and finally, with the indefinite postponement of the fact even the doctrine was surrendered. Alfred Loisy's remark applies to Saul even more than to Jesus: "What Jesus preached was the Kingdom of God, what happened was the Church."

Saul's improvisation, contrived to cope with a specific historical situation, proved to be infinitely elastic. It was dramatic enough and psychologically, i.e., timelessly, moving enough to transcend the failure of the glorious return and, via the concretization engendered by just that failure, to provide a model for popular worship as well as for mystical devotion. The glorious return, shelved forever, was replaced by the Church and by the magical procedures that infused it as it congealed.

Thus Saul's miscalculation of the timing of the glorious return brought it about that in the Church the sacraments once again became timeless, psychological; they were embodied in a structure of daily ritual that could constantly and repeatedly tap the well-springs of emotion in believers. Abstracted from their historical context—the sociopolitical circumstances of the Jews, i.e., the context of the historicization of the divine plan on earth—they became calcified in and for themselves, efficacious within an earthly edifice claiming divine resonance.

Saul's theory, by virtue of its very formulation, proved capable of providing access to nature itself. It proved capable, after the failure of the Kingdom of God to appear, of projecting believers into a Kingdom of God that *need never appear.* His passionate thought was to demonstrate, as it were inadvertently, that for human aspirations the projection of a hope can replace a reality that has never come about. In short, "it is better to travel hopefully than to arrive."

This insight, writ large, applies to Saul's handiwork; he had thought of it as a bridge to salvation, but it was a bridge that was never to be built. It was to hang in the air, so to speak, with its farthermost end hovering eternally over the suggestion of bliss.

In reality this possibility was already contained, without Saul's being aware of it, in his basic invention. If the World's End had already begun, though it remained indiscernible, it meant that people could already be part of the Kingdom of God even when that, too, was missing. Though Saul himself thought the Kingdom infallibly about to arrive, his formula nevertheless bridged over a nonexistent material situation with the aid of hope. By accommodating the "more or less," the "sooner or later" of the advent of the messianic kingdom, Saul created a formula that *also* encompassed "not at all"—the situation in which the messianic kingdom was eternally postponed. And that alone was enough to make his formula endlessly extensible. Saul's thought proved to be plastic enough to encompass indefinite deprivation.

Inventing a belief in Jesus as the Messiah who was both on his way and already there, Saul enveloped this with such passion and precision that it could be freed from its temporal anchor and float aloft forever.

He himself, to be sure, could never have accepted, even understood such a notion. For him the advent of the Kingdom was guaranteed in advance, so to speak, by its having already begun; at the same time strenuous efforts were required for its materialization. It was far from his temperament to repose in the world as it was; the action it called for led to his scurrying about the world to fill up his quota of recruits for the elect, his envisaging a trip as far as Spain to make sure that the quota was filled with as many members as possible, his reasoning that all this was indispensable as a way of convincing the Jews by "jealousy" to see the light.

Plainly, none of this has anything to do with the passive exhilaration of mystic union with the body of Christ as a permanent condition of the world. Though his intellect was to provide an anchor for a permanent world order in the shape of the Church, the world order itself, with its built-in magicality, its static "thereness," its all-encompassing immovability was the antithesis of Saul's personal, Jewish, history-tormented, dramatic and altogether active *struggling*—his wrestling with the world.

What made Saul's situation a problem for him was that in his own mind he could not shake loose from Judaism at all; he was obliged, as a normative Jew, entirely devout, simply to reconsider his position in the new circumstances. He could not, accordingly, take the Torah away from the Jews—how, indeed, would that have been possible? This was to happen afterwards, as an unforeseeable consequence of the failure of his ideas. With the failure of the glorious return Saul was to find himself, all unwittingly, the first of an endless line of ideologists who transferred all Jewish "privileges"—the status of chosen people as beneficiaries of the divine plan—from flesh-and-blood Jews to the new "Israel of God," constituted by simple exegesis rotating around the establishment of allegorical categories.

Saul thought he was merely consummating his Jewish faith by crystallizing it in Jesus as the "end of the Torah"—both its termination and its purpose (the Greek word *telos* has the same ambivalence as the English). Yet in the new age the consequences of this entire shift of emphasis were incalculable. By simultaneously spiritualizing and concretizing the nature of the covenant between the Jews and God, by magicalizing the instrumentality of the covenant's transmission, Saul made it possible to distribute the promise to pagans—all mankind—by means of a magically potent faith. He arbitrarily interpreted Abraham's "seed" as referring to all human beings, on the one hand, and on the other—through his interpretation of the word as a reference to a single individual—to Jesus Christ.

At bottom this, too, like so much else in Saul's driven mind, was a purely Jewish notion ultimately the old conception of the "righteous remnant" common in apocalyptic writings, which under the influence of the tension brought to a head by the Roman yoke had been given greater emphasis than before.

Saul had solved his puzzle by eternalizing delay. It was that delay, indeed, that had started him off on his attempt to solve the problem it constituted. While he naturally thought of it as an *ad hoc* situation, infallibly to be superseded by the imminent advent of the Kingdom—the ad hoc itself became eternal. The bridge flung by Saul over the gap between Jesus' resurrection and the installation of the messianic kingdom, a bridge implying a time-span of mere months or years, proved to contain an angle of elevation that, just because of the powerful abstractness of Saul's thought, could encompass all horizons seen and unseen. He had cast the contortions of his own temperament—his anguish—into a formulation that constituted a framework for the anguish of untold generations.

The process may be summed up, broadly. Saul had contrived a mechanism that for the recruits to the new fraternity had created an arc of immediate hope of salvation through absorption into the mystic body of Christ at the World's End.

But this arc of immediate hope was widened into an arc of timeless reassurance by the generation after Saul, dominated by a blanket misunderstanding of World's End theories. When pagans set about explaining salvation not as due to the installation of the messianic kingdom in a universe of Jewish drama, but as due to the fact of Jesus Christ himself, Savior of the Universe, the substance of Saul's thought was radically twisted.

Saul, while expanding the potential magic of the original, rather modest Jesist conception of Jesus as the usher of change, had not carried his realization of that potential to its farthest limit. His magic, linked to the World's End and hence auxiliary, was efficacious in an entirely different way from the magic embedded in the structure of the pagan Mysteries.

Saul utilized a partial magic, a sort of gimmick, an auxiliary to a historical event. Though modeled on the Mysteries, his idea was confined by its Jewish historical framework. When the glorious return failed, and the Church flowered in the void of Saul's shattered ideas, his system was unconsciously twisted into a total, timeless amplification of the magical procedures. But these selfsame procedures, misunderstood, survived the failure of the messianic kingdom to erupt; thus they became elements in a world order that with the collapse of Saul's historical assessment itself became part of the static, timeless world.

In that world, Saul's devices, in his own mind provisionally and transiently magical because of the impending great change, became fully, autonomously, and timelessly magical within the Church engendered by the misunderstanding of his ideas. Put concisely, Saul's mystical improvisation, that an event originally linked to some other event in a chronologically sequential future—i.e., the benefitting of the elect in the imminent future from Jesus' resurrection, after his glorious return—was transformed into a state of mind and emotion with a real existence in the present. Believers, who in the beginning had believed they would be saved after the glorious return, were gradually replaced by believers who believed in the salvational effects of their belief in the real presence of the deity at that moment. That was what created the Church; from then on it was a receptacle for dynamic transformations within itself while it itself remained static. It became an institution anchored in the humdrum world precisely as a vehicle for dynamic transformations: It could, through the dynamism it encompassed, offer salvation there and then.

In a word, history-minded monotheism, based on an absolute distinction between God and his handiwork, was replaced by dynamic magic, capable of transforming the world-stuff it was itself a part of. Saul had created a new and autonomous constituent of the primordial world-stuff.

More specifically, the potentialities inherent in Saul's apotheosis of Jesus were finally realized; the magicalization of the sacraments was globalized. This was a natural consequence of the magnification of Christ; the modalities for communion with him were correspondingly magnified. The limitless magnification of Jesus brought about the limitless magnification of the Eucharist.

Though the Eucharist had its roots in a piece of Jewish symbolism, it was soon transformed by this magnification and above all by the transference of its function to a magical contrivance. It ceased being a symbol, and instead became a modality of power. It is a sacrifice in which God once again becomes a voluntary victim at the very moment the rite is consummated. The result of this train of thought is that a "force (*dynamis*) is produced that is magical, and that generates mystical benefits for the participants that are incalculable."[3]

Saul's generalizing formula, originally linked to a time- and space-bound event in history, was emancipated from all considerations of time and space; it soared aloft as an absolute abstraction that at the same time was bound up with the new condition of the cosmos, i.e., the magic institution of the Church. Like pagan thought, Saul's formula attributed a new sort of reality to the natural world; his formula created a situation in which a believer could tap a reservoir of natural power quite independent of God. It was a piece of magical legerdemain within the reach of everyone.

Saul's personal anguish, his morbidity, his fear of death, his obsessive compulsiveness, his yearning for relief, had restored to the universe a broadened, streamlined, infinitely extended conception while at the same time creating procedures for coping with it. He had restored, magnified, deepened, and internalized magic. And he had structured that magic. Saul's ideas, originally devised to contain the immediate hysteria of those inflamed by the expectation of imminent bliss in the messianic kingdom, were given an algebraic formula, so to speak, that could be expanded at will. Flexible in its essence, the formula, by overcoming the awareness of human mortality in the minds of its believers, could express a condition of the universe.

In sum, Saul's thought involved the concept that whatever is instituted in the way of resurrection is linked to the world change; i.e., Jesus makes resurrection possible for the elect because he institutes the messianic kingdom. Later, after the idea was transformed, Jesus was conceived of as making immortality possible because of the magic inherent in his substance. Jesus brings about *in his own person* the hitherto inexistent conditions for resurrection.

Once again, materials invested by Saul with semimagical elements created for a situation in which they would automatically be nullified after the world-change, were paganized back into timelessness. Saul's historical conception had been converted into the magical conception of guaranteeing immortality through a procedure embedded in the world.

It was through the articulation of a lapse in analysis—Saul's failure as a historian!—that his general ideas, frustrated during his lifetime by his subordination to a central Jewish authority, could, with the disappearance of that authority, soar aloft as a paradigm for the anguish of all mankind, the basis of a universal religion.

The net result of all these transpositions was simple; Saul repaganized the universe.

Pagan configurations flowered in Christianity, not merely in the arts and in general culture, but in the very hierarchy headed by the Son of God and mediated by the magical Church interposed between the one unreachable God and men. The actual figure of worship in Christianity became Jesus, boldly linked to God the Father much later through the ingenious contrivance of the Trinity.

Jesus thus remained in some sense God, too, but as a son figure substituting for the Father, Jesus required an altogether different kind of commitment; the Jewish Yahweh, transcendent, could be trusted, loved, and obeyed, but was beyond identification with. Jesus, the suffering Man-God, could restore the ancient pagan intimacy with a divinity. It may be said that the symbol of the cross was potent enough to reach any human being, however base he felt himself to be; he could find a brother, a son, when he could not reach the Father. The rehumanized divinity, Jesus, became a magnet for multitudes. Christianity became the most influential religion in history.

Pagan religions, with their countless hierarchies of gods, wrestling with each other and with the world, and themselves subject to vast impersonal forces, like fate, embedded in the world-fabric, provided cozy divinities that anyone could identify himself with. Highly accessible, they could become the safety valves of all the forces at play within the human imagination. Judaism, perceiving with a clarity that after generations of rumination had become blinding, that all such notions of deity were the purest nonsense, had substituted for them a single grandiose concept of one God, articulated on the plane of ethics by sequestering all morality within the competence of that one God, thenceforth the source of all authority and subject to nothing whatever.

This simplified endlessly the crazy quilt of paganism, but it must have been frustrating for many whose identifications had to be made with something nearer at hand, who were deprived of the gratifications to be derived from the frivolous gods, their war games, their sexual diversions. Paganism as an unconscious restructuring of thought must also be considered the profound reason for the subsistence and, in the modern era, the reemergence of the devil as a cornerstone of Christian theology, not merely as a superstition lurking in the unconscious of the masses but as an explicit formulation in authoritative Catholic and Protestant milieus.

This surely may be linked to two intellectual alloys of Saul's, the deployment of the God-championing forces against the God-opposing forces and above all the implantation of the most fundamental, the primordial element in all paganism—the notion of God's pedigree.

Paganism is rooted in the singling out of aspects of the world, of nature, for contemplation and worship. Its gods reflect the universe; they are begotten and beget; they acquire authority and bequeath it; they die and live again. In monotheism God neither inherits his authority from progenitors nor bequeathes it to progeny. As he does not end, so he does not begin.

And it is just at this point that what was for Saul a historical, i.e., time-linked fact, though a fact that pointed the way to timelessness, became intertwined with the countless myths in which the deity is resurrected as part of an endlessly recurrent world order of divine contention. Saul's mystery-myth, originally contrived to span the historical chasm between one event and another, incorporated the notion that God's struggle against the forces of evil in the universe included a role for his son!

The cardinal distinction of monotheism is not, after all, the mere concept of a Supreme Being—that is common to various paganisms—but the conviction that a Supreme Being is the sole source of the universe and everything in it, *including* evil. All forms of paganism, contrariwise, postulate a world order in which there are contending sources of autonomous authority, of which evil is one. The world order itself is timeless, above history and *prior to the Supreme Being.*

It is just at this point that the unforeseen consequences of Saul's creativity become discernible. In Judaism, the one God, himself transcendental, had created history, which is itself real. Hence, while God contains all sources of divinity, and is himself the ultimate source of evil, the historical process can work itself out on the human plane. Human beings, morally responsible for their own behavior because of their free will, and subject only to God's intent in the world order, are actors on the stage of history, which in its final phase will be reconciled to God, who for purposes of his own had alienated the world from himself.

In the pagan world order, however, evil stands above divinities or is an equal divinity among other divinities; evil is itself timeless, primordial, yet subject to magic.

Thus paganism, established on an autonomous basis merely through the apotheosis of Jesus, was amplified and ramified, even in Saul's construction, by the notion of clashing powers leading to a victory for the God-forces. Then, when Saul's system was further dislocated and magic reinstated within the edifice of the Church, all the paganism overcome in Judaism flowered as never before. The devil as an autonomous force epitomizes this whole development.

If monotheism is the utter supremacy of the One, if the sovereignty of the One is limited by no laws, compulsions, or powers, if the One is, indeed, the source of all being, neither subject to nor produced by a pre-existent realm, it is plain that the notion of an independent source of authority in the form of the devil is a throwback to the paganism antedating Judaism.

The concept of a real, i.e., an autonomous devil, is even more paganistic, so to speak, than paganism, which defers to the sublime totality of the universe. When man puts himself on the level of nature, by projecting his own abstractions on a par with natural cycles, and then worships those abstractions, it would seem, indeed, the perversion of an originally sane and humble paganism.

But putting it that way would, of course, miss the whole point. The devil is encompassed, after all, by the Church, which is both the object of worship and its channel. The Church explains not merely God but the devil, too, and indeed all aspects of life, to which it gives meaning and purpose. By linking, mediating, and elucidating the world, God, the devil, and man, the Church itself becomes the structured locus of real authority.

The survival of the devil as an autonomous force of nature, subordinate to God, in a way, but fundamentally invincible—the containment of the devil is one of the main raisons d'être of the Church—was to have portentous consequences, as we shall see, for the Jews, whose kinship with the devil was by no means to be considered metaphorical, but a fundamental attribute of their nature.

The misunderstanding of Saul was natural, and no doubt inevitable. His own personal situation was unique in history. A pious Jew, suffering a uniquely personal anguish, he had worked out what he thought of as an adaptation of Jewish tradition to a specific unique historical situation. But since he could not convince other Jews, nor could his specific views have the slightest meaning for pagans, who became Christians in response to various sources of their own distress in the milieu they had come from, Saul had to be accepted by the early Church as a mere symbol, so to speak, of what he had really said.

Perhaps the most illuminating element in this historical process, looked at from outside, is that even though it took place with such rapidity it was impossible for those undergoing it to admit or even, no doubt, to perceive it. The concept of the World's End, though it had plainly vanished a few generations after Saul, had become an article of faith.

It may be said, indeed, that because of the omission from well-nigh all considerations of Saul (until Albert Schweitzer at the beginning of this century) of the absolutely fundamental element in his thought—the imminently looming World's End—all Christian views of Saul constitute a seamless tissue of historical misunderstandings. Saul's ideas were, essentially, fossilized the moment the World's End was forgotten. Any interpretation of Saul that disregards his view of the World's End as urgent and imminent, is bound to make him utterly incomprehensible.

At the same time, it may be particularly curious that in their singular ardor, their moving passion, Saul's improvisations could have had significance *only* for Jews. Saul's thought was senseless for pagans; it could appeal only to those for whom the Torah had become the center of life, those whose personal morbidity made the Torah a problem. Saul's system was utterly incomprehensible to all the pagans trickling into the congregations based on his key concept of a new covenant. What could the *old* covenant have meant to them?

Thus the new conception, obliged to create its own spiritual ambiance, to establish its own theory and symbols, was bound to be misconstrued. Saul's ideas were smothered in current world-views: as the end of history receded into history, as the World's End was replaced by real life, Greek ideas, which permeated the minds of the earliest non-Jewish coteries of Jesists in the Hellenistic world, created an entirely novel, unforeseen connection between the resurrection of Jesus and the pious believers' hopes for their own resurrections.

Apocalyptic was abandoned by both nascent Christianity and Judaism around the same time. After the crushing of the Bar Kochba revolt in 135, the notion that history would bring about its own rectification by a cataclysmic upheaval demonstrating God's will withered away.

With the definitive shriveling of faith in the World's End, as expectation of an upheaval in the real world faded, Christian speculation had to consider other ways of handling the intellectual and spiritual seeds embedded in the primitive Kerygma, the rather skimpy message thought to epitomize Jesus' career.

As the glorious return kept failing to be realized, and Jesus himself inevitably ceased being thought of as on his way back to a regenerated cosmos, speculation was obliged to concentrate on the meaning of the concept of Jesus Christ here and now on earth, and what that in turn implied for the hereafter. By the middle of the second century this had to be acknowledged by Christian thinkers, and though they were obliged to go on referring to the glorious return, solidly embedded, as it was, in all the documents, the references had become no more than a form of lip service. Whatever Christians preferred to think, they could no longer live in expectation of the glorious return, now totally dislocated from its formerly focal position.

For Hellenistic society the World's End could retain no sense. The philosophic dualism between the flesh and the spirit that had been prevalent—buttressed, to boot, by a leaning toward spiritualism—disinclined the ordinary run of Christianized pagans from a belief in the resurrection of the flesh and all the other material aspects of the messianic kingdom that Jewish thought had felt itself at home in.

For the Church, assuming a definite shape around this time, the definitive elimination of a Jewish center was to open a way once and for all to the triumph of all pagan material in the nascent faith. This meant the outright elimination or submergence of the Jewish elements, of which those that survived became encysted as it were within the core of the nascent faith, to be fossilized by layer after layer of thought drawn from the pagan milieu. The schism was consummated by the time of the Bar Kochba revolt in 135; after that it was no longer possible to be both a Jew and a member of the new sect.

This anchoring of Christianity's cosmic speculation in the here and now, coincident with the fading away of the hope for the cataclysm, gave the nascent faith a different framework. Remaining in the very nature of its thought other-worldly, the Church had to ground its evolving institutional life in a new theory. The extinction of living Jewish influence was reflected in or paralleled by a replacement of Jewish historicism—the notion that history, actual or imaginary, is what counts—by timeless theologizing.

With Greco-Roman pagans now constituting by far the bulk of the new fellowships, Saul's melange of Hellenistic ideas, stitched into a Jewish background, and the ethereal propositions scattered about the Gospel of John, equally rooted in pagan thought, were necessarily amplified. Most important of all, the amplification was accomplished in a society that was being shredded. The convulsions that established the Roman Empire provided nascent Christianity with a fertile seedbed.

By the end of the apostolic age, about 100 C.E., people calling on the name of Christ Jesus, Lord of the Universe, were discussing Jesus in ways that would, no doubt, have flabbergasted him. Very soon Jews were to be denied all knowledge of the truth, and for that matter of the Torah itself, which the new faith could take over in its entirety by appending to it an entirely novel interpretation. Indeed, the documents gathered together in various fellowships and soon to be canonized in what became the New Testament were so exiguous as a whole, so elusive as a corpus of historical reminiscence and still more so as a body of thought, that the bulky Hebrew Scriptures, a massive library accumulated over a millennium, were plainly indispensable to lend the new canon any weight.

The scattered Christian fellowships drawn from among practicing Jews who still looked up to the apostles and their Jewish disciples remained small and impoverished. They still existed in Syria, Egypt, perhaps in Rome, but had been swamped by massive congregations thronged with pagan converts. Around 160 St. Justin could say that Christians observing Jewish practices would be saved as long as they did not attempt to impose such practices on others, but he added that many Christians would not rub shoulders with them.

By the beginning of the second century, Christianity could stand forth as an independent religion, which even though its rites, dogmas, and institutions were still elementary, was no longer to be confused with Judaism. Anchored in the pagan world, it could offer personal salvation to all men without distinction.

14

A New Faith Articulated

The Jewish debacle of 70 did not bring about a general repression of Jews in the Roman empire; the Romans did not blame Jews as such for the insurrection. There had, after all, been a substantial Jewish peace party, headed by the Jewish royal family; Berenice, Agrippa II's sister, had a lengthy relationship with Vespasian's son Titus, the conqueror of Jerusalem. It was Agrippa II and Berenice, indeed, who had financed Vespasian's and Titus's campaign for the Roman throne.

The Temple, to be sure, was never rebuilt. This put an end to the sacrificial cult and to the high priesthood, hence to the influence of the Jewish aristocracy and the Sadducees, linked to both. The only general measure affecting Jews in the Empire at large was the *fiscus judaicus,* a Temple tax levied even after the destruction of the Temple.

Still, Judaism survived; in effect this meant the mainstream of Pharisee opinion, purged, very largely, of the militancy that had led to the debacle.

A Pharisee scribe, Yohanan ben Zakkai, had slipped out of Jerusalem during the last siege and reconstituted a new Sanhedrin in Jamnia, a village near what is now Rehoboth.

In effect the authority of the Torah was perpetuated; the tradition was ensured; the canon of the Hebrew Scriptures was closed; the apocrypha, books included in the Greek canon, remained excluded.

From this time on official Judaism consciously protected itself. A principal Jewish prayer, recited to this day, included a section directed against heretics, which came to include the Jesists.

From then on the rabbis who had inherited the legacy of Pharisaism were to be considered the chief enemies from within of the evolving faith. Though the Jews could not use force against the Jesists they could still expel them from their enduring socioreligious commonwealth. This is echoed in a number of passages in John (9:22; 12:42; 16:2) and especially in Matthew, which often sounds as though the author were still contending bitterly against dominant Pharisaism.

Jerusalem retained a small population, which was to be practically wiped out again during the last insurrection of the Jews under Bar Kochba in 132–135; some Jesists came back again as the city more or less settled down under Roman dominion.

We have already seen the interest of the Roman police in Jesus' family, the tracking down of all descendants of King David, started by Vespasian, was continued under Titus and Domitian, Titus's brother and successor, and even under Domitian's successor Trajan.

In short, Jesus' kin were regarded as potentially dangerous as late as the end of the first century. There was evidently a real fear of pretenders to Jewish sovereignty.

No doubt the Davidic origin of Judah the Galilean, whose grandsons had played insurrectionary roles down to the war of 66–70, was a factor in this, especially if there is some truth in the report of an "ambiguous oracle," presumably derived from the Hebrew Scriptures, to the effect that someone from Palestine, in the turmoil preceding the uprising of 66, was supposed to become ruler of the world. The insurgents were reported as having "interpreted this falsely to mean one of their own people"[1] while it was taken advantage of by our sole chronicler, Josephus, to hail Vespasian himself as fulfilling the prophecy. Thus an actual prophecy, interpreted in favor of Jewish would-be messiahs, and hence another cause of the intractable opposition to the Romans, still retained its force after the war.

Just before the outbreak of the war Upright Jacob had been succeeded by a cousin[2]; some dynastic principle was evidently involved. There was also a tradition that a community of Jesists in Jerusalem was headed by an uninterrupted succession of fifteen Jewish "bishops." After the Bar Kochba revolt in 135 Hadrian attempted to wipe out the name and the recollection of Jerusalem, christening it Aelia Capitolina; the Jesist community there seems to have abruptly become entirely non-Jewish.[3]

In any case, though the original Jesist coterie in Jerusalem vanished in the debacle of 70 together with the other insurgents, some community of believers in Jesus existed in Jerusalem down to the Bar Kochba revolt, in which some kinsmen of Jesus played a role independently of the Jesists themselves (Bar Kochba persecuted them). After the abortive Bar Kochba revolt the Romans forbade all Jewish settlement in Jerusalem, as well as all Jewish Jesist settlement, for some time. Jews were forbidden even to visit Aelia Capitolina. Hadrian's initiative was, in fact, the first attempt at genocide, in this case arising exclusively out of the long-drawn-out—two centuries—history of Jewish resistance.

For all the Jewish Jesists, of course, Jerusalem as such had been the object of reverence. That was why they prayed toward it, and that was why Upright Jacob had become celebrated for his incessant praying in the Temple, that is, in the true place of prayer. This tradition was carried over to the earliest Christians, who interpreted the destruction of Jerusalem as a punishment for Upright Jacob's murder by the Sadducee high priest.

In 66 the Jesists, completely at one with the other Kingdom of God activists, had formed an integral part of the upheaval directed by the rival militant factions. Like the other activists they must have been heartened by Gallus's incomprehensible retreat as well as by Vespasian's sluggish campaign. Like the other activists they must have thought that with the issue engaged at last the denouement must now be at hand. The World's End would come about for all people, the Kingdom of God would be installed, and world dominion would be bestowed on Israel.

The whole of the Jerusalem population, as we have seen, was submerged in the frightful siege and its indescribable sufferings. The carnage, exacerbated by famine and disease, had affected the entire population. Not merely was Qumran (the Dead Sea Scrolls community) wiped out in 68, but the Jesist coterie itself vanished two years later, when Jerusalem was laid waste and the Temple burned. (The legend of its flight to Pella, on the other side of the Jordan River, is a pious fabrication devised to substantiate the continuity claimed by a much later tradition [see critical appendix]).

Those Jesists who retained the essential views of the original Jesist coterie in Jerusalem were dealt a deathblow by the Jewish debacle of 70. In and around Palestine groups of Jewish Jesists (the two main groups were called "Nazarenes" and "Ebionites") who clung to the Jewish Torah and refused to accept, for instance, the legend of the virgin birth and in general the "Son of God" theory—i.e., whose faith in Jesus was limited to a belief in a mere Jewish Messiah expected to "restore sovereignty to Israel"—shriveled rapidly. Only a couple of generations later they were to be vilified as heretics, while at the same time the original Jesist community that such Jewish-oriented groups had descended from became fossilized and mythologized under the entirely misleading name of the "Mother Church," and brought into line with the emerging Greek ideas.

To be sure, a major Jewish idea, the Kingdom of God, by now to all intents and purposes, apparently, wholly extinct, was to retain enough potency to burst through its shroud and in specific situations to restimulate human imaginations. This was to happen periodically for centuries, indeed, down to the present day.

In those days, of course, religion was a communal matter; the place of individuals in society was defined by their religious status. The question of personal belief was not to arise, in a social sense, for many centuries. Thus the coteries of Jesists scattered throughout the area wherever there were Jewish communities initially benefited by the privileged position of Jews, and were not, in fact, substantively distinguished from Jews for generations after Jesus' execution.

The spread of the new religion was fairly rapid, though not remarkably so. A couple of centuries passed before it became a factor of importance in the State.

Budding Christianity offered its potential believers many advantages. For those who despaired of reason as a path to personal salvation it offered a divine revelation, the message of the Hebrew Scriptures (however that message was interpreted) plus the titanic fact of the risen Jesus. For those in need of philosophy it could put itself forward with composure as the finest philosophy in history. Because of the manner in which the early Christian thinkers fused together in their own minds as it were organically all the ideas taken from Judaism, from the presumed history of Jesus, and from their own Hellenist education, Christianity could plausibly be presented both as the direct link between Greek philosophic speculations and the Hebrew Scriptures, and as their joint consummation.

This stitching together of the Hebrew Scriptures and Greek ideas had already had the terrain prepared for it by the work of Philo, a devout Alexandrian Jew who had applied a system of allegory and exegesis to the Hebrew Scriptures to make them dovetail with the ideas of Plato. By this Philo had unwittingly facilitated a cleavage, in the world of thought, between Judaism and Christianity.

In the Gospel of John, for instance, Jesus the Messiah was presented as an earthly incarnation of the Logos, the Word (of God), according to Alexandrian exegetics an executive agency of Yahweh, and of course coeternal with Yahweh. This was really no more than an extension of Philo's own ideas, though on the other hand, it was an extension that, unsuspected by Philo, instantly led to the staggering proposition, in Diaspora Jesist circles, that since the Crucified One was identical with the Word of God, he was also a direct manifestation of God, and therefore, in fact, God himself.

Now, this idea of confining God within a mere human body was, of course, from the point of view of any Jew—Philo's as well—both blasphemous and incomprehensible. But it was child's play to reconcile it with the train of thought implied by Saul's flat statement that "the Lord is the Spirit," no more, in fact, than a parallel development of the identical conception—the boundless magnification of Jesus.

This flowered mightily on the terrain of Hellenism with the flexibility and abstract potentiality of the Greek language, for it was both natural and seductive to bring together God and Jesus in a union that simultaneously permeated and enveloped the universe. The major consequence of the Jewish debacle of 70 was this. It doomed the Jewish Jesists and their ideas and at the same time rooted the new beliefs throughout the Greco-Roman world.

By the end of the first century, the pagan believers in Jesus, in whom we can now see a sort of proto-Christianity slowly coagulating under the influence of Saul's misunderstood ideas, already formed a distinct entity, with the rudiments of an organization that was both cohesive and potent, very nearly to a degree equaled only by the continuing organization of Judaism. Perhaps the cardinal difference, at this time, was the absence of a Scripture, i.e., a canon, in sharp contradistinction to the majestic antiquity and amplitude of the Hebrew Scriptures.

On the other hand, despite its various frictions, internal rivalries, and the absence of an agreed-on body of beliefs, the proto-Church was unique in the Hellenistic world. Perhaps its chief distinction, socially speaking, lay in its embodiment in a relation to the individual over and above the social bonds that linked him to his past. The proto-Church cut across all past tradition and past attachment. It could appeal, therefore, to any individual merely as a human being.

This democratic appeal was sharply at odds with the vogue of current philosophies, which essentially appealed primarily to an elite. The newly evolving Christian faith cast a vast net, for all mankind without differentiation.

At the outset, after all, the doctrine, before its definitive formulation in the imposing edifice of theology that was to characterize Christianity in its consummation, was so simple that it required no education or training to grasp. At the same time it quickly evolved a sort of philosophy that could be found attractive to an elite too. In effect, what the first generations of Christian thinkers did was to absorb all Greek philosophy, especially neo-Platonism. St. Augustine of North Africa (end of the fourth century) was to say that he had discovered in neo-Platonism exactly the same ideas as in Christianity; all he missed were the incarnation and the humility of Christ.

The earliest Christianity appealed to both sexes equally; the appeal of its rivals (such as Mithraism) was restricted to men. And whereas the Mysteries on which the structure of the evolving faith was modeled so closely generally appealed to the affluent, since initiation fees were high, the Church welcomed rich and poor alike.

At the same time, though Christianity from its very beginnings was modeled on the Mysteries and salvation was offered its believers in much the same way, the one element inherited from Judaism—the belief in an all-knowing, all-powerful God, creator of the universe, even though diluted, as it were, by the necessity of finding a place for the Son of that God—made Christianity entirely intolerant of the Mysteries, which were, each within its own boundaries, generally quite willing to live and let live alongside all rivals. Still, despite this exclusive attitude vis-à-vis rival Mysteries, the Christian mystery was inherently flexible. The simplicity of its basic idea enabled it to adjust to many current beliefs and popular practices in a way that Judaism, linked to its ancient Scriptures, had scarcely found possible.

The prestige attached to Judaism in the ancient world—the prestige of antiquity and of a venerable tradition propped up on incontestably ancient, sacred scriptures—was of immense value to early Christianity. Thus the extinction of the Bar Kochba revolt, whether or not it was supported by Jewish Jesists (Bar Kochba had been hailed as a Messiah by the celebrated Rabbi Aqiba, himself tortured and executed by the Romans) had a direct effect on Jewish Jesism. The collapse of the revolt definitely extinguished an idea that for generations had galvanized the most energetic minds among the Jews, the idea that history was about to accomplish its own rectification through the Kingdom of God at the World's End. After the revolt collapsed, Jews as a body abruptly turned away from apocalyptic visions in general. The evolving Christian community, around the same time, dropped the idea of the glorious return.

As hopes faded for a transformation of the natural world, symbolized for the earliest generations of Jesist believers by the glorious return, Christian speculation was obliged to amplify its treatment of the spiritual and intellectual implications embedded in the primitive Kerygma—the "message" about Jesus. Since with the subsidence of emotional conviction about the glorious return Jesus himself was distanced from the workaday world, it was natural for speculation to be shifted to another axis; what Jesus Christ meant *here and now* on earth, and what that in turn might imply about the hereafter.

It was this emergence of an anchorage for the new faith in the here and now that transformed the faith. It retained its other-worldly thrust, as it were, but since it had to accommodate the needs of life in a workaday world whose permanence had come to be accepted, the evolving institutional life of the new religion was given a different cast.

This paralleled, to be sure, the extinction of Jewish influence implicit in the destruction of the Jewish State and Temple. Jewish historicism—the notion that history, actual or fanciful, is what counts—was replaced by timeless theologizing precisely as the proto-Church took root in the here and now.

Though Christians went on referring to the glorious return, it became a concept that was both emotionally and intellectually fossilized. References to it were no more than lip service; the emotional and intellectual expectation of the glorious return was dislocated entirely. Ousted from its focal position, it became, in fact, a mere traditional ornament, no more than a metaphor. Believers could no longer live in its expectation.

For the Hellenistic world, after all, the World's End had no sense at all. An integral part of Jewish history and historical thought, in spite of all its visionary elements, it could survive in Hellenistic thought only as an aspect of the magnified Lord Jesus; when the expectation of this glorious return shriveled, the locus of belief became radically different. The philosophic dualism of the Hellenistic world, fortified by a general leaning toward spiritualism, nullified the idea of a resurrection of the flesh, together with the material aspects of the messianic kingdom and the Kingdom of God that Jewish thought had found natural.

By the end of the first century and the beginning of the second, Greco-Romans were no doubt by far the bulk of the recruits to the new faith. This meant that there was an audience for the ideas projected both by Saul and by the Gospel of John, representing an attitude that was to sweep the field. By the end of the so-called Apostolic Age the rupture between Jews and Jesists was consummated; Jesists were Christians.

Even after Judaism and Christianity became formally distinct, there were countless communities throughout the Mediterranean area where Christians remained fascinated by Judaism. In many places it was quite usual for Christians to "attend the synagogue, keep the Jewish fasts, and even make gifts of oil on taking part in the festivals celebrated in the synagogue. In Spain there were people who persuaded the rabbi to pronounce a blessing over their fields; so, too, Africa seethed with the observance of Jewish customs and festivals."[4]

As late as the end of the fourth century John Chrysostom, the celebrated Greek Bishop of Antioch, felt obliged to vilify the Jews. People made a point of calling in Jewish doctors whose ceremonial prescriptions were complied with. Important oaths were sworn in the synagogue; everyone believed that oaths sworn before the ark of the Torah were peculiarly potent. People hoped to derive an advantage from joining in Jewish fasts and festivals, especially on New Year, when the blowing of the trumpet impressed many. A great many people thought, said Chrysostom in a sermon from autumn 386, that there was something particularly valuable about Judaism, and that Jews worshipped the true God.

In a sermon that may be taken as a model for the attitude of the Church for many centuries, Chrysostom denounced the Jews root and branch as idol worshippers and their synagogues as the home of the Devil and his demons.[5] The very heat of attack on the Jews must be taken as an index of the sympathy felt by many ordinary Christians.

Under the Caesars culture consisted mainly of a form of literature, rhetoric, and philosophy. Thus, in spite of the upheavals in the social and political spheres during the first centuries of the Empire, education from one end of it to the other was basically similar. In fact a general culture exemplified the same reasoning habits that served as a matrix for religious ideas.

Philosophy consisted of an attempt to strip the world of its appearances to ascertain the meaning of life and to lay down ethical principles independently of any form of science, still rudimentary. This was complemented by rhetoric, a mere technique for putting together ideas and words. The flowering of the early Greek interest in science had vanished; countless absurdities could plausibly be presented uncurbed and uncontrolled by common sense.

Without empirical controls, what passed for philosophy might, of course, be eloquent and ingenious, abounding in ideas, but with no grounding in factual enquiry it would naturally crumble into systems of thought that revolved, essentially, around arbitrary metaphors. These systems were scarcely more than traditional literary themes on which virtuosos would demonstrate their prowess by improvising variations. After being elaborated in ways that might be entirely divorced from the original architects of the ideas the themes could be transposed with ease.

Just as at the very outset of these attempts at the harmonization of ideas, Philo had integrated the Hebrew Scriptures and various themes of Greek philosophy that interested him, so the Neo-Platonists could extract from their fund of ideas a kind of revealed religion that could then be combined by the Christian scholars of Alexandria with the elements of Christian faith and so produce still another system of dogmatics. And even though the exposition of these ideas could not be defended rationally, it could also dispense with defense, since their basic elements were in fact already taken for granted in the minds of the elite and so were universally accepted by the educated as well as by the ignorant. Unchallenged premises were thus unconsciously the bedrock of all discussion and propaganda. Indeed, every interpretation of life, of destiny, had to start off from what at bottom were no more than conventional prejudices.

All creeds and cults had their followers, who adapted them all to the general pervasive longing for a future of eternal bliss in a mysterious hereafter. The given conglomeration of religious material was rich and diverse enough for each cult to combine its credo with rites of the most diverse origins.

The state religion had absorbed not only the nationalities conquered by Rome, but also their deities. Thus, from now on the religious upsurge, focused by the concentration of state power and aiming only at the salvation of the individual, formed a natural seedbed for Christianity.

Ordinary people took for granted a distinction between matter and spirit. The spirit represented the good, i.e., the aspirations of the soul; matter was bad. Hence salvation, to ordinary people, meant the emancipation of the soul from the thralldom of matter and the achievement of immortality through a union with God, not, of course, the God of the Jews, but a somewhat nebulous view of the divine that had been evolving for many generations.

It was this aspect of personal salvation, the immortality of the soul disencumbered of its material straitjacket, that was the objective of the Mystery Cults, of Gnosticism—a widespread current of thought aiming at the penetration of the secrets of reality through a mystically acquired and privately guaranteed "knowledge" (*gnosis*)—and of Neo-Platonism as well.

This longing, very general at the time, was satisfied by evolving Christianity. The redemption of the individual from the fetters of materialism, with its myriad afflictions, was achieved by the resurrection of an incarnate God, in a way structurally similar to the Mysteries and the ancient myths underlying them. But not merely did Christianity democratize and universalize its Mystery; the central fact of the new cult, the killing of a God, was linked to a historical reality; it had actually *happened*. On the other hand, that awesome fact, the incarnation, focused the torrent of emotionality released through the profound symbols of the new faith articulated by Saul's ardor.

Christianity, entering the maelstrom of contending cults in the first and second centuries, was regarded as another oriental religion, strange only, at the outset, in propping itself up for a short time on the ancient religion of the Jews, but otherwise a mystical and practical procedure for bringing about the salvation of its believers. Resting, on the one hand, on divine revelation and promising eternal salvation through an all-powerful Mediator, on the other it claimed to establish on earth, too, a new life through love and virtue.

It was also, of course, as I have indicated above, relentlessly hostile to all forms of syncretism—the fusion of forms, rites, and myths aiming at a common objective. At the same time its dogma as well as its practice was still very simple, that is, malleable. It could digest, inadvertently, the most fundamental of the religious aspirations and ritual practices it encountered when transplanted onto Hellenistic terrain. For that matter they were unavoidable. There was a constant interplay in the great capitals of the Hellenistic world between masses of people, both elite and plebeian, all longing for the same solutions to the same problems.

Thus, during the third century, as Christianity became embedded in Hellenistic society, it could meet and vanquish all forms of pagan syncretism for the simple reason that it had meanwhile itself become a syncretism; it had absorbed and digested all the essential rites, the fertile ideas, metaphors, and symbols with which pagan religions themselves were pullulating. It was able to harmonize these through its central concept, the seemingly simple fact of the incarnation and redemptive crucifixion, and without being inferior on any point could grapple with and incorporate or overcome all the inchoate beliefs and practices of its adversaries in the campaign to recruit adepts.

The unique attraction of Christianity—the only belief that could point to the execution of its own god—gave the metaphysical and transcendental embroidery that was soon to encrust that fact an unshakable anchorage, far removed, it must have seemed, from the whimsical fiddle-faddle of the cults and rites whose justification could be found in the minds of men alone.

The absorption of Hellenistic culture was not accomplished overnight. The new faith made its way through various strata of pagan society, borrowing from each stratum and laying the foundations of the hierarchy still extant in the Roman Catholic Church. A graph of its ascension would rise from the most primitive faith of the most ignorant classes of the population to the philosophical sophistication of the intellectuals. The backbone, so to speak, of the new faith was strong enough to sustain it all.

The very first steps had been taken among the plebeians, initially the "God-fearers" who for many reasons found solace in clustering around Jewish synagogues. On the other hand, not all the God-fearers were plebeian; they included many upper-class women and no doubt some men. Still, until the Antonines in the mid-second century the upper classes could have been only a tiny minority in the Church, whose chief recruits were slaves and laborers. Yet just such slaves carried the new idea into the milieu of free women, and accidentally, some learned men. Thus it was through the learned men that the new faith finally penetrated the upper classes, and concomitantly the circles of the professional intellectuals—the philosophers—during the second century.

The collision with thinkers close to the upper classes and the integration of their ideas with the simplicities of the new faith and with the explanation of the destiny of its deity Jesus Christ, both real-life and transcendental, were to make the ramifications of the encounter endless.

Philosophers like Justin Tatian and Tertullian, tormented by problems that could not be solved by current metaphysical speculation, became Christians, as it seems, as part of the logical outcome of a personal crisis. It seemed to them that the Christian faith solved all problems and satisfied all aspirations. On the other hand, that psychic fact, as it were, did not in itself substantiate the somewhat simple postulates clustered around the bedrock of the incarnation and the redemptive crucifixion. Such new converts naturally brought their extensive philosophical training to bear on their new faith.

Their whole style of thought, their intellectual achievements, were simply put in the service of a new emotional current. Whether or not they expressed this notion explicitly, they were aware that the religion they

had adopted lacked something or other, not, to be sure, in its substance—
i.e., the incarnation, an idea as unfathomable as infinity—but in its formulation. In propagating their new faith, accordingly, they naturally found
themselves fitting it out with the apparatus of ideas and formulations that
gave it all the attraction of a philosophy with the additional potent charm
of being *revealed.* They buttressed, amplified, and enriched its apologetics and dogmatics with all the interpretations and intellectual configurations derived from the metaphysics that had trained them all.

Both Saul's ideas and the somewhat dissimilar though cognate views
outlined in John (no doubt composed around the turn of the second century) were alike in being general enough to allow for immense elasticity.
The guiding ideas of the first period in the formation of the nascent cult
were in fact too general to control the movement of Hellenization, which
in its very nature tended to become a hotch-potch.

It was natural for early Christians to borrow from the surrounding
culture everything that seemed capable of making the initially inchoate
religion more profound as well as more satisfying aesthetically. It was
easy to find a *modus vivendi* between the basic postulates of the early
faith and the major Hellenistic ideas. The Alexandrian school associated
with the name of Origen (around the middle of the third century), for
instance, turned Christianity into a revealed and flawless philosophy by
splicing together all the large-scale ideas borrowed from Hellenistic culture and the axioms of the new faith.

It was no doubt natural, too, for this process, inherently uncontrollable,
to go to extremes. What had begun as a simple confession of faith was
transformed during the third century into a complex edifice of ideas that
looked entirely different. In the process of intertwining the axioms of the
new faith with beliefs and notions taken over from the Hellenistic environment, it absorbed without inhibition practically everything it found. The
general process had run riot. Everything was taken in indiscriminately—
Olympic paganism, Orphism, various oriental religions and philosophical
systems, all of this quite independently either of the historical data, skimpy
to begin with, or for that matter of the traditions handed down in the preceding few generations within the community of the believers. Many
"gnoses" had large followings.

This tendency pretended, in fact, to have a special revelation of its
own, which itself justified the most extravagant combinations, all of which
together made up a syncretistic system in which Jesus Christ was merely

an element. Thus Christianity was twisted out of the historic context in which it had begun and became, in fact, well-nigh unrecognizable. It had become no more than one part of a complex cosmogony and abstruse system of metaphysics, neither of which was inherently dependent on it at all.

All these "gnoses" flourished in the second century. Precisely because of their complexity, capriciousness, and endlessness, they inspired a need for some hierarchical organization, which during this same period began to take shape.

The evolving faith plainly required both a discipline and an authority that would defend that discipline as well as represent it. Thus the power of the as yet somewhat inchoate clergy was focused, that is, enhanced and fortified, by the quasi-monopoly it rapidly acquired in dispensing the magical power inherent in the sacraments and in institutionalizing the theory underlying them and the organization embodying them. The shapeless debates of the second century were the most potent factor in organizing a central authority—the Church.

Christianity also developed its ritual, for the same reasons and through the same processes, in line with the evolution of its dogmatic framework. It was natural for the Hellenistic milieu to channel pagan ritualism into what had been the simple worship of the earliest period, when that worship had been grounded in nothing more than the "spirit" and "truth." The whole of pagan ritualism came to be distributed somehow throughout the evolving Christian ceremonies, even though the genetic relationship between a Christian and a pagan rite may be obscure. In the fourth century, to be sure, some of these pagan rites were uprooted, but this merely accelerated the assimilation of the others.

Thus the simple practices inherited from Judaism and familiar to the earliest coteries—baptism, breaking of bread, laying on of hands, prayer, fasting—were permeated with a more and more profound and above all mysterious meaning. They were amplified, deepened, and decked out by rites taken over from the pagan surroundings, charged with the endless projections encompassed by the Greek and oriental Mysteries and thus infused with all the ancient powers of magic.

15

Institutionalization

The Jews were a considerable force in the Roman empire; in numbers they came to about 10 percent of the population, perhaps some seven million. In Egypt every seventh or eighth person was a Jew; a third of Alexandria was Jewish. A *religio licita,* Judaism was sanctioned by Roman law.

Jews were famous as the oldest living people, except, of course, for the Egyptians, whose elite, however, had been obliterated by Hellenism. The Hebrew Scriptures seemed to go back to the very beginning of time.

Jews had some constitutional privileges; they were exempt from army service and did not have to pay tribute to local gods. Famous as mercenary soldiers, they were generally considered vigorous, manly, and stubborn; at that time they had no reputation for cleverness. The Jews seemed to be respected by the Romans even though Palestine itself was a source of constant irritation.

In Jewish doctrine pagans were to be bound by the seven "Noachide" laws (concerning idolatry, blasphemy, unchastity, bloodletting, robbery, eating the flesh of still-living animals, and justice in general). Any pagan actually dwelling on Jewish land was obliged to obey these Noachide laws, though not the Torah.

Countless pagans were attracted to Judaism, the culmination of a movement of missionary activity that had been promoted by the Hasmonean kings. Before the war against Rome, Jews were very friendly to converts; as we have seen, Judaism had even penetrated the topmost strata of the empire, indeed into Nero's court.

Partial converts to Judaism, God-fearers, in addition to living up to the Noachide laws, were expected to obey the Ten Commandments, observe the sabbath, abstain from outrageous behavior, and pay the Temple tax. Though not admitted to sacrifices, they would take part in rituals and ceremonies. They did not have to be circumcised or to obey the dietary laws. The final stage was, of course, actual conversion. A full convert was simply a Jew in all respects.

It took a couple of generations after the execution of Jesus for the Jewishly-oriented Jesists to be submerged in the throngs of pagan recruits, and a little longer for the ideas associated with Saul to be wrenched out of their historical context to become the theology of a new institution.

For Saul, as we have seen, there was no point in creating an actual institution, either speculative or organizational; for him the Kingdom of God at the World's End was imminent. And even after the destruction of the temple in 70 all Jesists still felt themselves to be on the threshold of the only-slightly-postponed Kingdom of God, and had no need for organization.

Thus at the outset the unity of believers was simple. They formed the one people of God, the body of Christ—"one body and one spirit. . . . One Lord, one faith, one baptism, one God and Father of us all."[1]

At first the organization of the Jesist coteries was hesitant, groping. With no rationale, no attempts at systematization were made, but as soon as the initial disappointment in the failure of the Kingdom of God to appear immediately began to be felt, and it steadily became clearer and clearer that the Kingdom was not in fact arriving from one day or month or year to the next, the first attempts at organization were made. A couple of generations after Saul we can discern the emergence of two offices, the bishop and the elders (presbyters).

By this time the bishop as the apex of a pyramid might have been established, though it is difficult to generalize. There was no division into clergy and laity, no priestly consecration (only an ordination in the presence of the group), and no idea that the bishop had been empowered by any authority. It is not even sure that the bishop, when there was one, was the sole leader of the group. The difference between the bishop and the elders was not formalized, i.e., not substantive.

By the time of Ignatius, bishop of Antioch, around 110, things had evolved into bishop, elders, and deacons. The organizational structure, moreover, was now intertwined with the basic ideas of the nascent

Church—the Christology, the doctrine of the spirit, the sacraments, and the idea of the Church, all of which, taken together, constituted the spiritual as well as organizational justification of the hierarchy. By then God was represented within the community by the bishop. To be sure, it is impossible to analyze the progression from a lay leader of a group in which all are equal to the monarchical position of the bishop, the holder of a sacral office (consummated much later on by the papal office, in which the first bishop of the Roman See became the first bishop of the Church, and much later the pope).

With hindsight we can, of course, see that the cardinal concepts of the incarnation and redemptive crucifixion, embedded in real life, necessarily entailed a clarification of social relationships that led to the ramified structure of the later Church. Was it necessary to have an intermediary between Christ and the believer? What made a sacrament effective? Organizationally, what was the function of the bishop in the mediation needed between God (or Christ) and man? How did this mediation function? Was someone special—a priest—needed to dispense a true, i.e., effective sacrament? Could a priest in his turn be consecrated only by a superior, i.e., a bishop? Was the Church as a totality needed to serve as mediator between God and man? Was the Church itself the agency of salvation? Why was it, in fact, needed at all?

At the beginning of the second century these peremptory questions had not yet been raised, let alone settled.

Meanwhile, how were the Hebrew Scriptures to be dealt with? For the earliest Jesists they were the only Scriptures; the first coteries were in no sense consciously leaving Judaism. The God they believed in was still the Yahweh of the Hebrew Scriptures; when they said "Scriptures" or "Scripture" that was what they meant. The expressions "canon," "Old Testament," and "New Testament" were not to come about until much later.

But though Saul refers to the Old and New Covenants as new facts, and though the word he used in Greek was to be translated into Latin as Testament and has thus come down to us in that form, it was long after Saul before anyone would refer to the books of the Old Covenant and later of the New Covenant, and later still before the word *testament* came to mean a collection of books of any kind. For Saul himself the Hebrew Scriptures remained unconditionally valid. It was, for him, only a question of interpretation.

From the very beginning Jesus was necessarily integrated with the

Hebrew Scriptures. Since in real life he had been wholly identified with normative, though messianic Judaism, it was only natural for the earliest coteries to cling to that primal fact. The belief in Jesus as Messiah was itself, after all, anchored in the Hebrew Scriptures, since the very concept of the Messiah, drawn from the ancient past, was an element in the later, refocused view of Judaism as standing on the threshold of a new age. The assertion that the Messiah had come in and for itself entailed a positive acceptance of the Hebrew Scriptures, which in turn generated a polemic against official Judaism about their interpretation.

Around the beginning of the second century the idea of there having been twelve apostles was worked out. By then the believers, feeling themselves to belong to the "third generation," called for a definition of the "second"—"apostolic"—generation succeeding the first.

By this time the notion of the glorious return, containing within it the bedrock concept of the World's End, was well-nigh extinct, though the weight of the earlier ideas was such that individuals could still go on giving it at least lip service. Nevertheless, despite instances of a faith that still clung to this formerly explosive idea, it was already, functionally speaking, a fossil. For that matter even the delay in the glorious return no longer needed an explanation. Saul's Letters, full of ardent expectation of an imminent transformation of the world, have been by now, as we have seen, entirely relocated on earthly terrain. The World's End means nothing, and the henceforth authoritative reading of Saul's writings simply ignores his fundamental point of view. With the extinction of his real view the metaphorization, so to speak, of the Kingdom of God may be said to have begun.

To clarify the status of the Scriptures Justin Martyr (ca.150) distinguished between three elements in the Hebrew Scriptures: the moral law, the prophesying of the Christ, and the cultic law. The first two were still valid, but the cult was extinct.

This attempt at differentiation between the various elements in something accepted as divine itself, necessarily implied a radically different approach. When the question was asked about the validity of the Torah as divine, reason had to be applied. The "valid" elements had to be separated from the others. This opened the way for the blanket rejection of the Hebrew Scriptures and led to the emergence of what was to become known as the canon of the New Testament, meant either to supplement the Old (i.e., the Hebrew Scriptures) or to replace it.

The process naturally involved a further deployment of the authority now being centralized.

The original authority for the Jesist coteries had, of course, been simply the Lord. This in itself simply implied an absolute supremacy for the words attributed to Jesus, however scanty they were. Even though Saul says practically nothing about the real-life Jesus, the few things he does mention had absolute authority, e.g., the Last Supper (1 Cor 11:23ff) and one or two direct commandments (prohibiting divorce and defining marriage [as in 1 Cor 7:10]) which Saul attributes directly to Jesus while nevertheless interpreting them, to be sure, in his own way. Saul does not, after all, analyze the historic background of what he reports Jesus as having said at the Last Supper; it has already, en route to Saul, been wrenched out of its historic context.

The somewhat tortuous path that led from an original free form of the Lord's extremely uncomplicated authority to the canonization of the books purporting to contain that authority is too obscure to trace. In fact, down to the middle of the second century we have no documents, nor does any book have any authority whatever. At the same time, two foci of crystallization seem gradually to have acquired recognition. Saul's Letters contained an outline of the faith now coagulating, and the Gospels rounded off the relationship of that faith to the world.

Though the Gospels—at any rate the first three—presented themselves as a chronicle of Jesus' life on earth, they consisted, in fact, of material designed to give instruction about the meaning of that life on earth. (It took some eighteen centuries before this simple, though fundamental distinction was recognized.)

At first the two collections were independent of each other; when they were combined the first Christian canon may be said to have emerged. The common presupposition for both collections was that the current believers of the second century were separated from the very first believers by an epoch. This came to be known as the "apostolic" epoch, though this very conception was, as I have indicated, itself a construction of the later theory. It was taken for granted, around the middle of the second century, that the two were essentially a unity, even though Saul by this time had become entirely authoritative for the literary or theological collection, i.e., Saul's status had risen and he had become what he has in fact remained down to our own day—the paramount theologian of Christianity.

In any case, though the details remain unknown, after his death Saul gradually rose in authoritativeness until his victory toward the beginning of the second century. Soon after 100 the collection of his epistles numbering ten (Saul's present Letters without the three to Timothy and Titus, which came later), had already been formed.

The impact of Saul's brainwork on the evolution of Christianity can hardly be overestimated. With very minor exceptions it was Saul's Letters that shaped or substantially influenced all early Christian epistolary literature and subsequently all Christian doctrine.

As for the Gospels, their somewhat camouflaged catechetical structure replaced whatever had been the oral tradition about Jesus, assuming one existed. The oldest Gospel was that of Mark, the model for Matthew and Luke, though by the second century it was still far from canonical. Matthew and Luke supplement Mark, and while retaining its ground-plan give it to some extent a new shape. John, no doubt written around the beginning of the second century, represents an entirely different theological tradition. In the absence of authority, to be sure, anyone could handle traditional material as he wished.

There is no way of knowing exactly how these particular gospels came to be regarded as authoritative; each one had been revered in some particular community. One can only assume that in the give and take of intracommunal relations as the Church came to be organizationally shaped, the contention and compromise were worked out in the canon that has come down to us.

The tradition was not yet extinguished by the emergence of the Gospels in the second century; Bishop Papias of Hierapolis in Asia Minor, for instance, says stoutly that he esteems the "oral tradition"—we have no way of knowing what it was—far more than the books being put together at that time in what was to become the canon.

Throughout the first half of the second century, in fact, the idea of a canon consisting of the four Gospels had not yet emerged. What was required for the very concept of a canon, of course, as well as its corollary, the antithetical idea of apocryphal material, which had to be excluded, was a central authority.

The first attempt to form a canon, in fact, came about as the result of a determined effort to take another approach to the Hebrew Scriptures, i.e., to drop them. This attempt was made around 140 by Marcion, the son of a Jesist, as it seems, who came to Rome from Sinope on the Black Sea.

Marcion made a systematic effort to justify discarding the Hebrew

Scriptures altogether. The logic of the evolution of a new faith had persuaded him that the Hebrew Scriptures were now simply pointless. The God of the Scriptures was no longer the same as the God of Jesus Christ. Yahweh was no more, he thought, than the Creator of the World—the God of mere "righteousness." The real God dwells outside the world altogether, and it was this God, who out of compassion for men, embroiled in the iniquities arising out of the world created by Yahweh, has revealed himself in Jesus Christ. For Marcion, accordingly, redemption meant redemption from the world and from the Torah whose meaning was only for the world. He maintained, further, that this had been the same view as that of Jesus himself, and of Saul, and that the teachings of both had been warped by Jewish interpretations.

Accordingly, Marcion put together a canon, his own—the first Christian canon. It consisted of nothing but the ten Letters of Saul and the Gospel of Luke. Saul's far-reaching mythology was logically independent of the Hebrew Scriptures, despite his personal view of them as indispensable. As I have said, Saul regarded his whole system as justified, so to speak, only by the titanic event of the Kingdom of God, imminently to be installed. When that failed to happen a different logic supervened, the same logic that turned Saul's history-bound explanation of the resurrection into a timeless theology. Marcion was merely drawing different conclusions from premises that had been altered by the collapse of the Kingdom of God theory and the consequent need for the Church to go on living in this world after all.

Marcion dropped from Luke as a mere forgery whatever clashed with his doctrine. Thus he eliminated the account of Jesus' birth (Lk 1 and 2), designed to demonstrate to Jews that Jesus came of the royal line of King David (marred toward the end only by the insertion of the myth of the virgin birth); since for Marcion the redeemer was not born as a man at all. He merely appeared from heaven in the 15th year of the reign of Emperor Tiberius. Marcion started his Luke with the opening of chapter 3.

In this way the first Christian canon eliminated the Hebrew Scriptures entirely from the substance of the evolving faith. There was to be a complex clash of views revolving around the very essence of the new faith as such, around the very idea of God, as manifested in the relationship of God to the world, in the creation and the redemption, in the relationship between God and the Christ, in the *nature* of Christ, and in the validity of the tradition underlying the "truth" of the evolving Church.

For some time, to be sure, this remained totally unorganized. There was still no center for the far-flung coteries professing, with varying emphases, the cluster of ideas of which a few were soon to emerge as "orthodox," i.e., official. Still, toward the end of the second century the idea of a canon permeated the Christian coteries even without an organizational focus. This became a canon in which what was now to be considered the Old Testament, i.e., the Hebrew Scriptures, themselves canonized a relatively short time before, was rounded off by an agreed-on collection of Christian writings. Though some details remained a subject of debate—and were, indeed, never settled—they were mere details. Marcion's single Gospel was replaced by the familiar four Gospels. This number was explained by the Church Father Irenaeus (ca. 186) as embodying the concept of the four winds, i.e., the four points of the compass. In addition, the number conforms with the number of heavenly beings mentioned in Revelation 4 (cf. Ezekiel 1), e.g., man/angel (for Matthew), lion (for Mark), ox (for Luke), and eagle (for John).

Irenaeus, the mentor of Tertullian in Africa, Clement in Alexandria, and Hippolytus in Rome, represented a critical stage in the standardization of beliefs and institutions. His enterprise of orderly centralization was continued by ecumenical councils and much later by the papacy, to be culminated, logically, in the Papal Infallibility Decree of 1870.

It was some time before this collection of four Gospels itself became sacred. For a long time the Syrian Church, for instance, accepted a sort of "harmony" of the Gospels, all four being reworked into one. Also, the Gospel of John, which fits so badly, from an integrated point of view, with the other three (Synoptic) Gospels, was occasionally challenged, but without result; on the other hand those who disputed its authenticity, i.e., its aptness, were never accused of heresy.

The "apostolic" section of the evolving canon took in the ten Letters ascribed to Paul and never challenged, augmented by three more (two to Timothy and one to Titus), and the "catholic" epistles, though variously in different places. There was a consensus in favor of recognizing 1 Peter and 1 John, gradually added to by the five others, making up the seven that have since been accepted as official.

The question of the criteria involved in the establishment of a canon was scarcely raised in a self-conscious manner. There was simply a widespread desire for information about the Savior that could be considered reliable. The legacy ascribed to the earliest phase of the faith was thought of as calling for documentation. It had its roots in an era when the production of gospels as such was not thought of as a peril to the community, i.e., well before the formation of a central authority. After the first philosophical campaign of Marcion around 130–140, the feeling was accentuated that the broader the basis for documents attesting to Jesus' life on earth and its meaning the better. If an individual passing as an "apostle" could produce a "gospel" there was no objection to it. But in the absence of a central authority, the validity of such a gospel was not established by an ecclesiastical office, but only by the consensus that the witness was reliable.

This very fact, to be sure, had to be buttressed, ultimately, by just such an authority. What standard of common sense, for instance, could decide the validity of the varying accounts in the four Gospels? How could the reliability of the authors, whoever they were, be assessed? The notion that Matthew and John were apostles, for instance, was itself a decision of *some* ecclesiastical authority, even before the emergence of a center; the reliability of the two nonapostles, Mark and Luke, also had to be laid down from above.

In this period, inspiration, too, was irrelevant: it was not until the following generation (under the influence of Origen) that the notion of inspiration was transferred from the Old Testament to the New. Beforehand the question of inspiration versus a formal book was meaningless; it was essentially an idea that could prove attractive to people preoccupied with the subject only after the concept of Scripture as distinct from spirit had achieved a substantial degree of formalization. In the early period there could be no conflict in principle between spirit and book; the book itself was intertwined with the life of the Church.

The fledgling faith had to contend, of course, with many rivals, not merely the Mysteries themselves, of which it could present itself as the seal and simultaneously the obliterator, and Judaism, which it could claim to have superseded, but others of which we have only hints, such as the cult revolving around one Simon the Magus, a Samaritan who seems to have been a genuine rival. He is, indeed, the only head of a non-Christian sect mentioned in the New Testament (Acts 8:9ff), where he is treated as a mere self-styled embodiment of the "great power" inherent in God. Later on he was to be treated by the Church Fathers (apparently with no historical information) as the father of the "Gnostic heresy."

It was, indeed, Gnosticism in all its forms (asceticism, ritualism, libertinism, docetism) that at one time seemed to be about to become the standard form of the new faith. By taking a radical interpretation of the Christology, i.e., by making absolute the incarnation and thus splitting off from the concept of Jesus any form of humanity at all, Gnosticism split God and the world, as well as salvation and the world. Had this prevailed it would no doubt have transformed Christianity into an unorganized group of individuals with a merely spiritual view of the world.

But this was soon swept aside by the tide of secular organization that was to turn Christianity into a cosmic institution. By the beginning of the second century the way was open to its establishment both as a new religion and as a new organization.

Two or three generations after Saul, accordingly, the Torah was no longer a problem. Consummated by the destruction of the Jerusalem Temple, the problem whose solution had been adumbrated early on by Stephen and the "Hellenists" had been solved—the Torah was dropped. What had been a potential conflict between Jews and full pagans within the new Jesist sect had evaporated.

That alone, however, did not solve the problem of the Scriptures, which had formed an integral element of the day-to-day belief of the early Jesists as well as the bedrock of their religious feelings and world view. Yet how could the Scriptures be adapted to the changing views of the Jesist community at the very moment their essential elements had been discarded?

From the point of view of the functioning of the evolving faith, a new role had to be devised for the Hebrew Scriptures. Basically, of course, they were held to prophesy the advent of the Christ (as in Matthew). In addition, they were still regarded as the repository of God's commandments, of which the major ones, in particular the Ten Commandments, were still held to be valid. If a figurative style was in favor, what became the Old Testament was thought to have prefigured salvation by the demonstration of God's intervention in history; it also contained a sort of prototype of Christian life (as in I Clement, which has a substantial admixture of material drawn from the Hebrew Scriptures).

Throughout the formative period of the new Church, indeed, all the major elements were drawn from Jewish precept, even after the structure of belief itself had been transformed by the expanding concept of the Savior.

The ritual itself was drawn from Jewish experience; scripture reading, preaching, prayer, all reflected the preponderant influence of the synagogue.

Sunday, as a day of reunion, is taken for granted in Saul's day (1 Cor 16:2 : apparently for the purpose of taking up a collection for the "saints" in Jerusalem). There was also a regular custom, around the beginning of the second century, of meeting for morning worship and instruction. By the second century the essential elements of the Sunday liturgy, as we are familiar with it today, were established.

In the first part of the service the congregation would hear a reading from the Gospels or the prophets, over a fixed period of time. Then the officiant would give a sermon of exhortation to the congregation, including catechumens plus serious non-Christians.

In the second part the congregation would be reduced to the baptized. It would begin with a prayer for the salvation of Christendom and its moral perfecting for achieving eternal salvation. The members would then give each other the kiss of brotherhood as a symbol of Christian unity. Then the "offertory" would be made: The members of the congregation would bring the officiant bread, wine, and water; he would recite, over the gifts arranged on the table, the prayer of thanksgiving; the congregation would respond with "amen" and invoke the Logos, which the officiant would pray to descend into the bread and wine so that it could become the saving body and blood of Jesus.

After this culminating rite, deacons would distribute the consecrated gifts to those present, later taking them to the absent, to the sick, and to prisoners. The service would conclude with the collection of voluntary offerings, deposited with the officiant to enable him to succor the sick, widows, orphans, etc.[2]

From the earliest times on Easter was celebrated at the date established for Passover in the Jewish calendar, the day of the full moon of the spring month (14th Nisan); only the content, of course, now encompassed the passion and crucifixion of the Christ.

By the middle of the second century, accordingly, or, more precisely, after the Bar Kochba insurrection against the Romans in 135 was crushed, the chasm between Judaism and Christianity could no longer be bridged without a special act of conversion, though, as we have seen from the example of Chrysostom, social relations between Jews and Christians were to be relatively intimate for centuries. These complex developments took place against a turbulent background. The relations of the new sect with the Roman state took on basic political importance.

In modern terms the Roman Empire was not highly organized. There was, for instance, no imperial police force, nor were the provinces, governed by more or less sovereign governors, in any way homogeneous; they were a congeries of allies, free cities, vassal rulers (themselves with variously defined relationships with the central government), and territories under direct rule. Hence the treatment of the evolving faith was not uniform.

Before the collapse of the Jewish state and Temple in 70, the Roman government had acted against the Jews only in special circumstances, since Judaism, a *religio licita*, constitutionally authorized, was institutionally anchored in special privileges. The Jewish rejection of divine images, for instance, was accepted even after the Roman-Jewish war.

Before that the Roman authorities had done nothing to track down the Jesists after the crucifixion of Jesus, though, as we have seen, special measures were taken against the members of Jesus' family. It was, apparently, the Jewish authorities who took sporadic action against the new sect of Jesists in Palestine before the debacle of 70 (Acts 4).

Under Claudius in the forties the expulsion of the Jews from Rome, as well as the riots in Alexandria around the same time, were probably due, as we have seen, to the eruption of some messianically inspired riots our sources shed no light on. Similarly, the action undertaken by Nero in 64 might have had something to do with that too, though it is not clear what. After a great fire, "death penalties were pronounced on Christians, a sect that had succumbed to a new superstition dangerous to the public." There is some indication that repressive measures remained in effect for some time.[3]

On the other hand, though the Christians were not convicted of arson, but only of "hatred of the human race," part of the "absurd and repugnant Jewish way of life,"[4] it would have been only natural for the Roman state to be hostile to the new sect, whose founder, after all, had been executed for sedition. That made them *ipso facto* a criminal sect.

In any case, the destruction of the Zealot movement in the debacle of 70 inevitably attenuated, after a time, the culpability of the Christians, who were themselves changing very rapidly vis-à-vis the Roman state. From 70 on the Roman authorities were affected by the new sect only if it caused riots or other disorders.

Around 112, for instance, Pliny, Governor of Pontus-Bithynia, wrote Caesar Trajan asking whether the "name itself" of a Christian was punishable, i.e., whether the Jesists as such were still a criminal sect, or whether it was necessary to specify particular crimes they had actually committed.[5] Pliny's letter may imply some social problems, such as damage to business, that on various occasions played a role.

As late as 112, accordingly, it remained a question in law whether the association was itself illegal, in which case a confession would have been the equivalent of condemnation, or whether specific evidence had to be presented to the authorities. As governor, Pliny himself, for instance, had the Christians condemned if they refused to abjure their specific beliefs, a procedure that was, in fact, approved of by Trajan, who nevertheless laid it down that Christians were not to be hunted down by the authorities, nor were anonymous denunciations to be heeded.

Popular prejudice was, to be sure, widespread. It conceived of the meetings of worship, culminating in the banquet of believers (the Agape) as orgies. The notion was that Christians slaughtered and devoured children (apparently a misinterpretation of the Eucharist).

Trajan's orders to Pliny held good for some time. If valid accusations were laid before the authorities, Christians had to offer sacrifice or die. That is, the question of tolerating Christians was dealt with not judicially, but politically. Christian hostility to the state, even though it was not articulated, was regarded as judicially well-established, but not punished as such. All Christians were given the opportunity to demonstrate the contrary by sacrificing before a statue of Caesar. It was only when they expressly refused, and hence violated the reverence felt to be due the majesty of Caesar and the tutelary gods, that the death penalty would be incurred.

In any case, the State did not persecute Christians as such; even the imperial edicts prohibiting the profession of the religion never led to general persecutions. The edicts themselves were mere repetitions of Trajan's guidelines; the manner in which they were carried out was left to the judgment of the provincial authorities.

Despite a widespread impression, the Caesar cult apparently played no role in state intervention. The notion that Christians had to exchange the formula "Jesus is Lord" for "Caesar is Lord" is legendary.[6]

The Roman governors, to be sure, had extensive powers. They could make their own enquiries into facts, evaluate them and pronounce judgment. Thus, under Trajan as well as his successors it was always possible for the situation of a given Christian coterie to deteriorate in a particular province. The result was that in spite of the exaggerations of Christian martyrdom made by the later Church it seems that under the early Roman

Empire "the actual outbreaks of persecution were limited in area and duration."[7]

On the other hand, the new sect never became an enemy of the state. This stemmed, very naturally, from the interpretation given to the crucifixion from the very beginning, perhaps most markedly by Saul, i.e., the interpretation that eschewed a violently hostile view of the Roman Empire and that was, in fact, the theme of all the Gospels. From the time of the Jewish debacle on, the Jesists distinguished themselves from the obvious other alternative taken by Jewish apocalypticism and by one Jewish political tendency—the Kingdom of God activists. Thus, it was this strand—the otherworldly theme of the Jewish visionaries—that became an integral part of the triumph of the new sect, especially after the collapse of its this-worldly violent rival, the Zealots, whom the original Jesist coterie in Jerusalem had been intimately allied or identified with and who were submerged together with them in 70.

On the level of theology, to be sure, the book of Revelation is, of course, the precise opposite. For the author of Revelation the universe is filled with an out-and-out war in which the Beast—obviously the Roman Empire—has emerged from the abyss demanding worship, etc. Nevertheless the whole scene is mere fantasy. Set in heaven, it does not purport to give any flesh-and-blood people any instructions that would involve the authorities. For this very reason, perhaps, it could ultimately survive to be included in the Christian canon. It could satisfy theory without endangering the believers.

The text of Romans 13:1–7 (as well as related passages in 1 Peter 2:13–14) tells the believers, quite simply, to obey the authorities and be still. In Saul's formulation of the World's End theories he shared with others there was no need to involve the new sect in trouble with the authorities of this world when it was about to pass away at any moment.

This theory was bound to prevail. Since all World's End theories put a foreseeable, indeed imminent term to the workaday world, there was no need for the new sectarians to emigrate from this world even in theory. The ones who chose to emigrate from this world and did so, in practice as well as in theory, either perished physically in Palestine after the Jewish debacle in 70 or else survived with their disappointment.

In the passage from Romans cited above Saul avoids mentioning cases in which the State might require a religious confession that would inevitably be repugnant to sincere believers, but the related passage in 1

Peter 2:13 specifically enjoins the believer to wear a mask on all occasions: "Be subject for the Lord's sake to every human institution, both to Caesar and . . . to the governors" (1 Peter 2:13). It is evident that this prudent advice is given with an eye to possible persecutions. This was part of the advice given to pray for the well-being of the authorities, not, of course, for their conversion (1 Tim 2:1–2 & 1 Clement 61). In theory the Church, generally speaking, was not supposed to lay itself open to martyrdom at all, but simply to defend itself against false accusations and to propagandize on behalf of the new faith.

In its early formulations this theory, too, was connected with the World's End.

The early Jesists, as they diverged from Judaism, found themselves grappling with a social problem; life in the Hellenistic environment was universally characterized by religious and cultic practices of all sorts. The Mysteries, of course, could participate in anything, since the adept's commitment to the rites and theory of his particular mystery did not prevent him or her from participating in any other cult whatever while preserving a mystery commitment within a special sphere.

Though Judaism was still a *religio licita,* the Jesists were in a peculiar position. Still considered, in a way, an offshoot of Judaism, they were the target of growing hostility from the leaders of the various Jewries scattered throughout the empire. At the same time they required of their membership an active denial of all other religious connections, an echo of course of the exclusiveness characteristic of monotheism.

If we cast a glance backward at the Church as it took shape around the beginning and until the end of the fourth century, and compare it with the small Jesist coterie of the first generation, we find a dramatic transformation. Instead of a small group of Kingdom of God activists integrated with Jewry, assiduously praying in the Temple of Jerusalem, distinguished from most Jews only through a hope linked to a specific Jewish hero, and playing a role in the Kingdom of God agitation holding the country in its grip, we see, two and a half centuries later, a religious organization encompassing a cross section of a vast congeries of peoples. All members of the organization have a unique awareness; they are the Church of Christ, the elect of mankind.

This Church has by now rejected Israel root and branch; Israel is said to have abandoned the ways of the Lord and to be abjectly straying far from the truth. Moreover, Israel's rejection of the incarnation has made it a natural ally of Satan. Saul's nuanced relationship to Jewry has been dropped together with his time-table.

For Saul, the failure of the Jews to grasp the implications of the resurrection, the proof of the incarnation, had been a mystery. As the premier people in the world, the only one with whom God had had a covenant, they would inevitably perceive, very soon, the titanic significance of the incarnation and be present to usher in the Kingdom of God together with all converts.

But with the forgetting of the Kingdom of God as a palpable reality, and with the institution of an eternal Church, the role of the Jews as *de facto* allies of Satan itself became eternalized. This did not, of course, entail their extinction. Jewry was bound to survive, even though in abject circumstances, as witness to the triumph of Christianity. (This essentialization of evil in the Jews was to play a persistent role in history.)[8]

Yet aside from doctrine, though the Church has rid itself of all the practices of the Torah except for some customs that have been charged with an entirely different meaning, it has, at the same time, managed to preserve the Hebrew Scriptures, now the Old Testament, part of a new canon of its own whose rationale is established by the New Testament.

This in itself is, on reflection, surprising, since whether or not one might claim that the Hebrew Scriptures remain valuable because they lead up to the New Testament, the massive texts of the Old Testament, which took well nigh a millennium for the composition of its various sections, are restricted, after all, to the history and ideas of the Jews, one people among others. One might have thought that Christianity might, perhaps, have gained from discarding the Torah altogether (the aim of Marcion and his school).

Yet the historical origins of the early Jesist coteries, with the primitive habit of relying on the Bible as prophetical for the early purpose of propagandizing among Jews and semi-Jews, had congealed into a veneration for the Hebrew Scriptures despite the logic of the detachment from the tradition they embodied. The veneration of Christians, following the Jesists, for the divine authority of the Bible was thus firmly anchored. The attempts to get rid of all aspects of Judaism had been unable to overcome its original genetic connection with the new faith.

Thus the Church, for which the faith of Israel had been a mere starting point, has gradually pieced together a new and complex system of dogmatics revolving in its essence around the speculation dealing with the person of Christ—Christology—by now, of course, long since expanded to identification with God.

This whole work of inflation and expansion was dependent for its elements on the reflections I have indicated as arising out of the earliest magnifications of Jesus within the framework of Jewish history, buttressed and ramified by the rich material taken from the philosophical and religious doctrines of the Greco-Roman (Hellenistic) milieu. This whole system of dogmatics, expressed in the rule of faith presumably based on the opinion of the majority, as interpreted, of course, by a central authority, has arrived at the stage of being presented to the world as a revealed, perfected system of philosophy, an all-embracing, changeless explanation of the world, of life, of destiny.

From the merely organizational point of view the Christian Church has the aspect of an established institution. Originally organized in private assemblies modeled on the Jewish synagogue or on pagan associations, by the beginning of the third century it has assigned both its administration and its spiritual functions—conceptually a seamless web—to a body of clergy in a hierarchical order. The chief clergy have adopted the habit of consulting about the ensemble of activities involving morals, faith, and discipline. A majority opinion from among these higher clergy is expressed in concerted public pronouncements.

The clerical authorities preside over rites that have been borrowed more or less directly either from Judaism or from the pagan Mysteries. These all have been integrated with Christian aims. The principal rites have been recharged with the magical power familiar to adepts of the secret cults of Greece and of the Middle East.

By the beginning of the third century, then, Christianity has become a full religion, plausibly presented as the most complete of all religions, since it has taken what it can regard as the best from them all. It can also maintain that it is the most comforting, the most compassionate of all. To achieve salvation an ignoramus need only believe without understanding and obey the authorities, while the philosophically minded can speculate endlessly on the dogmas, which, rooted in the bedrock of the incarnation and the redemptive crucifixion, are themselves endless.

At the same time, though manifestly itself a complex syncretism, Christianity proclaims a comprehensive and indeed fanatical exclusiveness; it cannot share believers with any other religion, nor can it tolerate rivals. Ramified, articulated, and insulated against other social entities, the

Church stands out against the animosity of the state as well as that of the larger society it has not yet won over. Challenging the fabric of that larger society, and permeating it steadily, the Church will be ready to assume its leadership in another century, when through the conversion of Constantine the Great in 325 it will become not only an unchallengeable repository of spiritual authority, but a source of state power.

Epilogue

Saul's Longbow

It is strange that Saul's defeat made him a world-shaker. His survival as the founder of Christian theology would seem to be a baffling, indeed indigestible phenomenon. His complex, logical, passionate thought—a stupendous success, as it must have seemed to him, in solving the problem set for his generation by the risen Jesus—was frustrated, after all, by the fiasco of his analysis.

Saul's grand ideas shaped the Church; taken up by the scattered communities of believers in Jesus, they were transformed into the fundamental institutions of the new religion—the incarnation, the redemptive crucifixion, the mystic body of Christ, the mystic body of the Church, the sacraments.

Yet Saul's key concept—the imminent Kingdom of God and the cosmic struggle preceding it, was simply dropped, consigned to oblivion, and replaced by the Church, an eternal institution Saul could never have foreseen.

His very career was brought about by the failure of the glorious return that enthralled him. It was just that failure that he had to explain away. It made him something he could scarcely have understood—a *theologian,* a category that in Judaism, with its stark simplicity, could scarcely exist at all. Contrived to explain the meaning of an extraordinary fact, his analysis, wholly falsified by events and hence profoundly misunderstood, became the bedrock of a unique doctrinal edifice. Nor could he have digested what surely would have seemed to him the most grotesque of all ironies—that his own writings, assuring his audience that in spite of all appearances the Savior was bound to return in the imminent future, would themselves become the cornerstone of actual institutions built on the collapse of his predictions.

How was it, then, that the failure of the World's End to take place was not understood by his followers, quite simply, as a flat contradiction of everything he had said? If the premises of a deductive chain are shifted, the edifice they underly must crumble. How could Saul's logic withstand its self-destruction? Why did the final generation, realizing that it was, in fact, the first generation, not simply abandon Saul's ideas and turn elsewhere? How could a Church arise on the debris of its initial hopes?

Saul's canonization was rooted in the outright falsification of his thought, made indispensable, very naturally, by the evolution of the Church that replaced the glorious return. A doctrinal unity had to be attributed to the mythological founders of a mythological entity; Saul was integrated with and subordinated to the doctrine of the Church itself. The oddity was only—it remains a puzzle—how anyone could fail to perceive the authentic ideas in Saul's exposition, and how the Protestant reformers, in particular, could throw the Scriptures open to the laity and still cling to their misinterpretations.

It is curious to recall that until Luther it was an unshakable axiom that Saul held exactly the same views as Simon the Rock and the twelve apostles—i.e., was at one with the views of the Mother Church, the fictitious construction of a much later age that was, indeed, the initial dislocation of real history.

This notion of harmony is of course the foundation of the Christian canon; anchored in Acts, it may in fact be said to have launched the entire preposterous misunderstanding not merely of the scraps of real life embedded in the amber of the earliest documents, but of the actual reading of Saul's Letters, which in their broad outlines, after all, are luminously clear.

It is curious to see how small a switch was needed to shift Saul's ideas full circle and to lead to their massive misunderstanding. His views have served not only as the cornerstone of Christianity in its major historical forms—Greek Orthodoxy, Roman Catholicism, Protestantism—but in their distorted form have seeped into what may be called the generalized religious consciousness of the modern age.

The concepts underlying Saul's view of faith, sin, spirit, and love, while radically different from their reformulation in later Christianity, proved capable, nevertheless, of serving as their anchor.

For Saul faith was, quite simply, faith in the historical overturn predicted by him on the basis of his analysis of the true meaning of Jesus' death and resurrection. Because of this it was not absolute. It was not an anthropological insight, so to speak, or the recommendation of an enduring psychological stance. It was simply linked to a certain event, the imminent World's End, which was, after all, what warranted the cancellation of the Torah.

If we can imagine, say, a Saul grown older, surviving until he became convinced that he had somehow or other miscalculated, that Jesus was *not* returning in glory, that the messianic age had *not* been initiated by his death, that God, in short, had other plans, Saul as a pious Jew would have been obliged to acknowledge the continuing validity of the Torah in the unredeemed world. Because of its very logic his argument, so ingeniously contrived on the basis of the Hebrew Scriptures, would have had to revert to the alternative, what was to happen now, with the messianic kingdom still in the unknowable future?

When the Kingdom of God failed to come, Saul's views were unconsciously transformed by succeeding generations. His concept of faith was absolutized. Congealing in the vacuum of a frustrated hope, faith was salvaged by its very generality. It was abstracted, generalized, streamlined, and held aloft as an imperishable ideal. Even though Saul's concept of baptism and the Lord's Supper simply evaporated with the failure of his predictions, the formulation Saul had given both rites proved to be general enough to survive as a source of abiding glamour, mystery, and authority for the Church's countless believers.

The Protestant scholarship of the nineteenth and early twentieth century was engaged in a juggle with Saul's focal concept—justification by faith—since from that point of view it seemed possible to treat Saul as though he were, somehow, relevant to the modern age. He was made out to be subject to lofty struggles; his ideas were thought to arise out of personal integrity, conscience, and so on. But with the demonstration, made so effectively two generations ago by Schweitzer (1912), that Saul was simply taking for granted a crudely physical notion about the fusion of identity between different entities, and that this physical notion was at the core of his central concept of the being-in-Christ, Saul could scarcely be taken seriously any longer. His ideas, dead for millennia through misunderstanding, were even more dead when understood.

Similarly for Saul's view of sin. The inner consistency of his solution for sins committed after baptism was necessarily bound up with his view of the bliss that was to be attained for the faithful at the World's End.

For Saul suffering was, of course, an aspect of dying. Thus it was the fellowship with Christ in suffering and in death that solved the whole question of sin after baptism, since according to Saul—in accord with the Jesists generally—the atoning death of the Christ did not bring about forgiveness of sins on a continuing basis; it merely released the individual from sins committed *before* baptism. Sins committed after baptism could be atoned for only through suffering with Christ.

Since this view is entirely logical, it is valid only when the World's End is actually being awaited, while the whole concept of the tribulations to be endured in the premessianic period is still vigorous. But once believers lost their conviction that they themselves were in the process of premessianic tribulation, and because of that were at that very moment suffering along with Christ, there was no way for them to secure the forgiveness of sins committed *after* baptism.

For Catholics, of course, the problem was solved very tidily as part of the general solution provided by the Church's magical system; the Church itself could bring absolution! Protestants, having abandoned the Church as an authority of that kind, find themselves thrown back on their own resources; for them the problem of postbaptismal sin cannot, in theory, be solved at all.

Thus once again Saul's personal anguish, irrelevant to history—except for its side effects!—made a reentry into real life through the institutionalization of magic; a Church set up on scriptures based on the misunderstanding of his own historical posture used his writings to sanction magical remedies. In the same way Saul's original idea, based on the limitless magnification of the person of Jesus, was so ample that the concept of redemption could survive the collapse of the messianic hope by the simple transference of the vehicle of redemption to the person of Jesus.

Like his doctrine of salvation in general, the ambiguity of Saul's doctrine of the Spirit, too, has enabled it to play a role in the modern era.

Despite the physicality of Saul's idea of redemption, the qualities associated with it as a sort of by-product necessarily exercise a spiritualizing influence. Though Saul's personal mysticism was indissolubly linked to participation in a natural, historical, though transcendent process, it was bound to entail ethical consequences once it was looked at from an individual's point of view. Though what was significant for Saul had to do with the grandiose installation of the messianic kingdom on earth, even when that fizzled out it brought about an entirely different system of values rooted in a logic of its own.

Thus, understanding the spirit as the sum total of all emanations of an otherworldly spiritual universe under the dominion of God, Saul could express it in a form that seems to fit people's ordinary ethical impulses even today. And since for Saul the messianic kingdom had already begun, without having been consummated, he was able to create a framework in which it was natural, while on earth, to live as though one were, if not in heaven, at least thinking of heaven. Thus in spite of himself, in spite of his own logical extrapolations from the cosmic transformation, Saul created an enclave of religiosity in the workaday world.

Indeed, by using the word "love," Saul had an effect he could never have foreseen. Love, for him, was quite different from its vulgar meaning. It was simply the highest of all spiritual gifts, because it inheres in God. Scattered abroad in the human heart by means of the Holy Spirit (Rom 5:5), it is eternal. For Saul love was a mere modality of the manner in which the solidarity of the body of Christ—of the members of the elect among themselves and between the elect and the Savior—was expressed. In speaking of the love of God he really meant the love that is in God; thus, by the love of Christ (Rom 8:35) he meant the love derived from God that inheres in Christ (Rom 8:39). Hence he could hope (on behalf of the Corinthians) that the love of God will be with them (2 Cor 13:14), indeed that his own will be, too (1 Cor 16:24).

But this notion, while thoroughly metaphysical, is of course ethical at the same time. He is after all speaking of *love*; hence, as was the case with the spiritual benefits that flow timelessly from his own time-bound view of the Kingdom, the mere formula he used could exercise a spiritualizing influence through the ages, since the passion poured into his formulae lends them potency even in a different situation.

A similar consequence in the modern age of misunderstanding Saul's time-bound view of the world can be seen in the peculiar effect of his view of the state. Saul, whatever his motivation, sounds (in Romans) as though he were commending the state as such; hence it could be given a high ethical assessment that would sound as though stemming from Saul's views. And just as Saul's ideas congealed into permanence as the eternal Church replaced the Kingdom of God, so the positive assessment of the state, expressed by Saul in his own day as required by the imminence of the Kingdom, became a permanent assessment.

At the outset the Church did, indeed, try to sanction the state, but the demand conventionally made by various rulers of the early period that they be treated as themselves divine collided head on with a fundamental requirement of the burgeoning religion. Hence for a short period there was an irreconcilably violent split between Church and state whose consequences for posterity were momentous.

Saul's views were anchored in a modified theory of the World's End; his own modification diverged from the mainstream of World's End hysteria, which roundly condemned all powers as outrageous, without beating around the bush as Saul in his own immediate situation found it expedient to do. All he had done was to advise believers, prudently, to take it easy while the state was being annihilated.

The Protestant Reformation returned to a positive evaluation of the role of the state, in sharp contrast with the early Church tradition that had become embodied in the Roman Catholic Church and generated the celebrated Catholic theory that the Church itself, in view of the noxiousness or at least insufficiency of the civil state, should undertake to rule the world in the name of God. It was in contrast with this that the Reformation returned to a positive, even servile lauding of the state's role.

Thus the great Protestant reformers, basing themselves, in a way, on the celebrated passage in Romans, simply defended the state as such. Many Protestant thinkers went out of their way to exalt the state as a vehicle of progressive thought. Fichte and Hegel praised the civil state in a well-nigh psychopathic style. The monstrosities that this chain of thought has led to since the First World War, most notably with the elephantiasis of the state in Bolshevik Russia and its satellites, need only be mentioned. Perhaps the high point of this adulation of the state was the refusal of the German Lutherans, as well as of the Roman Catholics, because of Saul's endorsement, to react effectively to the Nazi state.

Saul was really entirely unsuitable for the nascent faith of the early Church; he was taken over as it were negatively, *faute de mieux,* and positively, because his general ideas could serve as a doctrinal foundation, however misunderstood, for the new community. This could be done, of course, only by diluting the brainpower behind his theories.

More especially, perhaps, the new community had to have *something,* and what else was there? The Jerusalem Jesists had written nothing, nor would any of the Jewish messianists have had any occasion to write down anything; they were coping with an explosive immediate situation. And why write? It was all written down already. They simply had to await—or bring about!—the explosion already foretold. The quietist Jews had still less reason to write; they were simply carrying on their lives as usual.

Thus, Saul, by temperament and virtuosity, was doubtless the only serious writer; it was natural to scour the early fellowships for his fragmented, urgent, hurried, sketchy, but powerfully thought-out ideas as adumbrated in his Letters, and to patch them up somehow—or mutilate them—to make them fit. Saul was revived *despite* the details of his analysis, and no doubt because of the broad overriding fact of his potential audience—the throngs of semi-Judaized pagans, the "God-fearers" who accepted the God of Israel but not yet circumcision or the dietary laws and who were a commonplace of the Greco-Roman world.

In sum, Saul's real views were abandoned by all successors. If there is a practical differentiation to be made in the style of abandonment, or rather the selection of topics of principal disregard, it may be said that the Greek Orthodox Church and its affiliates leaned toward Saul's mystical expressions and his theory of the Spirit, encompassing the gifts of the Spirit and the doctrine of the sacraments, all wrenched out of context, to be sure, like everything else in Saul's Letters.

In the Roman Catholic Church, on the other hand, and more particularly in the Protestant Reformation, Saul's doctrine of righteousness through faith, also dislocated and misunderstood, was to produce much thought and many shifts of perspective. In one of its characteristic misunderstandings, in fact, it was to lead to the Reformation itself—from a historical point of view a colossal misunderstanding.

The psycho-history called for by Saul remains peculiarly obvious, perhaps poignant, in the case of Luther, who like many others, though with more emotional drive, rediscovered in Saul's writings his own pathology.

Misunderstanding Saul as he misunderstood the Hebrew Scriptures, Luther, too, found Christ, readily enough, in the Old Testament. Inflamed by the short and quite subsidiary passage I have already mentioned ("righteousness through faith" [Rom 1:17]), he took it to be the core of belief.

It is illuminating to see how this phrase of Saul's, squeezed by so much thought and emotion out of his need to bypass through cleverness a piece of Jewish argumentation based on the Torah, should be snatched up so many centuries later and, because of its correspondence with a compulsion obsession that echoed Saul's own wretchedness, influence thought to such a degree.

Attempting to wrest some contemporary significance out of the Bible, Luther was pouncing on one of the least important fragments of Saul's writings, a mere element of a long-dead polemic in a historical situation that could no longer even be recalled, and elevated this to the heart of Saul's thought. This fragment of hysteria, too, became the foundation stone of a mighty Church.

It is strange indeed that Protestantism, struggling to evade the Catholic Church and its well-founded claims to an antiquity that could in its own way be traced directly back to Saul, should have found in him its patron saint. Disregarding the true content of his Letters, Protestants could utilize a stripped-down, lobotomized version of these ancient documents as the clarion-call to a new version of Christianity. The entire Lutheran doctrine, and to some extent the Calvinist doctrine of faith, justification, and election by grace were retrojected into Saul's Letters. Because of this entirely capricious identification of so much of Protestant doctrine with a misunderstood Saul, it was only natural for the attacks on Saul's person and thought that became rife in the nineteenth century to be simultaneously attacks, scarcely veiled, on Protestantism and to some extent, of course, on Christianity itself.

Saul proved to be a convenient repository for Nietzsche's hatred of all history (he thought it demonstrated a cosmic principle of decay); for him Saul was the "eternal Jew par excellence"—by definition loathsome. He thought Saul a "genius in hatred, in the vision of hate, in the ruthless logic of hate," in short, a "morbid crank . . . tormented, pitiable, repellent both to himself and others. . . . Such was the first Christian!"[1]

Leo Tolstoy, too, in his search for faith, tried to bypass Saul. Tolstoy's attempt to reinterpret Christianity was, indeed, perhaps the most modern of such latter-day revisions as it has been the most influential. At the turn of the century, and for decades afterwards, "Tolstoyanism" was a real force.

Indifferent to history—to the true ambitions of his heroes—and in his middle age tormented more and more by a harrowing *tedium vitae,* Tolstoy sought to exorcise his misery by a journey back to the core of Jesus' originality. He soon came to the conclusion, no doubt inevitably, that *all* current versions of Christianity were a tissue of falsehoods, misconceptions, and stupidities. He wanted to slash beneath the irrelevant excrescences of tradition and learn what had *really* happened, to extract from the vast accumulation of pseudodata the specific, unique, and indispensable essence of what Jesus himself had thought. For him it was a matter of course that the Kingdom of God was within the human soul, in no way a manifestation of God's omnipotence.

He learned Greek and Hebrew—the first, it seems, passably—to read the original documents. While reading the Sermon on the Mount (Matthew 5–7) together with a learned Moscow rabbi, he kept hearing from the rabbi very specific Jewish parallels for all the statements attributed to Jesus; the only exception was the celebrated injunction "not to resist evil by violence." The rabbi could find no Jewish parallel for this; when he shrugged it aside with a cynical reminder that Christians paid no attention to it anyhow, Tolstoy thought he had won the debate, as it were. He had finally distilled the quintessence of Jesus' ideas.

All else in Christianity—the incarnation, the redemptive crucifixion, the mystic body of Christ, the Church itself, indeed all Christian doctrine—was simply dropped. By singling out a single phrase and expanding its range endlessly, Tolstoy founded, in fact, a new religion or, at least, a minireligion.

The idea itself, wrenched out of context, was surely no more than another instance of Jesus' practice of making a principle "still more so" to drive it home. It is hard to withstand the impression that Tolstoy's obsession with nonviolence stemmed from a deep-laid cruelty in his own character—whether or not he was aware of it—that made him lean all the way over backwards to repress a fundamental element in his self-loathing. And it is all the more ironical to recall that the force of his obsession, plus its stark simplicity, enhanced, no doubt, by his aristocratic origins, was to give it a vast resonance. It moved Mahatma Gandhi, who as a student corresponded with Tolstoy, to launch his nonviolent campaign against the British in India, and, still more recently, provided Martin Luther King with his aura of loftiness. To this day, indeed, Tolstoy's model for self-improvement, both personal and social, has its devotees.

Tolstoy's mulishness, rooted in a deep stratum of anachronistic phobias, even drove him to a distinction between Jesus and Saul already made by Nietzsche. Tolstoy derived the tragedy of all mankind from their "racial" incompatibility! He wanted "to write something to prove how the teachings of Christ, who was not a Jew, were replaced by the very different teachings of Paul, who was a Jew."[2]

In our own day a general malaise that takes the form of hostility to Christianity may be said to be crystallized in such estimates of Saul. In a yearning, surely of remarkable naiveté, to get back to the beginnings of things, to a state of purity, to the true founder, to an ideal unencumbered by institutional encrustations, Saul has been thought of as a barrier. He is regarded as a monster, an evil genius, perhaps, who has obscured the luminous figure of Jesus, the perfect man, fully human, fully divine, by creating a maze of corrupt theology.

Saul is thought of as having misunderstood Jesus, and for that matter, precisely because of his "Jewish" gift for abstract thought, plus the extremist passion that permeates his writing, as having reimposed on Christianity—whatever that might be thought to have been without him!—an original Jewish element after all. The many anti-Christians (like Nietzsche) who misunderstand Saul's passionate invective and paint him as having had a special capacity for hatred lay on him the blame that should more properly, no doubt, be laid on Luther himself, a notable hater if ever there was one. Much is made, accordingly, of a psychological analysis of Saul, he is *too* Jewish, *too* split, *too* angry.

In this entirely artificial portrait of Saul it is curious to see how Saul, regarded as characteristically Jewish, is counterposed to another Jew, Jesus, and, since nothing is known of Jesus' personality it is easy to dislike the Jews, through Saul, while exalting the figure of Jesus as divinely human.

It is hard to exaggerate the superficiality of all this; it rests, ultimately, on a most unhistorical refusal to accept Saul and his age for what they were. It is at bottom part of the entire unhistorical approach to Saul that for almost two thousand years was to hamper the appreciation of his true gifts, a refusal to accept the seriousness with which he confronted the paramount event of his life—the intervention of God in history through the resurrection of Jesus and the consequent imminence of the World's End.

In broad summary it may be said that the two halves of early Christianity—personal salvation and the Kingdom of God—were reworked by posterity in different ways that while clinging to the allegiance necessitated by the authority of a canon were entirely alien to Saul's world view.

Christianity, as a vehicle for personal redemption, has of course survived—in a way. Diffuse, attenuated, even eroded as the idea may now be, at least for elites long battered by science and history-mindedness, the very longing for a religious anchorage, no doubt a constant of the human psyche, has kept alive the need for a feeling of personal redemption in the great majority of believers. Thus, even today, personal redemption must surely be considered a fundamental datum of the religious life. The ecstatic movement of reversions to "fundamentalism" that go far beyond the Protestant area in America and Europe must attest the need for a feeling of redemption that can still inflame masses of people.

But the other half of primitive Christianity, the Kingdom of God, has proved to be an explosive idea. Its specific formulation in the first century constituted the background not only for the Jewish insurrection against Rome but, as we have seen, for Saul's principal ideas. And even after it would have seemed to have been entirely extinguished, through the Jewish debacle in the war against Rome and through the misinterpretation of Saul's ideas in the generation after his death, the conception proved pregnant with potentialities for upheaval.

In Judaism, of course, world history is a seamless web, created by God's will once and for all. The world was created good, and remains good, despite the distortions, absurdities, and atrocities brought about by man's free will.

Still, if Messianism may be seen as a way of counterbalancing disagreeable reality, the Jews, too, succumbed to the fever of changing things, of "forcing the end," in the outburst of activist messianism that destroyed their communal existence for millennia. In its inflamed, hysterical form messianism lasted, to be sure, only a few generations, taking shape in an acute form during the collision with Greek thought and coming to a boil under the Roman Empire. For about 130 years, from the institution of the Zealot movement proper to the collapse of the Bar Kochba revolt in 135, messianism fascinated many, then it shrank back, becoming a remote though no doubt comforting perspective in the lives of observant Jews since then. Only a few generations later, when the Talmud was being compiled, the whole concept of "forcing the end" was to be rejected, indeed, like all forms of headstrong voluntarism. It was agreed—perhaps because of the reality principle!—that the advent of the Messiah was entirely a secret of God, whose action could not be influenced.

Because of this, activism, for Jews, has remained, generally speaking, inert. Jewish messianism gave up the ghost; it became a dimmed, blurred, remote hope, deferred to the World's End, or postponed to the unforeseeable future.

The three hundred years of World's End tension—between 168 B.C.E. and Bar Kochba's revolt in 135 C.E. represented the struggle of monotheistic Jews to defend their faith on their own soil. Afterwards, when the Jews were dispersed and monotheism, concentrated in messianism and the fevers of apocalyptic, was defeated, the religion hypostatized itself, becoming the unique hallmark of the Jews. By then the expectation of the World's End had shrunk to the dimensions of a mere theory, an emotional adjunct to a religion otherwise anchored in the here and now.

Thus Jewish messianism could on occasion surface, ironically enough among Jews who had lost their faith in Judaism. While for observant Jews, who have acquiesced in the indefinite postponement of the Messiah's coming, life must be ameliorated in the here and now, those who have lost their faith may try to "force the end" in their own way. Jewish messianism, originating in the tension of the contrast between the Jews as beholders of the one God and their situation as downtrodden pariahs, could find itself continuously reincarnated in Jewish history whenever civic breakdowns and calamities heightened latent Jewish exaltation.

In the modern era, the involvement of Jews in the civic life, for instance, of the West in disadvantageous, inhibited, or fragmented situations has led to recurrent outbreaks of millennial Jewish messianism. Singling out, with enthusiasm, specific social afflictions, Jews have secularized messianism in revolutionary effervescence on behalf of outsize ideas for world reform, like Marxism, or in the messianism embodied in Zionism and the establishment of the state of Israel, which may, perhaps be looked on as the attempt to realize a world change in the modest form of a nation "like all the nations."

In the Middle Ages the activism inherent in the concept of the Kingdom of God could, in a deflected form, emerge within Christendom again. Jewish messianism directly inspired numerous chiliastic Protestant movements of social salvation, whipped up with great dynamism on the basis of the Old Testament—Taborites, Anabaptists, radical Puritans—and acquiring world-historical importance.

Within Christianity it was precisely the commingling of the divine and the human that overcame the Jewish separation of the two. But the Christian search for divine sanction, which in the Old Testament found all the nuances of world-reforming messianism promised, and hence guaranteed, by God, created an explosive force.

The indefinite postponement of the Kingdom of God exercised a negative effect on civil society in Christendom. Though it was put off indefinitely, it lived on, in a way, as an ideal, however unattainable, and hence gave the Church an organic disdain for life in the workaday world. This made it natural for the city of God to be distinguished fundamentally from the city of man, and for the Church to leave law-making to the secular authorities.

Here the irony has been consummated, in the twentieth century, by the social activism that has surged into the vacuum left in civic consciousness by the millennial remoteness of the Church.

With religiosity battered by secularism, it became natural for countless Christians, primarily Protestants at first, but since the First World War increasingly Catholics, to find in Marxism an outlet for their faith, now adrift.

In a turn that would surely have seemed surprising both to Marx and to the Church Fathers—to say nothing of Saul himself!—social activism, both in overt Marxism and in veiled and open contact with Marxism, became a tidal wave in the Church, both Protestant and Catholic (in both major branches).

The great Protestant confederations—the World Council of Churches, the National Council of Churches, countless eminent divines—were strongly influenced by Marxist activism from the First World War on; after the Second World War the Roman Catholic Church was submerged in a tidal wave of Marxist exhortation, centering on the roots of poverty and agitating for the general overhaul of society.

Colloquies were held in Europe between Roman Catholics (Franciscans and Dominicans) and Marxists of various nuances. Liberation theology in Latin America presented itself openly as a Marxist movement; eminent liberation theologians openly called themselves Marxists, for whom the Gospels are Marxist documents whose message they propagate in the name of Jesus Christ.

The Kingdom of God, which for Saul was a divine enterprise about to be consummated by reorganizing the universe so that God, ruling directly, could provide salvation for the elite, was entirely stripped of its connection with God, and its message was taken to be no more than the elimination of poverty. The whole of Christianity, accordingly, was discarded, or rather, its essence was now claimed to be summed up by this goal.

The Kingdom of God proved, indeed, to have been a protean factor in its very conception that has enabled it to serve as the expression of plainly disparate ideas.

Perhaps the basis of it, essentially, is the rejection of the world. Initially this was taken to mean the rejection of this world, which for Jewish messianists and early Christians meant this world of pagan oppression of the chosen people and of the messianists, but for Marxified Christians now meant this world of "capitalist exploitation." Hence, on the basis of an accord that this world, evil by nature, had to be replaced, both Marxists and pious Christians could unite to promote the renovation of society.

There would seem to be a similarity of pattern in these universalistic formulations that may indicate a profound dynamic of the psyche. Just as the "forcers of the end" could not wait for God to implement his own plan, so the Marxist activists, the Bolsheviks, and neo-Bolsheviks could not wait for Marx's "iron laws" to work themselves out.

Just as the believers in the Kingdom of God fell naturally into quietists and activists—the ordinary Pharisees and the Zealot Pharisees—so the Marxists, under the pressure of events in the First World War, split into the old-fashioned Social Democrats who clung to Marx's "iron laws" and hoped to be carried along by the momentum of abstract ideas, and the activists—in the event the Russian Bolsheviks—who plunged into action in an attempt to force the "iron laws" to make a forward jump. And, by seizing the power in a backward peasant society previously considered by all Marxists to be totally unfit for the transition to Socialism, to compel Russia, by an act of will, to carry out the social mission that justified Marxism, or was at least inherent in it.

In this respect a similar division can be discerned among the Christians who piously assumed that the Kingdom of God would be realized within one's own heart by acts of mercy and compassion, and those activists in movements like liberation theology who wished to force society to demonstrate compassion institutionally and to realize the visions of the prophets in the here and now.

It need hardly be pointed out that liberation theology bypassed, in effect, both Christianity and Marxism simultaneously. The naiveté of thinking that all Christianity can be reduced to the egalitarian satisfaction of material needs is paralleled by the naiveté of thinking that Marxism will end poverty out of compassion.

After all, Marxism merely postulates a sociohistorical mechanism through which, because of the evolution of the bourgeoisie, the proletariat rectifies society by seizing power and then, in theory, ends poverty. If it were a question of compassion alone, it would obviously be more sensible to take into account the achievements of the free enterprise system in generalizing abundance, in contrast with all the powers that claimed the sanction of Marxism.

In view of this curious myopia it is fitting that in preaching that compassion for the poor is the essence of both Christianity and Marxism, the ally found by the liberation theologians was, in practice, the KGB.

It need hardly be added that in the modern age there has been a confluence of this form of messianism between Christians and those Jews who have also been stirred to their depths by the ferment of Marxism. It has been natural for Jews, seeking a way out of their isolation by an identification with programs of world reform to become active agents on behalf of universal ideals. The visions of social justice foreseen by the Hebrew prophets in the remote and unknowable future have, on occasion, been adapted to the agitational slogans propagated by universalist Jews.

Curiously enough, this aspect of Jewish behavior in the twentieth century may be linked directly to Saul, since it seems plain that Saul's conception, in its broadest focus—the obliteration of the Jews in the name of a universal project—was itself a typically Jewish initiative. Saul was, indeed, the first in a long series of Jewish self-immolators—Jews so ill at ease in their own identities, for various reasons, that the only solution has seemed to be their collective dissolution under the aegis of large-scale ideas.

Saul's specific origins in Tarsus duplicate the situation of countless individual Jews in the Diaspora since then. His parents' comfortable circumstances, their origins in a center of Jewish dissidence in Galilee (Gush-Halav) parallel the many Jews whose parents had been adherents of some world-shaking ideology and have grown up dynamically disaffiliated from their own people. It has been possible for them to realize their alienation from their immediate background by projecting themselves into the abstract on the wings of a pure idea. Thus what seems to have been Saul's overriding concern for the unification of Jews and the rest of mankind may parallel the experience of those Diaspora Jews who see in such a large-scale unification—all mankind!

If the collision with Hellenism was a problem for observant Jews, Saul may be said to have sublimated, projected, magnified, and generalized the Jewish problem to make it encompass the whole human race. Thus Saul's enterprise was doubly ironic—the projection of his private misery onto the world and the success of his Jewish ideas mediated by the extinction of Jewry as a territorial entity.

Yet what is perhaps oddest of all, in this intertwining of historical ironies brought about by Saul's handiwork, is the effect it has had on his own people.

In early Christianity the split away from Judaism was grounded fundamentally in Romans (9–11), which created a doctrinal justification for destroying Jewish propaganda. More directly, it led to the attitude of indifference to Judaism, sharpening to hostility, that was to set its stamp on Christendom to the present day. It also contributed, no doubt, to a loss of heart within Judaism with respect to its own view of the World's End—the ultimate reconciliation between the world and God. It was no longer possible for Jews to remain preoccupied with the fate of the pagans in the workaday world; in the present-day world, from which Jewish apocalyptic was to recede for millennia, it was the Christian Church—the eccentric offshoot of a fragment of Jewish emotionality—that was to corral countless pagans.

In our own day, of course, the consequences of millennial anti-Semitism have become notorious; here the true significance of Saul's magical system can be grasped. For what makes anti-Semitism altogether different in kind from all conventional xenophobia lies precisely in the role bestowed on the Jews not by doctrine as such, but by the magical structure of the Church.

In the cosmic drama of Christianity, in which the God-forces are arrayed against the devil-forces, including the devil as a real entity, the essential role assigned to the Jews at the outset was bound to be satanic.

They had, after all, given the universe a Savior, an aspect of God; but then they had rejected him. What could that mean? Obviously, they were playing out a cosmic role, which could be only that of the devil. As the Church evolved, the explicit description of their nature in the Gospel of John ("You [the Jews] are the Devil's children" [8:44]) was infinitely reinforced and at the same time submerged in the unconscious of believers when Church doctrine, building on this idea, assigned the Jews the dynamic role of contending against the God-forces as agents of the devil.

This primordial concept explains the singular potency of anti-Semitism, which revolves around the fundamental idea that the Jews, seemingly a small, dispersed, and essentially powerless people, are nevertheless in reality agents of Satan—a palpable, living entity who was the sole element to survive the complex array of devil-forces contending with the God-forces as part of the drama of the installation of the Kingdom of God. As with the elaboration of Christian theology the devil-forces coalesced in the form of an easily conceived and symbolized living entity, it became all the easier to perceive the Jews as *not really human.*

Saul himself, to be sure, could never even have dreamed that the Jews could be assigned such a role; for him they were the warranty of the divine plan. But in the system of magic established by the dislocation, transposition, and escalation of his symbols, the basic notion underlying the pagan system he had superimposed on the divine plan originally conceived by the Jews, there was only one conceivable role for them once they had rejected Jesus as Messiah. It is here that the irony implicit in Saul's timetable has become most poignant.

For Saul the obtuseness of the Jews about the incarnation was part of a great mystery; they had simply been blind, unaccountably. "This partial blindness has come upon Israel only until the Gentiles have been admitted in full strength; when that has happened the whole of Israel will be saved" (Rom: 11:25, 26).

But, while mysterious, their obtuseness could not last very long; it was merely part of the very brief period—not more than forty years—between the resurrection, the signal of the titanic change, and the onset of the messianic kingdom leading to the Kingdom of God. Before the installation of the messianic kingdom the Jews had to see the light, and all would be well.

But as Saul's timetable was forgotten, together with the inward logic of his key concepts, as the Church that replaced the Kingdom of God itself became an eternal institution, as those key concepts, misunderstood, became frozen in the motionlessness of an enduring theology, so the nature of the Jews, from having been bafflingly obstinate but inherently curable, became timelessly and essentially evil.

Thus, as the Church Fathers harmonized Saul's logical relationships into a theology for a universal Church, the Jews themselves became agents of Satan by their nature, while of course being capable nevertheless of salvation through conversion.

On the face of it, to be sure, Christian doctrine focuses no particular attention on the Jews. Christianity, after all, presents fallible mankind with a divine Savior. In principle Jews are merely a fragment of the human race, part of the two-thirds that have not yet become Christian.

It is a sort of irony that during the first couple of centuries, with the early Church competing, in a way, with Judaism for the allegiance of pagans, the early historical conflicts were fixated in texts, eventually canonized, that came to be inculcated in the young of each generation.

The ultimate twist of this irony was arrived at after theology itself, emasculated by the history-mindedness that began stirring at the end of the eighteenth century, lost its grip on society. Christendom as a whole, far more capacious than its theology, had been suffused for so many centuries in stereotypes portraying the Jews as symbolizing some aspect of evil that all Christians, regardless of their attitude toward religion proper, found it natural to consider Jews both evil and alien. Mystical anti-Semitism found a mass base.

And that mass base, most ironically, was created by the very attack on religion that led to the proliferation of the preposterous "race" theories that proliferated from the nineteenth century on.

These theories, disregarding the theological principle that the Jews had to be preserved, though in abject circumstances, as a witness to the triumph of Christianity, shifted the guilt of the Jews from theology to biology. When the burden of Jewish evil was no longer claimed to be rooted in beliefs, which could be cured by conversion, but in genes, which are incorrigible, conversion became laughably irrelevant. There was no longer any reason for Jews to survive at all.

Saul's thought, despite its energy and brilliance, was so physical, so concrete, indeed so crude, that it might seem difficult to retain for it any conceivable foothold in the modern world.

Yet nowadays, oddly enough, it might be said that psychoanalysis has come to his rescue. It has restored what is surely a key insight into the identity of the superstructure of man's ideas and the profoundest needs of the organism as a psychobiological entity. If it were to be true that art, mythology, religion, and philosophy themselves are merely objectified expressions of the organism's need of psychophysical gratification, there would seem to be a place for Saul's own regression to the earlier era prior to Judaism's sublimation or repression of so much instinct-gratifying material.

For surely the potency of Saul's images, his struggle with his own repressions, their bursting forth into the open accompanied by a solid panoply of reasoning plus a justified hopefulness, are due ultimately to their deep roots in the psyche. This is the only justification for talking about Saul's "genius" and no doubt what Freud meant when he referred, euphemistically, to Saul's reversion to the "dark layers of the past." Depth psychology can turn his brainwork to its own purposes!

It may be true that Saul could plumb the depths of his own psyche because of a regression that for him was justified intellectually by the combination of his doubtless pathological experience on the road to Damascus and the messianic fever he shared with so many other Jews. His conception of the body-of-Christ, in which the ego of the individual believer is effaced through absorption in a larger entity—the core of mysticism— by grounding itself in a stage of development preceding individuation, could restore to consciousness what had been unconscious for untold generations, the primal state of identity between the organism and its environment, encapsulated within the infinite solace of the certainty that life was eternal.

If Saul had merely undergone transports on this level of obliterating realities—the reality of the psychophysical world, in which egos are distinct, and people are not the same as their environments—it would be easy to dismiss him as an outright psychopath. But the psychopathic elements in his personality did not prevent his living an active, rationally directed life—at any rate a life in which he had full command of abundant energies, pouring them out on behalf of a deeply felt, palpable goal. His conception of the divine timetable entailed fruitful activity—he had to prepare everyone for something already happening. He was grounded, in fact, on two levels of being simultaneously—the deepest levels of his unconscious, which gave him full energy, and the topmost levels of conscious thought, his ego constructions. Both a mystic and an organizer, he had restored equilibrium to the two sides of his nature that, unreconciled, might well have torn him apart.

The peculiar power of his remark that "God's foolishness is better than human wisdom" (1 Cor 1:25) lies in the composure with which it transcends mere common sense while at the same time projecting an intellectual prediction based on longing. The result is ardent faith. "The language of the cross may be illogical to those who are not on the way to salvation, but those of us who are on the way see it as God's power to save" (1 Cor 1:18).

Psychologically Saul had conceived a sort of salvational strategy by finding his way to the Father, whom he could not hope to satisfy because of his inability to live up to the Father's law, i.e., his obsessive-compulsive inadequacy. Accordingly, he had managed to find his way back to the Father by way of a brother he could identify himself with. In this way he could assert his omnipotence not in an absolute form, like an out-and-out psychotic, but through the risen Jesus, a concept he could then invest with all his longings. This created a mechanism for articulating the faith of countless recruits. All believers could benefit from this simple strategy; they could, in a word, regularize their relations with the Father by identifying themselves with his son.

A troubled Jew, Saul had contrived an ingenious cure for himself. Simultaneously conquering death and establishing his peace with the Father, he could go on at the same time believing in the Torah for the space of time left before the World's End.

All this may, of course, be looked on as a form of Jewish extremism. Perhaps Saul had been disappointed by the failure of Jesus' enterprise, and so his need to realize unconscious yearnings had to turn to a much more comprehensive scheme to compensate for the fiasco of a narrowly conceived enterprise—the salvation of the Jews. In compensation for the magnitude of his disappointment in Jesus' movement, Saul expanded his requirements by projecting God's salvation to all mankind. His personal needs had become so demanding that any scheme he could devise intellectually had to be equated with the largest possible factor. Only a cosmic upheaval seemed big enough to counterbalance his wretchedness. The equation had to be, accordingly, between him and the world!

In a curious way this may round off the pervasive irony of Saul's career. For it may well be that despite the magnetism exercised on his emotions by the glamour of paganism, it was his Jewish piety, after all, the fundamental monotheism underlying his brainplay, that enabled him to surmount the magical accretions of his theories and to give his personal anguish a wording that had universal application.

Since monotheism creates, essentially, a link between the individual and a transcendental principle, a principle that soars far beyond all cleavages of mundane contingency, it confronts the individual human being with the totality of the world. Thus Saul's passionate commitment in itself provides the bridge between his world view—altogether extinct—and any modern world view. His emotion, perhaps his hysteria, was indispensable for the working out of his influence, since it was anchored in the overwhelmingly direct experience, the psychic explosion, which he personally confronted. It was first and foremost his redemption, the seeming solution of his own psychic torment, his directly and personally experienced feeling, that made his prose soar aloft. For without such personal emotion, without deep feeling, mere mental activity would, no doubt, seem to be frivolous agility.

Saul expresses, in short, a personal emotion. Calling it Christ, he expresses it in terms of a living relationship to an abstract ideal; his depth of feeling injected a permanent element, however distorted, into the vast institutions that were to claim his ideas as their own. Even though Saul's ideas were falsified, his ability to reinvest long-suppressed psychic material with new life by novel formulations could eventually be expressed in the institutions engendered even by his falsified ideas. Masses of people could dredge up from their unconscious much of the repressed material and aerate it within the framework of institutionalized symbols.

Saul's conditioning had been no different, after all, from that of countless contemporary Jews; what made him an innovator, or at least a successful promoter, was his private, clinical need for special succor—his fear of death. He had found his refuge in contriving a public answer to his private miseries. Ablaze with the notion that all mankind, in its ancient, familiar sheath, was coming to an end, to be reborn in a new sheath in a new universe, Saul could conquer death, for him now no more than the beginning of a new life in glory. The old idea of death as a mere cessation was replaced by the more attractive idea of death as the equivalent of birth. Saul's metaphor of baptism as meaning the death of Christ and hence a rebirth "with Christ" had a magnetism that for many proved compelling.

With the frustration of Saul's hopes after his death, the institutions anchored in his writings were to disregard his real ideas, which thus became pegs to hang an altogether alien theology on. With the abandonment of all World's End theories, the Church rooted in Saul's writings achieved stasis; it was now itself a component of the world order!

Saul, organizing his own anguish, organized the anguish of countless individuals—the bewilderment, despair, insecurity, and wretchedness of the millions of people torn away from their moorings, from villages, cities, tribes, countryside, in the wake of the upheavals that established the Roman Empire and, more generally, in the abiding travail of the human condition. Saul's Letters, throbbing with the certainty of the imminent World's End, were to implant in the generations governed by the Christian Scriptures, the feeling of an imminent world destruction that hitherto, and for only a few generations, had characterized the Jews in their specific situation as victims of rapacious idolaters.

In its turn this meant that the psychohistorical anguish of the Jews, translated into the pagan world milieu and expressed in formulas that, even though historically determined in origin, became for the pagans timeless facets of the universe and from then on were to embody the longings and the neuroses of countless individuals.

Looked at from a structural point of view, Saul originated a cosmic drama by transposing the Jewish drama of national redemption at the World's End to a drama, equally Jewish, located in the here and now. He made the Jewish drama of history, in which God makes the world, alienates the world, and returns to the world, a constant, day-to-day drama through the establishment of a pregnant relationship to the body of Christ.

Historically the effect of this—since the messianic kingdom never came—was to suspend the believer in this dramatic tension *in the present.* This anchored the believer in daily life in a dramatic relationship established by the sacraments so that, even with the messianic kingdom indefinitely postponed, the edifice built over Saul's fantasies had a built-in tension with immense impact.

The very notion that had seemed to the Jerusalem Jesists headed by Jesus' brother a deeply repugnant, doubtless incomprehensible idea—the escalation of the person of Jesus into a surrogate for the Eternal One—was to be a springboard for expansion among pagans who found it natural to worship a man, or rather, who took it for granted that in the right circumstances a man could turn into a god and vice versa. Thus it was Saul's version of the Gospel of Jesus Christ and not Jesus' own initiative for the Jews of his milieu that was to find an echo in the pagan world.

This idea, even when transformed, could appeal to the deep longings of mankind. Saul's mental activity was so intense, even on its narrow base, and so filled with emotion that the formulas it had worked out retained an appeal even when wrenched out of their organic matrix and transposed to an utterly alien realm of ideas. By opening a passageway into the depths of the workaday world, by piercing the camouflage of naturalistic appearances, Saul's intellect created an abstract framework that was well sprung enough to survive its unattainability for generation after generation.

And how simple the transformation was! By the mere designation of Jesus as "our Lord" Saul established an abstraction of endless potentiality. The notion of the "Lord" could achieve comprehensibility, organically, as it were, since it could be used to define a being who by definition could not be defined. As long as there was a deep substratum of uncertainty, inadequacy, or weakness in countless individuals—and how, after all, could there not be?—a Being who transcended all approximations to a description could become hypostatized as the repository of a universal human longing for self-definition, succor, and comfort. He could easily be imagined as the locus of the true reality that human beings could look to as a replacement for the mundane, deeply unsatisfactory reality they were embedded in by virtue of their very inferiority. Saul's theory of the divine timetable, which freed him from his misery, constituted a formula that in its nature could be extended to all men in the grip of the human condition. It institutionalized a safety valve for suffering.

His neuroses, maintaining a minimal contact with the workaday world, had created a vehicle for the religious, perhaps the neurotic needs of mankind. Generalizing out of existence the original Jewish scheme, Saul's pervasive, oceanic misery, his incapacity to feel at ease with himself, provided a paradigm that could be turned into the armature of a universal myth, and thus a universal institution—the Christian Church, the tangible embodiment of endless hope.

Thus Saul's basic attitudes, understandable in his own time only as personal effusions revolving around a specific historical situation—the incipient messianic kingdom, part of the World's End theory—lost their organic meaning and acquired a totally different meaning as part of the institutionalized complex of a universal religion. The modalities devised to relieve his unbearable misery were expressed with such generality that they could relieve *all* guilt via a general idea.

Jewish messianism, in its two phases—that of Jesus and that of Saul—by stretching toward the unfulfillable had created a longbow. In the tension created by yearning between ideal aspirations and down-to-earth needs, the stupendous edifice of the Roman Catholic Church could take shape and root itself. Embodying and expressing such longings, the cosmic institution could encompass them.

Jesus and Saul longed for the Kingdom of God. Their longing created an ideal that lent enthusiasm to its followers. The enthusiasm established institutions. The ideal, unattainable, was calcified in rhetoric; the institutions lived on.

Fantasy, soaring, had created a world order.

Critical Appendix

The Lost Continent

The reader will have observed that the story he has read is not the traditional one. Its background, the real-life roots of what came to be Christianity, is centered in a set of circumstances that are only glancingly and indeed incomprehensibly referred to in the New Testament.

The crux of the problem inherent in the establishment of Christianity is the transformation of the initial belief in the imminent Kingdom of God, shared by Jesus, John the Baptist, and Saul of Tarsus, into a salvational religion rooted in the incarnation, that is, in the worship of Christ Jesus, Son of God.

Jesus evidently never declared himself to be the Son of God, or even the Messiah awaited by many Jews. Saul reports only the most meager details about Jesus the man, while linking his own view of the Kingdom of God to the resurrection of Jesus Christ as a guarantee of its imminence.

The key to this puzzle will be found in the answer to a simple question. Why was a herald of the Kingdom of God executed as a rebel against the state? No real-life explanation of this seemingly strange fact is given in the documents themselves. The deep meaning extracted by Saul of Tarsus from the crucifixion is, of course, the foundation of the Church, but the Kingdom of God itself, the starting point, is not explained at all.

That would seem, nevertheless, to be the nub of the matter. How is it, then, that the Kingdom of God has been misperceived for almost two thousand years?

How is it that the movement of the Kingdom of God activists—Zealots and others—which occasioned the Roman destruction of the Jewish state and thus launched Christianity, has been entirely disregarded? How is it that the interconnection between Judah the Galilean and the Zealots, and Jesus the Nazarene, John the Baptist, and Saul of Tarsus is not obvious?

To grasp the reasons for this the organizing principle of the scanty documentation that supports the vast literature on Christian origins must be established. We can start from the plain fact that all these documents were composed after the death of Jesus and against the background, moreover, of growing Zealot agitation that brought about the Roman war, the destruction of the Temple in Jerusalem, the end of the Jewish state, and the enslavement and large-scale dispersion of Jewry in Palestine.

The Zealot movement, which took in a variety of anti-Roman activists, was to swing the masses of Jewry in a desperate attack on the Roman power and also on the Jewish peace party—the royal family and the bulk of the aristocratic Sadducees. Saul's ideas were not to have their dynamic impact, as we shall see, until after the Zealot fiasco in the war against Rome.

Saul's Letters uniformly describe a situation full of contention, friction, and struggle. He is not merely expounding his ideas abstractly to innocent readers, he is combating the Jerusalem Jesists. The violent polemical tone is due to his grudging acknowledgment of their authority.

Now, whatever agitated the congregations of the Diaspora, it must have been encased by the massive edifice of normative Judaism. Within the larger concentric circle, so to speak, of the effervescent messianism that had gripped many strata of the Jewish community inside and outside of Palestine, the partisans of Jesus the Jewish Messiah must have been thought innocuous. They had not fallen foul of the Temple authorities in any sense; otherwise they could easily have been ejected. We know the Temple heads could do as much, because Judaism was still an authorized religion (*religio licita*), hence under the specific protection of the Roman state even at a time when various strata of the Temple hierarchy itself were fermenting with sedition.

Similarly, within the smaller concentric circle of the Jesist tendency itself, the Jesist leaders in Jerusalem could easily have cut short the activities of the Antioch congregation or Saul's own activities, as we can see from Saul's trip to Jerusalem and his acceptance of Jacob's dilemma.

In the perspective of an imminent world upheaval heralded by the

Jewish Messiah, with God transplanted within the orbit of history at any moment to end the natural world and install the messianic kingdom, the shoots of a new and different belief could not have been seen as such. In that framework they were quite meaningless, mere pointers to be shrugged aside, since without any direction to point to they would simply have been obliterated, like all else in the natural world, with the installation of the messianic kingdom.

Thus, if different Jewish congregations emphasized one point or another of differing opinions about the validity of specific rites outside normative Judaism, they did so diffusely and unsystematically. The outstanding Jesists were unaware of the implications of such innovations, or might not have been concerned with any of them except precisely the two cardinal points that did give rise to friction between them and Saul, circumcision and table fellowship with pagans, both taken to imply the rejection of the Torah. It is also possible, of course, that this happened only in a few places, and acquired importance only after the Jesists of Jerusalem vanished with the destruction of the Temple in 70 C.E.

Thus the falling out between Saul and the Jerusalem Jesists was subordinated to the Jewish clash with the Roman authorities. During his lifetime Saul was not important; the Jewish leaders in Jerusalem had no difficulty in getting rid of him. The authority of the Jesists was merely one element in the activist movement against Rome that after simmering for decades, during and after the revolt linked to Jesus, had begun swelling around 55 to culminate a decade later—well after Saul's death—in the war against Rome.

When the Romans put down the desperate resistance of the Jews four years later, more than a million Jews were massacred; the remainder were deported as slaves. Only a remnant was left. The war, destroying the ancient shrine and extinguishing the Jews as a people rooted in their land, had the deepest repercussions throughout the Diaspora, which from then on was to encompass Jewry down to the modern era.

It was after the Roman-Jewish war and the destruction of the Temple that the documents of the nascent sect were created and/or reworked in an exclusively tendentious way. They naturally obscure the fundamental fact that a new sect was in the very midst of being articulated. The development of the new institutions was completely overlaid, eventually, by the harmonizing official version.

Since Christianity incorporates secular history, whatever its theological interpretation, and since the incarnation and the resurrection revolving around the crucifixion are taken to have been real events in human as well as in divine history—that is, indeed, their point—the five documents making up the historical element of the New Testament—the Four Gospels and Acts—are vital; they establish the historical framework that Saul's Letters give the meaning of as seen from the vantage point of a much later belief.

Saul's posthumous ascension, and the doubtless unconscious manipulation of history in the early documentation, are easily demonstrated once we look at the surviving sources with an eye just as much for what has been left out as for what has been included.

Saul's Letters are, of course, the oldest source for the history of the new faith, but Saul was writing some years after the events described in the Gospels. His own viewpoint influenced the writers and editors of the Gospels and Acts. More particularly, Saul died before the Roman-Jewish War of 66–70, which was surely uppermost in the mind of the author of Mark, whose ground plan was followed by the other two Synoptic Gospels.

Not only that; Acts, in which Saul is the star, describes his career wellnigh independently of his Letters, from the vantage point of a much later era, when the entire perspective of the evolving sect had been transformed and when Saul himself, in consequence, was misunderstood. Saul's powerlessness during his lifetime is plain not only from the sustained disputatiousness of the Letters, but from their actual physical condition.

It is obvious, from Saul's own Letters, that he must have written a great many. He was active, as it seems, from shortly after the execution of Jesus—say 35–36—for another two decades, i.e., until a short time before Upright Jacob's death. These two decades were surely productive; since Saul was in the habit of writing there is no reason to regard his surviving Letters as his total literary production.

His major Letters seem to have been written long after his seizure on the road to Damascus, e.g., some fourteen years, really a *very* long time. The small number of letters that now form the backbone of the New Testament cannot be all he wrote. The very condition of the Letters indicates as much; they are plainly random selections, often fragmentary to boot. One of the major ones, 2 Corinthians, is practically incomprehensible; it is best understood as a mosaic of scraps of other, left-over letters gathered together after the phenomenon of "Paulinism" made its appearance.

Many scholars concur in considering a whole chapter in Romans (16) a separate document. An important Letter known to have been written to a congregation in Laodicea has been lost altogether; a trivial note (Philemon) has survived, no doubt by accident.

Moreover, it is evident from the content of the Letters we have that a dominant theme in all his major Letters—the theme that often makes them sound hysterically demanding—is his conflict with others; he is plainly describing a situation in which he is promoting his own ideas against *rivals*. And the rivals include, equally plainly, the leaders of the Jesist community in Jerusalem.

The apology in Acts thus plasters over facts that in Saul's own lifetime had been too obvious, that on certain cardinal points Saul's views had been considered indigestible; they were rejected by the authorities of a state institution with well-nigh governmental power and did, in fact, lead to his undoing.

Hence Saul's writings must have been slighted while he was alive; they were, in fact, disinterred from the archives of a few congregations only after the destruction of Jerusalem. It was then that Saul emerged as the author of documents that could be used by a small, still somewhat shapeless community that was short of writings and had to make do with Saul's scrappy, casual Letters.

This is the background that must be kept in mind for a consideration of Saul's ascension—the replacement of the short tradition of Jesus' real-life activities by a complex of new ideas revolving around a unique interpretation of Jesus' *meaning*. Because of Saul's passionate temperament and brainpower these could at least be presented as a corpus of belief by the evolving bureaucratic structure. To be sure, the central thrust of his thought was to be radically misinterpreted for a long time, beginning almost immediately, but it could be seized on by leaders of the following generation as an intellectual framework for the nascent faith; then the actual copies of his Letters were scrambled for and patched up to produce what is now grandiloquently called the Corpus Paulinum.

Negatively, this curious quirk of evolution is paralleled by the total absence of any writings whatever from the Jerusalem Jesists. It is true they had no need to write anything down—why? After all, they were embedded, as they thought, in the bedrock of an ancient, established religion; the novelty of their views about Jesus was in no sense alien to the Jewish community as a whole. Their hopes, moreover, had crystallized in an expectation whose realization was thought to be so close at hand that there really must have seemed hardly anything whatever to do about it. It was merely an aspect of the well-nigh universal messianic agitation against the Roman Empire. Even if they had a regulatory role to play vis-à-vis the small congregations in the Diaspora that were accepted as fellow believers, there was no reason to write anything ideological.

The casual construction of Saul's Letters, our sole authority, with respect to the embryonic phase of Christianity for the period before the destruction of the Jewish community in 70, and the total absence of any other sources from before 70, indicate that there could scarcely have been even the beginnings of a bureaucracy in the Jesist community that was shattered in that year. Since it is plain that all were living in the immediate expectation of the World's End there would not, in fact, seem to be the slightest reason for anything else. A bureaucracy must have evolved much later.

There is only one mention of a bureaucratic process in Acts—the reference (15:23, 30) to the circularization to various churches of the "decision" of the "General Council" in Jerusalem. Saul's failure even to mention this thrusts it completely outside the realm of possibility, and it no doubt represents a situation after the collapse of the Jewish state. Acts itself is the first harmonizing, i.e., organizational apologia.

The reason for the absence of a bureaucracy is obvious—time. There was neither the time nor the occasion for an organization of any kind to be engendered. In the feverish atmosphere of the age a bureaucracy would have been the last thing to plan for. The Jesists needed no theology, no bureaucracy.

Nor can their silence be explained as due to the destruction of Jerusalem in 70. If anything had been written it would normally have circulated far and wide in the Jewish Diaspora; the Jerusalem community, after all, was linked to a huge network of synagogues abroad.

The paucity of documents for the century or so spanning the birth of Jesus is accentuated to utter nullity for the two decades spanning the rebellion against Rome—nothing whatever has survived, not a scrap. There is in fact a total silence about the Jewish war in all Christian documents, except for a few casual remarks made in the second century about the so-called "Mother Church," an altogether mythological, fictional misnomer whose very existence invites attention to the factual situation it was created to camouflage.

Silence was imposed on accounts of the Jewish uprising against Rome by the very magnitude of the event. If Jesus himself died as an insurrectionist against the Roman Empire, if the Temple was wiped out as a result of the ferocious war against Rome, if the Jesist community was thereupon itself eliminated in the obliteration of the Jewish community as a whole, there could have been no reason for the fragmented, diffuse, shapeless congregations of believers scattered throughout the Roman Empire even to mention the catastrophe of the Jewish nation. It was, in fact, in the vacuum created by the absence or destruction of documents that the traditional theory of Church history could be set up on a firm foundation, enabling the far-flung sectarian foci to develop an altogether different conception of their own salvation and elaborating, exclusively for purposes of harmonization, an entirely mythological attachment to the putative founders of the emerging religion.

It was in the scattered collectivities of these towns and cities, as the Church slowly coagulated, that the concept of an organized religious fellowship was conceived and embodied, in a form that could not have been foreseen by anyone in the Jesist community of Jerusalem, or by Saul, or by Jesus—least of all!

We have seen the initial magnification of Jesus as due to an event commonplace in the history of religion—a vision, Simon the Rock's on the Sea of Galilee very soon after the execution.

This had an electrifying effect on Jesus' immediate entourage. Yet for that entourage, which moved to Jerusalem very quickly, the vision, while representing a unique event, was nevertheless held within the framework of Jewish ideas; the vision merely confirmed, so to speak, Jesus' status as Messiah. His messiahship was still in accordance with the basic conception of the Kingdom of God—a transformation of the real world brought about by God's decision. Hence the function of Jesus the Messiah was now merely to come again, this time bringing with him the Kingdom of God.

But another tendency, a schismatic, anti-Torah tendency, began to make itself felt in this coterie of Jews who believed in Jesus' special status. Epitomized by the name of the first Christian martyr, Stephen, this tendency elevated Jesus far beyond the status of the Jewish Messiah to that of Lord of the Universe and Savior of Mankind. When Stephen was stoned to death as an apostate and his followers expelled from Jerusalem, they took their views to Antioch in Syria and, no doubt, many other Jewish centers in the Diaspora. It was these views that were expanded, elaborated, and streamlined by Saul, and provided the doctrinal framework that served as superstructure for the Gospel-writers' apologetic aim in camouflaging the true history of Jesus' career. Yet while the Temple stood, the anchor and magnet of world Jewry, this deification of Jesus had no potential.

It was thus a natural development, around the time the Zealot movement was swinging the masses of Palestinian Jewry into the titanic war against Rome, for the author of Mark not merely to suppress and distort the real-life meaning of the Kingdom of God—that is, its political element—but simultaneously to stress the transcendentalization of Jesus that had been going on in the Diaspora anyhow.

There are two factors in the genesis of the first three Gospels.

The global transformation of perspective between the events of Jesus' own lifetime and the germination of a new belief founded on Simon the Rock's vision of the risen Jesus were paralleled by a sociopolitical upheaval—the destruction of the Temple in Jerusalem, the consequent emancipation of the new belief from its institutional restraints, and the concomitant fact that for generations after the destruction of the Temple the new sect of believers in Jesus was opposed by the Jewish elite, the rabbis who had inherited the Pharisaic tradition.

Here the writers and editors of the Gospels, whose belief in the vision of the risen Jesus necessarily distorted their view of the world before the vision, found it natural to transpose their own contemporary disputes with the rabbis to the lifetime of Jesus, especially since by then the Jews were no longer regarded as targets for conversion and the leaders of the new sect were directing their propaganda at all mankind.

Thus the Gospels, written under the pressure of a specific situation, are structurally biased. This accounts for their timelessness, their motionlessness. Jesus expresses various ideas without the reader being able to see their meaning against a historical background. It is hard to see, from the text alone, what there was about the Kingdom of God, or about his ideas in general, that could have led to his crucifixion. As we have seen, Jesus' whole career as outlined in the first three Gospels could scarcely have lasted more than a few weeks; the Kingdom of God he proclaims at the outset of all three accounts seems peculiarly abstract and anodyne.

The homey, small-scale, intimate atmosphere that emanates from some parts of the Gospels does not make them histories; they are in fact full of disguised polemics whose fossilization makes them inaccessible to a naive reading. The key element in this obscuration of real life is the comprehensive elimination of the Romans.

The Gospels and the Church tradition founded on them indicate no friction at all between Romans and Jews in Palestine. Everything that happens to Jesus takes place in a Jewish milieu; even his trial before the Roman procurator is explained, as we shall see, as a Jewish plot. The stateliness of the seemingly simple anecdotes, shot through with camouflaged theological motifs, casts an atmosphere of frozen pageantry over what we know was a most turbulent era.

The Gospels suppress *any* criticism of the Romans. The word itself, indeed, occurs only once (Jn 11:48), and the Romans are assigned a role only twice; Pilate himself and the Roman centurion who, seeing Jesus on the cross, calls him "Son of God" (Mk 15:39).

The Romans, who crucified countless thousands of Jews, so that the cross became the conventional symbol of Jewish resistance to Roman power, go completely unnoticed by the writers and editors of the Gospels. Contrariwise, the Pharisees, equated with the rabbis, the chief opponents of the nascent sect by the time the Gospels were composed, are more or less constantly reviled (though here too numerous indications of the opposite peep through the web of apologetics).

The Acts of the Apostles (the sole Christian source for this period) also says nothing of the violence endemic in Judea in the first century. The Romans are scarcely mentioned; the Jewish authorities are treated ambiguously—the followers of Jesus are described as eminently pious, the hostility of the religious leaders remains unexplained. All is seen through the prism of much later theological propaganda whose purpose is to harmonize everything. The vast movement of religious-political disaffection that churned up the country is never referred to.

It was the global transformation of perspective inherent in the germination of a new belief inspired by Simon the Rock's vision of the risen Jesus, reinforced by the reaction of the new sect to the Jewish debacle of 70, that distorted the Gospels systematically. All the basic ideas that had a living context in the life of Jewry beforehand—Kingdom of God, the Messiah, Son of David, salvation—were wrenched out of their true context of national insurrection. In Jesus' lifetime not a single day could have passed without some inflammatory incident; the mere presence of the Romans constituted a constant provocation. All this is glossed over in the Gospels.

It was part of the natural habit of the proto-Christian fellowships to fling a blanket of harmony plus a theory of origins over the entire complex process of evolution. Documents were piously assembled, piously sifted, piously forged, and the results canonized. Authority was established, reinforced, and generalized; a harmony between history and ideas was contrived, itself becoming canonized, authoritative, and unique. The scraps of real history were forgotten, reassembled, and integrated in an entirely different structure. Little was left.

It must be admitted that the unconscious technique, so to speak, of building on silence and suppression was a great success. In fact, it took almost two millennia for the real situation in Judea to edge its way, tentatively, gropingly, well-nigh unconsciously through the wall of mythology petrified in the traditional documents. It is only our own generation, in fact, that has been able to leap over the chasm of tendentious distortion onto a vantage point from which it may be possible to restore the historical situation that through unconscious misdirection engendered the mythology.

The mere fact, in short, that no Jesist documents have been conserved and that Saul's Letters have survived sheds light on the principal anomaly of our sources, the utter failure of the documentation preserved by Christian tradition to account for the dramatic transformation of perspective during the two pregnant decades spanning the destruction of the Jewish state. The silence of all Christian historians on the events that wiped out the community of those who were closest to Jesus socially and temporally, merely confirms what one knows from the fundamental composition of these documents. They were designed precisely to transform the meaning of what had actually happened to the Jews during this turbulent era.

To put it in semilogical terms, the scholarly consensus that seeks to explain the genesis of Christianity on the basis of the surviving documents is the victim of a vast *petitio principii*; it takes for granted what must be proved. It uses the documents justifying a certain turn of events not as the result of those events, but as their explanation.

If there is a conundrum in the evolution of the nascent faith it plainly revolves around the manifest contradictions embedded not merely in the Gospels, with their reiterated echoes of a Jesus pious in the ancient faith of Israel and executed by the Romans as a Jewish national leader, but in the contrasts between Saul and Acts. The scholarly consensus that has endured for so long cannot be understood as scholarship alone. It is comprehensible only as an illustration of a bias in interpretation that has prevailed, and whose authority, accordingly, is unconsciously accepted.

And surely the most striking element in this well-nigh total muddle is the peculiarly intense silence muffling the fate of the Jesists, the very community that gave rise to the new faith. The destruction of the Mother

Church, part and parcel of the destruction of Jerusalem, is scarcely mentioned either in the New Testament or elsewhere.

The reason for the deep silence on roughly the decade spanning the Jewish War of 66–70 is only too manifest. The real-life Jesists had become irrelevant, indeed alien to the evolving mythology, which with the elimination of the institutional brake on the new faith in 70 could lash out on a majestic scale in the Greco-Roman world.

It was only after the destruction of the Temple in Jerusalem that a few of Saul's Letters—those embroidering on general ideas applicable to a novel situation—were disinterred from oblivion and patched together to serve as the foundations of a new theology that Saul himself never dreamed of.

It is an additional irony that this extraordinary phenomenon is hardly suspected. In the Gospels the Romans are barely mentioned, and Josephus, whose detailed, action-packed, lively history of the Jewish War is our only source for the whole period, has been of interest to the Church only because it contains a forged reference to Jesus as Messiah. Jews, on the other hand, have traditionally shrugged Josephus aside as a traitor, and single out the destruction of the Temple as the only episode worth remembering.

The result of all this has been that the Jewish War, studied chiefly by scholars with parochial interests, has had no impact whatever on popular consciousness, Jewish or Christian.

The Jewish catastrophe of 70 had fateful consequences. By obliterating the Jewish core of messianism it cleared the way for the popularization of the quietist, transcendental, and mystical features of Saul's ideas, which could now be aimed without hindrance at the pagans who had become their only target.

Thus the baffling enigma posed by the dense obscurity overhanging the two crucial decades (roughly 60–80 C.E.) is illuminated by the contrast between the Letters written by Saul, a real individual, and the anonymous compilations in the Gospels that came into being one by one after the destruction of the Jewish state and the Temple in 70.

This contrast enables us to see graphically displayed a profound, inexplicable, and of course camouflaged disjointing between the official version of Christian origins and the realistic glimpses tantalizingly suggested by Saul's urgent, passionate, real-life struggle, and by the nuggets of historical actuality embedded in the Gospels themselves.

From this point of view the indifference of both Church historians and academic scholars to the fate of the Jesist coterie in Jerusalem, headed, after all, by Jesus' brother, is bewildering. If the Mother Church ever existed as a Christian institution its total silence is incomprehensible. If its leaders had ever had anything self-aware to say, it would have been easy and natural for whatever it was to be circulated throughout the far-flung Jewish Diaspora. It is obvious that the very concept of this Mother Church, as well as the phrase itself, is profoundly misleading.

Around the middle of the fifties, that is, the time of the riot occasioned by Saul on the Temple premises, it is possible to infer a crisis in the history of the Jewish state and hence within the coterie of the Jerusalem Jesists. From then on all remains blank. We are thrown back on the evolution of the Zealot crisis that erupted in the Roman War of 66–70, and then, as the Gospels, the earliest documents after Saul of the new sect, began to be assembled, beginning with Mark, we can once again see the beginning of a continuity, in which, however, the first phase in the evolution of the new faith—the lives of Jesus, John the Baptist, Upright Jacob, and Saul himself—is twisted to conform with the later tradition embodied in Mark, Matthew, Luke, Acts, and John.

For the author of Mark, the problem, as indicated, was simple.

To nullify any identification of Jesus with the Zealots whose agitation had launched the war of 66–70, he had to exculpate him from the charge of being an activist in general and an enemy of Rome in particular. To do this he had to denature the Kingdom of God—to depoliticize it by twisting its undeniable association with Jesus out of its sociopolitical background and by giving it an elusive, other-worldly meaning. The corollary of this was to slide past the attack on the Temple and the resulting trial of Jesus for sedition.

It was the convergence of two concerns that led to the apologetic distortion of the historical account in the Synoptic Gospels. One concern was to stress the transcendentalization of Jesus that had been going on in the Jewish Diaspora side by side with the initial tradition of Jesus the Messiah and his glorious return as bringer of the Kingdom of God. The other concern, desperately urgent because of the bitterness surrounding a war, was to free the Jesist congregations in the Roman Empire from the stigma of the Zealots.

On the other hand, since there was no way of twisting the basic facts out of shape, i.e., the indictment and execution of Jesus as "King of the Jews" by a Roman official, it was necessary to create a narrative structure that, while accommodating the irrefragable fact of Jesus' execution, plausibly explained it away.

This was by no means due to hypocrisy. We have seen how, in the Diaspora, under the primary influence of Saul, Jesus the Messiah had been escalated into Lord of the Universe, Son of God, and Savior of Mankind. Psychologically, indeed, the same impulse that divorced the real-life Jesus from his historical background was parallel to the original impulse in the psyches of Diaspora Jews like Saul that made them, too, transcendentalize all traditional Jewish national ideas while remaining convinced that that itself represented the realization of a Jewish idea.

Nevertheless it is obvious that the mere fact that what Jesus was announcing was the Kingdom of God—i.e., a world transformation in which the pagan powers, preeminently Rome, were to be destroyed—together with his execution by the Romans for sedition, irresistibly brings to mind the Kingdom of God agitation that had dominated life in Palestine from the installation of direct Roman administration in 6 C.E. until it brought about the Roman-Jewish War in 66, and even later flared up in the abortive Bar Kochba revolt in 132–135.

It is evident, in short, that any discussion of Jesus' career, even if limited to the Gospels alone, will bring us face to face with the Zealots. These diehards, capable of swinging the bulk of the Jewish population of Palestine into the desperate rebellion against Rome, represented the culmination of a mood that had been intensifying for a long time.

And we know that with certainty through the histories of Flavius Josephus, our only real source for the study of the long-drawn out turmoil leading up to the Roman-Jewish war. His histories not only are indispensable for an account of Jewish politics for the generations preceding the war, but fill in the background obliterated largely, though not wholly, by the Gospels.

An aristocratic priest, Josephus was a commander in the war. After defecting to the Romans he became an outstanding propagandist of the Flavian dynasty that came out of it victorious. The Church Fathers took over the texts of Josephus's works very early on—he died at the end of the first century—because his was the *only* account covering this densely packed epoch and because it served as vehicle for a very early forgery designed to make Josephus a "witness" to the supernatural status of Jesus, a forgery whose blatancy, while obvious in any dispassionate examination, was not appreciated until the sixteenth century.

Yet Josephus has become a special subject. Specialists concentrate on the fine points called for by each one's speciality. Thus, by segregating

Josephus's chronicles within a special area of biased, though recondite scholarship, and by projecting its own version of events as exclusively authoritative, Church tradition insulated the whole era against empirical inquiries. At the same time, Josephus's writings were spurned by "official" Jewish tradition, even though that had long since turned against the "forcers of the end" as Josephus himself had. His renegade image overshadowed his acceptably negative view of the Zealots.

Josephus's account is packed with action and personalities; it conveys unmistakably the throb of life in Palestine for the generations preceding the outbreak of the Roman-Jewish war. It is steeped in blood; murders, revolts, cruelty, rapacity, cataclysms of all kinds are intertwined. Grinding oppression on the part of the Romans, desperate uprisings on the part of the Jewish Kingdom of God activists, against a background of well-nigh total corruption, ferocity, and deceit, are routine. His descriptions provide a blanket contrast with the eerie calm of the Gospels.

Josephus's account, dense with real-life detail and vivid characterizations that articulate a long-drawn-out process of alienation leading to a last-ditch insurrection, fills in the background of the Zealot agitation.

He has, to be sure, a bias of his own. He comprehensively vilifies the Zealot movement in all its variations, partly in the conviction, no doubt sincere, that the Kingdom of God activists were destroying Jewry and that God himself had favored the Romans by giving them victory, and partly, of course, because he was making propaganda on behalf of his Roman patrons.

Even more serious, he plainly minimizes their importance. It is evident from the balance and thrust of his narrative that the agitation capable of launching the masses of the population against the Roman Empire must have involved huge numbers of people, yet Josephus, while vilifying and denigrating the activists, says as little about them as possible. He emphasizes, in contrast, the behavior of the Roman procurators, personal intrigues, acts of individual heroism, etc.

Nevertheless, the texture of his chronicles is so close-knit that the broad outlines of the Zealot agitation, beginning with Judah the Galilean's initiative in 6 C.E., are unmistakable. It is easy to discount Josephus's bias. When he refers to "thieves" and "brigands" as being tortured to death for refusing to call Caesar lord, we are bound to conclude that they could not, after all, have been mere thieves and brigands.

On the other hand, he says nothing whatever about Jesus (aside from the forged paragraph mentioned above). He does mention John the Baptist, innocuously, and also Upright Jacob, in a brief, equally innocuous passage that by mentioning Jesus as Messiah without explanation implies a previous mention in some deleted passage.

But for the fleshing out of life in Palestine around this time and for the study of the earliest phase of the belief in Jesus, Josephus is priceless. His Chronicle creates a broader, deeper, and more ramified framework for judging the historical material in Saul's Letters, the Gospels, and the Acts of the Apostles.

If we compare Josephus's treatment of the Zealot movement with the treatment given by the Gospels, especially Mark, to the complex of ideas, personalities, and events involved in the Kingdom of God movement, we see a striking parallel. Both, for substantially the same reasons, ignore the true content of the whole movement. Josephus describes the Kingdom of God activists in such a way as to downgrade their ideological, idealistic concerns; the Gospels wholly disregard their political aims, too.

Most illustrative of this negative attitude of the Gospels is no doubt Jesus' complete silence about the Zealots. The Gospel writers, intent on whitewashing the Romans and dissociating the nascent sect from any connection with the Kingdom of God activists who after harassing the Romans for so many decades had brought about the ferocious war of 66–70, would surely have found it very convenient to set down Jesus' denunciation of the architects of the catastrophe, if he had ever made any.

In Rome, especially (where Mark was written during or shortly after the war), some negative remarks attributed to Jesus would have eased the embarrassment of his followers. But since the author or authors of Mark did not forge anything, they were obliged to disregard the subject altogether; this is all the more striking since they did find, in the reminiscences they had at hand, echoes of Jesus' opinions about real people (Pharisees, Herodians, even, occasionally, Sadduccees).

Taken together, however, both Josephus and the Gospels enable us to divine the presence of a turbulent, grandiose movement capacious enough to bring the Jewry of Palestine to destruction during the Roman-Jewish War. Both accounts, accordingly, radically contrasting with each other in all respects, confirm, through this same negative attitude, the existence of a vanished movement that in the desert of our documentation can be pieced together only through deduction.

Thus the basic problem in assessing the official tradition arising out of the Gospels is not merely the scantiness of the historical material. The missing evidence is actually replaced by the tradition.

The Gospels are accordingly *tendentious*; much has been disregarded, omitted, or distorted, not through a desire to falsify, but because the faith in the incarnation had become the perspective in which the past was recalled. And this shift in perspective naturally produced a corresponding forgetfulness.

Efforts were evidently made, as those who had been in contact with Jesus' milieu began to die off, to set down reminiscences, not for the sake of the information itself but as a way of fleshing out the earthly background of the glorified risen one. From the skimpiness of these scraps we can see both how meager the surviving information was and how a different reality peeps out from between the disharmonious fragments that were later harmonized—more or less.

Because these reminiscences were focused through a much later point of view, and at the same time handled with reverence, many fragments were dislocated, becoming unintelligible in a naive reading. Some parables, for instance, referred more or less clearly to an early view of the Kingdom of God; other material had evidently lost its anchorage in real life, so that some parables remain enigmatic (since a parable is devised to clarify something obscure, a parable that is itself obscure must be explained as a displacement of one kind or another).

In the nature of things revered relics could not be tampered with; what happened, in the event, was that a framework arising organically out of the new perspective of Jesus as Son of God and the Savior of the World integrated, up to a point, the mass of fragments and gave them meaning—the meaning, in short, of that new perspective.

If the Gospels had been fabricated, after all, there would be no way of knowing anything whatever about the career of Jesus the man. If we recall the sweeping powers assumed by the Church when Christianity became a state institution under Constantine the Great in the first quarter of the fourth century, and the severity of the censorship he authorized, which after him, from the fifth century on, was applied with energy, the survival of the few scraps of information we have is remarkable. We owe such scraps essentially to an indifference to mundane history and to the piety that forbade tampering with traditional texts. This comprehensive bias certainly helps explain the absence of explicit written references to the insurrection led by Jesus, which from the surviving fragments, and from the very nature of the enterprise, were evidently massive.

Some principle for distinguishing between grades of evidence is indispensable. It seems sensible to me to take as a starting point the global transformation of perspective I have mentioned, i.e., the germination of the belief in the vision of the risen Jesus, which intervened between the events and their chroniclers.

I mentioned a "cardinal criterion" above. Anything in the traditional texts that conflicts with that global transformation of perspective is likely to be historically accurate. This would make it possible to segregate those texts countering the prevailing tendency in the Gospels and elsewhere to exalt Jesus, preach his universality, and emphasize his uniqueness.

We have already seen that very soon after the execution of Jesus and until the Roman-Jewish War, the predominant attitude among the believers in the vision was that of the Jerusalem coterie, and that, at the same time, a contrary tendency—against the Torah and toward the escalation of Jesus as Lord of the Universe—had already made itself felt even in Jerusalem, when the so-called Hellenists, epitomized by the name of Stephen, were expelled. Saul himself, after attacking the new sect, as he himself says, was then converted and began to express a point of view he shared with some unknown predecessors. Indeed, Saul's own hostility toward the Jesists is doubtless to be explained as due to the anti-Torah views of such Hellenists, since before his conversion Saul had devoted his passion, as it seems, to the defense of the Torah, and only afterwards went to the opposite extreme.

In the discussion of Saul, we saw that his views were necessarily overshadowed and repressed by the Jesists of Jerusalem, in control of the Temple. We have seen that his audience was inevitably composed both of Jews and of converts to Judaism, both full and partial. His view of the Kingdom of God, which he also, like Jesus and John the Baptist, considered urgently imminent as long as he lived, and which was ultimately to triumph and incidentally to serve as matrix for a new religion he could never have foreseen, was intensely Jewish in its very conception; but it was nevertheless grounded in a nonnational, i.e., universal idea.

Saul, in his skimpy comments on Jesus the man, discarded the parochial, or at least national aspect of the Kingdom of God as conceived of by Jesus and John the Baptist, and by not mentioning Rome as oppressor and by omitting, accordingly, the specific occasion for Jesus' execution, enabled his own version of the Kingdom of God to survive long enough to supply the impetus for a new religion.

Thus the abundance of parochial Jewish references we have already seen was, despite Saul's own Jewishness, entirely superseded in his grandiose, ethereal, but still palpably real (to him) Kingdom of God. Saul's ideas won out, in short, against the nation-bound ideas of the Jesists in Jerusalem and no doubt elsewhere, and also against the views of his rivals, whoever they were (chapter 11).

This has been obscured, as I have noted above, by the fact that though Saul's Letters were written long before the Gospels, they describe a situation that came into being substantially *after* all the events of Jesus' lifetime.

We have already seen the specifically Jewish, indeed Zealot background of Jesus and John the Baptist, the assault on the Temple, and Saul's various rivals, muted, but not eliminated from the traditional texts.

It is evident, from even a cursory glance at the traditional texts, that many nuggets of real-life history have been tucked into a framework unconsciously pieced together to accommodate a much later situation. And the historical rationale for this is obvious. On the face of it, it must have been a source of acute embarrassment for believers living in Rome during the years preceding the Zealot war against Rome that their own leader, Jesus of Nazareth, had himself been executed only a few decades earlier for just the same reason—sedition. It was vital for them to dissociate themselves somehow from the opprobrium naturally clinging to followers of an enemy of Rome at a time when Rome was engaged in a ferocious struggle against Kingdom of God activists.

It was this crisis in the Roman Jesist community, indeed, that led to the composition of Mark, the first Gospel, whose author solved the problem more than adequately. He created a model, in fact, that still enthralls the hundreds of millions of people indoctrinated by the Gospels and by the vast cultural heritage they underlie.

We have already seen that in the Palestine of Jesus' day the statement "Pay Caesar what is due to Caesar, and God what is due to God" (Mk 12:13–17), would be taken by any Kingdom of God agitator in a real-life situation as self-evidently insurrectionist. To such an agitator it went without saying that the Holy Land was God's alone and no pagans could profit from it, and in particular that the taxation imposed in 6 C.E. was an outrage; but Mark places it in a context in which it sounds unmistakably as though Jesus were *endorsing* the tribute to Rome. He uses the phrase as Jesus' response to a trap set for him by the "Pharisees and the Herodians." It was natural for the Romans to expect a subject people to pay tribute, just as it was natural for a Kingdom of God agitator to refuse to pay tribute. By transposing the context of the question, accordingly, the architect of the Markan theme extracted its political taint, as it were, and soothed his readers among the Jesists in Rome as the Zealot war erupted.

In general, Mark depicts the Jewish authorities as hostile to Jesus from the outset: "Pharisees" plot with "Herodians" (the pro-Roman Jews headed by sons of Herod the Great and ruling Galilee at the time) against Jesus (even though it is the high priests who finally engineer the crucifixion [Mk 15:10–11]).

By the time the Gospels were established the high priests had vanished with the Temple cult, while the Pharisaic tradition was sustained by the rabbis who were now the chief opposition to the new sect. Thus, for the Gospel writers, the word "Pharisees" stood for the Jewish authorities in a comprehensive, absolute sense. Jesus in turn vilifies all Jewish authorities as cultically, legally, and spiritually sterile, even evil.

The hostility attributed to the Jewish authorities is extended to the Jewish people as a whole, who fail to perceive that someone they are familiar with since childhood is meritorious; hence Jesus' comment that "a prophet is without honor in his own country, and among his own people, and in his own house" (6:1–6); the Jewish people as such are condemned for ritualism (7:6–8) and, to cap the process, the Jewish mob actually calls for his death and derides him (15:11ff., 29–30).

Moreover, Jesus is described as cutting himself off from his kinship not only with his people, but with his own family:

> And his mother and his brothers came; and standing outside they sent to him. Jesus replied: "Who are my mother and my brothers? Whoever does the will of God is my brother, and my sister, and my mother."
> (3:31–5)

Mark tells us, in short, that mere biology is meaningless; the Roman Jesists can be as close to Jesus as his own family. If we recall the importance of the dynastic factor in the emergence of Upright Jacob in the Jerusalem coterie before the Roman-Jewish War, we discern a polemical thrust at Jesus' family at the time the Gospel was set down.

Hence, when the preeminence of Jesus' family in the Jerusalem coterie was made obsolete by its extinction together with the Temple, it was possible to defy the vanished authority and virtuously separate the Roman Jesists from it.

Thus, the family of Jesus is presented as having thought him out of his mind, to begin with, and as explicitly repudiated by him.

This is complemented by the contemptuous description of the apostles, who also constituted, together with Upright Jacob, the core of the Jesist coterie in Jerusalem. They are constantly described as bickering over precedence and rewards (9:34., 10:34–45) and as devoid of Jesus' own remarkable powers (9:6, 10, 18). One betrays him (14:10,11, 20,21,43–5); on his arrest they all abandon him and flee (14:50). For that matter the leading apostle, Simon the Rock, though acknowledged as the first to see in Jesus the Messiah, is said to "rebuke" Jesus for speaking of his future resurrection and because of that, indeed, is called by Jesus "Satan." On top of that there is an account of Simon the Rock's unappetizing denial of any acquaintance with Jesus. Not only is it excessively long in such a short document, but it is negative through and through.

The counterposition of these two attitudes—that Simon the Rock recognized Jesus as Messiah but denied the salvational function of the resurrection—is no more than a way of indicating that the Jerusalem group headed by Upright Jacob did not believe in Jesus except as the Jewish Messiah, that his role as Lord of the Universe, of Divine Savior of Mankind, meant nothing to them. In short, the viewpoint of Paul is put forth in Mark in such a way as to take advantage of the Jewish debacle.

The ground plan of Mark goes far beyond details; it has a profound apologetic aim. While bound to accept the historic fact that the Roman indictment was followed by a Roman execution, Mark tells us that Pilate was forced by the Jews to do what they wanted. In the narration this has already been built up—"planted," in literary parlance—by clear-cut suggestions of a Jewish conspiracy to destroy Jesus.

The assignment of an executive role to the Jewish authorities in explaining away the Roman indictment and execution of Jesus in and of itself expresses the anti-Jewish tendency of Mark's ground plan.

It is more than likely, of course, that the Kingdom of God agitation engaged in by Jesus would have set him against the Jewish aristocracy as well as the Romans, but there was no need at all for them to be involved in an actual trial. Indeed, it is hard to see why the Romans had any need for a trial either. Regardless of the importance of Jesus' religious/political agitation, a perfunctory hearing would seem to have been sufficient.

In any case, as we have seen, any number of Kingdom of God agitators, would-be messiahs, and pretenders of all kinds were routinely exterminated by the Romans. There was no need for the Jewish authorities to intervene at all.

Moreover, since the tendency in Mark is in any case to highlight the evil intentions of the Jews, had there been, in fact, any Jewish intervention to undo Jesus it would have been both natural and easy to stress that theme and omit the Roman role altogether.

The fact that the original writer of the ground plan for Mark was obliged, despite his reluctance, to record a vital role for the Romans confirms the matter-of-fact historicity of the Roman charge on the cross itself—"King of the Jews"—and demonstrates the tendentious artificiality of Mark's emphasis on the role of the Jews.

The theme was vital for Mark. To amplify it he enlarges on how Jesus, though of course a Jew, was not appreciated by Jews and how he expressly denied the importance of any kinship.

From the outset, the reader is informed that Jesus did not follow the tradition represented by the "scribes"; he, in contrast, "has authority" (Mk 1:22). Jesus, by absolving the sins of a paralytic he has just healed, forces the scribes to charge him with blasphemy (2:6–7). Then he attacks the "scribes of the Pharisees" for their objections to his eating with "tax collectors and sinners," and, in explaining that his disciples do not fast like "John [the Baptist's] disciples and the disciples of the Pharisees," he uses a metaphor—the futility of using new cloth to repair an old garment or of putting new wine into old wineskins— evidently intended to drive home the point of Judaism's obsolescence.

This metaphor would have had compelling force precisely in the wake of the destruction of the Temple, *and not before*. It gives lapidary cogency to what has now become a historic fact; the Roman Jesists, with a large admixture of converts and semiconverts, have found the solution to a problem that, as we know from the evolution of Saul's ideas, must have begun to weigh on them beforehand, i.e., the authority of the Torah and of Jewish traditions in general.

This has little to do with the much later theory of the organized Church. In that generation, after the belief in the incarnation had sprung up and with the transcendental concept of the Kingdom of God still alive, what was taken for granted was Jesus as the Son of God, not Jesus as the architect of a new religion.

Of course, it is quite possible that some actual statements of Jesus could be tucked into the evolving cult. In Judaism Jesus seems to have belonged to the lenient, nonliteral school of Hillel, as against the rigorous school of Shammai; Saul considered Jesus' hostility to divorce binding, to be sure, yet Jesus' indulgent view of adultery—"let him who is without sin cast the first stone"—might seem to strike a milder note. This may indicate that he disregarded some aspects of the Torah, and that he did, indeed, speak as one having "authority," unlike the "scribes."

But since there is no record of Jesus having actually formulated a "creed," it is obvious that the basic documents in the New Testament were shaped only much later into a vehicle for a systematic body of beliefs. In the era of the Gospels writers and editors that still lay in the future.

The fundamental theme of Mark can be tersely summarized: the Jews, both leaders and masses, are responsible for Jesus' death; his immediate family thought him crazy; and his apostles, having misunderstood him, also abandoned him.

Jesus himself provides the counterpoint to this series of negatives; he rejects those who reject him, emphasizes the importance of worshipping God through him in contrast with blood-relationships, and denounces the chauvinistic limitations of Simon the Rock, his preeminent follower. In short, Mark, while depicting Jesus in a Jewish environment, has extracted him from it and glorified him far beyond it.

There may be a further complication in Mark's treatment of Jesus' Jewish background. If, as seems likely, the agitation linked to Jesus, which must be deduced from the apologetic harmonization of the texts, was the true beginning of the upheaval foreshadowed by Judah the Galilean's more restricted rebellion, and if it was Jesus' movement that triggered the rapid, explosive concentration of insurrectionary forces in Palestine from Pontius Pilate on, the possibility of Jesus' royal status and more particularly of his importance in the politics of the era cannot be dismissed.

If we recall Saul's forthright, though casual statement, in a context of no spiritual or intellectual significance for him, that Jesus was a descendant of King David, and the fact that Jesus was crucified as King of the Jews—there is no evidence that any of the countless thousands of Kingdom of God activists crucified by the Romans were attributed a similar status—it seems reasonable to suppose that the rebellion he led was exceptionally important.

It is certainly a monumental fact that an imperial edict condemning all "Davidides" to death on sight was still current two generations after Jesus' insurrection. Jesus' action must have been considered particularly important if the members of his immediate family, specifically, were still being hunted by the Roman police in the reign of Domitian (see pages 131–32).

Nor should still another element be forgotten. There are indications in the Gospels (Mt 19:23–4) that Jesus might have thought the rich were disadvantaged vis-à-vis the Kingdom of God.

We know from Josephus that some of the Zealots were levellers (the reason for burning the ledgers containing debtors' receipts). We also know that of the two main leaders of the Jewish revolt of 66–70 one, Simeon Bar-Giora, was a leveller, while the other, John of Gush Halav (John Gischala), had conventional views on property, etc. Bar-Giora was executed, John of Gush Halav merely imprisoned for a time. This , if it is relevant to Jesus' seeming prejudice against the rich, might be a further reason for the Romans to look on his enterprise with particular hostility.

Mark, too, in its determination to slight the element of Jesus' lineage as part of its downgrading of the whole of Jesus' Jewish background, disregarded the down-to-earth, political sense natural to the times. Only the emblematic, honorific element survived.

In any event, Mark's detachment of Jesus from his Jewish roots is driven home explicitly in what is, thematically, the crux of the Gospel. After demonstrating how the Jews had failed to understand the divine nature of Jesus, the narrator puts a key statement—"truly, this man was the Son of God"—into the mouth of the Roman centurion directing the crucifixion. (The fact that Mark uses a Latin word, "centurion," where Matthew and Luke use a Greek one, reinforces the impression that Mark was indeed composed in Rome.) Thus the basic idea, perceived beforehand in Mark only by demons (responsible in antiquity for the supernatural knowledge ascribed to madmen), is expressed by a normal human being, that is, by a pagan, like perhaps the bulk of the Jesists in Rome.

Though it took varying lengths of time before the World's End idea was wholly extinct, it is plain that by the time Luke was written, some ten years after the destruction of the Temple, the idea had become at least quiescent. It was no longer held seriously. Most important, it was not *felt*.

Thus the general mood has moved definitively away from Saul's state of mind. He wrote because he felt the World's End was imminent despite delay, but by the time this had evolved into the conviction that the delay was no longer a delay but a condition of nature, it was possible, indeed indispensable for something to be written down authoritatively.

Hence, some time after Mark, Luke plus Acts was drafted (parts of both of which were, as it seems, the work of the same hand). Acts is, indeed, our sole source for the earliest period of the new sect. It carries the process of sociopolitical accommodation begun by Mark still further.

The sources embodied in Acts are so fragmentary that no coherent account is possible; still less does it say anything about any individual except Saul himself. There is almost literally no information about anyone mentioned. The individuals are given names, to be sure, and an occasional sentence or two purports to flesh out an inchoate narrative, but there is no way of apprehending motive, character, or activity.

The writings set down in this very early period had the function of defining, that is, establishing the leadership of the new sect; they were a major attempt at organization. And to do so, decades after the destruction of the Temple and two generations after the death of Jesus, it was vital for the leaders to claim a living link between Jesus and themselves.

Accordingly, the newly evolving Church was defined by the twelve apostles, or rather, more accurately, by apostles in the plural. This claim, wedded to the claim, implicit and explicit, that the founding apostles' authority was binding, became the theological principle underpinning the Church.

This principle in and for itself was never to be challenged by the great divisions of the later Church (Catholics, both Roman and Greek Orthodox, and Protestants); the only dispute was to be the manner in which the authority attributed to the apostles was, in fact, binding (the Protestants, of course, accepted the Scriptures alone as binding; the Catholics considered the Church tradition an indispensable complement).

But in fact the apostles were simply part of a theory. In the very beginning there was no such institution as the twelve. The figure itself, reflecting the World's End expectations of the Kingdom of God activists, merely stood for the twelve tribes of Israel. Historically, however, the twelve never played a role of any kind. After their first mention (in late sources) they are never, except for Simon the Rock, mentioned again, even though a major associate of Jesus, Jacob ben-Zavdai, lived for a decade after Jesus' crucifixion and must have been both eminent and active, since he was executed in 43 by Agrippa I.

Most striking of all, in discussing his trips to Jerusalem Saul makes no mention of the twelve whatever; he talks only of the three "pillars," the only ones he confers with. They are obviously the leaders of the Jerusalem coterie. That is, even if there was such a group as the twelve, it was no longer in existence in the middle or perhaps end of the forties (44 or 48). Later on only Upright Jacob, Jesus' brother, is mentioned as leader of the Jerusalem coterie (Acts 32:15f).

It is obvious, then, that the statement that there were apostles is part of the early Church tradition itself. It is the way the tradition substantiates itself.

Though the Church "theory" is very old, it goes back, accordingly, only to the time when there was already a huge gap between the real-life background and an awareness of that gap—that is, about 100, when the Jewish Temple had been extinct for a whole generation and when the Jesists themselves were swiftly being transformed into the first stage of what could now be called "Christians," or perhaps only "Proto-Christians," since although Saul was now accepted and the foundations of the religion accordingly laid, the organization of the Church itself was still rudimentary and uncertain, and a dogma that was to be indispensable—the Trinity—had not yet been thought of, let alone worked out.

But the generation of 100, aware that they were different as it were in essence from the historical Jesus, Simon the Rock, Upright Jacob, and Jacob and John ben-Zavdai, and aware of the gap between them, conceived of themselves as being not the second link in the chain of generations—the gap made that impossible—but the third. i.e., they had to create a link between themselves and the first generation. This was what the concept of the apostles fixed and amplified. It became the "apostolic tradition," as though it were a tradition about a historical situation.

Thus the traditional definition of the "apostolic age" as ending with the deaths of Simon the Rock (Peter), Paul, and probably Upright Jacob (James) rests on the claim that until a few years before 66 reminiscences directly derived from Jesus were still alive. Nevertheless this "living tradition" about Jesus itself consists of assertions made about it by—the tradition.

Hence the Gospels and Acts, while containing particles of historical fact or probability, as I have indicated, no longer reflect the circumstances of Jesus' real life, but the pseudotradition about them embodied in revered documents. The handful of what might have been historic reminiscences, committed to writing as the real-life first generation began to die off, survive merely as fragments embedded in theologically tinctured and slanted texts that began to be assembled as a canon around the middle of the second century.

Even the earliest current of belief in Jesus was already expressed in two different styles. One had to do with the homely tradition of Jesus the Jewish Messiah who had lived in Palestine, had been crucified and seen resurrected at the right hand of God; the second was the visionary Jesus stripped completely of all earthly attributes and embodying a simple principle, to wit, that he had died and been raised again in glory.

Basically the two traditions were to become one, since the tradition about the earthly Jesus, though it underlies what seem to be the facts in the Gospels—sayings, miracles, snippets of statements, etc.—has actually been twisted around as a form of adaption to the disembodied, spiritual, abstract, principled framework of the confessional formula inherited by Saul from his own predecessors very early on. Hence the significance of the seemingly historical framework of the Gospels is in fact found only within the capsule of the confessional formula of the death and resurrection of Jesus Christ. That is, the seemingly factual framework of the Gospels was itself an adaptation of historical or semihistorical fragments about Jesus' life on earth only from the point of view of fleshing out the formula of the confession.

This had little to do with a lapse of time; it was a transformation of view that took place very rapidly. It was already given a sort of schematic representation by Saul. Whereas before his resurrection Jesus was the son of David, i.e., the Jewish Messiah, afterwards he was the Son of God, Lord of the Universe (Rom 1:3–4). Thus the process of transforming historical into theological materials that took place after the destruction of the Temple was the same, writ large, as the transformation already seen at work in Saul's Letters, written before 55.

For Saul, too, a communal repast had already become sacramental. It can be summed up in a single sentence:

> When we bless "the cup of blessing," is it not a means of sharing in the blood of Christ? When we break the bread, is it not a means of sharing in the body of Christ? (1 Cor 10:16)

The transition from the time in which the early Jesists interpreted the Lord's Supper as a Passover meal—a seder—to the time when Christ was himself called a Passover lamb is evident.

Though the factual information in Saul's Letters is peripheral as well as scanty—he was arguing a case, exhorting his audience, justifying his position—it is, to be sure, illuminating. It gives us an insight, for instance, into the authoritative position of Upright Jacob and his possible role in Temple politics just before the Roman-Jewish War. Negatively, too, Saul's

Letters tell us that before the destruction of his Temple Saul was overshadowed by the Jerusalem Jesists. We can also estimate the speed of expansion in the very earliest tradition. When Saul mentions the appearance of the risen Jesus to more than "five hundred brethren" (1 Cor 15:6), it is obvious, even if we accept the figure, that he is referring to a stage some time, though evidently fairly soon after Simon the Rock's vision.

The Jerusalem coterie, as we have seen, did not interfere with the new speculations that under Hellenistic influence began in the Jewish Diaspora after the vision; no doubt they were shapeless, unsystematic. Perhaps such speculations came to the surface in only a few centers, such as Antioch, that were to become important after the extinction of the Jerusalem coterie in the debacle of 70. And it was just this fact that after the debacle was concealed by the instinctive creation of a legendary, mythological fabric to manifest the continuity claimed by all institutions.

The conventional view of theologians today would have it that the anti-Torah, transcendental conception of Jesus held by Saul and Stephen had already struck deep roots throughout the Christian community long before the destruction of the Temple in 70. From that point of view, accordingly, the elimination of the "Mother Church" and all the more so of the Temple and the Jewish state meant nothing—a mere clearing away of the debris long since left behind by the evolving faith.

This conventional view is also the grand theme of Acts—indeed, its purpose. Yet it can hardly be historically valid. We have already seen the evidence of Saul's second-class status, as recorded in his Letters, written years before the destruction of the Temple and long before the evolution of any theological views at all. We have seen his irritation about the contending Gospels he kept colliding with, the hostile attitude of the Jerusalem pillars, the atmosphere of contention and self-justification. The impression left by these striking motifs in Saul's Letters is reinforced negatively, as we have seen, by their physical condition.

Saul does, to be sure, attack "the Jews" for persecuting the Jesists in Judea (1 Thes 2:14–15), but this cannot have been so, since there is no indication that, after the expulsion of the "Hellenists" in the wake of Stephen's execution in the forties, the Jesist coterie was molested at all, up to and during the Roman-Jewish War. This is all the more obvious since the background of Saul's trial under Upright Jacob during his last trip to Jerusalem takes for granted his entire acceptance by Upright Jacob and the Jesist coterie within the Temple milieu. In any case the anti-Jewish remarks in

Thessalonians comprehensively contradict Romans 11. Most scholars doubt Saul's authorship.

Saul died long before the triumph of his ideas. The destruction of the Temple cleared the way for the tendentious slanting of the Gospels, beginning with Mark, away from the real-life career of Jesus, executed by the Romans for sedition, into the Pacific Christ, Lord of the Universe and Savior of Mankind, whose salvational powers were to be mediated to believers via the magical Church.

In one respect proto-Christianity carried on the tradition of Judaism. It was grounded in mundane history as well as in reflections on its meaning. Yet the difference was vital. The incarnation, propped up on two great events, the crucifixion (and its meaning) and the vision of the risen Jesus (and its meaning) were the very core of the new faith.

For this reason the combination into one canon of the pseudohistorical Gospels and Acts of the Apostles and the theological framework provided for them by the surviving Letters of Saul is fundamental for grasping the significance of the factual material so painstakingly camouflaged.

With the destruction of the Temple in 70 Saul's ideas could flower fully. And since, at the same time, the new sect of believers in Jesus was opposed by the Jewish elite—the rabbis who had inherited the Pharisaic tradition—the Gospel writers and editors, whose transcendentalizing tendency dominated their view of history, found it natural to develop limitlessly their hostility to the rabbis and the Jews they represented.

This was all the more tempting since after the destruction of the Temple and the state the Jews were no longer worthwhile targets for conversion; the leaders of the new sect were directing their propaganda at all mankind.

Thus Saul's ideas, originally conceived of as an explanation of what was, for him, a current historical crisis—the hiatus between the installation of the messianic kingdom, hence the Kingdom of God, and the resurrection of Jesus—became, through a systematic and tendentious misunderstanding of the key phrase, the Kingdom of God, the foundation of something undreamed of by Saul or Jesus—a timeless theology.

Saul's views, sincerely conceived of by him as a response to a Jewish problem—how could God delay the installation of his kingdom once he had begun it?—themselves naturally shunted attention away from the down-to-earth background of the agitation against Rome. His views, further misunderstood as the Kingdom of God idea shriveled rapidly after the debacle of 70, became a mere spiritual metaphor by the middle of the next century, after the debacle of the Bar Kochba revolt in 132–135.

This whole process, coinciding with the gap in Jewish historiography, created a fundamental hiatus in Jewish history, and this hiatus was itself bridged over on the level of secular as well as religious history by a vast edifice—the edifice of Christian mythology.

Jewish historians, accordingly, like historians in general, hamstrung by a dearth of documentation and prejudiced by the radical distaste for the Kingdom of God activists (if only because their failure demonstrated the loss of God's favor) have perforce slid by the real import of the Kingdom of God movement.

This constitutes, of course, a remarkable irony. Jewish historiography has lost the century that saw the transformation of the Jews into a Diaspora people; i.e., Jewish self-consciousness lacks a real-life anchor for its own condition.

Although the Jewish debacle of 70 did not eliminate the Jewish population of Palestine, the bloodletting was vast; also, huge numbers were sold off into slavery abroad. And with the destruction of the Temple the scattered Diasporas, long a feature of Jewish life, no longer had a center. The abortive Bar Kochba revolt two generations later, by putting the seal on the territorial phase of Jewish history, established the Jews as the people they have since remained.

Just as Christian mythology obliterated its own real-life background, so in Jewish consciousness, during the long-drawn-out Diaspora, the debacle of 70 led organically to a stressing of religion—in any case, to be sure, the leitmotif of the very genesis of the Jews as a people. Thus the catastrophe of 70 was fitted into just that strand of Jewish historiography anchored in the contemplation of God's will in history.

Because of this the secular components of the catastrophe of 70 have been perceived through a religious prism; in the religious consciousness of Jews the destruction of the Temple wholly overshadows the destruction of the state itself, or rather, the dual destruction is conflated to constitute the identical religious disaster.

This surely accounts for the fact that conventional Jewish historiography does not make much of what was, on the face of it, a remarkable gap in national evolution—from a people with a center, at least, rooted in a land of its own to the special case of a people with no territorial anchor surviving through portable documents.

It is true that the antiquity of the Jews makes it easy to tuck the debacle of 70 into the endless succession of triumphs and calamities stretching from the captivity in Egypt through the glory of the monarchies into the complexities generated by the triumph of Hellenism in the ancient world, when the Jews, after a brilliant but brief resumption of sovereignty under the Maccabees, began to collide with the Roman Empire in the chain of setbacks leading from Pompey's conquest of Jerusalem in 63 B.C.E. down to the penultimate, but decisive defeat by the Romans a century later.

Nevertheless the extinction of the Jewish center in 70 was unique. It was qualitatively different from the Babylonian Captivity six centuries before, which merely relocated the upper classes for a short time. It would be reasonable to expect Jewish historians to highlight the radical turning point in Jewish history constituted by the obliteration of the territorial foundation of Jewish life and its replacement through institutions shaped and implemented by abstract ideas.

The powerful tradition of explaining the debacle of 70, like all debacles, as a divine punishment, meant that Jewish historians were trapped, so to speak, by the amputation of the secular background of the Exile into believing the mythology encasing the New Testament.

The failure to appreciate the qualitative uniqueness of this caesura in Jewish history, the radical turning point that made the Diaspora coextensive with Jewish national existence for almost two millennia, is due to the fact that Jewish historians, too, have accepted the Christian view of the origins of Christianity.

To summarize, the Kingdom of God activists, of whom Jesus was one, kept Palestine churned up for two generations. Their agitation culminated in the massive insurrection that destroyed the Temple and Jerusalem in 70 C.E. Christianity at its inception was a by-product of messianist ardor. The destruction of the Temple and the state removed the barrier to the spread of a new faith elaborated by Hellenistic ideas from a messianist germ.

In short, the grand arch of Christian doctrine spans two deficits: the refusal to accept the recollection of the Kingdom of God in its first phase—Jesus' expectation of an immediate transformation of the natural world, destroying the pagan powers, and restoring the fortunes of the Jews—and Saul's conviction of an imminent installation of an ethereal, but somehow real-life world pruned of the pro-Jewish and anti-Roman motifs, guaranteed by the resurrection of Jesus.

The emotional need for the Kingdom of God, transposed to a Hellenistic milieu, was absorbed, simplified, magnified, and elevated through the deification of the man who had announced the Kingdom. With the deification of Jesus the Kingdom of God could be dropped altogether.

The documents that have come down to us were organized through the convergence of two tendencies. The need for the nascent movement of faith in Jesus to gloss over the real-life reasons for his crucifixion as a rebel against Rome and the parallel rejection, though for different reasons, by authoritative Jewish opinion of the Kingdom of God as a formula for political action.

The warping of perspective inherent in our sources can scarcely be exaggerated. Because of the very fact that Christian tradition was itself fabricated by biased documents, the conventional view today accepts without question a transcendental interpretation of Christian origins, an interpretation that, overshadowed at first by the historical expectations of the first Jesist coterie, later swept the field after the Jewish debacle in 70 and was later amplified, magnified, ramified, and consolidated precisely as the institutional expression of the triumphant tendency.

This vacuum in the vast bulk of the literature on Christian origins is all the more disturbing since the key to a realistic treatment of the Gospels was indicated some two centuries ago at the very inception of the Higher Criticism in Germany.

Hermann Reimarus, the first scholar to scrutinize the Gospels realistically, thought it obvious that Jesus was, quite simply, executed by the Romans for sedition—sedition inevitably arising out of the activist interpretation of the Kingdom of God. But for generations after Reimarus this simple, commonsense explanation of Jesus' death was ignored; the countless biographies of Jesus that proliferated through the nineteenth and twentieth centuries reverted to the apologetic claim that while Jesus was indeed executed as a rebel the execution was based on a mere misunderstanding.

Nevertheless, the simple explanation of Jesus' execution is also the correct one; it is, indeed, the very obviousness of this fact, as we have seen, that explains why the Gospels were composed to begin with. The political and emotional need to detach Jesus from his immediate roots led to the obliteration of the Kingdom of God movement and, accordingly, to the genesis of Christian mythology.

That obliteration, which radically warped the framework of the scanty documents that have survived in the New Testament, has imposed itself even on secular historians, who might have been expected to pierce the veil created by the combination of bias in the compilers and flimsiness in the documents. It has led to a permanent crippling of scholarship. It is more or less taken for granted that the origin of Christianity and the Jewish debacle in the revolt against Rome, despite their intimate symbiosis in the Kingdom of God agitation of the first century, are unrelated.

This scholarly bias was reinforced, negatively, by the curious absence of any Jewish historiography for several centuries, from the last book of the Hebrew Scriptures (Daniel, around 165 B.C.E.) to the fixing of the Talmud centuries later. And since the Roman writers themselves said practically nothing about the beginnings of Christianity, there was nothing from any other source to fill the vacuum left by the neglect of the real-life circumstances of the earliest agitation. The result has been that the secular history of the first century, the fundamental era in the establishment of the modern world, has been veiled for almost two thousand years.

The reluctance to grasp the true dynamics of the history underlying the present skimpiness and confusion of our traditional documents is surely the reason for the radical failure of the Higher Criticism of the New Testament. Scholarship, confined to documents inherently and unconsciously tendentious, necessarily arrived at the unhistorical conclusions entailed by the unhistorical premises. The historical puzzles created by the apologetics, both theological and practical, that generated the New Testament as a whole, and in particular the Gospels and the Acts of the Apostles, cannot be solved without incisive analysis.

Because of this, even the most industrious probing of the only texts expressly relevant to Jesus—the Gospels, the Acts, Saul's Letters—gives us no real information about Jesus the man. After almost two centuries of the most painstaking, intense study by scores of thousands of able, conscientious scholars, the amount of information refined out of the sources can be contained in a few lines.

There is no assurance of the most primitive facts about Jesus the man; the significance of the word "Nazarene," the date and place of his birth, his parents, his family, his milieu. All such information is summed up in a disconcertingly barren statement. In the words of Charles Guignebert, Jesus was "born somewhere in Galilee in the time of Emperor Augustus, in a modest family that aside from him numbered a good half-dozen children."[1]

Moreover, the paucity of information about the background and personality of Jesus the man is reinforced, as it were, by the utter absence of any indication of original teaching. Whatever Jesus thought about religion, and in particular about Judaism, his own ideas failed to survive his death. He could neither have foreseen nor desired the state of affairs that replaced the Kingdom of God he was inspired by, and even though the genetic relationship between himself and Christianity is evident, it can only be in the narrow sense that the new religion coagulated through speculations around the meaning of his death.

This gap between the historical circumstances of Jesus' life and the later faith in his resurrection and what it meant entailed the incapacity of documentation to bridge that gap. The evolution of faith made it impossible for the faithful even to conceive of a historical situation that would contradict their faith; even the primordial fact of the Crucifixion required the transformation into metaphor of the deep meaning that constituted the faith. The crucifixion—summed up in Saul's celebrated aphorism: "I preach Christ crucified, to the Jews a scandal, to the pagans a folly"—is, indeed, the model for all such transformations.

But what was understandable for the believers of the first and second centuries is bewildering in scholars of the nineteenth and twentieth. Generations of Higher Critics have stubbornly disregarded the fact staring at them from out of the desert of the documentation—the causal connection between Jesus' initial emergence as a herald of the Kingdom of God and his execution by the Romans as an insurrectionist. They have accepted as plausible what was a mere apologia on the part of the believers of the first phase of the evolving faith.

Scholars have in fact failed to see the cardinal element in the history of the germination of Christianity—that it was the history of a transformation. The faith having, let us say, germinated, was then shaped, absorbing in the process the cardinal events and the various views and ideas felt to be important by the earliest founders of what became the Church.

Thus the Higher Criticism, which has generated hundreds of thousands of books analyzing the texts of the Gospels and the New Testament generally, the parallels, echoes, repetitions, nuances, duplications, enveloping the sparse account of Jesus' life and Saul's ideas, has inevitably bypassed the prime factor in the origin of the new sect—the Kingdom of God agitation that alone can explain it.

But once it is accepted that the thought of founding a new religion never even crossed Jesus' mind, it becomes obvious that Christianity derives not from anything Jesus did, but from what happened after his death. Thus, it was after his death that the germination and efflorescence of a new religion took place, rooted in the primordial vision of Jesus resurrected and glorified.

This in itself is simply another way of repeating Saul's aphorism. If Jesus was not resurrected the faith was in vain. In the most literal sense, it was the vision of Jesus resurrected that launched the process culminating in Christianity.

But if this is so, it means that the entire vast library of literature on Christian origins, to the extent that it struggled to fling a bridge from the religion itself to the figure of its putative founder, was condemned to sterility.

And the labor underlying that literature! The hundreds of thousands of books, all dissecting the Gospels, the Acts, Saul's Letters, sentence by sentence, crystallizing out of this meager source material layers, sublayers, parentheses, quotations, minutely scrutinizing the texts, all on the theory that if you could grasp the genesis of the texts you would somehow know more about Jesus. This was so even for critics who at the same time accepted the fact that Jesus had originated nothing in the religion that sprang up over his dead body.

Yet the lesson to be drawn from this divorce between the living Jesus and the later religion is clear. Although it was Jesus who was taken as the object of the evolving religion from its earliest phase on, his own emergence as a figure in Israel must be explained against the background of the Kingdom of God agitation whose echo, faint and distorted, has survived in the documents incorporated in the new religion's early phase.

Jesus, accordingly, may be inserted in the series of Kingdom of God agitators spanning the period between 6 and the outbreak of the anti-Roman insurrection of 66–70. Once that is understood, and the aims of the Kingdom of God agitators are known, we shall be in a position to understand how it was that a Kingdom of God visionary, whose followers loved him after death, could be plucked from the oblivion normally the lot of failures in this world and transformed, over the space of a generation or two, into the object of an entirely unforeseen cult.

The ideas kindled by the vision of a risen Jesus, in short, served as a pivot for switching one Kingdom of God agitator out of the fate that befell all other such agitators and transforming his memory, seen now in celestial perspective, into an element of a new religion for which it was, while historically irrelevant, metaphysically indispensable for the purpose of anchoring in the real world the staggering uniqueness of the incarnation.

If the rationale of the church is summed up in the phrase ascribed to the risen Jesus—"I am with you always, until the World's End"—and if its institutional continuity is guaranteed by the passage aimed at Doubting Thomas—"Blessed are those who have not seen [the risen Jesus' wounds] and yet believe" (Jn 20:29)—we see how essential it was for Christian theology from the very beginning to wrench both Jesus and the Kingdom of God out of their historical matrix.

Theology itself was a product of history. Its need to rationalize, on its own terms, the paramount events—the execution of Jesus, its putative founder, as King of the Jews, and the failure of the Kingdom of God to materialize—created an imaginary history whose web of myth smothered the real-life history of real people.

What is, perhaps, astonishing is the durability of that imaginary history. Christianity is the only major religion whose essence is substantiated by supernatural claims made on behalf of a historic individual—claims, moreover, expressed in actual documents. One might have thought, once the documents were scrutinized, that the real-life background of the supernatural claims would eventually edge aside or at least modify the claims themselves. Yet to this day the tradition has withstood the counterweight of probability, of rank impossibility, of pervasive discrepancies, of manifest contradictions.

The hundreds of millions of Protestants—recently joined by Catholics, now also allowed to read the Bible freely—who even in childhood read and study the New Testament, including the Gospels, which constantly hint at real-life situations, look—and see nothing. Huge motion pictures have been made depicting, in a naturalistic setting, the supposed events of Jesus' life in Roman Palestine. These motion pictures, conscientiously constructed with the guidance of sincere experts, are so foolish when held up against their real-life background in the vividness called for by naturalism that one might well think the insulating walls of traditional perception would surely be pierced.

They seem to elicit no reflection. Audiences are so conditioned by the theological interpretation of the historic setting that the setting itself is apprehended dimly or not at all; the mythology is potent enough to plaster over all the fissures between itself and real-life plausibility.

Nor has the vast literature on Christian origins had much influence on the broad public. By and large the Higher Critics, after two centuries of analysis, have become, in effect, a vast bureaucracy processing its own materials. Even those critics who have shredded the traditional account of Christian origins have failed to fill in the empirical void left behind. No doubt this, too, is due to a reluctance to venture into conjecture, to abandon the haven of documentation even when the documentation can be shown to be self-annihilating. Thus the Higher Criticism, in Albert Schweitzer's words the "masterwork of German theology," has wound up in a dead end. Its sum total has boiled down to practically zero.

All this, of course, is only another way of saying that the framework of Christian theology, the brainwork of Saul of Tarsus, has withstood the countless factors of the modern world that unite in demanding rational, naturalistic explanations of the past. Saul's personal agony, by creating a symbolical structure infused with a profound emotionality, has safeguarded traditional beliefs against the corrosion of analysis.

It is true that the idea of the Kingdom of God—the profound feeling that God should and must rule the world directly—was to be expressed repeatedly throughout the history of Christendom. It was, so to speak, implied by the Bible, and during the Middle Ages found expression in numerous outbreaks of "millenarian" fever. Subsequently, in the twentieth century, as we have seen, it flared up in the contagious effect on the major Churches of a stripped-down version of Marxism that in the wake of the Bolshevik putsch in 1917 involved many elements of the Christian establishment in political action.

Yet the original formulation of the Kingdom of God idea was wholly forgotten, and the Kingdom of God agitation against Rome in the first century, obliterated by the cosmic surge of its offshoot, the Christian Church, has become a sort of lost continent.

Nevertheless we have seen that a general history can be assembled via the factual debris discernible in surviving documents; the piety of countless writers, editors, and compilers forbade forgery and ensured respect for elements of history that were merely misunderstood. Above all, the three paramount facts that soar above analysis—the Jesus who preached the Kingdom of God, his execution as "King of the Jews," the densely Jewish background of Jesus and John the Baptist—give us a tripod sturdy enough to clarify the roots of Saul's brainwork and thus sustain a real-life account of Christian origins.

The foregoing account has situated Jesus, John the Baptist, and Saul of Tarsus in time and space; it has described how real-life events came to be transformed into a great Church with mythological, mystical, and magical underpinnings, embodying the theology that after Jesus' death was layered around the concept of the Son of God, Lord of the Universe and Savior of the World. And it makes it possible to discern the true importance of the event that made that possible—the Roman-Jewish war of 66–70.

The general ignorance of the connection between the launching of the Christian faith and the destruction of the Jewish state and the Temple in Jerusalem is all the more bizarre because of the latter's global consequences.

The destruction of the Temple removed the fundamental obstacle to the spread of Christianity in the vast areas touched by Judaism.

In addition, the Zealot debacle drove substantial numbers of Jewish exiles, as well as a scattering of early Christians—no doubt schismatic Jesists hostile to the deification of Jesus—into the interior of Arabia. Muhammad, inspired by both Jews and Christians, declared himself "envoy of Allah" with the mission of propagating the "message of Moses" to the world in the "noble tongue of the Arabs."

The West, integrated with Christendom, generated cosmic processes— the French and American revolutions, democracy, Marxism.

In short, ideas shaped by Jews in the first century were to mold Christianity and Islam—half the human race directly, the other half indirectly.

Notes

Chapter 1

1. Josephus, *The Jewish War* 7.327.
2. Ibid.
3. In the Apocrypha, the Pseudepigrapha, and still later in rabbinic discourses.
4. Silver; Josephus, *Ant.* 17.2.4.

Chapter 6

1. Herbert Danby, *The Mishnah,* p. 391.
2. A comment on "Jewish malice" (1 Thes 2:15) is omitted; most scholars consider it spurious. It completely contradicts Rom 15:18.

Chapter 7

1. Robert Eisler, *The Messiah Jesus and John the Baptist,* p. 443, citing Acts of Paul and Thekla, by some presbyter of Asia Minor, around 170 (Tertullian, *De Capt.* 17).
2. Philo of Alexandria, *Leg. ad Gaius,* ed. E. M. Smallwood, p. 128; Brandon, *Jesus and the Zealots,* p. 68.

3. Josephus, *Ant.* 17.55ff. Josephus does not explain Theudas's enterprise. Also Brandon, *Jesus and the Zealots,* p. 69.

4. Josephus, *War* 7.389–390.

Chapter 8

1. Cf. Daniel, Enoch; it may be echoed in some of the sayings attributed to Jesus in the Gospels.

2. The Apocalypses of Baruch and Ezra.

3. Saul's train of thought seems similar to the ideas expressed in Baruch and Ezra (above), apparently written after the destruction of Jerusalem in 70, but circulating even in Saul's day as a school of messianist thought.

4. As in the Apocalypse of Ezra (4 Ezra 9:39–10:57).

5. For some time Protestants have rejected this idea because of their preoccupation with denying the Catholic claim of continuity going back to the earliest days of the Church. Yet it is plain that the Catholic claim is based here on historical fact. Saul often, to be sure, uses the world *ekklesia* for a specific community (some twenty times), but he also uses it in contexts referring, clearly, to the community of believers as a collectivity. He takes the blame, for instance, for harassing the "community of God" (Gal 1:13; 1 Cor 11:22), and calls on them to be guiltless toward them (1 Cor 10:32). Thus the Catholic view goes back to the World's End community of saints at the outset of Church history—the community founded on the original expectation of the World's End. Hence it is obvious that the realistic idea of the Church was grounded on a mystical abstraction at the very beginning.

6. Schweitzer, *The Mysticism of Paul the Apostle,* p.110.

Chapter 9

1. Ass. Mos. 10:7; Enoch 1:3ff.; 4 Ezra 7:33; Sib. 3.308.

2. Baraita in Sanh., 97a.

3. In Enoch, for instance, what can it mean for "angels in heaven" to live in accordance with the Torah? The Psalms of Solomon, which describe the inhabitants of the Messianic Kingdom not as resurrected but simply as living in an ideal situation, nevertheless do not portray the messianic kingdom as one in which the Torah is lived up to with perfection.

Chapter 10

1. Those of Basilides and Valentinus, respectively, in the second century.
2. Pirqei Aboth 3:2.

Chapter 11

1. Klausner, *From Jesus to Paul,* pp. 398–99, note 6.
2. Ibid., p. 278.

Chapter 12

1. Josephus, *Ant.* 18.85–89; see also Brandon, *Jesus and the Zealots,* p. 80
2. Josephus, *The Jewish War,* 2.I.7, translation Ber.-Grass, p. 233; Eisler, *The Messiah Jesus and John the Baptist,* p. 259.
3. Ibid.
4. Suetonius *Claud.* 25; also, Letter of Claudius to the Alexandrians, cited in Bell, *Jews and Christians in Egypt.*
5. Eisler, p. 552, quoting a passage in Sulpicius Severus considered authentic by Bernays, *Gesammelte Abhandlungen,* pp. 159–81; and many other authorities; also Weber, *Josephus and Vespasian,* p. 72, note 1.
6. Josephus, *Ant.* 20.180–81; also Eisler, p. 543.
7. Ibid., pp. 182–84.
8. Ibid.
9. Schweitzer, *Geschichte der Lebens-Jesus Forschung,* pp. 393–95.
10. Eisler, p. 448.
11. Josephus, *Ant.* 20.197–200.
12. Ibid., 200–203.
13. Eusebius, *Hist. Eccl.* 2.23.5–6, quoting Hegesippus.
14. Epiphanius, *Haeres.,* 1.28 (P.G. x.1.ii.714).
15. Ibid., 29.4 (P.G., 10.1.1. 396); Eisler, pp. 540–41.
16. Eusebius, 3.31.3–5.24.2 seq.
17. Brandon, *The Fall of Jerusalem and the Christian Church,* pp. 89–90; cf. *Beginnings of Christianity,* vol. 4, pp. 133–34; Goguel, *La Naissance du Christianteme,* pp. 491–96.
18. Eusebius, 2.23.18, quoting Hegesippus; cf. Eisler, p. 543.
19. Josephus, *Ant.* 20.9.1; Eisler, p. 543.
20. Eisler, p. 544.

21. Cf. note 14.

22. Josephus, *Ant.* 20.204.

23. Eusebius, 2.23.1, 3.9, derived, as it seems, from the second-century writers Julius Africanus and Hegesippus, the latter from Palestine.

24. Eusebius, 3.20.

25. Ibid., 3.32.

26. Josephus, *The Jewish War,* chapter 8, p. 137.

27. Epiphanius, *Patrologia Graeca Haer.* 29.3–4 (ed. J. Migne).

28. Eusebius, 2.23.13–14.

29. Strabo, quoted in Josephus, *Ant.* 14.7.2.

30. Josephus, *Ant.* 20.8.II (195).

31. Josephus, *War,* 7.3.3. (45).

32. Josephus, *Ant.* 20.2.3. (34).

33. Josephus, *War,* 2.19.2 (520); 6.6.4. (356).

34. Rostovtzeff, *Social and Economic History of the Roman Empire,* p. 179.

35. Josephus, *War,* 2.17.6. (427).

36. Ibid., 4.9.3. (508).

37. Josephus, *Ant.* 19.6.3. (299).

38. Matt. 9:10–11; Mark 2:11,17; Luke 5:30.

39. Josephus, *Ant.* 20.i.4 (214).

40. Ibid., 11.1 (255).

41. Tacitus, *Hist.* 5.10.

42. Josephus, *Ant.* 21.5 (204–15).

43. Josephus, *War,* 2.9.10 (560 f.).

44. Ibid., 4.9.10 (560 f.).

45. Ibid., 5.10.2.4. (424; 440–41).

46. Ibid., 3.7.32 (307f.).

47. Ibid., 3.1.2.(3).

48. Ibid., 2.16.4 (346).

49. Aberbach, *The Roman-Jewish War,* p. 31, quoting Git. 56a; Lam.R. 1.5.31.

50. Josephus, *War,* 2.7.2 (409).

51. Ibid., 2.18.2–5, 7–8; 20.2 (461–68, 487–98, 559–61).

52. Ibid., 2.19.7–9 (540–555).

53. Ibid., 3.4.2. (64–69).

54. Ibid., 2.434.

55. Ibid., 5.3.1; vi.9.3; (99–102, 421).

Chapter 13

1. See, notably, Brandon, *The Fall of Jerusalem, Jesus and the Zealots, The Trial of Jesus of Nazareth.*

2. Notably Ignatius, Polycarp, Papias. Papias, Bishop of Smyrna around 150, had such faith in the imminence of the messianic kingdom that Eusebius (*Hist. Eccl.* 3:39) belittled him because of it. Papias even quotes Jesus as saying that the messianic kingdom was so fertile that every vine would have 10,000 branches, every branch ten thousand clusters, every cluster ten thousand grapes, and every grape would produce twenty-five measures of wine. The same sort of thing was said about other plants; animals were to live at peace with each other and with man. All this was merely an echo of fantasies ultimately based on the Hebrew Prophets. Justin, too, in his *Dialogue with Tryphon,* believes in the imminence of the messianic kingdom. In his attack on Tryphon (a Jew) he says: "You have only a short time now to attach yourselves to us; after the return of Christ your weeping will be of no avail, for He will not listen to you." (Dial.28:2) The tenacity of the World's End theory in certain enclaves, despite its general decline, can be seen, further, in the spread of Montanism around 150; that was an energetic revival of the earliest doctrine of the imminence of the messianic kingdom. The incomprehensible delay of the glorious return also, to be sure, led to some doubts (Hebrews, 6:11–12; 10:23,35; 12:12–14. 2 Peter, 3:4–9; Jude, 17–23).

3. Guignebert, *Christianisme antique,* p. 201.

Chapter 14

1. Josephus, *War,* 6.312ff.
2. Ibid., 3.11.
3. Ibid., 4.5.1–4.
4. Hans Lietzmann, *A History of the Early Church,* vol. 4, p. 113.
5. Ibid., 114.

Chapter 15

1. This passage in the new Testament, traditionally attributed to Saul, was no doubt written much later, around 100, by one of his "school."

2. H. Conzelmann, *History of the Primitive Church,* Appendix II.

3. Suetonius, *Nero* 16.

4. Tacitus, *Hist.* 5.5.

5. Hans Lietzmann, *Cambridge Ancient History,* vol.12, pp. 516–17.

6. Conzelmann, p. 129.

7. Ibid., p. 131.

8. Joel Carmichael, *The Satanizing of the Jews.*

Epilogue

1. Nietzsche, *Werke,* ed. K. Schlacht, 3:656: *Aus dem Nachlass der achtziger Jahre.*

2. Troyat, p. 589: letter written 16/11/1906 (to Chertkov).

Critical Appendix

1. Charles Guignebert, *Jésus,* p. 148.

Bibliography

Aberbach, Moses. *The Roman-Jewish War.* London, 1966.

Baeck, Leo. *Der Menschensohn.* MGWJ, 1937.

Bammel, Ernst, and C. E. D. Moule, eds. *Jesus and the Politics of His Day.* Cambridge, 1984; *Jewish Quarterly,* in association with R. Golub.

Baron, Salo. *Social and Religious History of the Jews.* Vol. 1., New York, 1937.

Batey, Richard, ed. *New Testament Issues.* New York, 1970.

Bell, H. Idris. *Jews and Christians in Egypt.*

Bernays, Jacob. *Gesammelte Abhandlungen.* Vol. 2.

Bornkamm, Günther. *Paul, Apôtre de Jésus-Christ.* Paris, 1971.

Brandon, S. L. F. *The Fall of Jerusalem and the Christian Church.* New York and London, 1957.

———. *Jesus and the Zealots.* New York and London, 1967.

———. *The Trial of Jesus of Nazareth.* New York and London, 1968.

Carmichael, Joel. *The Death of Jesus.* New York and London, 1962.

———. *Stehe auf und Rufe Deinen Herrn.* Munich, 1982.

———. *The Birth of Christianity: Reality and Myth.* New York, 1989.

———. *The Satanizing of the Jews.* New York, 1992.

Cohn, Norman. *The Pursuit of the Millennium.* New York, 1957.

Conzelman, H. *History of the Primitive Church.* New York, 1973.

Cullmann, Oscar. *Jesus und die Revolutionäre seiner Zeit.* Tubingen, 1970.

Cumont, Franz. *Religions orientales dans le paganisme romain,* rev. ed. Paris, 1929.

Danby, Herbert. *The Mishnah.* Oxford, 1933.

Davies, W. D. *Christian Origins and Judaism.* New York & London, 1962.

———. *Paul and Rabbinic Judaism.* New York, 1967.

Eisler, Robert. *The Messiah Jesus and John the Baptist.* London, 1931.

Goguel, Maurice. *Jean-Baptiste.* Paris, 1928.

———. *La Naissance du christianisme.* Paris, 1955.

———. *Vie de Jésus.* Paris, 1950.

Guignebert, Charles. *Jésus.* Paris, 1933.

———. *Le christianisme antique.* Paris, 1921.

———. *Le Christ.* Paris, 1948.

Hengel, Martin. *Die Zeloten.* Leiden, 1976.

Jackson, F. J., and Kirsopp Lake, eds. *Beginnings of Christianity.* 5 vols. London, 1920–33.

Jastrow, M. *Dictionary of the Targumim, Talmud Bavli and Yerusahlmi, and the Midrashic Literature.* 2 vols. New York, 1959.

Josephus, Flavius. *The Jewish War.* London and New York, Loeb edition.

———. *Antiquities of the Jews.* London and New York, Loeb edition.

Kaufman, Yehezkiel. *The Religion of Israel* (abridged by Moshe Greenberg). New York, 1972.

Klausner, Joseph. *From Jesus to Paul.* Trans. W. Stinespring. Boston, 1961.

Lietzmann, Hans. *A History of the Early Church.* 1927.

Loisy, Alfred. *The Origins of the New Testament.* London, 1950.

Maccoby, Hyman. *Revolution in Judea.* London, 1973.

———. *The Mythmaker.* New York, 1986.

———. *Paul and Hellenism.* London, 1991.

Robinson, John A. T. *The Body.* London, 1952.

Rostovtzeff, M. *Social and Economic History of the Roman Empire.* Oxford, 1921.

Rubenstein, Richard. *My Brother Paul.* New York, 1972.

Schoeps, J. J. Paul. *The Theology of the Apostle in the Light of Jewish History.* Philadelphia, 1961.

Schürer, Emil. *A History of the Jewish People in the Time of Jesus.* New York, 1961.

Schweitzer, Albert. *Geschichte der Leben-Jesus Forschung.* Tübingen, 1913.

———. *The Mysticism of Paul the Apostle.* London, 1931. Paperback 1968.

Silver, Abba Hillel. *Messianic Speculation in Israel.* New York, 1927.

Spiegel, Shalom. *The Last Trial.* New York, 1967.

Tarn, W. W. *Hellenistic Civilization,* 3rd ed. London.

Weber, Wilhelm. *Josephus and Vespasian.* Stuttgart/Leipzig, 1921.

Name Index